Computer-Aided Oral and Maxillofacial Surgery

Computer-Aided Oral and Maxillofacial Surgery
Developments, Applications, and Future Perspectives

Edited by

Jan Egger

Institute of Computer Graphics and Vision, Graz University of
Technology, Graz, Austria; Computer Algorithms for Medicine
Laboratory (Café-Lab), Graz, Austria; Department of Oral and
Maxillofacial Surgery, Medical University of Graz, Graz, Austria

Xiaojun Chen

School of Mechanical Engineering, Shanghai Jiao Tong
University, Shanghai, China

ACADEMIC PRESS
An imprint of Elsevier

Academic Press is an imprint of Elsevier
125 London Wall, London EC2Y 5AS, United Kingdom
525 B Street, Suite 1650, San Diego, CA 92101, United States
50 Hampshire Street, 5th Floor, Cambridge, MA 02139, United States
The Boulevard, Langford Lane, Kidlington, Oxford OX5 1GB, United Kingdom

Notices
Knowledge and best practice in this field are constantly changing. As new research and experience broaden our understanding, changes in research methods, professional practices, or medical treatment may become necessary.

Practitioners and researchers must always rely on their own experience and knowledge in evaluating and using any information, methods, compounds, or experiments described herein. In using such information or methods they should be mindful
of their own safety and the safety of others, including parties for whom they have a professional responsibility.

To the fullest extent of the law, neither the Publisher nor the authors, contributors, or editors, assume any liability for any
injury and/or damage to persons or property as a matter of products liability, negligence or otherwise, or from any use or
operation of any methods, products, instructions, or ideas contained in the material herein.

Library of Congress Cataloging-in-Publication Data
A catalog record for this book is available from the Library of Congress

British Library Cataloguing-in-Publication Data
A catalogue record for this book is available from the British Library

ISBN: 978-0-12-823299-6

For information on all Academic Press publications
visit our website at https://www.elsevier.com/books-and-journals

Publisher: Mara Conner
Acquisitions Editor: Tim Pitts
Editorial Project Manager: Isabella C. Silva
Production Project Manager: Sojan P. Pazhayattil
Designer: Miles Hitchen

Typeset by Thomson Digital

Working together
to grow libraries in
developing countries

www.elsevier.com • www.bookaid.org

Contents

Antonio Pepe, Gianpaolo Francesco Trotta, Christina Gsaxner,
Antonio Brunetti, Giacomo Donato Cascarano,
Vitoantonio Bevilacqua, Dinggang Shen, Jan Egger

Contributors

Victor Alves
Centre Algoritmi, University of Minho, Braga, Portugal

Vitoantonio Bevilacqua
Department of Electrical and Information Engineering, Polytechnic University of Bari, Bari, Italy

Antonio Brunetti
Department of Electrical and Information Engineering, Polytechnic University of Bari, Bari, Italy

Giacomo Donato Cascarano
Department of Electrical and Information Engineering, Polytechnic University of Bari, Bari, Italy

Ti-chiun Chang
Siemens Technology, Princeton, NJ, United States

Xiaojun Chen
School of Mechanical Engineering, Shanghai Jiao Tong University, Shanghai, China

Jeroen Van Dessel
Department of Imaging and Pathology, OMFS IMPATH Research Group, KU Leuven, Leuven, Belgium; Department of Oral and Maxillofacial Surgery/Faculty of Medicine, KU Leuven, University Hospitals, Leuven, Belgium

Ulrich Eck
Computer Aided Medical Procedures & Augmented Reality, Technical University of Munich, Garching, Germany

Jan Egger
Institute of Computer Graphics and Vision, Graz University of Technology, Graz, Austria; Computer Algorithms for Medicine Laboratory, (Café-Lab), Graz, Austria; Department of Oral and Maxillofacial Surgery, Medical University of Graz, Graz, Austria

Marius Erdt
Fraunhofer Singapore, Nanyang Technological University, Singapore

Maria Gonçalves
Institute of Computer Graphics and Vision, Graz University of Technology, Graz, Austria; Computer Algorithms for Medicine Laboratory, Graz, Austria; Centre Algoritmi, University of Minho, Braga, Portugal

Christina Gsaxner
Institute of Computer Graphics and Vision, Graz University of Technology, Graz, Austria; Computer Algorithms for Medicine Laboratory, Graz, Austria; Department of Oral and Maxillofacial Surgery, Medical University of Graz, Graz, Austria

Yifei Gu
Department of Imaging and Pathology, OMFS IMPATH Research Group, KU Leuven, Leuven, Belgium

Firdaus Janoos
Squarepoint Capital, LLC, New York, NY, United States

KengLiang Lan
Department of Second Dental Center, Shanghai Ninth People's Hospital, College of Stomatology, Shanghai Jiao Tong University School of Medicine; National Clinical Research Center for Oral Diseases; Shanghai Key Laboratory of Stomatology & Shanghai Research Institute of Stomatology, Shanghai, China

Ping Liu
Shenzhen Institute of Advanced Technology, Chinese Academy of Sciences, Shenzhen, China

Jianning Li
Graz University of Technology, Institute of Computer Graphics and Vision, Graz, Austria; Computer Algorithms for Medicine Laboratory (Café-Lab), Graz, Austria

Xiangyun Liao
Shenzhen Institute of Advanced Technology, Chinese Academy of Sciences, Shenzhen, China

Yongfeng Mai
School of Mechanical Engineering, Shanghai Jiao Tong University, Shanghai, China

Wang Manning
Digital Medical Research Center, School of Basic Medical Sciences, Fudan University; Shanghai Key Laboratory of Medical Image Computing and Computer Assisted Intervention, Shanghai, China

Nassir Navab
Computer Aided Medical Procedures (CAMP), Technical University of Munich, Garching, Germany; Whiting School of Engineering, Johns Hopkins University, Baltimore, MD, United States

Antonio Pepe
Institute of Computer Graphics and Vision, Graz University of Technology, Graz, Austria; Computer Algorithms for Medicine Laboratory, Graz, Austria

Constantinus Politis
Department of Imaging and Pathology, OMFS IMPATH Research Group, KU Leuven, Leuven, Belgium; Department of Oral and Maxillofacial Surgery/Faculty of Medicine, KU Leuven, University Hospitals, Leuven, Belgium

Yinling Qian
Shenzhen Institute of Advanced Technology, Chinese Academy of Sciences, Shenzhen, China

Chunxia Qin
School of Biomedical Engineering, Shanghai Jiao Tong University, Shanghai, China; School of Mechanical Engineering, Shanghai Jiao Tong University, Shanghai, China

Dieter Schmalstieg
Institute of Computer Graphics and Vision, Graz University of Technology, Graz, Austria

Michael Schwaiger
Department of Oral and Maxillofacial Surgery, Medical University of Graz, Graz, Austria

Dinggang Shen
Department of Research and Development, Shanghai United Imaging Intelligence Co., Ltd., Shanghai, China

Philipp Streckbein
Department of Oral- and Cranio-Maxillo-Facial Surgery, University Hospital Gießen, Gießen, Germany

Yi Sun
Department of Imaging and Pathology, OMFS IMPATH Research Group, KU Leuven, Leuven, Belgium; Department of Oral and Maxillofacial Surgery/Faculty of Medicine, KU Leuven, University Hospitals, Leuven, Belgium

Baoxin Tao
Department of Second Dental Center, Shanghai Ninth People's Hospital, College of Stomatology, Shanghai Jiao Tong University School of Medicine; National Clinical Research Center for Oral Diseases; Shanghai Key Laboratory of Stomatology & Shanghai Research Institute of Stomatology, Shanghai, China

Gianpaolo Francesco Trotta
Moxoff S.P.A., Milan, Italy

Jürgen Wallner
Department of Oral and Maxillofacial Surgery, Medical University of Graz, Graz, Austria; Department of Cranio-Maxillofacial Surgery, AZ Monica and the University Hospital Antwerp, Antwerp, Belgium

Feng Wang
Department of Oral Implantology, Shanghai Ninth People's Hospital, College of Stomatology, Shanghai Jiao Tong University School of Medicine; National Clinical Research Center for Oral Diseases; Shanghai Key Laboratory of Stomatology & Shanghai Research Institute of Stomatology, Shanghai, China

Qiong Wang
Shenzhen Institute of Advanced Technology, Chinese Academy of Sciences, Shenzhen, China

Yiqun Wu
Department of Second Dental Center, Shanghai Ninth People's Hospital, College of Stomatology, Shanghai Jiao Tong University School of Medicine; National Clinical Research Center for Oral Diseases; Shanghai Key Laboratory of Stomatology & Shanghai Research Institute of Stomatology, Shanghai, China

Wolfgang Zemann
Department of Oral and Maxillofacial Surgery, Medical University of Graz, Graz, Austria

Song Zhijian
Digital Medical Research Center, School of Basic Medical Sciences, Fudan University; Shanghai Key Laboratory of Medical Image Computing and Computer Assisted Intervention, Shanghai, China

About the editors

Priv.-Doz. Dr. Dr. Jan Egger has over 10 years of experience in developing algorithms in medical image analysis and computer vision, including 5 years of postdoctoral research and development in the healthcare industry. He has extensive experience in implementing algorithms and software in the field of surgical planning, and published over 100 peer-reviewed papers and several patents (~50 of these as first author). Jan holds a PhD and a German Habilitation in Computer Science, and an interdisciplinary PhD in Human Biology. He is the Principle Investigator of *Studierfenster* (www.studierfenster.at) a cloud-based platform for medical image processing, founder of the multi-institutional *Computer*

Algorithms for Medicine Laboratory, and Principle Investigator and organizer of the MICCAI AutoImplant challenge with over 100 registered participants in 2020 (https://autoimplant. grand-challenge.org/) and editor of the Springer LNCS challenge proceedings *Towards the Automatization of Cranial Implant Design in Cranioplasty*. Further, Jan is the PI of the *en-Faced* project, the only *KLIF* proposal that has ever been awarded by the *Austrian Science Found (FWF)* to the Graz University of Technology. His main research interests are Translational Science in Medical Image Analysis and Image-Guided Therapy. Jan is currently *Privatdozent* and has a dual appointment at the Graz University of Technology and the Medical University of Graz, which allows him to conduct his interdisciplinary research at a technical and medical side.

Prof. Xiaojun Chen is with Institute of Biomedical Manufacturing, School of Mechanical Engineering, Shanghai Jiao Tong University (SJTU), China. He received his PhD from SJTU in 2006, and then furthered his research as a postdoc at the same institution until 2008. After that, he has been working at SJTU as assistant professor (2008-2010), associate professor (2010-2018), and full professor (2018-now). As a visiting scholar, he had worked at the Surgical Planning Laboratory, Harvard Medical School during Oct 2011–Oct 2012; the TIMC-IMAG lab, CNRS, France, during Sep–Dec 2013; the OMFS-IMPATH lab, KU Leuven, Belgium during

Jun–Aug 2015; and the CISTIB lab, the University of Sheffield, UK during Jun–Aug 2016. His research focuses on computer assisted surgery, including biomedical image analysis, image-guided interventions, artificial intelligence in biomedical physics and analysis, VR/AR/MR technology in medicine, medical robotics, biomedical manufacturing, etc. He is the author and co-author of more than 200 peer-reviewed papers, and delivered more than 30 lectures in the prestigious international conferences including IEEE-EMBC, IEEE-ITAB, MICCAI, CARS, CAI, etc. He is the PI of more than 30 research projects, including 7 funded by National Natural Science Foundation of China and several international collaboration projects. He is an associate editor or editorial board member of 8 journals including *Computerized Medical Imaging and Graphics* (Elsevier), *Physics in Medicine & Biology* (IOP), *International Journal of Computer Assisted Radiology and Surgery* (Springer), *Medical Engineering & Physics* (Elsevier), *Frontiers in Bioengineering and Biotechnology* (Frontiers), *Computer Assisted Surgery* (Taylor & Francis), *Journal of Healthcare Engineering*, etc. He was granted Second Prize of National Science & Technology Progress Award of China (2019), Chinese Society of Stomatology Science and Technology Award (2018), China Medical Science and Technology Award (2016), Shanghai Science & Technology Award (2010), a laureate of "France Talent Innovation (FTI) Program" (2011), etc.

Jan (left) and Xiaojun in fall 2019 at the Minhang campus of the SJTU in Shanghai.

Preface

Ni Hao and *Willkommen* to our interdisciplinary—but also somehow intercultural—book about *Computer-Aided Oral and Maxillofacial Surgery: Developments, Applications, and Future Perspectives*!

The aim of our book is to provide an understanding on the latest technologies applied to oral and maxillofacial surgery as an ideal resource for biomedical engineers and computer scientists, clinicians, and clinical researchers. In facial surgery, computer-aided decisions supplement all kind of treatment stages, from a diagnosis to follow-up examinations. In this regard, our book gives an in-depth overview of state-of-the-art technologies, such as visualization, deep learning, radiomics, augmented reality, virtual reality, and intraoperative navigation, as applied to oral and maxillofacial surgery. It covers applications of facial surgery that are at the interface between medicine and computer science. In addition, our book gives insights into the clinical practice from facial surgeons in Austria, China, and Germany. The numerous expert contributors of this book have various backgrounds, coming from technical and clinical academia, but also the industry, and work mainly in China and Europe.

Hence and summarized, the key features of the book are:

- providing a comprehensive, state-of-the-art knowledge of interdisciplinary applications in facial surgery;
- presenting recent algorithmic developments like deep learning, along with recent devices in augmented reality and virtual reality; and
- including clinical knowledge of several facials surgeons who give insights into the current clinical practice and challenges of facial surgeons in university hospitals in Austria, China, and Germany.

The idea for this book was born when Jan Egger was awarded the Overseas Visiting Scholarship from the Shanghai Jiao Tong University (SJTU), allowing him to join Xiaojun Chen's group as visiting professor in 2019. During his stay, Jan was also able to meet Professor Yiqun Wu at the Shanghai Ninth People's Hospital and observe several research experiments there, which gave him additional impressions to the research and interventions he regularly observes at the university hospital in Graz, and previously in Germany. Discussing these experiences and impressions with Xiaojun over some Hong Kong-style milk tea lead ultimately to the decision to jointly tackle this book endeavor.

Xiaojun and Jan met already in 2012 in Boston, when they were doing research at the Harvard Medical School and kept remotely collaborating and working together over the years, resulting in dozens of joint works and publications. Occasionally meeting at conferences around the world, like the 29th Conference of the International Society for Medical Innovation and Technology (SMIT) in Torino, Italy, where they both got a fine for buying the wrong bus ticket to visit the Basilica of Superga (they wanted to do some sightseeing in the afternoon, after the conference ended), Jan already visited Xiaojun and his team for a few days in 2015. A longer research stay by Xiaojun at Jan's site is still outstanding. It was originally planned for 2020, but had unfortunately to be postponed due to the COVID-19 pandemic.

Please Stay Safe and Healthy!

Jan Egger

Xiaojun Chen

Medical image segmentation in oral-maxillofacial surgery

Jianning Li[a,b], Marius Erdt[c], Firdaus Janoos[d],
Ti-chiun Chang[e], Jan Egger[a,b,f]

[a]INSTITUTE OF COMPUTER GRAPHICS AND VISION, GRAZ UNIVERSITY OF TECHNOLOGY, GRAZ, AUSTRIA; [b]COMPUTER ALGORITHMS FOR MEDICINE LABORATORY (CAFÉ-LAB), GRAZ, AUSTRIA; [c]FRAUNHOFER SINGAPORE, NANYANG TECHNOLOGICAL UNIVERSITY, SINGAPORE; [d]SQUAREPOINT CAPITAL, LLC, NEW YORK, NY, UNITED STATES; [e]SIEMENS TECHNOLOGY, PRINCETON, NJ, UNITED STATES; [f]DEPARTMENT OF ORAL AND MAXILLOFACIAL SURGERY, MEDICAL UNIVERSITY OF GRAZ, GRAZ, AUSTRIA

1 Introduction

Image segmentation is a key task in image-guided therapy. Overall, end-to-end systems for image-guided therapy in use today perform segmentation, registration, as well as navigation and visualization. Segmentation in particular involves identifying meaningful regions and structures within a medical image, such as normal anatomical tissue, pathology, or resection, for the purpose of planning and guiding operations as well as measuring the outcome of a therapeutic procedure [1].

Hence, medical image segmentation algorithms are of special interest, as they play an important role in various medical fields for diagnosis and treatment support. Typically, segmentation is the first step in an image-based diagnosis, prognosis and therapy pipeline, and therefore incorrect segmentation affects any subsequent steps heavily [2,3]. As illustrated in Fig. 1.1, after the imaging data of the organ of interest is acquired with a certain imaging modality such as computed tomography (CT), CT angiography (CTA), magnetic resonance imaging (MRI), single-photon emission computed tomography (SPECT) or ultrasound (US), the organ of interest has first to be segmented from the imaging data so that relevant information regarding the organ can be extracted by the subsequent computer-aided diagnosis and treatment systems. This in turn helps surgeons in clinical decision-making for each specific patient. For example, thoracic endovascular aortic repair (TEVAR) is usually performed to repair the abnormality of the aorta (e.g., aortic dissection and aneurysm), which requires the aorta to be segmented [4] to enable 3D visualization of the aorta model and quantification of important aortic parameters such as lumen volume, diameters as well as the position of the intimal tear [3].

However, automatic medical image segmentation is known to be one of the most complex problems in medical image analysis [5]. Therefore, to this day, delineation is often

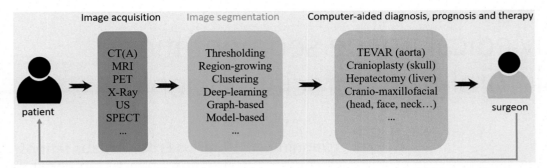

FIGURE 1.1 Medical image segmentation is the core step for various computer-aided diagnosis, prognosis and therapy systems, which help surgeons with clinical decision-making. With the decision, the surgeons are able to perform final treatment on the patients.

done manually or semi-manually, especially in regions with limited contrast and for organs or tissues with large variations in geometry [6]. In this chapter, we will start with a general introduction of current semi-automatic and automatic segmentation techniques and their applications to various computer-aided surgery scenarios. We will introduce these segmentation algorithms in an easily comprehensible manner and mathematical formulae are included only when necessary. Then, a comprehensive evaluation of the segmentation techniques specifically applied to oral-maxillofacial surgery will be covered in-depth.

1.1 Medical image segmentation: technologies and applications

Medical image segmentation, essentially the same as natural image segmentation, refers to the process of extracting the desired object (organ) from a medical image (2D or 3D), which can be done manually, semi-automatically or fully-automatically. The imaging modality of the medical images can be diverse such as CT, MRI, US, PET, X-ray, or hybrid such as PET/CT, depending on the organ to be imaged and the imaging purpose. The number of existent segmentation technologies (and their variants), from the naive manual delineation to the most up-to-date fully automatic segmentation technologies such as deep neural networks, is large. These technologies can generally be categorized into two groups: **intensity-based segmentation** and **shape-based segmentation**. The basic idea of the former group is that voxels within an organ of interest have similar intensity (gray value) while the inter-object voxel intensity is different. Fig. 1.2A shows an idealized example of intensity-based

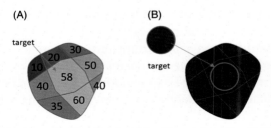

FIGURE 1.2 Illustration of idealized intensity-based segmentation (A) and shape-based segmentation (B).

segmentation, where the voxels within the target have a fixed gray value (i.e., 58) and the gray values in the surrounding objects are different from that of the target. Even if the difference among some gray values (e.g., 58, 60) is hardly recognizable by human eyes, the subtle difference can still be detected by computers so that different objects can be separated according to their gray values. However, the intensity distribution in real medical images is much more complex and has much greater inhomogeneity, that is, the gray values of voxels within a target tend to be different due to unevenly distributed contrast agent or pathological factors, while the inter-object voxel intensity can have some similarity. For shape-based segmentation, the idea is that the shape of the target to be segmented is approximately known, so that segmenting the object can be achieved by detecting a particular shape in the image. For example, in Fig. 1.2B, the target is circular and can be detected by hough circle transform (HCT). In this case, intensity-based segmentation tends to fail as target has identical gray values with its surrounding environment. Note that the shape of medical targets in medical images tend to be much more irregular and, most importantly, highly varied compared to the idealized example in Fig. 1.2B, so that the segmentation is still a challenging task. One of the most common applications employing shape-based segmentation techniques is the segmentation of the aorta, which is in generally tube-shaped [7,8]. This group of segmentation method, which exploits the prior knowledge of the shape of the target, is more widely known as model-based segmentation [9].

We use the term *shape-based* segmentation, as it is more intuitive than model-based segmentation according to the example in Fig. 1.2B. However, they refer to the same group of segmentation techniques in our chapter. Shape-based segmentation is among the most widely used and influential techniques for segmenting anatomical structures that depicts a particular shape with foreseeable variations.

1.2 Shape-based segmentation

Here, we will introduce the *shape-based* segmentation techniques, including **Statistical Shape Model**, **Statistical Appearance Model,** and **Atlas-based segmentation** in an unified way and distinguish them from another well known segmentation technique, the **Active Contour Model**.

1.2.1 Statistical shape model

The basic idea behind a statistical shape model (SSM) [10,11], sometimes also known as active shape model (ASM) and smart snakes, is to mathematically describe the geometric shape of an object and a set of shape variations. The shape variations can be learnt from a group of shape templates (training data). The application of SSM in medical image segmentation consists of three key components: (1) construction of shape templates, (2) creation of SSM from the shape templates, and (3) adapting an SSM to a new image. These components are explained as follows.

1.2.1.1 Construction of shape templates

The shape templates are used to learn shape variations. They should be large in number and representative of the shape variabilities of the target. The shape templates are usually created by segmenting the target manually from a number of representative training medical images.

1.2.1.2 Creation of SSM

An SSM is derived from a group of shape templates with the ability to represent shape variations of the target. The calculation of SSM requires that a correspondence should be established across the template shapes, which is a major consideration in SSM creation [12]. Take the creation of one of the most frequently used SSM point distribution model (PDM), for example. A set of landmarks is (manually) sampled from a reference shape template. Then, the reference template is registered with the rest of the templates respectively so that a correspondence can be established between the landmarks on the reference template and potential anatomical points on the rest of the shape templates. By doing so, the template shapes are represented by a set of landmarks and each landmark approximately represents the same anatomical structure for all the shapes involved. In this sense, establishing correspondence among shapes is being formulated as a registration problem [13,14]. Another commonly used approach for correspondence establishment is surface parameterization [14,15], where all the points of the shape templates are mapped onto a spherical surface after the templates are centered and normalized. The landmarks points are then sampled from the spherical surface. After the correspondence is established by using either registration or surface parametrization, a covariance matrix is calculated from the 3D landmark coordinates of all the shape templates. The PDM $\mathbf{S}$ can then be expressed as a linear combination of the eigenvectors $\Phi_i \alpha_i$, calculated using principle component analysis (PCA), of the covariance matrix, with the bias (i.e., the mean shape $\bar{\mathbf{S}}$) being the mean of the landmark coordinates:

$$S(\alpha_i) = \bar{\mathbf{S}} + \Phi_i \alpha_i \qquad (1.1)$$

Each eigenvector represents a shape variation and they are combined by a set of feature weights α_i.

1.2.1.3 Applying an SSM to new images: the segmentation phase

After the establishment of an SSM, the general shape and the shape variations of the target to be segmented become a **known prior**, which can then be applied to new images to segment the target. In particular, the segmentation of the new image requires an initialization of points, which can be just a rough estimation of the landmarks. The initialization can be based on the prior knowledge about the target, if known. The points are then adjusted iteratively to fit the boundary of the target more accurately while being constrained by the shape priors at the same time. The adjustment of the points dx has the following relationship with the feature weights α_i:

$$d\alpha_i = \Phi_i^T dx \qquad (1.2)$$

According to Eq. (1.2), the updates of the feature weights $d\alpha_i$ can be calculated using least square methods. Then, new shapes can be generated based on Eq. (1.1) after α_i has been updated. Readers are referred to [10,11,16] for technological details regarding how Eq. (1.2) is derived.

1.2.2 Statistical appearance model

Statistical appearance model (SAM), aka active appearance model (AAM) [17–19], is an extension to SSM, which incorporates, besides the shape, the appearance (e.g., color or texture represented by voxel intensity) of an object into the shape matching process. After the correspondence has been built among the template shapes, the correspondence of the voxel intensity of the landmark points can be established simultaneously so that, besides the 3D coordinates of the landmark points, the intensity of the landmarks (in and around) can also be sampled. Compared with SSM which only uses the 3D landmark coordinates for the computation of mean shape and shape variation, the SAM incorporates also the mean appearance (intensity) and appearance variations, which can be calculated using PCA.

1.2.3 Atlas-based segmentation

Similar to SSM, the atlas-based segmentation approach [20] requires a set of reference images and their corresponding manually (or semi-automatically) created segmentation templates (atlas). Given a new image, the reference images are registered with the new image so that a transformation matrix can be produced. Segmentation of the new image can be achieved by warping the corresponding templates to match with the new image based on the transformation matrix. In this sense, image segmentation is formulated as an image registration problem. Only a single atlas is used in the early stage of atlas-based segmentation due to the lack of computational resources, which tends to be insufficient as a single atlas is not representative of the population to be studied. Then, multi-atlas segmentation (MAS) is devised [21] with superior performance yet higher computational cost compared to using a single atlas. For multi-atlas segmentation, all the reference images are registered with the new image in a pair-wise manner, yielding a set of segmentation results. The multiple segmentation results are fused via, for example, majority voting, to form the final single segmentation [22–24]. Therefore, we can see that the two key components in MAS are image registration and label fusion.

1.2.4 Summary

The above introduced shape-based segmentation methods: **Statistical Shape Model**, **Statistical Appearance Model,** and **Atlas-based segmentation** can be put into the same category given the fact that they all exploit the prior shape knowledge of the target in an implicit way, that is, the shape priors are first learnt from a group of pre-created shape templates and then, the prior shape knowledge is applied to new images for segmentation. The selection of the template images, which should be representative of the shape variations as well as the diversity of the target, can have fundamental influence in the segmentation quality. The shape prior can also be exploited in an explicit manner, such as the use of HCT for aorta segmentation [25]. Some segmentation techniques make use of other anatomical priors besides shape, such as the spatial location of the target, the relative location of the target to other anatomical structures in an image, the range of gray level, the orientation and size of the target, in an implicit or explicit fashion. However, the use of a shape prior is the most prevalent among other anatomical priors and the shape-based approaches introduced earlier are the most well established and representative.

We will also show in the following sections of the chapter that making use of anatomical priors especially the shape priors, is the most prevalent for the segmentation of the mandible, which is one of the most important target in the oral and maxillofacial surgery.

1.2.5 Active contour model

We differentiate active contour model (ACM) [26], aka snakes, from SSM, SAM, and atlas-based approaches based on the fact that anatomical priors are not must-have ingredients for ACM and no training templates are required. Instead, the algorithm deforms an initial contour iteratively to fit that of the target through the minimization of so called contour energy. The initial contour, most of the time, needs to be provided by users manually even if sometimes a prior anatomical knowledge can be used to determine the initial contour automatically. The contour energy consists of two parts: the *internal energy*, which depends on the shape of the contour itself and measures the contour smoothness and continuity, as well as the *external energy*, which is derived from the gray value image [27]. The lower the energy combined, the better the contour matches that of the target. The internal energy is easy to understand. Briefly, the smoother the contour, the lower the internal energy. The external energy **E** is expressed in Eq. (1.3).

$$\mathbf{E} = w_1 I(x,y) - w_2 \left| \nabla \left(G * I(x,y) \right) \right|^2 \tag{1.3}$$

w_1 and w_2 are the weights of the two terms. $G * I(x,y)$ denotes the original gray value image $I(x,y)$ convolved with a Gaussian smoothing filter G. ∇ is the gradient operator. Looking at Eq. (1.3) alone might be confusing as it is unrelated to the contour and difficult to correlate the contour energy with the gradients of the original gray value image $\left| \nabla \left(G * I(x,y) \right) \right|^2$. Here we try to explain in a way that is intuitive and easy to understand. The contour energy is dependent on whether the contour falls on the low gradient area or on the high gradient area. If the contour falls mostly on the edge of the target, where the gradients are high, the contour energy is low according to Eq. (1.3). On the contrary, if the contour falls on an area away from the contour target, where the gray values are uniform so that the gradients are low, the contour energy is high.

Fig. 1.3 further illustrates the internal and external energy through an example of aorta segmentation. The left side of Fig. 1.3 shows a gray value CT image $I(x,y)$ containing the aortic lumen, which is the target of segmentation. The bottom shows the same image with the high intensity area the object edges as well as the low intensity areas, where the intensity distribution is generally uniform, marked. The right side shows contour (a) contour (f) that have a different internal and external energy. Contour (a), (b), (c), and (d) are smooth so that they have a low internal energy while contour (b), (c), and (d) fall mostly on the low gradient areas so that they have a high external energy. Contour (c) and (d) intersect with some object edges, where the gradient is high but the dominant contour portion is in the low gradient area. Contour (a) has both a low internal energy and a low external energy as it falls entirely on the edge of the target, where the gradients are high. Contour (d) and (e) have a high internal energy, as the contours are not smooth. As contour (d) falls entirely on

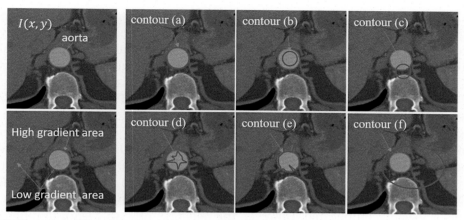

FIGURE 1.3 Illustration of the contour energy in active contour models (ACMs). Left, the original *gray* value image $I(x,y)$. Right: contour (a) -contour (f) show examples of high/low internal/external energies.

the low gradient area, it has a high external energy. Most of contour (e) falls on the edge of the target so that it has a low external energy.

1.3 Intensity-based segmentation

Most of existent segmentation techniques are intensity-based, such as thresholding, clustering, deep learning, watershed, and graph-cut (Strictly speaking, deep learning based approaches not only learn to differentiate between fore-ground and background voxels based on intensity but may have also learnt to recognize the shape of the target during the training process, depending on how the ground truth and the network is designed). These techniques are explained as follows:

THRESHOLDING is one of the most straightforward segmentation techniques applied to medical images [28], especially when the region of interest (ROI) in the image has distinct intensity from its surrounding structures. The common targets of thresholding-based segmentations are the bony structures, such as the skull, which have a high intensity in computed tomography (CT) images. An application scenario of thresholding-based skull segmentation is brain tumor surgery, which requires that the skull after craniotomy should be segmented from head CT scans. Professional designers make use of the defective skull for computer-aided design of the cranial implant [29–34], which can then be used in cranioplasty to repair the skull defect caused by the previous surgery. THRESHOLDING is also commonly used together with other segmentation techniques such as HISTOGRAM to determine the optimal thresholds for a specific object of interest. HISTOGRAM-BASED segmentation is based on the observation that the voxels within each ROI have similar intensities while the voxel intensities of different ROIs are different so that the minima of the image histogram can be used to separate different ROIs. Ref. [35] gives an example of abdomen segmentation using image histogram and thresholding.

CLUSTERING is one of the primary unsupervised learning methods that does not require ground truth and can cluster the voxels in an image based on their similarity (e.g., the Euclidean distance of a voxel to a cluster center). The initialization of the number of clusters and the cluster centers can affect the clustering results substantially. Ref. [36] uses K-mean clustering to segment the brain tumor, which assists brain tumor surgery. CLUSTERING can also be used in combination with image HISTOGRAM to determine the number and initial centers of clusters. In Ref. [37], histogram-based clustering estimation (HBCE) together with c-means clustering is used for skin lesion segmentation. Supervised learning techniques, predominantly deep convolutional neural networks (CNN), require that the ground truth segmentation should be provided so that the network can be trained either to learn to detect the edge [4] (EDGE-BASED) or to detect the region [38] (REGION-BASED), depending on how the ground truth is designed. The learning pattern of such networks is usually complicated. However, the networks primarily learn to differentiate voxels inside and outside of the ROI based on their intensity.

REGION-GROWING-BASED segmentation, as the name suggests, extracts the ROI by iteratively growing a region starting from a seed point, assuming that the voxels within a ROI have resembling intensities. REGION GROWING has several variants and the seeded region growing is the most representative of the technique. It requires that the seed points should be selected within the ROI and the growing criterion should be carefully designed (e.g., the growing criterion can be that the difference between the intensity of a candidate voxel and the mean voxel intensity within the region is smaller than a predefined threshold). Ref. [39] presents several segmentation tasks involving multiple imaging modalities and organs for different computer-aided surgery systems that can be fulfilled using the region growing technique. In Ref. [39], the initial seed points need to be selected manually based on the prior knowledge about the target.

WATERSHED TRANSFORMATION is also based on the observation that the intensities of voxels within a ROI are similar while there is a sudden change of voxel intensity in the border between a ROI and its surrounding environment (i.e., other objects and the background). This property can be described quantitatively using the intensity gradients: voxels with highest gradient magnitude form the ROI boundary, which separates it from surrounding environment and encloses voxels with a common minimum. The technique has been primarily applied to image segmentation considering its ability to separate different ROIs in an image. In Ref. [40], WATERSHED TRANSFORMATION is used to segment multiple facial structures from magnetic resonance (MR) images. First, the gradient magnitude representation of MR images is calculated using Sobel filter (a differentiation operator) and then THRESHOLDING is applied to the gradient magnitude image to discard weak edges (voxels with gradient magnitude not large enough to form a ROI boundary are excluded from the initial segmentation to avoid over- segmentation). Ref. [41] exploits the prior information of the target to be segmented to improve the performance of WATERSHED TRANSFORMATION on knee cartilage and brain gray/white matter segmentation.

GRAPH-BASED segmentation is a technique initially proposed in Ref. [42], which borrows the idea of graph cuts in graph theory. Under the framework, segmenting ROIs in an image is equivalent to partitioning vertices in a graph and the images are converted into a graph representation. Each voxel in an image is represented as a vertex and the (non-negative) weights of edges denote the similarity between neighboring voxels. The similarity is usually measured in terms of the voxel intensity. Egger and coworkers have applied GRAPH-BASED techniques (and its variants) in various medical image segmentation tasks [43–49]. In Ref. [43], the technique is used for the segmentation of brain fiber bundles from Diffusion Tensor Imaging (DTI) to assist preoperative planning and intraoperative guidance of related neurosurgeries. In Ref. [45], the pancreatic metastasis is segmented from liver ultrasound imaging for pancreatic cancer surgeries. In Ref. [46], a graph-based method is used to segment the pituitary adenoma for brain tumor surgery (neurosurgery). In Ref. [47], the segmentation target is the prostate central gland.

To conclude, these intensity-based segmentation algorithms, even if presented in different forms, all depend on the voxel intensity for segmentation.

1.4 Summary of the segmentation algorithms

We have introduced the commonly used image segmentation algorithms in Section 1.1.1–1.1.3 and the various algorithms are grouped into two categories: shape-based segmentation and intensity-based segmentation. For the former category, the segmentation is dependent on the shape priors of the target and for the latter; the segmentation is primarily based on the voxel intensity. Shape-based segmentation algorithms are prevalently used in tasks where the difference of voxel intensity among different structures is difficult to distinguish. A common use case scenario is the segmentation of a particular bony structure from a bony cluster consisting of multiple highly occluded bony structures. The intensity-based segmentation algorithms, however, are more effective in tasks where the target to be segmented is contrasted from the surrounding structures with, for example, contrast agent.

1.5 Segmentation in oral and maxillofacial surgery

Oral and maxillofacial surgery, as the name indicates, aims at repairing defects/injuries related to the oral-maxillofacial complex, which primarily includes face, teeth, mouth, mandible (i.e., the lower jawbone), and maxilla (i.e., upper jawbone). The preoperative planning of the surgery usually requires that these ROIs should be delineated, which in current clinical routine is usually done manually by surgeons and is subjective and prone to errors. Qualitatively, the delineation and outlining of these ROIs allows a 3D visualization of the targets, which help surgeons obtain an overall morphological understanding of each patient-specific anatomical structure. Quantitatively, segmentation also allows a precise and automatic measurement of the ROIs or the creation of 3D models for 3D printing. Considering that the surgery covers a broad spectrum of surgical operations in the above-mentioned anatomical ROIs, it is impossible to give all of them a comprehensive introduction in a single chapter. Therefore in this chapter, we investigate the segmentation of the mandible, which is the largest

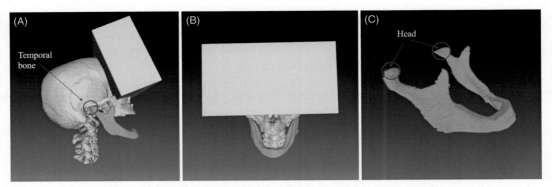

FIGURE 1.4 The relationship of the mandible *(blue)* to the skull bone *(gray)*. (A) and (B) the mandible in two different 3D views. (C) The mandible in 3D. The two mandible heads are connected to the temporal bone via the temporomandibular joint. For anonymization, the face of the patient was covered.

anatomical structure in the oral-maxillofacial complex and often the most common target in facial surgery [6].

Fig. 1.4 (A) and (B) show a 3D skull model without teeth, where the mandible is highlighted. Fig. 1.4 (C) shows the mandible model alone in 3D. The mandible is the largest bony structure of the human face and is connected to the temporal bone via the temporomandibular joint. As one of the primary functions of the mandible is for chewing food, it is the also the strongest bony structure in the facial area.

We can see that the difficulty of mandible segmentation lies in the separation of the mandible from neighboring bony structures such as the temporal bone, as these bony structures depict close intensity values in images. Therefore, as introduced in the former section, intensity-based techniques are not well suited for the segmentation of the mandible. Instead, the anatomical shape of the mandible is often used as a prior in the segmentation task [50–55]. Deep neural networks are also widely used in mandible segmentation [56–62]. Ref. [54] used watershed transformation. Ref. [6] gives a review of interactive mandible segmentation techniques using various open-source softwares. These publications are summarized in Table 1.1 and we will introduce these techniques in more detail in the remaining part of the chapter. These publications are primarily categorized into four groups based on the methods used:

- **Anatomical priors:** Mandible segmentation is achieved primarily using the prior knowledge of the mandible anatomy, either implicitly or explicitly. Note that the shape of the mandible is part of the mandible anatomy so that shape-based segmentation algorithms, such as SSM, SAM, and atlas-based methods belong to this category.
- **Intensity:** Mandible segmentation using intensity based segmentation algorithms such as watershed transform.
- **Contour:** Mandible segmentation by detecting the boundaries of the mandible, such as active contour model (snake) and edge detection algorithms (e.g., Canny).
- **Convolutional neural networks:** Mandible segmentation using CNN.

Table 1.1   Mandible segmentation publications.

Publications	Method	Image modality	Automaticity	Teeth
Aghdasi et al. [50]	Anatomical prior	CT	√	×
Abdi et al. [52]	Anatomical prior	2D panoramic X-rays	√	×
Spampinato et al. [54]	Anatomical prior	CT	√	√
Gollmer et al. [51]	SSM	CBCT	√	×
Kim et al. [53]	SSM	CBCT	√	×
Kainmueller et al. [55]	SSM	CBCT	√	×
Gollmer et al. [63]	SSM	CBCT	√	–
Kim et al. [64]	SSM	CBCT	×	×
Raith et al. [65]	SSM	CT	×	×
Wang et al. [66]	Convex optimization	CT + CBCT	√	√
Wang et al. [67]	Convex optimization + atlas	CBCT	√	√
Wang et al. [68]	Random forests + priors	CBCT	√	×
Lamecker et al. [69]	SSM + shape priors	CBCT	√	×
Brandariz et al. [70]	PSO + ACM	CBCT	√	–
Gamboa et al. [71]	ACM	CT	×	√
Chuang [72]	Atlas	CT	×	√
Egger et al. [56]	CNN	CT	√	×
Qiu et al. [57]	CNN	CT	√	×
Yan et al. [58]	CNN	CT	√	×
Qiu et al. [59]	CNN	CT	√	×
Abdi et al. [60]	3D Generative CNN	CT	√	×
Qiu et al. [61]	2D Recurrent CNN	CT	√	×
Ham et al. [62]	3D CNN	CBCT	√	×
Fan et al. [73]	Watershed transform	CBCT	√	√
Torosdagli et al. [74]	Random forest, FC	CT	√	×
Wallner et al. [6]	Interactive	CT	×	×
Abdullah [75]	Software	CT	×	√
Lilja [76]	–	X-rays	√	×
Nassef [77]	–	CT	√	×
Nassef [78]	–	CT	√	×

ACM, Active contour model; CNN, convolutional neural networks; FC, fuzzy connectivity; PSO, particle swarm optimization; SSM, statistical shape model. The √ (yes), × (no) in the final column of the table denotes whether the final mandible segmentation contains the teeth or not. – denotes no relevant information given in the publication.

- **Interactive segmentation:** Interactive mandible segmentation algorithms such as GrowCut and region growing.

1.5.1 Segmentation based on mandible anatomical priors

The anatomical priors, such as the shape and position of the mandible, are often used in mandible segmentation tasks. These anatomical priors can be involved in the segmentation process explicitly or implicitly.

1.5.1.1 Implicit use of shape priors: statistical models and atlas-based approaches

The implicit usage of anatomical priors means that the shape priors have to be learnt in the first phase and then the learnt priors are applied to new images in the segmentation phase. Representative approaches are SSMs. Related publications are introduced as follows. In [51,53,55,69], an SSM was used to segment the mandible from dental cone-beam CT (CBCT), which is a common imaging modality used in oral-maxillofacial surgeries [79]. SSM has widely been used in medical image segmentation tasks especially when it is difficult to separate the target from its surrounding structures based on intensity and the general shape as well as the shape variations of the target are known priors [16]. Briefly, an SSM of the mandible, which is trained from a set of mandible shapes, is representative of the mandible shapes and their variabilities, which can be statistically expressed under a unified framework [13]. The segmentation is achieved by matching the model with the candidate objects in an image.

Refs. [51,63] proposed an automatic scheme for both establishing correspondence among the training shapes and the initialization. For correspondence establishment, spherical parameterization was adopted. For automatic initialization in the segmentation phase, the author exploited the prior knowledge about the gray value and gradient distribution in the image. The proposed approach allows reasonable segmentation results while requiring significantly smaller training population.

Ref. [69] also use surface parameterization in correspondence establishment but in an interactive and patch-wise manner. In particular, each training shape is decomposed into several sub-regions (patches) and the correspondence is built in a patch-wise manner among the training shapes. The final correspondence is obtained by concatenating each individual parameterization. In the segmentation phase, the initialization is done by placing the average shape model to the center of the image data.

Ref. [64] built an SSM from 46 semi-automatically segmented mandible tem-plates. The cephalometric parameters measured from the average mandible model in SSM were compared with those measured from each template using conventional methods. The results show an agreement between the two sets of measurement, indicating that the SSM is a representative of the shape variations of the mandible. To establish the correspondence, the study adopted a similar approach to Ref. [69], where the correspondence is built in a patch-wise manner.

Ref. [65] requires manual creation of a standard mandible shape template with 555 vertices. On the template, several nodes are defined which are used to deform the template toward each training shape (mesh) manually through a graphical user interface. By doing so, all the training data can have a fixed number of vertices. The landmarks for correspondence establishment are the same as the nodes used for template deformation. Different from other applications, the authors used SSM to reconstruct complete mandible shapes from partial mandible shapes. First, an SSM is built from the 60 training data cases. Then, virtual defects are generated on three mandible shapes by removing a portion of the mandible bone from the complete shape to simulate the process of the tumor removal surgery.

Finally, the missing part, that is, the removed bony portion is reconstructed. The process is illustrated in Fig. 1.5. The SSM acts as a shape constraint that forces the reconstruction to follow the pattern of the shape variations in the training set and therefore guarantee a reasonable shape reconstruction. This study shows the feasibility of using SSM for

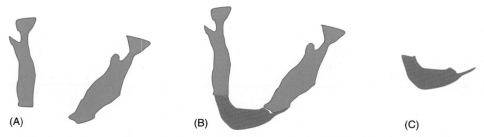

(A)   (B)   (C)

FIGURE 1.5 Illustration of mandible reconstruction using SSM. (A) The partial mandible mesh *(blue)*, which is the input of the algorithm. (B) The reconstructed mandible mesh with the missing part restored *(gray)*. (C) The mandible graft, which can be obtained by taking the difference between (A) and (B).

mandible (or dental) implant design. The implant model can then be 3D printed for the mandible repair surgery.

In Ref. [72], a set of mandible templates was created manually out of 54 CT scans. Given a new test CT scan to be segmented, the 54 CT scans are respectively registered to the new case using diffeomorphic registration. The registration step produces a deformation matrix that can be used to warp each mandible template so that the template can look similar to the mandibular structure in the test case. By doing so, all together 54 warped templates are created, each of which can be a rough segmentation for the test case. The last step merges the 54 segmentation results to form a final segmentation. The post-processing step is to manually edit the segmentation where necessary. The registration, warping, and merging, is fully automatic but the creation of the mandible templates and the post-processing requires human input.

Refs. [70,71] use active contour model (ACM) for mandible segmentation. Publications that are based on SSM and atlas are summarized in Table 1.2.

1.5.1.2 Explicit use of anatomical priors in mandible segmentation

The anatomical priors can also be used in an explicit manner in mandible segmentation. Compared with implicit usage introduced in the former section, explicit usage of anatomical priors means that the segmentation is achieved directly using the anatomical knowledge. Representative publications are Refs. [50,52,54].

Table 1.2   Mandible segmentation using SSM and atlas-based approach.

Publications	Correspondence	Dataset	Initialization	Landmarks (n)
Gollmer et al. [51]	Spherical parameterization ($\sqrt{}$)	30 (training) +6 (test)	$\sqrt{}$	4002
Lamecker et al. [69]	Patch-wise parameterization ($\times$)	13 (training) + 15 (test)	$\sqrt{}$	–
Kim et al. [64]	Patch-wise parameterization ($\times$)	46	–	18
Raith et al. [65]	Manual LM placement ($\times$)	60 (training) + 3 (test)	–	–
Chuang [72]	Diffeomorphic registration ($\sqrt{}$)	54 (training) +20 (test)	–	–

$\sqrt{}$ means the correspondence and initialization is done automatically and $\times$ denotes otherwise. n, number; LM, landmark.

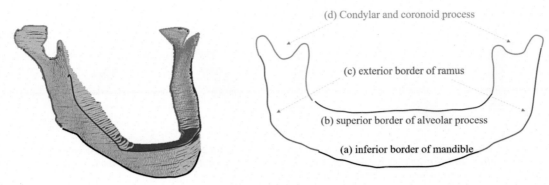

FIGURE 1.6 The contours of the mandible sub-regions described in [52]. *The figure on the right is adapted from Ref. [52].*

Ref. [50] makes use of the prior anatomical knowledge such as the spatial relations of the mandible to its surrounding bones in mandible segmentation. Specifically, the method first predefines a set of anatomical landmarks in the skull, such as the nasal tip point and the frontal bone, which are then used to extract a sub-volume that contains the target, that is, the mandible. In the sub-volume, the mandible structure is extracted by registering it with five pre-created mandible models represented in point clouds. The advantage of the approach is that it is using predefined anatomical landmarks to restrict the volume from where the mandible is segmented. This can help improve segmentation accuracy and decrease computation. The disadvantage, however, is that the registration may fail when the variation of the target mandible to the five pre-created mandible models is too large to be registered with sufficient accuracy.

Ref. [52] segments the complete mandible in four steps. In each of the steps, a sub-region of the mandible is segmented. Fig. 1.6A–D shows the contours of the four mandible sub-regions. The segmentation of (A), (B), and (C) is largely based on the prior anatomical knowledge, such as the shape and relative position, of each structure. For example, in the segmentation of the exterior borders of the ramuses (Fig. 1.6C), an SSM created from 30 manually segmented mandibles was used to guide the contour tracing of this sub-region. In the segmentation of the inferior border of the mandible (Fig. 1.6A), a set of modified edge detectors was adopted. For example, the canny edge detector was modified to preserve the horizontal edged while in the meantime weaken the vertical edges, considering that the inferior border of a mandible is generally horizontal. Then, a Prewitt filter was used to remove all the vertical edges. The extraction of the final target is based on the fact that the inferior border of a mandible is located the lowest among other horizontal edges. The segmentation of the condylar and coronoid process (Fig. 1.6D) was achieved via shape matching, where the query image was compared with a large group of pre-created shape templates.

Ref. [54] segments the mandible using a series of constraints based on the prior knowledge about the mandible anatomy (e.g., position, distance, and shape of the mandible). For example, the authors devised a criterion: $A/(A+B) < A'(A'+B')$, to separate the lower

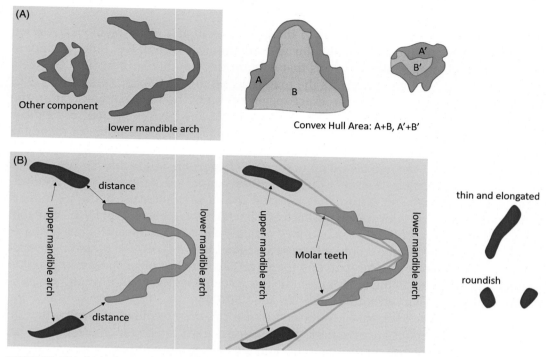

FIGURE 1.7 (A) Left: the lower mandible arch and other components in a 2D image slice. Right: the convex hull of the inferior mandible arch and other components. (B) The distance, position, and shape constraints used in the segmentation of the upper mandible arch. *Adapted from Ref. [54].*

mandible arch from other components in 2D slices, based on the prior anatomical knowledge that the ratio of the target area (i.e., the inferior mandible arch) to the area of the corresponding convex hull is the smallest among that of other components, as can be seen in Fig. 1.7A. A and B are the area occupied by the target and another object. $A + B$ and $A' + B'$ are the area occupied by the convex hull of the target and another object, respectively.

Similarly, the knowledge about the relative distance and position to the lower mandible arch, as well as the mandibular shape is exploited to segment the upper mandible arch among many other bony structures. As shown in Fig. 1.7B, the upper mandible arch falls within the region formed by four tangents from the midpoint of the previously segmented lower mandible arch to the right- and leftmost of the molar teeth (position constraint). The distance between the lower and upper mandible arch is also roughly a known knowledge, which can be used to further decide the potential candidates (distance constraint). Lastly, the shape of the upper mandible arch is also unique among other components that are coexistent with the target, that is, the upper mandible arch is thin and elongated in lower slices and roughly roundish in higher slices. The shape characteristic of the upper mandible arch can be helpful in separating the target from other components.

1.5.2 Intensity-based mandible segmentation

Ref. [74] segments the mandible from CT images in two steps and use an intensity-based segmentation technique in combination with anatomical knowledge. First, a random forest is trained to recognize CT slices that contain the mandibular bone and to create a bounding box that tightly encloses the mandible. Second, the fuzzy connectivity (FC) algorithm is used to delineate the exact region occupied by the mandible within the bounded area. The details of the FC algorithm are not covered in this chapter, as the focus of our chapter is to emphasize the importance of using anatomical priors in mandible segmentation. Readers are referred to Ref. [80] for a comprehensive overview of the FC algorithm. To decide the initial seed point for the FC algorithm automatically, the authors chose the voxel of highest intensity within the largest connected component in the bounded area. To separate the teeth from the mandible, the authors made use of the anatomical fact that the mandible is located in the back of the teeth in axial slices (Fig. 1.7B). Note that the mandible is segmented from a bounded area instead of from the entire image space, which is a useful technique commonly used in segmentation tasks. The bounding box allows the segmentation algorithm to find the target in a much smaller space compared to segmenting the target in the original volume, which can potentially improve the segmentation results. A similar technique is used in Refs. [50,72].

Ref. [73] used a marker-based watershed transformation for mandible segmentation, where the initial markers are automatically set using a pre-created mandible template, on which markers are placed on the mandible and the background, respectively. By registering a new image to be segmented with the template, the markers on the new image can be determined accordingly. According to the introduction of the watershed transformation algorithm in the first section, the sharp intensity change at the border of the target is fundamental in deciding the mandible boundary for the watershed transformation algorithm. To enhance the object boundaries, the authors transformed the original gray-scale image to its corresponding gradient image applying a Gaussian-based filter to the original image. On the gradient image, the two types of markers (in the mandible and the background) are dilated until their watershed lines meet to achieve the segmentation. The approach, however, did not distinguish between mandible and teeth and both structures are included in the final segmentation mask.

1.5.3 Convolutional neural networks

This section introduces mandible segmentation techniques based on CNNs. With the availability of adequate computation power and large amount of medical images, CNNs have been widely used in medical image processing such as segmentation [81,82], reconstruction [83], and registration [84]. Ref. [59] adopted three 2D UNets to segment the mandible from 2D CT slices. Each UNet takes as input three neighboring 2D slices from axial, sagittal, and coronal views, respectively, and produces the corresponding segmentation results in 2D. The 2D results from each network are then aggregated to form the final 3D mandible segmentation. Ref. [57] extends the method on a larger CT dataset. In Ref. [56], a 2D VGG-16 network [85] was first trained to identify whether the mandible is present in a CT slice. Then, fully convolutional networks (FCN) [86] were trained on slices where the mandible exists. Ref. [58] used a so-called symmetric convolutional network (SCN), where each encoding layer is symmetric to the corresponding decoding layer in terms of kernel size and number of feature maps. Ref. [58] used a technique to fuse the output of convolutional and deconvolutional layers with kernel size of multiple scales. Different from other deep learning approaches that use standard CNN, Ref. [61] adopted a 2D recurrent CNN (RCNN) [87] for mandible segmentation. The proposed RCNN is comprised of multiple segmentation units, each of which can be a conventional segmentation network such as a UNet and is responsible for mandible segmentation in a slice. Different slices in a 3D CT image are represented as different time steps in the RCNN. In inference, the 2D output of the segmentation units can be aggregated to form the final 3D segmentation. The advantage of the approach is that the contextual information among slices can be fully exploited compared to conventional 2D segmentation while avoiding the high computational requirement of 3D CNN. Ref. [62] proposes the usage of a 3D UNet to segment multiple facial structures, including the mandible, from CBCT (cone beam computed tomography) images. Ref. [60] proposed to use a generative CNN to generate mandible shapes represented as 3D voxel girds (dimension: 140^3), given as input the 3D coordinates of a set of mandible landmarks. The source data used in this work are 3D meshes, on which 28 landmarks are selected as the input of the generative CNN. The ground truths are the voxel grids voxelized from the 3D meshes. The approach is different from conventional CNN-based mandible segmentation methods which generate the mandible models (voxel grid) from source images fully automatically. Instead, mandible models are generated from a set of 3D coordinates, which needs to be selected manually (semi-automatic segmentation). Another point to note is that generating 3D models from a limited number of 3D coordinates is an ill-posed problem, that is, one set of landmarks may correspond to multiple mandible voxel grids as no constraint is applied on the edges of the mandible during the training process. Therefore, the evaluation of the results largely depends on visual inspection (the generated mandible is realistic/reasonable or not). Besides, the authors proposed to use the average distance of the landmarks to the reconstructed mandible surface for quantitative evaluation.

These deep learning approaches applied in automatic mandible segmentation are fully data-driven, without relying explicitly on the anatomical priors during the network design, training, and inference process. However, the creation of the ground truth segmentation required for supervised learning involves already intensive expert knowledge of the mandible anatomy. For example, the ground truth segmentation of the training dataset used in Ref. [62] was first created by in-house software and then corrected manually by experts in a slice-wise manner. The deep neural networks are then trained to learn this knowledge from the input image and the ground truth so that given a new image; the network is able to identify the mandible based on the learnt knowledge. Furthermore, most of the deep learning based approaches introduced above take as input 2D slices due to the high computational requirement of processing the entire 3D volume directly (Table 1.3).

Table 1.3   Mandible segmentation using convolutional neural networks (CNN).

Publications	Network	Dataset	Metrics	Loss function
Egger et al. [56]	2D FCN	20 3D CT	DSC	—
Qiu et al. [57]	2D UNet	109 3D CT	DSC, RMS	Dice Loss
Qiu et al. [59]	2D UNet	11 3D CT	DSC	Dice Loss
Yan et al. [58]	2D SCN	93 3D CT	DSC, IoU	L_2 loss
Abdi et al. [60]	AnatomyGen	103 meshes	L2S, DSC, HD, MSD,	Dice Loss
Qiu et al. [61]	2D RCNN	109 3D CT	DSC, ASD, HD	BCE + Dice
Ham et al. [62]	3D UNet	100 i-Cat CBCT	DSC, JSC, MSD, HSD	—

ASD, Average Symmetric Surface Distance; BCE, Binary Cross Entropy; DSC, Dice Similarity Coefficient; FCN, Fully Convolutional Network; HD, Hausdorff Distance; HSD, Hausdorff surface distance; IoU, Intersection over Union; JSC, Jaccard similarity coefficient; L2S, landmarkto-surface distance; MSD, mean surface distance; MSE, Mean Square Error; RCNN, Recurrent CNN; SCN, Symmetric Convolutional Network.

To conclude, using prior anatomical knowledge in combination with image processing algorithms is prevalent in mandible segmentation. Most of the introduced publications above use either shape-based segmentation techniques (e.g., SSM, atlas) or are based entirely on the anatomical knowledge about the mandible (Ref. [54] is representative of such methods). The prior anatomical knowledge is usually a robust indicator that can be dependent on for mandible segmentation but can fail when, in highly deformed cases, the mandible is irregularly-shaped and positioned. A few, such as Refs. [50] and [73] adopted intensity-based segmentation methods but still involved/used the anatomical knowledge of the mandible. The reason is that it is difficult to distinguish between the mandible and surrounding structures based purely on intensity since the voxel intensity of these bony structures is largely similar. Data driven approaches, such as CNNs, learn such anatomical knowledge during the training process from the ground truth segmentation by an expert or experts. Another important and challenging issue in mandible segmentation is the separation of the teeth from the mandible, considering that the teeth are fully occluded with the mandible. It can lead to an ambiguous mandible boundary especially when the intensity of the teeth is similar to that of the mandible. Precise delineation of the mandible boundary is therefore difficult in an automated manner. To achieve this goal, most of the above introduced mandible segmentation approaches rely on the knowledge of mandible and skull anatomy. For CNN-based approaches, the ground truth labels usually do not include the teeth (teeth and mandible are separated manually during manual labeling), so that the networks have already learnt to separate the teeth from the mandible during the training process [56]. Some approaches, such as Ref. [73] cannot separate the teeth from the mandible. Regarding the imaging modality, CT and CBCT are the most commonly used in the surgery according to Table 1.1. Compared with conventional CT, the image quality of CBCT is poorer (lower signal-to-noise rate and artifacts) and thus the mandible segmentation tends to be more challenging. Besides, the CBCT usually requires maximal intercuspation during imaging so that the upper and lower teeth are tightly occluded, which adds to the difficulty of mandible segmentation. However, the radiation to the patient is reduced compared to conventional CT due to the reduced dosage requirement.

1.5.4 Interactive mandible segmentation

In this section, we will introduce interactive mandible segmentation algorithms that are carried out on medical platforms (software) via user interface.

Ref. [75] evaluated the reconstruction quality of 3D mandible models from open-source software MITK (www.mitk.org) and made a comparison with the commercial software Mimics (Materialise NV, Belgium). It demonstrated that the reconstruction quality from MITK is comparable to that of Mimics and therefore the easily accessible MITK can be used as an alternative to the costly commercial software in 3D mandible reconstruction during pre-operative planning of mandible-related surgeries. The major factor affecting the quality of mandible reconstruction is the mandible segmentation process, during which the precise mandible anatomy should be delineated and separated from other bony structures. For both software (MITK and Mimics), the authors used the built-in region growing algorithm for mandible segmentation. After the mandible was segmented, the 3D surface model of the mandible was exported as stereolithography (stl) files from the two software, denoted as M_{MITK} and M_{Mimics}. The 3D reconstruction quality is evaluated by the agreement between the landmark distances measured from M_{MITK} and M_{Mimics}. The statistical analysis shows that the difference between the two groups of measurements is not significant ($P < 0.05$). The Hausdorff distance (HD) between M_{MITK} and M_{Mimics} is also less than 1%, meaning that the quality of 3D mandible reconstruction using MITK is comparable to that of using Mimics. The 3D mandible model can be used for various medical applications such as 3D medical printing, pre-operative planning, and surgical navigation. The key to the success of these applications is that the mandible can be segmented with clinically tolerable precision.

Ref. [6] conducted a thorough evaluation of the interactive (semi-automatic) and open-source segmentation algorithms that can be carried out on various easily accessible platforms such as 3D Slicer (www.slicer.org), MeVisLab (www.mevislab.de), and MITK for mandible segmentation. Several interactive segmentation algorithms including GrowCut, Robust Statistics Segmenter (RSS), 3D Region Growing, Otsu, ITKCannyLevelSet, and Geodesic Segmenter (Level set/active contour) have been evaluated. 10 head CTs with complete mandibles (teeth excluded) as well as the corresponding ground truth segmentation manually created by two experts were used for the assessment of these interactive algorithms. Some of the algorithms such as region growing have been introduced at the beginning of the chapter and in this section; we will focus on introducing how human interaction is involved in the segmentation process.

The **GrowCut** algorithm is initialized by specifying the foreground (i.e., the mandible) and the background with user-defined scribbles in the axial, sagittal, and coronal plane, as illustrated in Fig. 1.8A. The **RSS** and **3D region growing** (Fig. 1.8C) algorithms are initialized with user-specified seeds within the mandible in multiple slices. The difference is that the initialization is done in axial planes for **RSS** (Fig. 1.8B) and in axial, sagittal, and coronal planes for **3D region growing** (Fig. 1.8C). **Otsu** is a thresholding-based segmentation algorithm [88,89]. On the MITK platform, the user first specifies an initial number of regions for the segmentation. The **Otsu** algorithm can calculate the ideal thresholds, which are used for the determination and separation of the regions. Then, the user picks

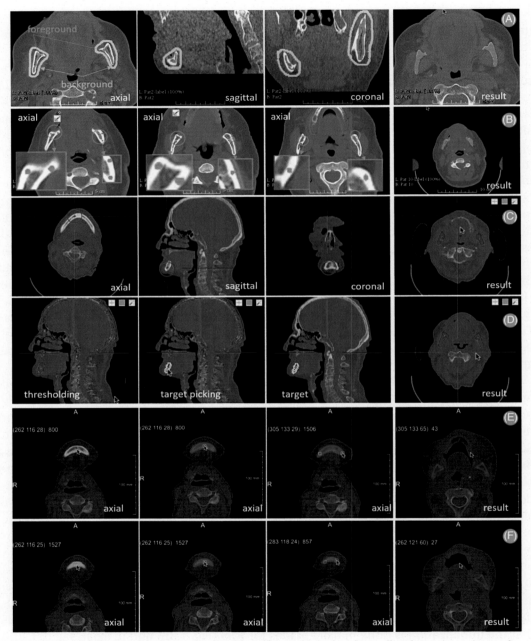

FIGURE 1.8 The initialization of the interactive algorithms (first to third column) as well as the segmentation results (fourth column, shown in axial view) described in Ref. [6] . The first to last row are the GrowCut (A) RSS, (B) 3D Region Growing, (C) Otsu, (D) ITKCannyLevelSet, (E) and Geodesic Segmenter (F), respectively.

Table 1.4 Human interaction involved in the interactive segmentation algorithms evaluated in Ref. [6].

Algorithms	Platform	Initialization	Plane	Category
GrowCut	3D slicer	fore/background scribbles	a/s/c	Intensity
RSS	3D slicer	foreground seeds	a	Active contour
3D Region Growing	MITK	foreground seeds	a/s/c	Intensity
Otsu and Picking	MITK	number of regions and picking	s (single slice)	Thresholding
ITKCannyLevelSet	MeVisLab	foreground seeds	a	Level set + edge detection
Geodesic Segmenter	MeVisLab	foreground seeds (one click)	a	Level set + active contour

a/s/c denotes the axial/sagittal/coronal plane. Unless otherwise noted, initialization needs to be done for multiple slices.

the target manually. The process can be done in the sagittal plane in a single slice as can be seen in Fig. 1.8D. **ITKCannyLevelSet** combines Canny edge detection with level set for segmentation. **Geodesic Segmenter** combines active contour model with level set. The initialization of both **ITKCannyLevelSet** and **Geodesic Segmenter** can be done by clicking on the mandible on the MeVisLab platform.

These algorithms are summarized in Table 1.4. Of the six algorithms, three (**GrowCut, 3D region growing**, and **Otsu**) are intensity-based and three (**RSS, Geodesic Segmenter**, and **ITKCannyLevelSet**) are edge-based. **RSS** and **Geodesic Segmenter** are based on active contour models (ACM).

1.6 Conclusion and future outlook

In this chapter, the publications related to mandible segmentation have been reviewed comprehensively. It can be concluded that the use of anatomical priors, especially the shape priors are widely used in mandible segmentation algorithms, while intensity-based segmentation algorithms are less prevalent in this field. With the prevalence of deep learning in medical image processing, pure data-driven approaches such as CNNs have become popular in more recent publications. The chapter covered only the segmentation of the mandible, as the mandible is the largest bony structure in the facial area and the most common target in oral-maxillofacial surgery. Most importantly, the segmentation algorithms used for the mandible are representative of that of other structures related to the surgery, such as the segmentation of the mandibular canal [90–93], jaw tissues [94], and the mandibular nerve [55]. In particular, anatomical priors and shape-based segmentation algorithms are widely adopted besides deep learning based approaches. However, despite the enthusiasm in automated mandible segmentation approaches, interactive (semi-automatic) segmentation methods remain to be the primary choice in applications requiring clinical precision. In clinical practice, interactive medical image segmentation is usually carried out on costly commercial platforms such as MIMICS (Materialise NV, Belgium). The study from Jürgen Wallner and coworkers [6,95] revealed that the easily accessible and free platforms such as 3D Slicer, MITK, and MeVisLab combining built-in open source segmentation algorithms can yield comparable segmentation accuracy to commercial software. The automated solutions can, nonetheless serve as a tool providing initial segmentations for the interactive segmentation approaches, which can potentially reduce the time and human interaction needed for a segmentation. It is also worthy of note that statistical models are a powerful tool for not only medical image segmentation but for shape reconstruction for the mandible [65], facial bones [96,97], skulls [98], and other bony structures. In these applications, the defects are created virtually and artificially to simulate the real surgical process. SSM allows a fast 3D modeling of the missing portion of the bones. The 3D models can then be manufactured using additive manufacturing (3D printing) and used as bone grafts (implants) in subsequent surgeries.

Acknowledgment

This work received the support of CAMed—Clinical additive manufacturing for medical applications (COMET K-Project 871132), which is funded by the Austrian Federal Ministry of Transport, Innovation and Technology (BMVIT), and the Austrian Federal Ministry for Digital and Economic Affairs (BMDW), and the Styrian Business Promotion Agency (SFG). Further, this work received funding from the Austrian Science Fund (FWF) KLI 678-B31 (enFaced—Virtual and Augmented Reality Training and Navigation Module for 3D-Printed Facial Defect Reconstructions) and the TU Graz Lead Project (Mechanics, Modeling and Simulation of Aortic Dissection).

References

[1] T. Kapur, J. Egger, J. Jayender, M. Toews, W.M. Wells, Registration and Segmentation for Image-Guided Therapy, Springer, New York, NY, 2014, pp. 79–91.

[2] J. Li, L. Cao, W. Cheng, M. Bowen, W. Guo, Towards automatic measurement of type b aortic dissection parameters: Methods, applications and perspective, in: D. Stoyanov, Z. Taylor, S. Balocco, R. Sznitman, A. Martel, L. Maier-Hein, L. Duong, G. Zahnd, S. Demirci, S. Albarqouni, S.-L. Lee, S. Moriconi, V. Cheplygina, D. Mateus, E. Trucco, E. Granger, P. Jannin (Eds.), Intravascular Imaging and Computer Assisted Stenting and Large-Scale Annotation of Biomedical Data and Expert Label SynthesisSpringer International Publishing, Cham, 2018, pp. 64–72.

[3] A. Pepe, J. Li, M. Rolf-Pissarczyk, C. Gsaxner, X. Chen, G.A. Holzapfel, et al. Detection, segmentation, simulation and visualization of aortic dissections: A review, Med. Image Anal. 65 (2020) 101773, doi: 10.1016/j.media.2020.101773.

[4] Z. Li, J. Feng, Z. Feng, Y. An, Y. Gao, B. Lu, et al. Lumen segmentation of aortic dissection with cascaded convolutional network, in: M. Pop, M. Sermesant, J. Zhao, S. Li, K. McLeod, A. Young, K. Rhode, T. Mansi (Eds.), Statistical Atlases and Computational Models of the Heart. Atrial Segmentation and LV Quantification Challenges, Springer International Publishing, 2019, pp. 122–130.

[5] I.N. Bankman, Handbook of Medical Image Processing and Analysis, 2009.

[6] J. Wallner, M. Schwaiger, K. Hochegger, C. Gsaxner, W. Zemann, J. Egger, A review on multiplatform evaluations of semi-automatic open-source based image segmentation for cranio-maxillofacial surgery, Comput. Methods Programs Biomed. 182 (2019) 105102.

[7] T. Kovács, P. Cattin, H. Alkadhi, S. Wildermuth, G. Székely, Automatic segmentation of the vessel lumen from 3d cta images of aortic dissection, Bildverarbeitung für die Medizin, Springer, Berlin Heidelberg, 2006, pp. 161–165.

[8] T. Behrens, K. Rohr, H.S. Stiehl, Robust segmentation of tubular structures in 3d medical images by parametric object detection and tracking, IEEE Trans. Syst. Man Cyber. Part B Cyber. 33 (4) (2003) 554–561.

[9] P. Suetens, R. Verbeeck, D. Delaere, J. Nuyts, B. Bijnens, Model-based image segmen-tation: Methods and applications, in: M. Stefanelli, A. Hasman, M. Fieschi, J. Talmon (Eds.), AIME, 91, Springer Berlin Heidelberg, Berlin, Heidelberg, 1991, pp. 3–24.

[10] T.F. Cootes, C.J. Taylor. Active shape models—'smart snakes'. *Proceedings of the British Machine Vision Conference (BMVC)*, pp. 28.1–28.10 (1992).

[11] T.F. Cootes, C.J. Taylor, D.H. Cooper, J. Graham, Active shape models-their training and application, Comput. Vision Image Understand. 61 (1995) 38–59.

[12] S. Wang, B.C. Munsell, T. Richardson, Correspondence establishment in statistical shape modeling: Optimization and evaluation, Statistical Shape and Deformation Analysis: Methods, Implementation and ApplicationsAcademic Press, 2017, pp. 63–75.

[13] F. Ambellan, H. Lamecker, C. von Tycowicz, S. Zachow, Statistical shape models: Understanding and mastering variation in anatomy, Biomed. Visual. Adv. Exp. Med. Biol. 1156 (2019) 67–84.

[14] G. Zheng, Z. Li, J. Gu. Evaluation of 3d correspondence methods for building point distribution models of the kidney. 2012 5th International Conference on BioMedical Engineering and Informatics, pp. 637–640 (2012).

[15] M. Styner, K.T. Rajamani, L.-P. Nolte, G. Zsemlye, G. Székely, C.J. Taylor, R.H. Davies. Evaluation of 3d correspondence methods for model building. *Information Processing in Medical Imaging: Proceedings of the ... Conference*, vol. 18, pp. 63–75 (2003).

[16] T. Heimann, H.-P. Meinzer, Statistical shape models for 3d medical image segmentation: A review, Med. Image Anal. 13 (4) (2009) 543–563.

[17] T.F. Cootes, G.J. Edwards, C.J. Taylor. Active appearance models. Proceedings of European Conference on Computer Vision, vol. 2, pp. 484–498, Springer (1998).

[18] T.F. Cootes, G.J. Edwards, C.J. Taylor, Active appearance models, IEEE Trans. Pattern Anal. Mach. Intell. 23 (6) (2001) 681–685.

[19] G.J. Edwards, C.J. Taylor, T.F. Cootes. Interpreting face images using active appearance models. Proceedings Third IEEE International Conference on Automatic Face and Gesture Recognition, pp. 300–305 (1998).

[20] M. Bach Cuadra, V. Duay, J.-P. Thiran, Atlas-based segmentation, Handbook of Biomedical Imaging: Methodologies and Clinical ResearchSpringer Science+Business Media, 2015, pp. 221–244.

[21] J.E. Iglesias, M.R. Sabuncu, Multi-atlas segmentation of biomedical images: A survey, Med. Image Anal. 24 (1) (2015) 205–219.

[22] R.A. Heckemann, J.V. Hajnal, P. Aljabar, D. Rueckert, A. Hammers, Automatic anatomical brain MRI segmentation combining label propagation and decision fusion, NeuroImage 33 (1) (2006) 115–126.

[23] A. Klein, B. Mensh, S.S. Ghosh, J.A. Tourville, J. Hirsch, Mindboggle: Automated brain labeling with multiple atlases, BMC Med. Imaging 5 (2005) 7.

[24] J. Wang, C. Vachet, A. Rumple, S. Gouttard, C. Ouziel, E. Perrot, et al. Multi-atlas segmentation of subcortical brain structures via the autoseg software pipeline, Front. Neuroinform. 8 (2014).

[25] Z. Turani, R.A. Zoroofi, S. Shirani, S. Abkhofte. Cardiovascular segmentation based on hough transform and heuristic knowledge. 2012 19th Iranian Conference of Biomedical Engineering (ICBME), pp. 309–312 (2012).

[26] M. Kass, A.P. Witkin, D. Terzopoulos, Snakes: Active contour models, Int. J. Comput. Vision 1 (1998) 321–331.

[27] B. Preim, C.P. Botha, Image analysis for medical visualization, Visual Computing for Medicine: Theory, Algorithms, and ApplicationsMorgan Kaufmann, 2014, pp. 111–175.

[28] N. Thresholding, P. Sauvola, Jaccard, Image segmentation by using thresholding techniques for medical images, CSEIJ 6 (2016).

[29] M. Gall, X. Li, X. Chen, D. Schmalstieg, J. Egger. Computer-aided planning and recon- struction of cranial 3d implants. Annual International Conference of the IEEE Engineering in Medicine and Biology Society (EMBC), pp. 1179–1183, vol. 08 (2016)

[30] X. Chen, L. Xu, X. Li, J. Egger, Computer-aided implant design for the restoration of cranial defects, Sci. Rep. 7 (2017) 1–10.

[31] J. Egger, M. Gall, A. Tax, M. Üçal, U. Zefferer, X. Li, et al. Interactive reconstructions of cranial 3d implants under mevislab as an alternative to commercial planning software, PLoS ONE 12 (2017) 20.

[32] J. Li, A. Pepe, C. Gsaxner, J. Egger, An online platform for automatic skull defect restoration and cranial implant design, arXiv:2006 00980 (2020).

[33] J. Li. Deep learning for cranial defect reconstruction. Master's thesis, Graz University of Technology (2020).

[34] J. Li, A. Pepe, C. Gsaxner, G. von Campe, J. Egger, A baseline approach for autoimplant: the miccai 2020 cranial implant design challenge, Multimodal Learning for Clinical Decision Support and Clinical Image-Based ProceduresSpringer, 2020, pp. 75–84.

[35] N. Sharma, L.M. Aggarwal, Automated medical image segmentation techniques, J. Med. Phys./ Assoc. Med. Physicists India 35 (2010) 3–4.

[36] H.M. Moftah, A.E. Hassanien, M. Shoman. 3d brain tumor segmentation scheme using k- mean clustering and connected component labeling algorithms. 10th International Conference on Intelligent Systems Design and Applications, pp. 320–324 (2010).

[37] Y Guo, A.S. Ashour, Neutrosophic sets in dermoscopic medical image segmentation, Neutrosophic Set in Medical Image Analysis, Elsevier, 2019, pp. 229–243.

[38] L.D. Hahn, G. Mistelbauer, K. Higashigaito, M. Koci, M.J. Willemink, A.M. Sailer, et al. Ct-based true and false lumen segmentation in type b aortic dissection using machine learning, Radiol. Cardiothorac. Imaging 2 (3) (2020).

[39] R.K. Justice, E.M. Stokely, J.S. Strobel, R.E. Ideker, W.M. Smith, Medical image segmentation using 3d seeded region growing, In SPIE Medical Imaging. doi: 10.1117/12.274179.

[40] H.P. Ng, S. Huang, S.H. Ong, K. Foong, P.M. Goh, W.L. Nowinski. Medical image segmentation using watershed segmentation with texture-based region merging. 30th Annual International Conference of the IEEE Engineering in Medicine and Biology Society, pp. 4039–4042 (2008).

[41] V. Grau, A.J.U. Mewes, M.A. Raya, R. Kikinis, S.K. Warfield, Improved watershed transform for medical image segmentation using prior information, IEEE Trans. Med. Imaging 23 (2004) 447–458.

[42] P.F. Felzenszwalb, D.P. Huttenlocher, Efficient graph-based image segmentation, Int. J. Comput. Vision 59 (2004) 167–181.

[43] M.H.A. Bauer, J. Egger, D. Kuhnt, S. Barbieri, J. Klein, H.K. Hahn, et al. Ray-based and graph-based methods for fiber bundle boundary estimation, ArXiv, abs/1103 (2011) 1952.

[44] J. Egger, R.R. Colen, B. Freisleben, C. Nimsky, Manual refinement system for graph-based segmentation results in the medical domain, J. Med. Syst. 36 (2011) 2829–2839.

[45] J. Egger, X. Chen, L. Bettac, M.M. Hänle, T. Gräter, W.G. Zoller, In-depth assessment of an interactive graph-based approach for the segmentation for pancreatic metastasis in ultrasound acquisitions of the liver with two specialists in internal medicine. 10th Biomedical Engineering International Conference (BMEiCON), pp. 1–5 (2017).

[46] J. Egger, D. Zukić, B. Freisleben, A. Kolb, C. Nimsky, Segmentation of pituitary adenoma: A graph-based method vs. a balloon inflation method, Comput. Methods Prog. Biomed. 110 (3) (2013) 268–278.

[47] J. Egger, Pcg-cut: Graph driven segmentation of the prostate central gland, PLoS ONE 8 (2013).

[48] M.H.A. Bauer, J. Egger, D. Kuhnt, S. Barbieri, J. Klein, H.K. Hahn, et al. A semi-automatic graph-based approach for determining the boundary of eloquent fiber bundles in the human brain, ArXiv, abs/1103.1475 (2011).

[49] M.H.A. Bauer, J. Egger, T.O'Donnell, S. Barbieri, J. Klein, B. Freisleben, A fast and robust graph-based approach for boundary estimation of fiber bundles relying on fractional anisotropy maps. 20th International Conference on Pattern Recognition, pp. 4016–4019 (2010).

[50] N. Aghdasi, Y. Li, A. Berens, K. Moe, B. Hannaford. Automatic mandible segmentation on ct images using prior anatomical knowledge. MIDAS 03 (2016).

[51] S. Gollmer, T.M. Buzug. Fully automatic shape constrained mandible segmentation from cone-beam ct data. 9th IEEE International Symposium on Biomedical Imaging (ISBI), pp. 1272–1275 (2012).

[52] A.H. Abdi, S. Kasaei, M. Mehdizadeh, Automatic segmentation of mandible in panoramic x-ray, J. Med. Imaging 2 (2015) 044003.

[53] J. Kim, L. Minjin, H. Helen, Automatic mandibular segmentation using shape restriction information from cranial face cbct image, J. Korea Comput. Graph. Soc. 23 (5) (2017) 19–27.

[54] C. Spampinato, C. Pino, D. Giordano, R. Leonardi. Automatic 3d segmentation of mandible for assessment of facial asymmetry. IEEE International Symposium on Medical Measurements and Applications Proceedings, pp. 1–4 (2012).

[55] D. Kainmüller, H. Lamecker, H. Seim, M. Zinser, S. Zachow, Automatic extraction of mandibular nerve and bone from cone-beam ct data, MICCAI 12 (2) (2009) 76–83.

[56] J. Egger, B. Pfarrkirchner, C. Gsaxner, L. Lindner, D. Schmalstieg, J. Wallner. Fully convolutional mandible segmentation on a valid ground- truth dataset. 40th Annual International Conference of the IEEE Engineering in Medicine and Biology Society (EMBC), pp. 656–660 (2018).

[57] B. Qiu, J. Guo, J. Kraeima, H.H. Glas, R.J.H. Borra, M.J.H. Witjes, et al. Automatic segmentation of the mandible from computed tomography scans for 3d virtual surgical planning using the convolutional neural network, Phys. Med. Biol. (2019).

[58] M. Yan, J. Guo, W. Tian, Z. Yi., Symmetric convolutional neural network for mandible segmentation, Knowl. Based Syst. 159 (2018) 63–71.

[59] B. Qiu, J. Guo, J. Kraeima, R.J.H. Borra, M.J.H. Witjes, P.M.A. van Ooijen, 3d segmentation of mandible from multisectional ct scans by convolutional neural networks, ArXiv, abs/1809.06752 (2018).

[60] A. Abdi, H. Borgard, P. Abolmaesumi, Fels.F S., Anatomygen: Deep anatomy generation from dense representation with applications in mandible synthesis, in: M.J. Cardoso, A. Fer-agen, B. Glocker, E. Konukoglu, I. Oguz, G. Unal, T. Vercauteren (Eds.), Proceedings of the 2nd International Conference on Medical Imaging with Deep Learning, volume 102 of Proceedings of Machine Learning ResearchPMLR, London, United Kingdom, 2019, pp. 4–14.

[61] B. Qiu, J. Guo, J. Kraeima, H.H. Glas, R.J.H. Borra, M.J.H. Witjes, et al. Recurrent convolutional neural networks for mandible segmentation from computed tomography, ArXiv, abs/2003.06486 (2020).

[62] S. Ham, A.-R. Lee, J. Park, Y. Byeon, S. Lee, M. Bae, N. Kim. Multi-structure segmentation of hard tissues, maxillary sinus, mandible, mandibular canals in cone beam ct of head and neck with 3d u-net. Proceedings of the international conference on medical imaging with deep learning (MIDL), pp. 1–3 (2018).

[63] S.T. Gollmer, T.M. Buzug, Relaxed statistical shape models for 3d image segmentation – application to mandible bone in cone-beam ct data, Curr. Med. Imaging 9 (2) (2013).

[64] S.-G. Kim, W.-J. Yi, S.J. Hwang, S.-C. Choi, S.-S. Lee, M.-S. Heo, et al. Development of 3d statistical mandible models for cephalometric measurements, Imaging Sci. Dentist. 42 (2012) 175–182.

[65] S. Raith, S. Wolff, T. Steiner, A. Modabber, M. Weber, F. Hölzle, et al. Planning of mandibular reconstructions based on statistical shape models, Int. J. Comput. Assist. Radiol. Surgery 12 (2016) 99–112.

[66] L. Wang, K.C. Chen, F. Shi, S. Liao, G. Li, Y. Gao, et al. Automated segmentation of cbct image using spiral ct atlases and convex optimization, MICCAI 16 (3) (2013) 251–258.

[67] L. Wang, K.C. Chen, Y. Gao, F. Shi, S. Liao, G. Li, et al. Automated bone segmentation from dental cbct images using patch-based sparse representation and convex optimization, Med. Phys. 41 (4) (2014) 043503.

[68] L. Wang, Y. Gao, F. Shi, G. Li, K.-C. Chen, Z.C. Tang, et al. Automated segmentation of dental cbct image with prior-guided sequential random forests, Med. Phys. 43 (1) (2016) 336–346.

[69] H. Lamecker, S. Zachow, A. Wittmers, B. Weber, H.-C. Hege, B. Elsholtz, et al. Automatic segmentation of mandibles in low-dose ct-data, Int. J. Comput. Assist. Radiol. Surgery (2006).

[70] M. Brandariz, N. Barreira, M.G. Penedo, M. Suarez-Cunqueiro. Automatic segmentation of the mandible in cone-beam computer tomography images. 2014 IEEE 27th International Symposium on Computer-Based Medical Systems, pp. 467–468 (2014).

[71] A. Gamboa, A. Cosa, F. Benet, E. Arana, D. Moratal. A semiautomatic segmentation method, solid tissue classification and 3d reconstruction of mandible from computed tomography imaging for biomechanical analysis. 9th IEEE International Symposium on Biomedical Imaging (ISBI), pp. 1483–1486 (2012).

[72] Y.J. Chuang, B.M. Doherty, N. Adluru, M.K. Chung, H.K. Vorperian, A novel registration-based semiautomatic mandible segmentation pipeline using computed tomogra- phy images to study mandibular development, J. Comput. Assist. Tomogr. 42 (2018) 306–316.

[73] Y. Fan, R. Beare, H. Matthews, P. Schneider, N.M. Kilpatrick, J.K. Clement, et al. Marker-based watershed transform method for fully automatic mandibular segmentation from cbct images, Dento Maxillo Facial Radiol. 48 (2) (2019) 20180261.

[74] N. Torosdagli, D. Liberton, P. Verma, M. Sincan, S. Pattanaik, U. Bagci. Robust and fully automated segmentation of mandible from ct scans. IEEE 14th International Symposium on Biomedical Imaging (ISBI 2017) (2017).

[75] J.Y. Abdullah, M. Omar, H.M.H. Pritam, A. Husein, Z.A. Rajion, Comparison of 3d reconstruction of mandible for pre-operative planning using commercial and open-source software, AIP Conf. Proc. 1791 (1) (2016) 020001.

[76] M. Lilja, V. Vuorio, K. Antila, H. Setaelae, J. Järnstedt, M. Pollari. Automatic segmen- tation of the mandible from limited-angle dental x-ray tomography reconstructions. 4th IEEE International Symposium on Biomedical Imaging: From Nano to Macro, pp. 964–967 (2007).

[77] T.M. Nassef, New segmentation approach to extract human mandible bones based on actual computed tomography data, Am. J. Biomed. Eng. 2 (2012) 197–201.

[78] T.M. Nassef, N.H. Solouma, M.A. Alkhodary, M.K. Marei, Y.M. Kadah. Extraction of human mandible bones from multi-slice computed tomographic data. 2011 1st Middle East Conference on Biomedical Engineering, pp. 260–263 (2011).

[79] A. Schramm, M. Rücker, N. Sakkas, R. Schön, J. Düker, N.C. Gellrich, The use of cone beam ct in cranio-maxillofacial surgery, Int. Congr. Ser. 1281 (2005) 1200–1204.

[80] J.K. Udupa, S. Samarasekera, Fuzzy connectedness and object definition: Theory, algorithms, and applications in image segmentation, Graphic. Models Image Process. 58 (3) (1996) 246–261.

[81] O. Ronneberger, P. Fischer, T. Brox, U-net: Convolutional networks for biomedical image segmentation, MICCAI (2015) 234–241.

[82] F. Milletari, N. Navab, S. Ahmadi. V-net: Fully convolutional neural networks for volumetric medical image segmentation. 2016 Fourth International Conference on 3D Vision (3DV), pp. 565–571 (2016).

[83] H. Zhang, B. Dong, A review on deep learning in medical image reconstruction, J. Oper. Res. Soc. China 8 (2019) 311–340.

[84] G. Haskins, U. Kruger, P. Yan, Deep learning in medical image registration: a survey, Mach. Vision Appl. 31 (2020) 1–18.

[85] K. Simonyan, A. Zisserman. Very deep convolutional networks for large-scale image recognition. International Conference on Learning Representations (ICLR) (2015).

[86] J. Long, E. Shelhamer, T. Darrell. Fully convolutional networks for semantic segmentation. 2015 IEEE Conference on Computer Vision and Pattern Recognition (CVPR), pp. 3431–3440 (2015).

[87] M. Liang, X. Hu. Recurrent convolutional neural network for object recognition. 2015 IEEE Conference on Computer Vision and Pattern Recognition *(CVPR)*, pp. 3367–3375 (2015).

[88] H.J. Vala, A. Baxi, A review on Otsu image segmentation algorithm, Int. J. Adv. Res. Comput. Eng. Technol. 2 (2) (2013).

[89] A.B. Patil, J.A. Shaikh, Otsu thresholding method for flower image segmentation, IJCER 06 (05) (2016).

[90] F. Abdolali, R.A. Zoroofi. Mandibular canal segmentation using 3d active appearance models and shape context registration. 21th Iranian Conference on Biomedical Engineering (ICBME), pp. 7–11 (2014).

[91] N.L. Gerlach, G.J. Meijer, D.-J. Kroon, E. Bronkhorst, S.J. Bergé, T.J.J. Maal, Evaluation of the potential of automatic segmentation of the mandibular canal using cone-beam computed tomography, Br. J. Oral Maxill. Surgery 52 (9) (2014) 838–844.

[92] D.J. Kroon, Phd thesis, Segmentation of the mandibular canal in cone-beam ct data. University of Twente (2011).

[93] J. Jaskari, J. Sahlsten, J. Järnstedt, H. Mehtonen, K. Karhu, O. Sundqvist, et al. Deep learning method for mandibular canal segmentation in dental cone beam computed tomography volumes, Sci. Rep. 10 (2020).

[94] S. Rueda, J.A. Gil, R. Pichery, M.A. Raya, Automatic segmentation of jaw tissues in ct using active appearance models and semi-automatic landmarking, MICCAI 9 (1) (2006) 167–174.

[95] J. Wallner, K. Hochegger, X. Chen, I. Mischak, K. Reinbacher, M. Pau, et al. Clinical evaluation of semi-automatic open-source algorithmic software segmentation of the mandibular bone: Practical feasibility and assessment of a new course of action, PLoS ONE 13 (2018).

[96] W. Semper-Hogg, M.A. Fuessinger, S. Schwarz, E. Ellis, C.P. Cornelius, F.A. Probst, et al. Virtual reconstruction of midface defects using statistical shape models, J. Cranio-maxillofac. Surg. 45 (4) (2017) 461–466.

[97] M.A. Fuessinger, S. Schwarz, J. Neubauer, C.P. Cornelius, M. Gass, P.J. Poxleitner, et al. Virtual reconstruction of bilateral midfacial defects by using statistical shape modeling, J. Cranio-maxillofac. Surg. 47 (2019) 1054–1059.

[98] M.A. Fuessinger, S. Schwarz, C.-P. Cornelius, M.C. Metzger, E. Ellis, F. Probst, et al. Planning of skull reconstruction based on a statistical shape model combined with geometric morphometrics, Int. J. Comput. Assist. Radiol. Surg. 13 (2017) 519–529.

2

Registration in oral and maxillofacial surgery

Chunxia Qin[a,b], Yongfeng Mai[b], Xiaojun Chen[b]

aSCHOOL OF BIOMEDICAL ENGINEERING, SHANGHAI JIAO TONG UNIVERSITY, SHANGHAI, CHINA; bSCHOOL OF MECHANICAL ENGINEERING, SHANGHAI JIAO TONG UNIVERSITY, SHANGHAI, CHINA

1 Medical image registration

1.1 Brief introduction of medical image registration

For disease diagnosis, treatment design, and minimally invasive operation, the surgeon often requires to collect various image series acquired in different time intervals or by distinct sensors at the same time, for an optimal description of anatomical structures and metabolic function of patients. Therefore, it is essential to transform different image sequences with respect to different modalities and dimensionalities to the same coordinate frame. The process of aligning two or more clinical image acquisitions based on certain matching criteria, is referred to as medical image registration, image alignment, image fusion, and image superimposition. Generally, medical image registration can be achieved by calculating or searching an optimal global or local spatial transformation for a source image (also called as moving image or sensed image), to make its pixels best align with the corresponding points on the target image (referred as fixed image or reference image). The corresponding point pairs of two image series are supposed to represent the same anatomical position after registration.

The chapter first depicts brief knowledge about medical image registration, including its basic framework, common categories, and clinical applications. After that, image registration algorithms in oral and maxillofacial surgery are introduced in detail. Specifically, subsection 1.1 introduces the definition of image registration and its clinical applications from five aspects: (1) clinical disease detection and diagnosis, (2) evaluation of surgical performance and surgery treatment follow up, (3) building of statistical atlases, (4) surgical navigation system, and (5) other applications. The registration approach classifications based on different criteria have been listed in subsection 1.2. Then, subsection 1.3 presents the several major components of image registration procedure, including similarity measure, spatial transform, image interpolation, and optimization strategy. Subsequently, subsection 1.4 illustrates the commonly used medical imaging modalities in oral and maxillofacial surgery and their characteristics, and then summarizes the reported image alignment algorithms in oral and maxillofacial surgery from three categories that are mono-modal approaches, multi-modal approaches, and deep learning based approaches. Mono-modal registration has been widely applied for surgery treatment follow up overtimes or the surgery operation evaluation via the comparison of the pre-interventional and post-intervention data. In addition, due to the limited view field, it is necessary to integrate multiple single data into a whole object by mono-modal alignment approaches. In term of multi-model image registration, more than one imaging modes are collected to obtain more descriptive and comprehensive information to improve the accuracy and efficiency of disease diagnosis, lesion delineation, or treatment planning. For example, compared with CT image which has superiority in depicting osseous tissue while less clear in soft tissue, MRI can complimentary provide more fair contrast of soft tissue. Therefore, the registration of CT and MRI can provide surgeons with information of both bone tissues and soft tissues. Furtherly, subsection 1.5 illustrates the image-to-patient coordinate registration method, which is one of the essential steps for image-guided surgical navigation systems. Finally, several common software tools developed for medical image registration and fusion are listed and briefly introduced in the last subsection.

1.2 The application of medical image registration technology

Because complementary information conveyed in different image sequences can be collected together to provide a better descriptive of patient's anatomical structures and metabolism functions, image registration has become one of the crucial technologies for computer assisted diagnosis and surgery. In the past several decades, medical image registration has found an increasingly wide utilization in image-guided radiation therapy, image-guided radiosurgery, image-guided minimally invasive therapy, and other fields. As shown in Fig. 2.1, we summarize these applications from five aspects: (1) clinical disease detection and diagnosis, (2) evaluation of surgical performance and surgery treatment follow up, (3) building of statistical atlases, (4) surgical navigation system, and (5) other applications.

1. Diagnosis of disease

Single modality imaging has its advantages and limitations for disease detection. For example, X-ray or computed tomography (CT) can provide dense structures like bones and implants with less distortion, but they cannot detect physiological changes. Similarly, CBCT scan can obtain high-resolution images with lower radiation and non- invasion, while it can only illustrate the tissue structures without functional information, and its quality can be easily affected by streak and scatter artifacts. Moreover, normal and pathological soft tissue can be better visualized by MRI images whereas PET can be used to provide better information on blood flow and flood activity with low spatial resolution. Therefore, complementary knowledge of both hard/soft tissues or metabolism/anatomical information can be obtained via the combination of multiple modality images. Multi-source medical image fusion, offering a larger diversity of medical features, has indicated significant achievements in facilitating disease diagnosis and treatment planning. For example, mammograms

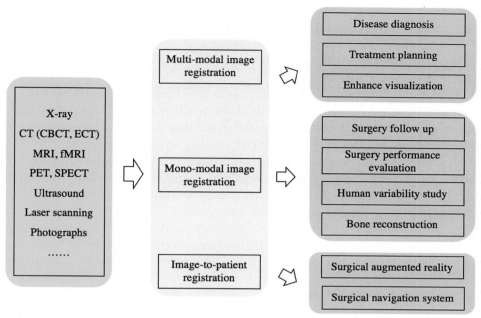

FIGURE 2.1 The clinical applications of medical image registration.

are the most widely applied imaging modality for breast cancer. The superimposition of function imaging PET has reported notable improvement in diagnostic accuracy. Similarly, the combination of CT and PET is widely used for the detection and localization of maxillofacial cancer.

2. Evaluation of surgical performance and surgery treatment follow up
   Both the applications of surgical performance evaluation and treatment follow up are based on mono-modal image registration. For the operation guided by preoperative planning, it is meaningful to match the pre-interventional data with the post-interventional image for the evaluation of surgical accuracy. Take for example, the zygomatic implant placement. As zygomatic implant is more than 3 times as long as traditional dental implant, preoperatively planned placement trajectories are important reference for the intra-operative guidance under computer assisted surgical navigation technology. After the surgery, the deviations between designed zygomatic implant paths and the actually placed implants are measured by aligning the pre-operative data to the post-operative data, to evaluate the operation performance, or to investigate the feasibility of the employed navigation system.

   Besides for the pre- and post-interventional data comparison, mono image registration technology is often conducted to track the temporal anatomical structure changes. As disease would dynamically develop or degenerate along time, the design and adjustment of some patient's therapeutic schedule not only depend on the patient's current condition, but also refer to the disease change over a period of time.

For example, the dentition displacement assessment during the orthodontic procedure is essential, as it is an important reference for the operator to verify and adjust the orthodontic treatment. In addition, the surgeon is also required to compare and analyze the image series collected at different times to follow up the treatment effects.

3. Building of statistical atlases

   Anatomical statistical atlas has become a useful method to investigate human anatomical variability and the detection of abnormal anatomical structures. Different types of statistical atlas have been reported in the past 2 decades, like statistical shape model (SSM), statistical shape model(SDM), and so on. SSM is a geometric model containing a mean shape and multiple compressed primarily shape variations of a collection of similar shapes. SDMs are regarded as statistical model to describe or infer the spatial or temporal changes in anatomy and function [1]. Due to the ability to represent prior geometric or intensity information, SSM and SDM have been widely applied in different medical modalities for the segmentation and registration of various anatomical structures, including the brain, bone, liver, heart, prostate, and so on. The alignment of a collection of similar data is an integral step for the building of those statistical atlases.

4. Computer-assisted image-guided surgical navigation system

   Since computer-assisted image-guided surgical navigation system (SNS) concept was proposed, great progress has been made in this technology in the past several decades, especially in the field of neurosurgery, otorhinolaryngology, orthopedics, and even in some soft anatomical structures. In surgical navigation systems, based on an employed position localization systems (like infrared or electromagnetic tracking devices), the relative positions among the surgical instruments, patient's anatomy, and planned surgical paths designed on pre-operative images can be obtained, guaranteeing the accuracy and reliability of the operation. There, alignment of pre-operative data and intra-operative scene is an enabling procedure of SNS. Furthermore, augmented reality (AR) has been paid wide attention recently. It can guide surgery by superimposing the critical anatomical organs like nerves, vessel, and preoperative planning into the intraoperative scene, by aligning the imported virtual objects with the real-time images captured by its embedded camera.

5. Other applications

   There are other applications of medical image registration that cannot be included by the aforementioned four classifications. For example, due to the view field limitation, it is necessary to integrate multiple single data into a whole object by registration approaches, like the partial laser scanned images.

2 The classification of medical registration methodology

Medical image registration methodologies can be classified based on different criteria. According to the review of Maintz et al. [2], the commonly used classification criteria contain spatial transformation, dimensionality of source and target images, nature of registration

Table 2.1 The classification of registration methodology according to different criteria [2].

Criteria	Categories
Spatial transformation	Rigid, similar, affine, projective, or non-rigid registration
Dimensionality	2D-2D, 2D-3D, 3D-3D, time series
Nature of registration basis	Intrinsic or extrinsic
Transform domain	Global or local
Modality involved	Mono-modal or multi -modal
Human interaction involved	Interactive, semi-automatic or automatic
Subject	Intrasubject or intersubject
Object	Head, thorax, abdomen, pelvis and perineum, limbs, and spine or vertebra, etc.
Optimization procedure	Parameter computed, or parameter searched for

basis, human interaction level, image modality involved, transform domain, object, subject, and optimizer type. Those criteria are summarized in Table 2.1, and each classification is elaborated as follows.

2.1 Spatial transform

According to the employed spatial transform, registration methodologies can be divided into rigid, similar, affine, projective, and non-rigid registration. Rigid transformation is capable for the presentation of osseous structure deformation in orthopedics, dentistry, and etc. While for soft structure, such as abdominal organs, non-rigid deformation is more descriptive compared with other types of transformation. The detailed description of each transformation is presented in subsection 3.2.

2.2 Dimensionality of source/target image

According to the dimensionality of source and target image, registration methodologies can be divided into 2D-2D, 2D-3D, 3D-3D, temporal series.

2D-2D. Prior to the wide application of three-dimensional image visualization, 2D radiographs are the most popular imaging for clinical diagnosis and disease detection. Therefore, different 2D images have been aligned to measure the changes of anatomical structures, like facial soft tissues, mandibular, and dentition. Compared with other 2D-3D, 3D-3D registration procedures, 2D-2D image alignment is relatively easier with processing smaller data volumes and operating fewer parameters.

2D-3D. It is referred to as volume-to-slice registration. One application of medical image registration is concerned with aligning the pre-operative image with intro-operative data in minimally invasive surgery. Generally, pre-operative imaging adopts 3D data with higher resolution for pre-interventional diagnosis and treatment planning, while the inter-operative data are 2D easily-available images such as ultrasound, projective X-ray, optical images, fluoroscopy in some situations. As most 2D-3D registration procedures are conducted intraoperatively, they are time-constrained with high requirements for the computational complexity and optimizer performance. It is worth mentioning that 3D images, including MRI, CT, CBCT, 3D surface point clouds are also widely used as the intraoperative image modality.

3D-3D. Besides the alignment requirement between 3D pre-operative data and 3D interoperative image, the surgeon also needs to analyze the operation performance which requires the alignment of pre-operative image and post-operative image. In addition, nowadays, 3D images in different modality are fused for the acquisition of more detailed information. For example, 3D MRI and PET image fusion is a popular hybrid image modality employed in oncology diagnosis and surgery, as the former contains anatomical structures with high resolution while the latter with low resolution exhibits functional characteristics.

Temporal series. Time sequences of a patient in different time intervals are registered to compensate for the physiological motion of the target. It can assist the surgeon in the analysis of patient's blood flow and metabolic process and other situations.

2.3 Nature of registration basis

According to the used registration basis, the alignment approaches usually can be sorted into two classes, based on intrinsic and extrinsic features, respectively.

Intrinsic features. Intrinsic method is mainly based on image intrinsic information, such as anatomical or geometrical landmarks, parts of surface or voxel values for image matching. The advantages of intrinsic methods are non-invasive, and low cost.

Extrinsic features. Extrinsic method depends on invasive foreign objects like stereotactic frame, bone-inserted screw markers, or non-invasive accessories, including skin-attached fiducial markers, occlusal splints, and mounts.

2.4 Transform domain

According to the coordinate transformation domain, image registration algorithms can be classified into either local or global.

Global transform. In this case, one transformation will be employed to warp the entire source image. The alignment between rigid structures usually adopted this kind of algorithms.

Local transform. Different from the global method, for the local transform case, each subsection of source image have their own specific transformation.

2.5 Modality involved

The image alignment tasks can be divided into two categories, that is, mono-modal registration and multi-modal registration according to the involved image modalities. Mono-modal registration assists in applications that grow monitor by tracking the temporal anatomical structure changes, intervention verification based on the comparison of pre- and post-interventional data and so on. For multi-modality, each imaging modality has its advantage and limitation, and then the combination of multiple modal data can offer more comprehensive information. Therefore it has been widely adopted among clinical diagnosis, planning, and treatment. For example, CT and MRI fusion have performed within the field of radiation oncology, orbital, skull base region, and pelvic tumor surgery.

2.6 Human interaction involved

Concerning image registration methods, they can be classified into three levels of human interaction: manual or interactive, semi-automatic, and automatic.

Interactive. For interactive case, the operator requires to conduct the alignment procedure manually with the assistance of feedback from the visual interface.

Semi-automatic. For semi-interactive methods, parts of user interactions are demanded, such as the initialization of spatial transformation, the guidance of algorithm optimization procedure, or the acceptance of alignment results.

Automatic. In terms of automatic registration algorithms, there is no human interference involved. The user only provides the algorithm with source and target image.

2.7 Subject

Intrasubject. If both the source image and target image involved are acquired from the same patient, these methods are referred to as intrasubject registration.

Intersubject. The registration methods whose source image and target image collected from different patients, are regarded as intersubject. The cases that one or both of source image and target image are atlases, they also be regarded as intersubject methods.

2.8 Object

Medical image registration technology has been used in whole body, both hard and soft structures. The imaging areas contain head, thorax, abdomen, pelvis and perineum, limbs, and spine and vertebrae.

2.9 Optimization procedure

Based on the inference method of parameters involved, there are two categories of registration algorithms.

Parameter computed. For this category, the transformation parameters can be explicitly calculated according to the corresponding mathematical formulas. The advantage of this kind of approach is the relatively lower computational complexity and better time-consuming performance. However, only part of registration process can use this method, like global rigid registration or other situation merely involved sparse information.

Parameter searched for. Most registration task can be formulated to a mathematical function (called as energy function/cost function/similarity function) based on the transformation parameters. Therefore, the parameters involved can be further determined by iteratively optimizing the target functions.

3 The general framework of image registration procedure

3.1 The general framework of image registration

Registration methodologies are also classified based on the utilized image information. If the registration method directly uses the information related to image gray level, like voxel gray, intensity gradient, or the voxel intensity statistic information, it is referred to as intensity-based registration approach. Conversely, instead of using intensity information, if the registration method extracts the features of the source or/and target images, such as anatomical landmarks, organ edges or contours, distinct surfaces, to conduct the alignment task, it is known as feature-based approach. Besides the intensity-based and feature-based approaches, the methodologies use the images information in the frequency domain based on Fourier transform are referred to as frequency-based approach. The following part mainly introduces the framework of the intensity-based and feature-based registration methodologies, due to their frequent clinical utilizations.

As shown in Fig. 2.2, Intensity-based image registration can be regarded as the research process of mapping/warping the source image to optimally match the target image by optimizing the image similarity degree or minimize the cost functions, which usually is defined as the inverse of the similarity plus a regularization term. Manual or semi-auto initial transformation can be alterative applied in advance to warp the source image and make it closer or more similar to the target image. This pre-process can accelerate the convergence of the optimizer. The feature-based registration methodologies share with the similar workflow as intensity-based registration procedure as shown in Fig. 2.2B. However, the features extracted are applied to evaluate the correspondence, rather than the original images. The interpolator Sometimes is not involved in feature-based registration. Generally, image registration contains four integral components, that are similarity/correspondence measurement, spatial transform, image interpolation, and optimization algorithm.

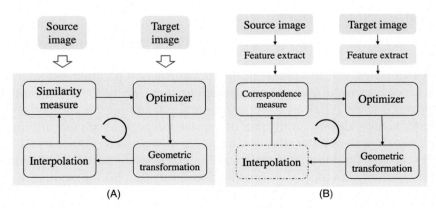

FIGURE 2.2 The general framework of image registration procedure, (B) based on (A) intensity and features, respectively.

3.2 Similarity measure, to judge the alignment quality

This section displays several commonly used similarity/correspondence measurements for intensity-based and feature-based registration. First, let S represent the source image, and G be the target image. The size of both S and G is n times n.

1. Mean square difference (MSD) can be applied for similarity measure of mono-modality image registration.

$$MSD(G, S) = \frac{\sum_{i=0,j=0}^{i=m,j=n}\left(\left(S(i,j)-G(i,j)\right)\right)^2}{m \cdot n}$$ (2.1)

Similar to MSD, Sum of squared differences (SSD), Sum of absolute differences (SAD) are another two commonly utilized metrics for the calculation of gray difference.

$$SSD(G,S) = \sum_{i=0,j=0}^{i=m,j=n}\left(S(i,j)-G(i,j)\right)^2$$ (2.2)

$$SAD(G,S) = \sum_{i=0,j=0}^{i=m,j=n}\left|S(i,j)-G(i,j)\right|$$ (2.3)

2. Normalized correlation coefficient (NCC)
NCC is a frequently used criterion for image similarity measure, with its value range from 0 to 1. The greater the NCC value, the higher the similarity between the two images. *NCC*(G,S) is defined as following:

$$NCC(G, S) = \frac{\delta(S, G)}{\sqrt{D_S}\sqrt{D_G}}$$ (2.4)

where, σ(S,G) is the covariance of image S and image G. D_S, D_G are the variance of S and G, respectively.

$$D_S = \frac{1}{mn}\sum_{i=0,j=0}^{i=m,j=n}\left(S(i, j)-\bar{S}\right)^2$$ (2.5)

According to the above two equations, NCC value of S and G can be written as:

$$NCC(G,S) = \frac{\frac{1}{mn}\sum_{i=0,j=0}^{i=m,j=n}\left(S(i,j)-\bar{S}\right)\left(G(i,j)-\bar{G}\right)}{\sqrt{\frac{1}{mn}\sum_{i=0,j=0}^{i=m,j=n}\left(S(i,j)-\bar{S}\right)^2}\sqrt{\frac{1}{mn}\sum_{i=0,j=0}^{i=m,j=n}\left(G(i,j)-\bar{G}\right)^2}}$$ (2.6)

3. Mutual information (MI)
MI-based approach is the most widely applied measurement, which is suitable for both mono-modality and multi-modality registration.

$$MI(S,G) = H(S) + H(G) - H(S,G)$$ (2.7)

Where, $H(S)$, $H(G)$, and $H(S,G)$ are the source image entropy, target image entropy and the joint entropy of S and G, respectively.

$$H(S) = -\sum_{i=1}^{N} P_i \cdot \log P_i \tag{2.8}$$

$$H(S,G) = -\sum_{i=1, j=1}^{i=N, j=n} P(i,j) \cdot \log P(i,j) \tag{2.9}$$

4. Linear correlation of linear combination (LC^2), can be used for mono- and multi-modal image registration.

$$CR = 1 - \frac{\sum_{x \in \Omega} \left(T(x) - f\left(S(x,t) \right) \right)}{|\Omega| \mathrm{Var}(T)} \tag{2.10}$$

In the correlation ratio framework of image registration, the transformation parameters t are obtained via the maximization of the above CR value. Where, f denotes the mapping function to estimate the intensities of the target image T from the transformed source image $S(t)$. Ω presents the shared image domain. Wein et al. [3] donated LC^2 measurement for MRI and US registration. They assumed that the intensity value T_i for pixel/voxel i in the target image T is either correlated with the intensity value p_i, or with the image gradient $g_i = |\nabla p_i|$ for pixel/voxel i in source image S. The mapping function can be written as following:

$$f(\vec{x}_i) = \alpha p_i + \beta g_i + \gamma \tag{2.11}$$

Based on the above two equations, the parameters (α, β, γ) have to minimize

$$\left\| \begin{pmatrix} p_i & g_i & 1 \\ \vdots & \vdots & \vdots \\ p_i & g_i & 1 \end{pmatrix} \begin{pmatrix} \alpha \\ \beta \\ \gamma \end{pmatrix} - \begin{pmatrix} T_i \\ \vdots \\ T_n \end{pmatrix} \right\|^2 ,$$ where n is the number of pixel/voxel in domain Ω.

Hence, the solution of the transformation $t(\alpha, \beta, \gamma)$ is:

$$\begin{pmatrix} \alpha \\ \beta \\ \gamma \end{pmatrix} = \left(M^T M^{-1} \right) M^T = \begin{pmatrix} T_i \\ \vdots \\ T_n \end{pmatrix}, \quad M = \begin{pmatrix} p_i & g_i & 1 \\ \vdots & \vdots & \vdots \\ p_i & g_i & 1 \end{pmatrix} \tag{2.12}$$

3.3 Spatial transform

1. Isometric transformation, which only involved translation and rotation, is widely used in osseous fields, such as orthopedics and craniomaxillofacial surgery. Rigid transformation, also referred to as rigid transformation, can be written as the following mathematic equation

$$X' = \begin{pmatrix} x' \\ y' \\ 1 \end{pmatrix} = \begin{bmatrix} \cos\theta & -\sin\theta & t_x \\ \sin\theta & \cos\theta & t_y \\ 0 & 0 & 1 \end{bmatrix} \begin{pmatrix} x \\ y \\ 1 \end{pmatrix} = \begin{bmatrix} R & T \\ 0 & 1 \end{bmatrix} X \qquad (2.13)$$

where, T depicts the translate component while R, an orthogonal matrix, represents the rotation component.

2. Similar transform, has an additional scaling factor s compared with isometric transformation, which can be depicted as following:

$$X' = \begin{pmatrix} x' \\ y' \\ 1 \end{pmatrix} = \begin{bmatrix} s\cdot\cos\theta & -s\cdot\sin\theta & t_x \\ s\cdot\sin\theta & s\cdot\cos\theta & t_y \\ 0 & 0 & 1 \end{bmatrix} \begin{pmatrix} x \\ y \\ 1 \end{pmatrix} = \begin{bmatrix} s\cdot R & T \\ 0 & 1 \end{bmatrix} X \qquad (2.14)$$

3. Affine transform, contains translation, rotation, scaling, and shear.

$$X' = \begin{pmatrix} x' \\ y' \\ 1 \end{pmatrix} = \begin{bmatrix} b_{11} & b_{12} & t_x \\ b_{21} & b_{22} & t_y \\ 0 & 0 & 1 \end{bmatrix} \begin{pmatrix} x \\ y \\ 1 \end{pmatrix} = \begin{bmatrix} B & T \\ 0 & 1 \end{bmatrix} X \qquad (2.15)$$

where, B is a nonsingular matric which contains the rotation, scaling and shear factors.

4. Projective/perspective transform

$$X' = \begin{pmatrix} x' \\ y' \\ 1 \end{pmatrix} = \begin{bmatrix} c_{11} & c_{12} & c_{13} \\ c_{21} & c_{22} & c_{23} \\ c_{31} & c_{32} & c_{33} \end{bmatrix} \begin{pmatrix} x \\ y \\ 1 \end{pmatrix} = \begin{bmatrix} c_1 & T \\ c_2 & c_3 \end{bmatrix} X \qquad (2.16)$$

5. Deformable transform/curved deformations

As most human anatomical tissues or organs are deformable structures, lots of medical image registration procedures are complemented based on deformable transformation. Free-form deformations and guided deformations, as two kinds of curved deformations, have been applied in medical image registration. The former allows any kind of deformations while the latter is constrained by a model considering the physical properties. In terms of free-form deformation models, a grid of control points is defined to describe the involved deformation. During the iteration registration process, the control points of the defined grid are moved individually according to the deformation field estimated by the optimizer. Then, deformation between control points is propagated by interpolation algorithms, such as linear interpolation, bilinear interpolation, cubic B-spline interpolation. In terms of guided deformation approaches, there are elastic-based registration and flow-based registration.

3.4 Image interpolation

Commonly used interpolation methods include nearest interpolation, bilinear interpolation, bicubic interpolation, and cubic interpolation, partial volume interpolation, and so on.

3.5 Optimization algorithm

Optimization strategy is used to search and optimize the transform parameters for the maximization of the similarity value between the warped source image and the target image. The optimization algorithms commonly used in medical image registration includes Gradient descent (GD), genetic algorithm (GA), partial swarm algorithm, simulated annealing algorithm, and so on.

1. Gradient descent

    Gradient descent (as shown in Fig. 2.3) is by far the most popular optimization algorithm used in computer vision and machine learning, to minimize a given cost function to its local minimum. A gradient can be defined as the slope of a function. The equation below shows the computational process of GD:

$$f(k+1) = f(k) - \gamma \cdot \nabla f(k) \tag{2.17}$$

    where $f(k)$ is the function value of iteration k, and $f(k+1)$ is the value after iterating $(k + 1)$ times obtained based on $f(k)$ and the function gradient. γ, a user-defined parameter, is called waiting factor, which determines the convergence rate of the optimization process.

    Three types of variants of gradient descent algorithm have been widely employed for optimization problems. (1) Batch gradient descent, also referred to as vanilla gradient descent. The most characteristic of batch gradient descent is that parameters of the given function will only be updated after all examples have been evaluated.

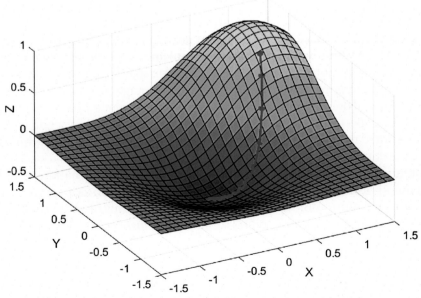

FIGURE 2.3 The procedure to search a minimum value by gradient descent optimism algorithm.

It can produce a stable convergence with higher efficiency. (2) Stochastic gradient descent, updates the parameters after calculating one example. It has a faster convergence efficiency with more expensive computational requirements. (3) Mini-batch gradient descent. It is a combination of stochastic gradient descent and batch gradient descent. It simply splits all the examples into numerous small batches, and conducts an update for each batch. Therefore, it is relatively robust and efficient.

2. Genetic algorithm

   Genetic algorithm is a metaheuristic inspired by the process of natural selection that belongs to the larger class of evolutionary algorithms (EA). Genetic algorithms are commonly used to generate high-quality solutions for the optimization and searching problems by relying on biologically inspired operators such as mutation, crossover, and selection.

   In a genetic algorithm, a population of candidate solutions (called individuals, creatures, or phenotypes) for the optimization problem is evolved toward better solutions. Each candidate solution has a set of properties (its chromosomes or genotype) which can be mutated and altered; traditionally, solutions are represented in binary as strings of 0 and 1.

   The usual approach of selection is: for a population S of size N, determine its chance of being selected according to the selection probability $P(x_i)$ of each chromosome $x_i \in S$, randomly select N chromosomes from S in N times, and make a copy.

   Crossover is the interchange of genes on certain positions of two chromosomes. There are several different crossover measurements, including one-point crossing, multi-point crossing, uniform crossing, sequential crossing and periodic crossing. One-point crossover is the most basic method. Mutation is to change a gene on a certain position of the chromosome. It randomly changes the value of the genetic gene (representing a certain bit of the chromosome symbol string) with a small probability. In a system where chromosomes are coded in binary, it randomly changes a certain gene of the chromosome from 1 to 0, or from 0 to 1.

   The genetic algorithm has the characteristics of high search efficiency, no objective function, and flexibility, etc. However, genetic algorithms do not scale well with complexity and easily converge towards local optima or even arbitrary points rather than the global optimum of the problem.

3. Particle swarm optimization

   Particle swarm optimization is developed by Eberhart and Kennedy in 1995 [4], which is a computational method that optimizes a problem by iteratively trying to improve a candidate solution with regard to a given measure of quality. This algorithm is developed by simulating the foraging behavior of birds, consider the candidate solutions (particles) as a population of birds, moving these particles around in the search space according to the particle's velocity and position, which is updated in Eq. (2.18) and Eq. (2.19), the best position is determined by the local optimal positions of all particles in each iteration.

$$V_{id} = \omega V_{id} + C_1 \, random(0, 1)(P_{id} - X_{id}) + C_2 \, random(0, 1)(P_{gd} - X_{id}) \qquad (2.18)$$

$$X_{id} = X_{id} + V_{id} \qquad (2.19)$$

In Eq. (2.19), ω is the inertia factor, it controls the power of global search ability. C1 and C2 are acceleration constant, it controls the behavior and efficacy of the PSO method.

PSO has been widely used in many fields such as function optimization, image processing, and geodesy due to its simple operation and fast convergence speed. However, the PSO algorithm has problems such as premature convergence, dimensionality disaster, easy to fall into local extreme values, etc., which need to be solved.

4 Image registration in oral and maxillofacial surgery

4.1 Different image modality in oral and maxillofacial surgery and their application

Computerized tomography(CT), contrast-enhanced CT (CECT), magnetic resonance image(MRI), optical images, 3D digital points or surfaces (scanner), 3D photography, are several most commonly utilized imaging modalities for disease diagnosis, treatment planning, and surgery follow up in oral and maxillofacial surgery. In addition, Cone-beam CT (CBCT), as an alternative to multi-slice spiral CT, has become integral to the field of orthodontics, implant dentistry, and other oral and maxillofacial surgery in recent years. Furthermore, Ultrasound, an easily available, relatively inexpensive, and non-invasive imaging modality, is often adopted for the identification of various soft-tissue pathologies in the orofacial region or the detection of fetal facial dysmorphisms and craniofacial malformation. Based on the acquired metabolism information, functional imaging (positron emission tomography (PET), single-photon emission computed tomography (SPECT)) is a useful adjunct for craniomaxillofacial clinical applications, such as the diagnosis and treatment of abnormal bone turnover, bone tumor, and osteomyelitis. Table 2.2 illustrates major image modalities employed in clinical oral and maxillofacial surgery, and summaries the advantages and disadvantages of each imaging modality.

4.2 Mono-modal image registration in oral and maxillofacial surgery

1. **Partial scanned dental surface**. The registration of partial laser scanned dental surfaces. Because of the similar intensity with nearby structures and artifacts, accurate dental delineation or segmentation in CBCT is challenging. Meanwhile, as CBCT is expensive and radiative, 3D laser scanning is regarded as a cheaper and faster alternative imaging to obtain the dental model. However, because of its limited view field, multiple laser scans are required to collect at different orientations and positions

Table 2.2   Major image modalities in oral and maxillofacial surgery and their characteristics.

Modality	Advantages	Drawbacks	Application examples
CT	• high resolution • osseous tissue	• radiation • cost	• depict intricate bony details of
CBCT	• lower radiation • less expensive • compact	• limited scan field • scatter artifacts	• visualize skeletal and dental
uCT	• non-destructive • non-invasive	• limited imaging field • partial volume effects • scatter artifacts	• analyze the new bone information following implant placement
PET/PED-PET	• metabolism information	• expensive • motion artifacts	• detect the nodal metastases and distinguish the recurrent or residual disease from the normal treatment-induced tissue change
MRI	• high resolution • soft tissue • nonradiative	• cost • time consuming	• visualize masticatory muscle, ligaments, and the cartilaginous disc
US	• noninvasive • inexpensive • fast	• low quality • deformation introduction	• delineate the thickness and extension of gingiva
3D laser surface scanning	• accurate • nonradiative	• limited scan field • time consuming • harmful to eyes	• rapidly acquire a digital dental model directly, without using gypsum dental model
3D photography	• nonradiative • fast • low cost • with color texture	• low quality on subnasal and submental region	• obtain the color texture information of patient's mouth

and further integrate into a unified coordinate frame for a whole dentition. For example, Park et al. [5] proposed a registration to integrate partially scanned dental surface into a whole. In their method, the 3D surfaces were firstly converted into 2D depth map images by applying a 3D rigid transformation. Then, the depth map images were used to estimate the initial transformation of the correspondent surface pairs. And ICP algorithm was employed to conduct the subsequent fine registration on the last step.

2. **Laser scanned image.** One application of laser scanned images registration is to assess the dental displacement in orthodontic procedures. Surgeons can verify the clinical treatment and conduct adequate adjustment based on aligned results between dentition scanned images acquired at different intervals. In Jang et al. [6] research, they investigated the accuracy of the registration method based on three inserted-screw landmarks, and further employed a new ruga-palate-superimposition method algorithm by using the medial points of the right and left third palatal rugae and the surface of the palatal vault. Similarly, instead of using 2D radiographs,

Thiruvenkatachari et al. [7] developed a method to measure the 3D tooth movement by comparing the pretreatment and posttreatment laser scanned models. They initially registered two data by manually selecting multiple anatomical landmarks, including the medial and lateral end points of prominent rugae on the palate. Then a specific region of the palate on both image data was chosen for further alignment. In addition, Gibelli et al. [8] proposed an automatic method to register dental models acquired by laser scanner at different times according to the least point-to-point distance of the respective dental surface. Their registration method can use to analyze dental changes during therapy by generating a chromatic map of dental arches, which can provide detailed movement of each tooth including translation and rotation.

3. **X-ray dental image**. Norollah et al. [9] developed a non-rigid registration method to compare two X-ray radiographs collected in different times by three steps: a series of control points were automatically selected from both images based on the voxel gradient magnitude; then a dental template was employed to calculate the displacement of the control points based on the similarity measure of normalized cross correlation; last step, the displacement over the whole image was deduced based on the displacement on the control points, to generate the registered image.

4. **CBCT**. In oral and maxillofacial, different CBCT images acquired at different times can be superimposed together to display the temporomandibular joint change, mandibular and craniofacial development. Ruellas et al. [10] performed a fully automated voxel-wise growing registration method based on 3D slicer software.

4.3 Multi-modal image registration in oral and maxillofacial surgery

1. **CECT(CT)/PET(FDG-PET).** Even CT shares high resolution for bone structures, while the erosion and remodeling of bone is challenging to distinguish from osteomyelitis based on CT images. Conversely, technetium bone scintigraphy can serve as a useful tool for dynamic physiological monitoring of bone, as radionuclide is absorbed to hydroxyapatite crystals in bone in proportion to both osteoblastic activity and regional blood flow. Yu et al.[11] described a new approach for the resection and reconstruction of recurrent maxillary squamous cell carcinoma (SCC) by the fusion of 18F-fluorodeoxyglucose (FDG)–positron emission tomography (FDG-PET)/computed tomography and contrast-enhanced CT (CECT). They used landmark-based approach of Brainlab software to register image series in different modalities for the visualization of the vessel, high metabolic tumor, nerves and other critical organs. According to their report, the average shift of two data was less than 1 mm. In addition, Loeffelbein et al. [12] despicted the beneficial use of the fusion of functional image and structural image in head and neck malignancies. Witjes et al. [13] study (from University of Groningen, The Netherlands) reported PET-MRI-CT data fusion for mandible tumor detection and reconstruction planning, as shown in Fig. 2.4.

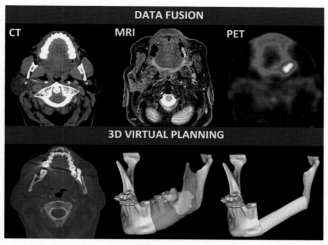

FIGURE 2.4 An example case reported in [13] with PET-MRI-CT data fusion for mandible tumor detection and reconstruction planning.

2. **CT(CBCT)/laser scanning.** Different methods have been proposed for the registration of CT and laser scanning, in order to fabricate a precision 3D maxillofacial model containing both the facial structures and detailed occilasal/ interocclusal data. For example, Kim et al. [14] proposed a matching algorithm to integrate the CT image with laser scanned dental cast by sequential point-based and surface-based registration. Two steps were conducted based on ICP algorithm: Six anatomical point pairs on the central groove or cusp tip of teeth were selected manually for the coarse integration; then surface on each model was chosen for further registration. Similarly, Sun et al. [15] integrated laser scanned images with maxillofacial CBCT data based on three different surface combinations. They firstly selected three anatomical points corresponding to CBCT and laser scanned image to perform the initial alignment. Subsequently, further registration was finalized by selecting different surface regions. They reported that CBCT/scanned image registration with a larger surface area had a better performance.

3. **CT(CBCT)/MRI.** In order to show the detailed information of tumors, including localization, extent, size and shape, characteristics, it is necessary to fuse MRI images to 3D CT bone images. Individual medical imaging modality is not enough for the tumor diagnosis. CT and MRI can offer complementary information for maxillofacial tumor diagnosis, as the former can show intricate bony details well, while MRI provides fair contrast to the soft tissue. Their fusion can display both osseous and soft tissues Dai et al. [16] fused CT and MRI based on five anatomic landmarks of both imaging modalities. The detailed registration method was not described in their report. Al-Saleh et al. [17–19] investigated two CBCT/MRI co-registration methods based on fiducial markers and voxel gray information,

respectively. For the first approach, several radio-opaque fiducial markers were fixed on the patients before data acquisition. The voxel based registration method analyzed the statistical dependence between the corresponding voxels of two images by calculating the normalized mutual information of image pair. Their research results showed the MI-based matching algorithm outperformed the fiducial-based registration method. In order to combine the advantages of MRI and CT, Nix et al. [20] implemented two deformable image registration methods to estimate the local transform based on block-wise MI (b-MI) and pseudomodality MI (b-pmMI). For the b-MI approach, image sub-blocks were selected according to the grey and standard deviation value. MI similarity metric was used to search the optimal local translations for better alignment. For b-pmMI approach, joint histogram variance-minimization greyscale remapping function was adopted firstly to generate reduced-contrasted pseudomodality image pair for each block. Then MI of the generated pseudomodality image was used for the local transform optimization. Fig. 2.5 is the schematic overview of CT-MRI fusion based 3D virtual surgical planning vorkflow for mandible resection and reconstruction surgery via software Mirada (Mirada Medical, Oxford Centre for Innovation, United Kingdom).

4. **Photograph/laser scanned image.** Current stereophotogrammetry is easily available, non-expensive and with high resolution. To map color photographs onto the 3D scanned digital model, which cannot provide satisfactory color texture information. Different integration approaches of oral photographs with 3D dental mesh were performed [21,22]. Those approaches usually include three steps: first, the feature point extraction in the photograph via color segmentation methods, like mean-shift, active contour model, maximally stable extremal regions, and so on. The

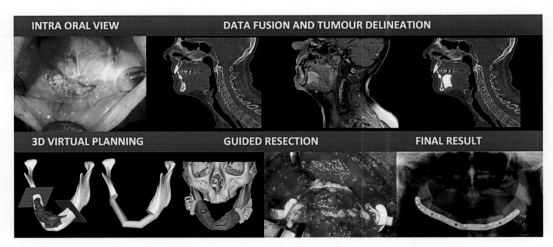

FIGURE 2.5 The registration MRI and CT images for mandible tumor detection and reconstruction [13].

feature points in dental color image mainly are occlusal points or those points on the boundary of gum and teeth. Second, feature points extraction on surface model. Local curvature is widely used for the extraction of singular 3D points on surface mesh. Third, 3D/2D feature point correspondences. Once the feature points on both image modality are captured, the match of photograph and 3D mesh surface can be calculated based on teeth number.

5. **CT(CBCT) /Ultrasound.** As ultrasound is an easily available and non-invasive imaging modality, it is often adopted for the identification of various soft-tissue pathologies in the orofacial region or the detection of fetal facial dysmorphisms and craniofacial malformation. Nguyen et al. [23] proposed a probability-based point set registration method to integrate oral ultrasound image with CBCT by using coherent point drift (CPD) algorithm. Ultrasound image can offer the thickness and extension information of gingiva, and partially illustrate the thickness of alveolar bones, which are important for the diagnosis of dental anomaly disease. A side-tracing strategy was employed firstly to extract the boundary points of tooth and bone on the CBCT images. Correspondingly, a growing segmentation method was adopted to determine the tooth and bone surface from US images. Both surface points extracted from CBCT image and US images were curve-fitted to remove outliers. Finally, two outlier-removed surface point clouds were registered by CPD algorithm.

4.4 Deep learning for image registration in oral and maxillofacial surgery

In recent years, several research groups have employed different machine learning methods for the process of oral and maxillofacial medical image, including classification, recognition, segmentation, and registration tasks [24]. The registration approaches based on neural networks can be divided into two groups: one is the unsupervised learning framework by measuring the similarity criteria, such as NCC, MI, another one is the supervised/ weakly supervised learning network which can learn from the provide images and ground truths. Torosdagli et al. [25] developed a learning framework for the automatic location of mandible anatomical landmarks, which can be applied for maxillofacial image registration according to aforementioned image alignment approaches. In their method, a Convolutional neural network (CNN) was proposed firstly to segment the mandible from CBCT scans. Then a learning-based method was presented for the geodesic map generation of each sparsely-spaced anatomical landmark. And the generated geodesic maps were used to locate the mandible landmarks based on a long short-term memory (LSTM) on the last step. For the direct superimposition of CBCT data and laser scanned images, a deep pose regression neural network was built by Chung et al. [26], for the initial registration of two image acquisitions. Next, optimal cluster-based algorithm was employed for the fine registration. The registration methods mentioned in Sections 4.2, 4.3, and 4.4 are listed in (Table 2.3).

Table 2.3 Multi-modal image registration in oral-maxillofacial surgery.

Publications	Class	Modality A	Modality B	Registration method
A. Mono-modal image registration in oral and maxillofacial surgery				
Jang et al. (2009) [6]	Mono-	Laser scanned	—	Point + surface
Thiruvenkatachari et al. (2009) [7]	Mono-	Laser scanned	—	Point + surface
Norollah et al. (2012) [9]	Mono-	X-ray	—	Voxel + Point based
Park et al. (2015) [5]	Mono-	Laser scanned	—	Point mapping
Ruellas et al (2016) [10]	Mono-	CBCT	—	Voxel
Gibelli et al. (2017) [8]	Mono-	Laser scanned	—	Surface based
B. Image registration of the facial skeleton and the dentition				
Gateno et al. (2003) [27]	Multi-	CT	Laser scanned dental cast	Fiducial markers
Gateno et al. (2007) [28]	Multi-	CT	Laser scanned dental cast	Fiducial markers
Nkenke et al. (2004) [29]	Multi-	MSCT	MSCT scanned dental cast	Fiducial markers
Schutyser et al. (2005) [30]	Multi-	CT	CT scanned dental cast	Point based
Swennen et al. (2009) [31]	Multi-	CBCT	CBCT of tray impression	Voxel based
Uechi et al. (2006) [32]	Multi-	MSCT	Laser scanned dental cast	Fiducial markers
Hoon et al. (2011)	Multi-	CBCT	Laser scanned dental cast	Surface based
Kim et al. (2010) [14]	Multi-	CT	Laser scanned dental cast	Point and surface based
Sun et al. (2017) [15]	Multi-	CBCT	Laser scanned dental cast	Point and surface based
Chung et al. (2020) [26]	Multi-	CBCT	Laser scanned surface	Neural network
C. Image registration of the facial soft tissue and facial skeleton				
Ayoub et al. (2007) [33]	Multi-	MSCT	3D photography	Surface based
Groeve et al. (2001) [34]	Multi-	MSCT	3D photography	Surface based
Khambay et al. (2002) [35]	Multi-	MSCT	3D photography	Surface based
Maal et al. (2008) [49]	Multi-	CBCT	3D photography	Surface based
Olszewski et al. (2008) [36]	Multi-	MSCT	MRI & laser-scanned dental cast	
D. Image registration for oral and maxillofacial tumor				
Dai et al. (2012) [16]	Multi-	CT	MRI	Point based
Yu et al. (2017) [11]	Multi-	FDG-PET/CT	CECT	Point based
Nguyen et al. (2019) [23]	Multi-	CBCT	US	Point based
Kraeima et al. (2018) [13]	Multi-	CT	MRI	---
Hu et al. (2020) [37]	Multi-	CT	FDG-PET	Voxel based
		CT	MRI	Point based(manual)
		MRI	PET-CT	
E. Image registration for other applications				
Al-Saleh et al. (2015) [18]	Multi-	CBCT	MRI	Fiducial Voxel based(MI)
Al-Saleh et al. (2017) [19]	Multi-	CBCT	MRI	Voxel based(MI)
Hsung et al. (2018) [21]	Multi-	Laser scanned	Photograph	Point based
Destrez et al. (2018) [22]	Multi-	Laser scanned	Photograph	Point based

Abbreviations: CECT, Contrast-enhanced CT; CPD, Coherent point drift; ICP, Iterative closet point; MI, mutual information.

5 Image-to-patient registration in oral and maxillofacial surgery

Nowadays, SNS is an adjunct to surgical procedure, allowing visualization of the tracked surgical instruments and relates them visually to the patient's anatomic images. As one of the key technologies of SNS, image-to-patient registration is regarded as the process to integrate the pre-operative data and intra-operative data into a unified coordinate frame. The pre-operative data usually contains the patient's radiology image acquired before intervention for the disease detection and diagnosis, and the design information of the surgery plan. The image-to-patient registration methodologies include marker-based registration and marker-free registration. Each registration category bears an individual level of registration accuracy and clinical feasibility.

In terms of the first methods, extrinsic markers, which also are referred to as fiducials, are fixed on the patient before the preoperative image acquisition, and are required to be easily localized during the operation. These markers can be split into three categories: (1) invasively inserted bone-implanted screws, (2) makers attached to skin or other surfaces non-invasively, (3) individual mounting frame, dental templates or splints fixed to the dentition, for example, a frame with artificial landmarks can be fixed to the skull of the patient before obtaining the pre-operative images. In addition, patient-specific templates or splint carried markers are alternatives for mounting frame to eliminate the invasive fixation. In the past 20 years, different marker-based registration methods have been proposed for the calculation of the geometric transform in the SNS field. For example, a couple of researchers [38–40] proposed automatic marker localization techniques which use the centroid of titanium screw as the bone-implanted fiducial. Hongmin Cai et al. [41] proposed a method in which nonlinear diffusion and mean shift were exploited to locate the cross-sections of the axon. Bettschart et al. [42] investigate the accuracy of the splint-based registration method, mainly fusing on the mandible.

There are three measures for the assessment of image-to-patient registration error, including fiducial localization error (FLE), fiducial registration error (FRE), and target registration error (TRE). FLE means the error in locating fiducial points. FRE is the root mean square distance of the registered corresponding fiducial points. TRE represents the distance between the registered corresponding point pairs except fiducial points. Currently, TRE is the most useful metric to analyze the accuracy of point-based registration.

In terms of the marker-free registration approaches, mainly intrinsic features are extracted to conduct the coordinate alignment task. One way is to capture a set of homologous anatomical landmark points, such as the anterior nasal spine, from both pre-interventional and intro-interventional data, respectively. Another more reliable matching way is based on laser- and video-surface scanners, ultrasound scan probes, or infrared pointers. Due to the expensive and time-consuming logistic costs and potential invasion of fiducial-based registration, surface-based image-to-patient registration has been paid lots of attention. Its principal is to align the surface collected by some non-invasive imaging devices (laser scanner, tracked US probe, camera, or infrared pointer) with the surface detected and generated from preoperative CT/CBCT/MRI data. Yan Zhang et al. [43] reconstructed the 3D point cloud of a patient's essential structures and then applied ICP (Iterative closest point) algorithm for surface registration. Wang et al. [44] achieved image registration by matching real-time 3D contour with a customized stereo camera tracking patient and surgical instruments. In addition, BrainLab (Munich, Germany), a company of precision radiotherapy and stereotactic radiosurgery, has produced handheld Z-touch and Softouch make image-to-patient registration quick and easy by touching the patient's skin surface based on surface matching with either a pointer or a laser. In terms of surface registration algorithm in commercial medical software, manual coarse registration is often required for the initial transform relationship.

6 Software tools for medical image registration

A large number of software tools have been developed for medical image registration. Several widely used are listed as following:

1. Insight segmentation and registration toolkit (ITK)/SimpleITK
   Implemented in C++, ITK is one of the largest open-source, cross-platform projects for medical image processing, including image qualification, segmentation, and registration. SimpleITK, a simplified interface built on top of ITK, is available for C++, Python, Java, R, and other code languages. ITK designs four components, that is spatial transform, interpolation, similarity measurement, and optimizer, for various matching tasks, including both mono-model and multi-model registration.
2. Elastix/SimpleElastix
   Elastix [45] is an open-source software based on ITK, which collects a board range of algorithms to solve medical image registration problems. The modular design of Elastix allows the user to quickly configure, test, and compare different registration methods for a specific application. Its advanced interface library SimpleElastix also made it available in C++, C#, Python, Java, R, Ruby.
3. 3D Slicer (have specific craniomaxillofacial registration model)
   3D Slicer (Slicer) [46] is an open-source software platform for medical image informatics, image processing, and 3D visualization. It is extensible with powerful plug-in capabilities for adding algorithms and applications. 3D slicer has several registration extensions, such as SlicerElastix, CMFreg, General Registration, Demon Registration. CMFreg is a specific package for craniomaxillofacial registration. It compares voxel by voxel of gray-level CBCT images to calculate rotation and translation parameters between two images, for the assessment of overall facial changes. Specific anatomic regions are used to create localized masks and aid regional superimpositions for the calculation of localized facial changes, like mandibular, maxillary growth, bone remodeling of the mandibular condyle, and tooth movement.

4. Advanced Normalization Tools (ANTs)

ANTs [47,48] is considered as a state-of-the-art medical image registration and segmentation toolkit. This toolkit designs different registration methods with various models including diffeomorphisms, independent evaluation, template construction, similarity metrics, multivariate registration, multiple modality analysis, and statistical bias.

There also are several other software coded in Matlab, Python, C, or C++ for medical image registration. Except the CMFreg extension of Slicer, none of them is designed specifically for craniomaxillofacial image registration.

References

[1] G. Zheng, S. Li, G. Szekely, Statistical Shape and Deformation Analysis: Methods, Implementation and Applications, Academic Press, (2017).

[2] J.B.A. Maintz, Viergever M.A., A survey of medical image registration, Med. Image Anal. 2 (1) (1998) 1–36.

[3] W. Wein, S. Brunke, A. Khamene, M.R. Callstrom, N. Navab, Automatic CT-ultrasound registration for diagnostic imaging and image-guided intervention, Med. Image Anal. 12 (5) (2008) 577–585.

[4] J. Kennedy, R. Eberhart, Particle swarm optimization, Proceedings of ICNN'95-International Conference on Neural Networks, Perth, Australia, November 27-December 1, IEEE 4 (1995) 1942–1948.

[5] S. Park, H.C. Kang, J. Lee, J. Shin, Shin Y.G., An enhanced method for registration of dental surfaces partially scanned by a 3D dental laser scanning, Comput. Methods Progr. Biomed. 118 (1) (2015) 11–22.

[6] I. Jang, M. Tanaka, Y. Koga, S. Iijima, J.H. Yozgatian, B.K. Cha, et al. A novel method for the assessment of three-dimensional tooth movement during orthodontic treatment, Angle Orthod. 79 (3) (2009) 447–453.

[7] B. Thiruvenkatachari, M. Al-Abdallah, N.C. Akram, J. Sandler, K. O'Brien, Measuring 3-dimensional tooth movement with a 3-dimensional surface laser scanner, Am. J. Orthod. Dentofac. Orthoped. 135 (4) (2009) 480–485.

[8] D.M. Gibelli, V. Pucciarelli, L. Pisoni, F.M. Rusconi, G. Tartaglia, C. Sforza, Quantification of dental movements in orthodontic follow-up: a novel approach based on registration of 3D models of dental casts, Orthodontics 4 (1) (2017) 57–63.

[9] M. Norollah, H. Pourghassem, H. Mahdavi-Nasab. Image registration using template matching and similarity measures for dental radiograph. In: 2012 Fourth International Conference on Computational Intelligence and Communication Networks, Mathura, India, November 3–5, 2012, IEEE (2012) 331–335.

[10] A. Ruellas, C.D.O. Yatabe, M.S. Souki, B.Q. Benavides, E. Nguyen, T. Luiz, et al. 3D mandibular superimposition: comparison of regions of reference for voxel-based registration, PLoS One 11 (6) (2016) e0157625.

[11] Y. Yu, W.B. Zhang, X.J. Liu, C.B. Guo, G.Y. Yu, X. Peng, Three-dimensional image fusion of 18F-fluorodeoxyglucose–positron emission tomography/computed tomography and contrast-enhanced computed tomography for computer-assisted planning of maxillectomy of recurrent maxillary squamous cell carcinoma and defect reconstruction, J. Oral Maxillofac. Surgery 75 (6) (2017) 1301.e1–1301.e15.

[12] D.J. Loeffelbein, M. Souvatzoglou, V. Wankerl, J. Dinges, L.M. Ritschl, T. Mucke, et al. Diagnostic value of retrospective PET-MRI fusion in head-and-neck cancer, BMC Cancer 19 (14) (2014) 846.

[13] J. Kraeima, B. Dorgelo, H.A. Gulbitti, R.J.H.M. Steenbakkers, K.P. Schepman, J.L.N. Roodenburg, et al. Multi-modality 3D mandibular resection planning in head and neck cancer using CT and MRI data fusion: A clinical series, Oral Oncol. 81 (2018) 22–28.

[14] B.C. Kim, C.E. Lee, W. Park, S.H. Kang, P. Zhengguo, C.K. Yi, et al. Integration accuracy of digital dental models and 3-dimensional computerized tomography images by sequential point-and surface-based markerless registration, Oral Surg. Oral Med. Oral Pathol. Oral Radiol. Endod. 110 (3) (2010) 370–378.

[15] L. Sun, H.S. Hwang, Lee K. M, Registration area and accuracy when integrating laser-scanned and maxillofacial cone-beam computed tomography images, Am. J. Orthod. Dentofac. Orthoped. 153 (3) (2018) 355–361.

[16] J. Dai, X. Wang, Y. Dong, H. Yu, D. Yang, G. Shen, Two-and three-dimensional models for the visualization of jaw tumors based on CT–MRI image fusion, J. Craniofac. Surgery 23 (2) (2012) 502–508.

[17] M.A. Al-Saleh, N.A. Alsufyani, H. Saltaji, J.L. Jaremko, Major PW, MRI and CBCT image registration of temporomandibular joint: a systematic review, J. Otolaryngol. Head Neck Surgery 45 (1) (2016) 30.

[18] M.A.Q. Al-Saleh, J.L. Jaremko, N. Alsufyani, Z. Jibri, H. Lai, Major PW, Assessing the reliability of MRI-CBCT image registration to visualize temporomandibular joints, Dentomaxillofac. Radiol. 44 (6) (2015) 20140244.

[19] M.A. Al-Saleh, N. Alsufyani, H. Lai, M. Lagravere, J.L. Jaremko, Major P W, Usefulness of MRI-CBCT image registration in the evaluation of temporomandibular joint internal derangement by novice examiners, Oral Surgery Oral Med. Oral Pathol. Oral Radiol. 123 (2) (2017) 249–256.

[20] M.G. Nix, R.J. Prestwich, R. Speight, Automated, reference-free local error assessment of multimodal deformable image registration for radiotherapy in the head and neck, Radiother. Oncol. 125 (3) (2017) 478–484.

[21] T.C. Hsung, W.Y. Lam, E.H. Pow, Image to Geometry Registration for Virtual Dental Models, 2018 IEEE 23rd International Conference on Digital Signal Processing, Shanghai, China, 2018, IEEE (2018) 1–4.

[22] R. Destrez, B. Albouy-Kissi, S. Treuillet, Y. Lucas, Automatic registration of 3D dental mesh based on photographs of patient's mouth, Comput. Methods Biomech. Biomed. Eng. Imaging Visual. 7 (2019) 605–615.

[23] K.C.T. Nguyen, N.R. Kaipatur, E.H. Lou, P.W. Major, K. Punithakumar, L.H. Le, Registration of Ultrasound and CBCT Images for Enhancing Tooth-Periodontium Visualization: a Feasibility Study, 2019 International Conference on Multimedia Analysis and Pattern Recognition, Ho Chi Minh City, Vietnam, May 9–10, 2019, IEEE. (2019) 1–5.

[24] J.J. Hwang, Y.H. Jung, B.H. Cho, M.S Heo, An overview of deep learning in the field of dentistry, Imaging Sci. Dentist. 49 (1) (2019) 1–7.

[25] N. Torosdagli, D.K. Liberton, P. Verma, M. Sincan, J.S. Lee, U. Bagci, Deep geodesic learning for segmentation and anatomical landmarking, IEEE Trans. Med. imaging 38 (4) (2018) 919–931.

[26] M. Chung, J. Lee, W. Song, Y. Song, I.H. Yang, J. Lee, Y.G. Shin, Automatic Registration between Cone-Beam CT and Scanned Surface via Deep-Pose Regression Neural Networks and Clustered Similarities (2019) arXiv preprint1907.12250.

[27] J. Gateno, J.F. Teichgraeber, J.J. Xia, Three-dimensional surgical planning for maxillary and midface distraction osteogenesis, J. Craniofac. Surgery 14 (6) (2003) 833–839.

[28] J. Gateno, J.J. Xia, J.F. Teichgraeber, A.M. Christensen, J.J. Lemoine, M.A. Liebschner, et al. Clinical feasibility of computer-aided surgical simulation (CASS) in the treatment of complex craniomaxillofacial deformities, J. Oral Maxillofac. Surgery 65 (4) (2007) 728–734.

[29] E. Nkenke, S. Zachow, M. Benz, T. Maier, K. Veit, M. Kramer, et al. Fusion of computed tomography data and optical 3D images of the dentition for streak artefact correction in the simulation of orthognathic surgery, Dentomaxillofac. Radiol. 33 (4) (2004) 226–232.

[30] F. Schutyser, G. Swennen, P. Suetens, Robust visualization of the dental occlusion by a double scan procedure. International Conference on Medical Image Computing and Computer-Assisted Intervention, Palms Springs, USA, October 26–29, 2005. 8 (2005) 368–374.

[31] G.R. Swennen, W. Mollemans, C. De Clercq, J. Abeloos, P. Lamoral, F. Lippens, et al. A cone-beam computed tomography triple scan procedure to obtain a three-dimensional augmented virtual skull model appropriate for orthognathic surgery planning, J. Craniofac. Surgery 20 (2) (2009) 297–307.

[32] J. Uechi, M. Okayama, T. Shibata, T. Muguruma, K. Hayashi, K. Endo, et al. A novel method for the 3-dimensional simulation of orthognathic surgery by using a multimodal image-fusion technique, Am. J. Orthodont. Dentofac. Orthoped. 130 (6) (2006) 786–798.

[33] A.F. Ayoub, Y. Xiao, B. Khambay, J.P. Siebert, D. Hadley, Towards building a photo-realistic virtual human face for craniomaxillofacial diagnosis and treatment planning, Int. J. Oral Maxillofac. Surgery 36 (5) (2007) 423–428.

[34] P.D. Groeve, F. Schutyser, J.V. Cleynenbreugel, P. Suetens, Registration of 3D photographs with spiral CT images for soft tissue simulation in maxillofacial surgery, Int. Conf. Med. Image Comput. Comput. Assist. Interven. 2208 (2001) 991–996.

[35] B. Khambay, J.C. Nebel, J. Bowman, F. Walker, D.M. Hadley, A. Ayoub, A plot study: 3D stereophotogrammetric image superimposition onto 3D CT scan images--the future of orthognathic surgery, Int. J. Adult Orthodont. Orthog. Surgery 17 (2002) 331–341.

[36] R. Olszewski, M.B. Villamil, D.G. Trevisan, L.P. Nedel, C.M. Freitas, H. Reychler, et al. Towards an integrated system for planning and assisting maxillofacial orthognathic surgery, Comput. Methods Prog. Biomed. 91 (1) (2008) 13–21.

[37] L.H. Hu, W.B. Zhang, Y. Yu, X. Peng, Accuracy of multimodal image fusion for oral and maxillofacial tumors: a revised evaluation method and its application, J. Cranio Maxillofac. Surgery 48 (8) (2020) 741–750.

[38] R. Balachandran, M.A. Fritz, M.S. Dietrich, A. Danilchenko, J.E. Mitchell, V.L. Oldfield, et al. Clinical testing of an alternate method of inserting bone-implanted fiducial markers, nternational, J. Comput. Assist. Radiol. Surgery 9 (5) (2014) 913–920.

[39] J.P. Kobler, J.D. Díaz, J.M. Fitzpatrick, G.J. Lexow, O. Majdani, T. Ortmaier, Localization accuracy of sphere fiducials in computed tomography images, Int. Soc. Optic. Photon. 9036 (2014) 90360Z.

[40] T.R. McRackan, R. Balachandran, G.S. Blachon, J.E. Mitchell, J.H. Noble, C.G. Wright, et al. Validation of minimally invasive, image-guided cochlear implantation using advanced bionics, cochlear, and medel electrodes in a cadaver model, Int. J. Comput. Assist. Radiol. Surgery 8 (6) (2013) 989–995.

[41] H. Cai, X. Xu, J. Lu, J. Lichtman, S.P. Yung, S.T Wong, Using nonlinear diffusion and mean shift to detect and connect cross-sections of axons in 3D optical microscopy images, Med. Image Anal. 12 (6) (2008) 666–775.

[42] C. Bettschart, A. Kruse, F. Matthews, W. Zemann, J.A. Obwegeser, K.W. Grätz, et al. Point-to-point registration with mandibulo-maxillary splint in open and closed jaw position Evaluation of registration accuracy for computer-aided surgery of the mandible, J. Cranio Maxillofac. Surgery 40 (7) (2012) 592–598.

[43] Y. Zhang, X. Shen, Y. Hu, Face registration and surgical instrument tracking for image-guided surgical navigation, International Conference on Virtual Reality and Visualization, Hangzhou, China, September 24–26, 2016, IEEE. (2017) 65–71.

[44] J. Wang, H. Suenaga, K. Hoshi, L. Yang, E. Kobayashi, I. Sakuma, et al. Augmented reality navigation with automatic marker-free image registration using 3-D image overlay for dental surgery, IEEE Trans. Biomed. Eng. 61 (4) (2014) 1295–1304.

[45] S. Klein, M. Staring, K. Murphy, M.A. Viergever, J.P.W. Pluim, Elastix: a toolbox for intensity-based medical image registration, IEEE Trans. Med. Imaging 29 (1) (2009) 196–205.

[46] R. Kikinis, S.D. Pieper, K.G. Vosburgh, 3D Slicer: a platform for subject-specific image analysis, visualization, and clinical support, Intraoperative Imaging and Image-Guided Therapy, Springer, New York, 2014, pp. 277–289.

[47] B.B. Avants, N. Tustison, G. Song, Advanced normalization tools (ANTS), Insight J. 2 (365) (2009) 1–35.

[48] N.J. Tustison, Y. Yang, M. Salerno. Advanced normalization tools for cardiac motion correction. International Workshop on Statistical Atlases and Computational Models of the Heart, Bston, USA, September 18, 2014. 8896 (2015) 3–12.

[49] T.J. Maal, J.M. Plooij, F.A. Rangel, W. Mollemans, F.A. Schutyser, S.J. Berge, The accuracy of matching three-dimensional photographs with skin surfaces derived from cone-beam computed tomography, Int. J. Oral Maxillofac. Surgery 37 (7) (2008) 641–646.

3

Deep learning and generative adversarial networks in oral and maxillofacial surgery

Antonio Pepe[a,b], Gianpaolo Francesco Trotta[c], Christina Gsaxner[a,b,d], Antonio Brunetti[e], Giacomo Donato Cascarano[e], Vitoantonio Bevilacqua[e], Dinggang Shen[f], Jan Egger[a,b,d]

[a]INSTITUTE OF COMPUTER GRAPHICS AND VISION, GRAZ UNIVERSITY OF TECHNOLOGY, GRAZ, AUSTRIA; [b]COMPUTER ALGORITHMS FOR MEDICINE LABORATORY, GRAZ, AUSTRIA; [c]MOXOFF S.P.A., MILAN, ITALY; [d]DEPARTMENT OF ORAL AND MAXILLOFACIAL SURGERY, MEDICAL UNIVERSITY OF GRAZ, GRAZ, AUSTRIA; [e]DEPARTMENT OF ELECTRICAL AND INFORMATION ENGINEERING, POLYTECHNIC UNIVERSITY OF BARI, BARI, ITALY; [f]DEPARTMENT OF RESEARCH AND DEVELOPMENT, SHANGHAI UNITED IMAGING INTELLIGENCE CO., LTD., SHANGHAI, CHINA

1 Introduction

Deep learning represents a subset of machine learning approaches [1]. The particularity of this type of algorithms is given by their capability to process the data in the original raw format. For the application of more classical machine learning algorithms, such as Support Vector Machines [2], a pre-processing step is usually necessary. In this step, meaningful features are extracted manually or semi-automatically. A common approach for the extraction of meaningful features is the application of the principal components analysis [2]. Deep learning approaches leveraged the extended capabilities for parallel computing provided by the recent breakthroughs in graphic processing units (GPU) [1], which allowed for automatic feature selection strategies. In the field of image processing, this is currently achieved using convolutional neural networks (CNN), which will be covered later on in this chapter. Although they were already suggested and applied at the end of the last century [3,4], they gained popularity after the CNN architecture AlexNet [5] won the ImageNet challenge (https://www.image-net.org) back in 2012. From that moment on, deep learning and convolutional neural networks have received an increasing attention in different communities, including medical image analysis [6].

2 Deep learning and its applications

The goal of deep learning approaches is to completely automate the task of learning without relying on the need for handcrafted features. In the field of medical image analysis, this is usually achieved by means of convolutional neural networks [6,7], which we introduce here. First, we provide an overview on neural networks and later on we describe the novelty introduced by convolutional neural networks and some of their successful applications.

2.1 Neural networks

Artificial neural networks (ANN) are biologically inspired computing systems that mimic the physiological neural networks of the human brains [8]. ANN are often described as a set of numerical techniques which have found initial applications in a range of fields ranging from solving ordinary and partial differential equations to modeling and control of non-linear systems [9]. In particular, ANN can be thought as non-linear, multi-layered, parallel regression techniques and can be used for signal processing, forecasting and clustering. The goal of this numerical framework is to learn specific distributions by examples, without providing explicit task-specific rules. For example, in medical image analysis, the network may learn to automatically generate patient-specific implants [10] or to detect cancer in medical images to support oncologists during the phases of diagnosis and management [11–13]. In common scenarios, the ANN detects the location of a cancer, if present, with a certain accuracy, after learning its representation from a collection of example images, referred to as *training set*, which have been previously labeled as either "cancer" or "non cancer" by one or more domain experts [6]. These networks are described with a graph-based representation, where the graph nodes, or artificial neurons, model the physiological neurons of a biological brain, while the connections model the synapses. The very first mathematical model of a neuron, the *perceptron*, was introduced by McCulloch and Pitts in 1943 [14]. In their model, the input variables are connected to a single node (Fig. 3.1, FFNN). The perceptron processes the inputs with a set of three rules. First, the inputs x_i are multiplied with individual weights w_i, then, the weighted inputs are summed up—sometimes a bias b is added. Lastly, the summed weighted inputs are evaluated with an activation function $f(.)$ that produces the output y of the node:

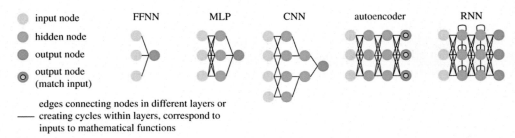

FIGURE 3.1 Different architectures of neural networks. *FFNN*, Feed-forward neural network; *MLP*, multi-layer perceptron; *CNN*, convolutional neural network; *RNN*, recurrent neural network. *From Ching et al. [1]. CC-BY 4.0*

$$y(x,\theta) = f\left(\sum_{i=1}^{D} x_i w_i + b\right), \tag{3.1}$$

where D denotes the dimension of the input, x is the input vector and θ is the state vector representing the weights w_i and bias b. The activation function is chosen depending on the problem the artificial neuron should solve. It can be a step function, a linear function or a non-linear function [15].

During the training phase, specific algorithms are used to train the ANN model $\mathcal{M}$ by finding the optimal values of w_j and b_i, $\forall$ j,i. The optimal weights of this model are those, which minimize the error on the training set. We will discuss this point later on in this chapter. A particular limitation of the perceptron lies in its capability to only act as a linear, binary classifier [16]. Minsky et al. [16] showed how a relatively simple task, such as mimicking the XOR function, cannot be performed with a perceptron. This caused a temporary decline of ANNs and researchers began to develop instead symbolic AI methods and systems, that is, expert systems [17,18]. Afterwards, newer connectionist models and training algorithms were introduced: associative memories [19], multi-layer perceptron (MLP) [2], the back-propagation learning algorithm [2], and many more. Based on these different graph-based models, many applications have been developed and used in a variety of fields. In particular, the limitations of the perceptron were surpassed by increasing the complexity of the neural network. The application of an intermediate neural layer (Fig. 1.1, MLP) allowed to obtain a surrogate model of more complex functions. We generally refer to this network as multi-layer perceptron (MLP). It consists of one hidden layer and each layer is fully connected to the following layer as shown in Fig. 3.2. Analytically, it can be formulated as:

$$y(x,\theta) = f^{(2)}\left(\sum_{j=1}^{M} w_{kj}^{(2)} f^{(1)}\left(\sum_{i=1}^{D} w_{ji}^{(1)} x_i + b^{(1)}\right) + b^{(2)}\right), \tag{3.2}$$

where M is the number of nodes in the hidden layer and the subscript denotes the layer number. Note that the input layer is usually not counted, making the multi-layer perceptron a 2-layer neural network. A network like the multi-layer perceptron in Fig. 3.2 is referred to as feed-forward neural network (FFNN). FFNNs propagate information from input to output in only one direction. Another important group of neural networks are recurrent neural networks (RNNs) that allow the information to flow also in the opposite direction.

Although different network families have been introduced, including Hopfield networks [19], self-organizing maps [20], and RNNs, we will here focus on two specific families: the convolutional neural networks (CNN) and the autoencoders. For any of these families, it is important to consider that, while increasing the complexity of a neural network enables the learning of complex tasks, as shown with the MLP, the optimal number of intermediate layers and intermediate nodes is generally unknown. This also applies for the node type and connectivity pattern: Should the nodes be fully or partially connected? For this, it is

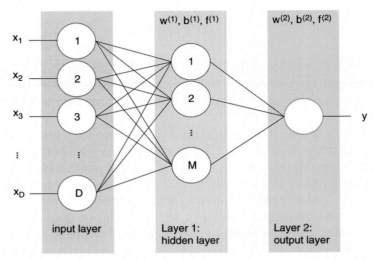

FIGURE 3.2 A multi-layer perceptron. It has one hidden layer and all layers are fully connected, meaning that each node of a layer connects with all nodes of the next layer.

generally recommended to follow the law of parsimony, or Occam's razor [21], for which the simplest model should be chosen among the best performing models.

2.2 Training of a neural network

In the previous section, we introduced how a neural network is defined and represented, and anticipated that a training algorithm is necessary for the retrieval of the optimal weights w_j and biases b_i. The connection weights and biases of each node, combined, form the parameter vector θ, which defines the overall behavior of a network. The identification of the optimal parameters, for a given task, can be formulated as the minimization of an error function $E(\theta)$.

The error function is a measure of discrepancy between the desired output and the actual output of the model. Its choice strictly depends on the problem being solved. For regression, a common choice is the mean squared error

$$E(\theta) = \frac{1}{2} \sum_{i=1}^{N} \left(y(x_i, \theta) - t_i \right)^2, \tag{3.3}$$

where N is the number of examples $x_1,...,x_N$ and $t_1,...t_N$ are the corresponding target values. For classification, a cross-entropy error function can instead be used:

$$E(\theta) = -\sum_{i=1}^{N} \left(t_i \ln(y_i)(1 + t_i) \ln(1 - y_i) \right), \tag{3.4}$$

where y_i denotes $y(x_i, \theta)$. The cross-entropy error function can be generalized to multi-class problems with K classes as [22]:

$$E(\boldsymbol{\theta}) = -\sum_{i=1}^{N}\sum_{k=1}^{K} t_{ki} \ln y_k(x_i, \boldsymbol{\theta}). \tag{3.5}$$

The error function can be viewed as a surface sitting over the parameter space defined by the vector θ. It is a smooth and continuous, but also a non-linear and non-convex function. Therefore, the parameter set θ that minimizes the function cannot be computed analytically, because the function possesses local minima besides the global minimum [23]. Therefore, the computation of the minimizing parameter vector is usually done iteratively, recalculating the parameter vector in each step:

$$\boldsymbol{\theta}^{(\tau+1)} = \boldsymbol{\theta}^{(\tau)} + \Delta\boldsymbol{\theta}^{(\tau)}, \tag{3.6}$$

where τ is the current iteration step and $\Delta\theta^{(\tau)}$ is the update of the parameter vector in this step. The most common way to calculate the update is by using gradient information:

$$\boldsymbol{\theta}^{(\tau+1)} = \boldsymbol{\theta}^{(\tau)} - \eta\nabla E\left(\boldsymbol{\theta}^{(\tau)}\right) \tag{3.7}$$

η is called learning rate. This procedure is called gradient descent algorithm. The gradient of the error function $\nabla E(\theta)$ always points into the direction of greatest rate of increase of the function. By moving in the opposite direction, the error is therefore reduced. Since $E(\theta)$ is a smooth, continuous function, a vector θ, for which the gradient vanishes, exists [22,23]. The learning rate η is used to control the length of each step taken in the current direction. This prevents over-correction of the current variables, which could lead to divergence. So to speak, the learning rate determines how fast a network changes established parameters for new ones. Often a decay function is used for the learning rate, so big steps are taken in the beginning of the algorithm, then learning rate is gradually decreased to make smaller steps. There are two different approaches for timing the update of the parameter vector. In batch gradient descent, the parameters are updated based on the gradients ∇E evaluated over the whole training set. In stochastic gradient descent, the gradient is calculated for one sample in each iteration step and the parameters are updated accordingly. In deep networks, stochastic gradient descent is more commonly used [24].

The gradient of the error function for a network with L layers is given by

$$\nabla E(\Theta) = \left[\frac{\partial E}{\partial\Theta^{(1)}} \cdots \frac{\partial E}{\partial\Theta^{(l)}} \cdots \frac{\partial E}{\partial\Theta^{(L)}}\right], \tag{3.8}$$

where the superscript denotes the layer index. For the gradient descent algorithm, this gradient needs to be calculated in every update step. To compute this efficiently, error backpropagation is usually used. The idea behind error back- propagation is to propagate the resulting error from the output layer back to the input layer [25]. For this, a so-called error message $\delta^{(l)}$ is calculated for every layer $1,...,l,...,L$. The error message of each node can be seen as a measure for the contribution of said node to the output error. Since the states and desired outputs for hidden layers are not known, error terms can not be calculated but

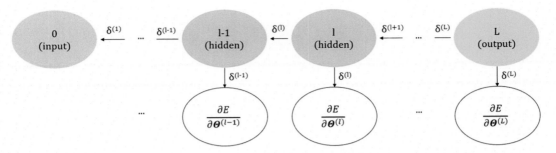

FIGURE 3.3 Error backpropagation. The error message δ is propagated from output to input and updated in every layer. In each layer, the partial derivatives with respect to the parameters $\Theta^{(l)}$ are calculated using the error message. Together, these partial derivatives make up the gradient of the error function ∇E.

have to be estimated by propagating the error messages backwards through the network. Layer l receives an error message $\delta^{(l+1)}$ from layer $l+1$ and updates it using

$$\delta^{(l)} = f'\left(z^{(l)}\right).\left[\left(\Theta^{(l+1)}\right)T\delta^{(l+1)}\right]$$ (3.9)

where $z^{(l)}$ is the input vector of layer 1 and $f'(\cdot)$ is the inverse of the activation function, and passes it on to layer $l-1$. Furthermore, the activation of layer $la^{(1)}$ is used to calculate the gradient of the error function with respect to the parameters of the current layer:

$$\frac{\partial E(\Theta)}{\partial \Theta^{(l)}} = \delta^{(l)}a^{(l)}.$$ (3.10)

This is repeated for every layer [23]. The basic concepts of error backpropagation are illustrated in Fig. 3.3.

2.3 Convolutional neural networks

In the multi-layer networks discussed in the previous sections, inputs were in vector form and network layers were fully connected. However, this is not practical for image data. Each pixel in the input image counts as one input dimension.

If each of these inputs were to be connected to a hidden layer with about 100 hidden units, an image of size 200×200 would already result in several 40,000 weights per neuron and over 4,000,000 weights for the whole layer. Training all these weights would require a large amount of training data and memory. Furthermore, a lot of information is gained from the topology of the input, in example local correlations among neighboring pixels. This information is destroyed when vectorizing image data. Therefore, convolutional layers are introduced into the network architecture. These layers force the network to extract local features by restricting the receptive fields of hidden units to a certain neighborhood of the input. Such features could be oriented edges, end-points or corners [26].

Each unit of a convolutional layer receives inputs from a small neighborhood of units in the previous layer. This neighborhood is also called receptive field. Sets of neurons whose receptive fields are located at different parts of the image are grouped together to have identical weight vectors (weight sharing). As an output, these sets produce so-called feature maps. A convolutional layer consists of several such unit sets, therefore, the output of these layers is a three dimensional volume where width and height are dependent on width and height of the input, and the depth is equivalent to the number of neuron sets in the layer. This process can also be understood as convolving the input with several different filter kernels, each kernel contributing one feature map to the output. The filters are defined by their values, given by the weights of the network, and their size, defined by the size of the receptive fields. Besides, the number of filters, there are two more parameters that influence the size of the feature map. First, the stride is the number of pixels by which the kernel slides over the input image in each step. A larger stride results in reduced width and height of the feature map, a stride of 1 would leave width and height unchanged. Second, zero-padding is sometimes applied to the borders of the image to allow for the application of the filter to bordering pixels. Since in convolutional layers many neurons share the same weights, the number of parameters to train is greatly reduced.

Furthermore, if the input image is shifted, the feature maps will shift in the same way but remain otherwise unchanged. This makes the network invariant to small shifts [22,26].

Since the convolution is a linear operation, but the transformation a CNN should learn is mostly non-linear, non-linearity must be introduced via a suitable activation function. Convolutional layers can use non linear activation functions such as the hyperbolic tangent or logistic sigmoid, but another type of activation function has been found to perform better, namely the Rectified Linear Unit (ReLU) function

$$f(x) = ReLU(x) = max(0, x). \tag{3.11}$$

Subsequently, another new type of layer is introduced, the pooling layer. Its purpose is to downsample an input feature map by reducing the width and height of each map, but leaving the depth unchanged. Similar to the convolution layer, each unit of the pooling layer is connected to a receptive field of units from the previous layer. There are several variants for pooling, such as max pooling where the maximal value inside a receptive field is taken, or average or mean pooling, where the average/mean value is calculated. Pooling has the purpose of decreasing the feature dimensions and therefore, further reduces the number of parameters (weights, biases) of the network. Furthermore, it makes the network invariant to small scaling. In a convolutional neural network, several convolutional and pooling layers are usually applied successively. Ideally, and provided that enough training data is available, the deeper the network becomes, or, equivalently, the more hidden layers it has, the better the ability of the network to extract useful features. The output of such a network consists of high-level, lower dimensional features, which are derived from the input and that are eventually used for tasks like classification. Fully connected layers with appropriate activation functions, as discussed in the previous sections, are usually used for this task. A typical neural network architecture can be seen in Fig. 3.4.

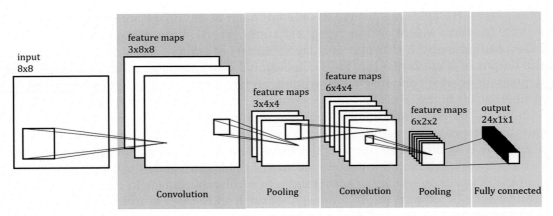

FIGURE 3.4 Convolutional neural network with two convolution and pooling layers. The input image of dimension 8×8 is convolved with three kernels to produce a 3×8×8 feature map. Width and height are reduced in the first pooling layer to the dimension 3×4×4. The feature map is then convolved and pooled for a second time in the same manner. The output layer is fully connected and produces a vector of 24×1×1.

2.4 Applications of deep learning in maxillofacial imaging

Deep learning techniques have been applied to different problems of maxillofacial imaging in the last years [27,28]. These techniques allowed to automate different processes such as anatomical landmark detection [29,30], bone or tumor segmentation [31], disease detection [32], image denoising and reconstruction [33].

2.4.1 Image segmentation

Classical segmentation methods, such as region growing and active contour models [34], have been largely applied to the field of maxillofacial imaging [35]. The strong contrast of bony structures in CT images and of tumors in PET images perfectly suited the application of such methods. For this, the hyperparameters of the methods have to be fine tuned for each target image and additional human interaction is needed to select the area of interest [35]. Additionally, such methods are not thought for objects of interest with inhomogeneous or weak contrast, such as tumors in CT images. In 2015, Ronneberger et al. introduced U-Net [36]. A CNN architecture for supervised learning, originally conceived for the task of 2D biomedical image segmentation. Afterwards, the architecture has been extended to 3D tasks [37] and adapted in a number of studies [38,39]. An example of the architecture is shown in Fig. 3.5. From this point on, U-Net-like networks, and other deep neural networks, have been widely applied to automate the task of segmentation, also in maxillofacial imaging. Qiu et al. [40] evaluated a CNN-based approach for the segmentation of the mandible in CT images. The mandibular bone usually presents a well-defined contrast in CT images. Nonetheless, dental implants can generate a non-negligible noise, which limits the applicability of classical methods. The supervised learning allows to ignore, or limit, the effects of noise and to separately segment mandible and teeth [41]. A task which is otherwise more difficult to achieve with less complex approaches [35]. Fig. 3.6 shows an

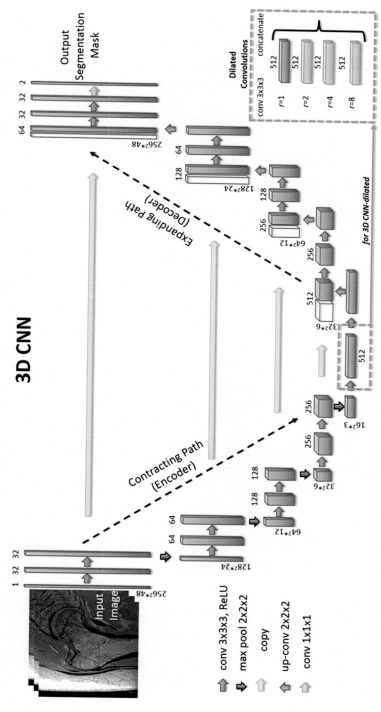

FIGURE 3.5 U-Net-like CNN architecture. Example of a 3D CNN architecture used for the segmentation of a femoral bone. The *blue* layers are convolutional layers. Max pooling operations are used for feature reduction *(black arrows)* and skip connections link the encoding layers to the deconding layers *(gray arrows)*. *From Deniz et al. [38]. CC-BY 4.0*

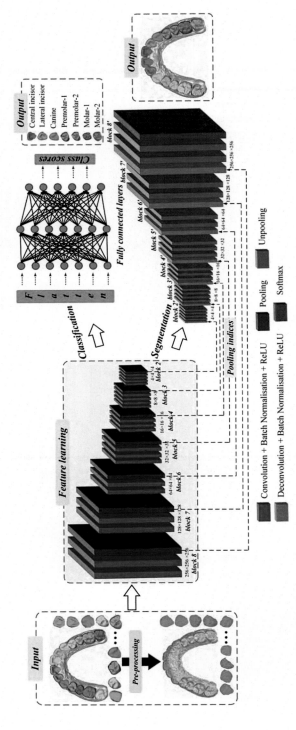

FIGURE 3.6 Example of semantic teeth segmentation with convolutional neural networks. *From Tian et al. [41]. CC-BY-4.0*

example of a CNN used for semantic teeth segmentation. In the selected work, the authors use convolutional layers to learn meaningful teeth features from an initial geometry. The learnt features are passed to a fully connected network for a semantic classification of each tooth and to a convolutional decoder, hence forming a U-Net-like architecture, which generates the actual segmentation. To support the segmentation of the mandible without any interference from the teeth, Wallner et al. [42] published a data collection of clinical head CT images of patients without teeth, together with a ground truth annotation of the mandibles. The absence of teeth allowed to remove their influence during the annotation process. Egger et al. [31] evaluated this collection with different fully convolutional neural networks, a less common architecture for biomedical image segmentation, which used to be applied before the success of U-Net. An evaluation of this collection with a U-Net-like network is currently still missing. Additionally, Gsaxner et al. [43] used the peak activations of PET images from combined PET/CT acquisitions, to automatically generate a ground truth for specific structures in CT images. This considerably reduces the time needed for the generation of the training set and reduces the chances of human errors during the annotation process. This could be applied, for example, to head and neck cancer segmentation, which can be difficult to segment with classic approaches [44,45]. Mimicking the behavior of interactive graph- based segmentation approaches [46], interactive CNN-based approaches have also been suggested [47]. The interactive selection of the areas to be segmented can be used to reduce the amount of training examples or as an intermediate tool to be used during the creation or extension of the training set. This is particularly applicable to vascular structures, like carotid arteries and jugular veins: by leveraging their regular shape, the learning task can be limited to a smaller portion of the vessel while through human interaction or other (semi-)automatic approaches the vessel can be tracked [39]. The segmentation and localization of the blood vessels can be useful not only for a vascular analysis but also to support surgeons during the resection of tumors and avoid unwanted damage to the vascular system [45,48]. A similar surgical problem arises also in dentistry, where it is essential to locate the inferior alveolar nerve, a part of the mandible, to avoid a nerve injury during the surgical procedure. To automate its detection, Kwak et al. [49] recently suggested to consider this as a segmentation problem and evaluated three different architectures: 2D U-Net, 3D U-Net and 2D SegNet [50]; a more recent alternative to U-Net which introduced batch normalization [51], and a softmax activation in the final layer. Although 2D SegNet strongly outperforms the original U-Net, the 3D information analyzed by the 3D U-Net outperforms both methods. Nonetheless, the comparison between U-Net and SegNet in 2D suggests that a 3D version of SegNet may potentially provide a higher accuracy than the 3D U-Net. Recently, Xu et al. [52] also suggested a pipelined model for the segmentation of the maxillary sinus: the authors first trained a VGG network, typically used for classification purposes, to automatically select the slices which contain the sinus, afterwards, these slices were processed with an improved variant of V-Net, a CNN architecture typically applied to 3D segmentation tasks [53]. In their work, Xu et al. [52] showed how the modified V-Net can outperform both the original V-Net and U-Net, suggesting that there is still potential for improvements in the field.

2.4.2 Anatomical landmark detection

Cephalometric analysis is the study of measurements and features that describe the morphology and the growth of the craniofacial skeleton. The analysis is based on the extraction of anatomical landmarks and allows for the identification of patient-specific features for evaluation, diagnosis, and surgical planning [54]. Manual landmarking on 2D or 3D images is a time-consuming, error-prone and imprecise task, requires a significant medical background, and is highly influenced by the clinician's expertise. Automatic landmarking algorithms have been proposed to reduce the task subjectivity introduced by the operator.

Machine learning methods showed promising results in anatomical landmark detection in 2D and 3D medical images [55,56] and, with the developing of deep learning techniques, several workflows based on convolutional neural networks (CNN) have been proposed [29,56–59]. The use of 2D or 3D data as input showed advantages and disadvantages: The direct use of the whole volume to predict the coordinates of landmarks is simpler because it does not require preprocessing, but, at the same time, it introduces higher computational costs and the need for a larger amount of memory. By contrast, the use of lower spatial representations, such as 2D or 2.5D image views, allow the use of simpler and faster models, but they may lack the capability of describing the spatial relationships among landmarks.

According to Ma et al. [60], manual and algorithm-based methods for landmarks detection are still the mainstream in different fields, including oral and maxillofacial surgery. Before starting a surgical treatment for oral and maxillofacial structures, surgeons need to analyze a patient's CT scan for surgical pre-planning. To reduce the surgeons' workload, the authors developed an automatic landmarking model based on real oral and maxillofacial surgery data. The model is based on a patch-based deep neural network with a three-layer CNN architecture. Li et al. [61] instead, proposed a robotic surgery assistant technology based on deep learning for cleft lip and palate repair surgery; the authors used an Hourglass architecture [62] and combined advanced face alignment and deep residual learning.

2.4.3 Disease detection

The segmentation and landmark detection tasks discussed in the previous paragraphs are usually two preliminary steps for the clinical work: the information retrieved with such methods can be used to detect a disease and support further clinical evaluations [39]. For example, odontogenic cystic lesions are usually diagnosed on panoramic and cone-beam CT images [63]. With a similar architecture as Tian et al. [41] (Fig. 3.6), Lee et al. [63] used a CNN to both detect and classify oral cysts. The authors evaluated the architecture Inception V3 [64]. This architecture received a considerable attention as it outclassed AlexNet [5] in 2014 during a follow up of the ImageNet challenge. Lee et al. showed how Inception V3 can provide state-of-the-art results for cyst detection, although the automation of the diagnosis procedure is more challenging: according to them, this relies on the fact that the decision making process usually also considers further information, which is not provided in the CT images. A similar evaluation was conducted by Kwon et al. [65] but limited to panoramic CT images and using a YOLOv3 architecture [66]. Laishram and Thongam [67] used a similar approach for the automatic detection and classification of dental pathologies with an overall accuracy of ≈ 90% for tooth detection. A relevant problem in maxillofacial surgery is tumor resection [45]. This is an invasive procedure and a thorough examination is usually required to assess the malignancy of a tumor. For this, Welikala et al. [68] suggested a CNN-based approach for the automatic scoring of oral lesions for early cancer detection. The authors used a CNN to detect and classify the correlated risk in one of four classes, from low to high risk. Kim et al. [69] instead used deep learning to predict the chances of survival for patients with oral cancer.

2.4.4 Image denoising and reconstruction

Cranial-maxillofacial defects restoration is a delicate task and several studies in literature describe systems based on statistical and deep learning approaches, which were developed to deal with this task. In particular, Wang et al. [70] used a system called EasyImplant that can easily and efficiently design customized cranio-maxillofacial implants with a porous structure using created sample points, distance field and marching-cube algorithms based on an tem- plate implant model. However, these methods are efficient, if the healthy side of the skull model can be used to obtain the initial implant model for the defective side by simply applying a mirroring operation. In their conclusions, the authors highlight this limitation and describe two further approaches that could improve the performance when a reference model is unavailable. More in details, Fuessinger et al. [71] propose and evaluate a computer-based approach which employs a statistical shape model (SSM) of the cranial vault. The suggested workflow is easy to apply and feasible for untrained users: Following image segmentation, the only manual interaction required is the placement of six anatomical landmarks. Moreover, a great benefit of this approach is the applicability to bilateral defects, which is, for obvious reasons, not possible when using a technique based on mirroring. Finally, Morais et al. [33] propose a deep learning approach towards the automated computer-aided design of cranial implants, allowing the design process to be less user-dependent and even less time-consuming. The problem is solved by applying a 3D shape completion task based on a Volumetric Convolutional Denoising Autoencoder. In particular, their work uses transfer learning and domain adaption approaches, starting from a trained deep learning neural network from Sharma et al. [72]. The unsupervised nature of this approach requires more training time than a fully supervised network. However, the described qualitative results are considered satisfactory and the completed skull surfaces can provide a good approximation for the reconstruction of the cranial defects in an automatic way, showing that reconstructing a cranial defect is possible by taking a 3D model of the defected skull and performing a single forward pass through a trained Volumetric Convolutional Denoising Autoencoder. Furthermore, deep learning approaches were also introduced to reduce noise and perform contrast enhancement in CT images. This preprocessing step is used to generate cleaner inputs for deep learning neural network removing some streaking artefacts produced by contrast medium. In particular, Sumida et al. [73] describe a new convolutional neural network structure using a residual network.

The results were then compared to the wellknown U-Net model [36]. The proposed CNN model showed to be suitable for reducing the contrast-enhanced regions in CT images and therefore helping reduce radiation exposure time of patients, and it is able to predict non-contrast CT images, which are available to use in a treatment plan for dose calculation. In the next sections of this chapter, generative adversarial networks are introduced and discussed. These networks are also used for image denoising. Chen et al. [74] describe an image denoising training framework based on Wasserstein Generative Adversarial Networks (WGAN) and apply it to cell image denoising. The problem is that current popular convolutional neural network-based denoising methods encounter a blurriness issue in which denoised images are blurry on texture details. In this study, the authors, to solve the blurriness issue, propose a framework with WGAN based adversarial learning. The authors employed WGAN instead of primary GAN because it solves the training difficulty problem of GAN and improves GAN's performance. More details are discussed in Section 3.

3 Generative adversarial networks and deep perceptual losses

In this section, we introduce generative adversarial networks. After providing a technical overview, we examine some of their variants such as the Wasserstein generative adversarial network and the key role of deep perceptual losses in the training of such networks. Finally, we provide a qualitative synthesis of selected applications of generative adversarial networks in maxillofacial imaging [75–77].

3.1 Generative adversarial networks

Generative adversarial networks have been first introduced at the *Annual Conference on Neural Information Processing Systems* in 2014 [78]. Since then, they have received attention from different research communities, including computer vision and medical image analysis [75–77]. Until that point, deep neural networks had been primarily used for classification tasks [78]. The originally proposed generative adversarial network (GAN), also known as vanilla GAN, was conceived to draw samples from a certain probability distribution by implicitly modeling the prior and, therefore, the probability density function by only knowing a subset of this [77]. The vanilla architecture is composed by two distinct networks, the generator, $G(\mathbf{z})$, and the discriminator, $D(\mathbf{x})$. G and D represent a generative and a classification function, respectively. These two networks are adversarially trained, following the framework of a minimax game [2,78] for the value function $V(G,D)$:

$$\min_{G} \max_{D} V(G,D) = \mathbf{E}_x\left[\log D(\mathbf{x})\right] + \mathbf{E}_z\left[\log(1 - D(G(\mathbf{z})))\right], \tag{3.12}$$

where the aim of the discriminator D is to maximize the likelihood of correctly classifying the vectors $<\mathbf{x}>$ as real data and the vectors $<G(\mathbf{z})>$ as generated data. The input of G, $\mathbf{z}$, is a random vector from the latent vector space of the network G, often referred to as noise vector. In practice, the generator performs the equivalent task of maximizing $\log\big(D(G(\mathbf{z}))\big)$ as this was empirically demonstrated to converge in a shorter time [78]. This training strategy aims to find the Nash equilibrium between the two adversarial tasks, so that, as a result, the generator can implicitly estimate the distribution of a known data collection [76]. Goodfellow et al. [78] showed how Eq. (3.12) implicitly minimizes the Jensen-Shannon divergence between the probability distributions of the real data p_{data} and of the generated data p_{gen}:

$$D_{JS}\left(p_{data}, p_{gen}\right) = \frac{1}{2}D_{KL}\left(p_{data}\left\|\frac{p_{data} + p_{gen}}{2}\right.\right) + \frac{1}{2}D_{KL}\left(p_{gen}\left\|\frac{p_{data} + p_{gen}}{2}\right.\right),$$

(3.13)

where D_{KL} is the Kullback-Leibler divergence:

$$D_{KL}\left(a \,\|\, b\right) = \int_x a(x)\log\frac{a(x)}{b(x)}dx.$$

(3.14)

The Jensen-Shannon divergence is characterized by being symmetric and having an absolute minimum of zero when $\forall x : a(x) = b(x)$. Radford et al. [79] extended the concept of GAN to deep convolutional neural networks, referred to as Deep Convolutional GAN (DCGAN). In DCGAN, convolutional, encoding layers are used to represent the discriminator D and transposed convolution is used to in the deep neural network representing the generator G.

3.2 Training optimization for generative adversarial networks

One of the most critical limitations of vanilla GANs is training convergence. Some of the causes have been analyzed by Salimans et al. [80]. In their work, the authors discuss how the training of vanilla GANs consists in finding *a Nash equilibrium of a non-convex game with continuous, high-dimensional parameters*. Nonetheless, the training of a GAN is typically done using gradient descent methods, which are generally conceived to find the optimum value of a differentiable function. Furthermore, the generator and the discriminator optimize their cost functions independently: no observation is done whether an update is also beneficial for the opponent. A solution to this problem is given by feature matching. Instead of directly training the generator to optimize the output value of the discriminator, the generator is trained to optimize for the statistics, which describe the discriminator. In case of deep neural network, this is equivalent to optimize for the output of the intermediate layers of the discriminator. In this way, the generator can directly optimize for the most relevant features, which determine the output of the discriminator. Another possible failure of GANs happens when the generator collapses to a certain parameter configuration and produces always the same output and the discriminator then learns that the sample is generated. This phenomenon is often marginalized by using minibatch discrimination, where the discriminator looks at a batch of samples at a time instead of a single sample. More foundations to this approach are given by Salimans et al. [80]. Radford et al. [79] showed also that, like for other families of neural networks, batch normalization can positively influence the training results. To overcome the limitation that, in batch normalization, the importance of a single sample is averaged with that of other samples, Salimans et al. [80] suggested to use a so-called "virtual batch normalization," where the normalization is performed in relation to the statistics of a reference batch.

3.3 Wasserstein generative adversarial networks

To solve the problem of mode collapse, Arjovsky et al. [81] introduced the so-called Wasserstein generative adversarial networks (WGAN). In Section 3.1, we described how the adversarial training of a GAN implicitly tries to reduce the Jensen-Shannon divergence (Eq. 3.13) between the two distributions. For this to be possible, the Kullbach-Leibler integral (Eq. 3.14) must be defined and finite $\forall a(x), b(x)$. In their work, Arjovsky et al. [81] focus on minimizing, during training, the Wasserstein distance between the distribution of generated samples p_{gen} and the distribution of the training samples p_{data}. They show that under this consideration the function describing the WGAN is defined as

$$\min_G \max_{D \in \mathcal{L}} V(G,D) = \mathbf{E}_x[D(\mathbf{x})] + \mathbf{E}_z(D(G(\mathbf{z}))), \tag{3.15}$$

where $\mathcal{L}$ is the set of Lipschitz-continuous functions with Lipschitz constant $k_{\mathcal{L}} = 1$. For deep neural networks, they indirectly enforced this condition by introducing weight clipping. Nonetheless, Gulrajani et al. [82] showed that the application of weight clipping can produce side effects like vanishing gradients. As an alternative, the authors replaced the weight clipping with a gradient penalty term to ensure that each gradient g_i is smaller or equal to one. This approach has been empirically shown to produce less side effects, although the application of a penalty term is not enough to enforce the gradients $g_i \leq 1$ at the beginning of a training. For this, Wei et al. [83] suggested the application of a consistency term. This term is directly defined following the definition of Lipschitz continuity where for each pair of samples $\mathbf{x}_1$ and $\mathbf{x}_2$ the following holds:

$$d\big(D(\mathbf{x}, D(\mathbf{x}_2))\big) \leq K * d(\mathbf{x}_1, \mathbf{x}_2), \tag{3.16}$$

where d is the Euclidean distance and K the Lipschitz constant. To penalize any violation of the Lipschitz continuity, the authors replaced the gradient penalty term with a so-called consistency term defined as:

$$CT = max\left(0, \frac{d\big(D(\mathbf{x}_1), D(\mathbf{x}_2)\big)}{d(\mathbf{x}_1, \mathbf{x}_2)}\right). \tag{3.17}$$

K' approximates K as it is calculated over a discrete number of sample pairs. The subtraction of the consistency term during the training helps to approximate the Lipschitz condition already during the initial iterations of the training but still follows the idea introduced with gradient penalty to avoid the limitations of weight clipping.

3.4 Image-to-image transformation with generative adversarial networks

The original architecture of GAN, or vanilla GAN [78], introduced a break- through in the field of stochastic image generation. This lead a number of experts to analyze the limitations of the suggested architecture and examine alternative versions which provide a more stable training convergence [80,81,83–85]. The formulation of unsupervised learning with DCGAN set the ground for a more diverse number of possible applications for GANs [75,76], also in medical imaging [77]. Isola et al. evaluated the efficacy of conditional GANs for image-to-image transformations [86]. Prior to their evaluation, GANs had been used for image-to-image transformations unconditionally [79]. Conditioning the output of a GAN on distinct labels, such as the expected edges for the generated images, has shown to particularly boost the performance of these approaches. Additionally, the authors showed how the application of skip connections between convolutional and deconvolutional layers of same size, that is, a U-Net-like architecture, also provides a raise in performance, as the input conditional label can then be easily forwarded to the deconvolutional layers of the CNN. Prior to this evaluation, the *de facto* standard was to utilize encoder-decoder CNNs without skip connections. While previous trials employed the L2 loss, that is, the Euclidean distance, Isola et al. [86] opted for the L1 loss. The results motivating this choice are discussed in their work, were the authors show how the sole application of the L1 loss provides the best results for vision tasks, for example, image labeling, while the graphics applications such as photorealistic image generation, benefit from the joint application of the L1 loss and conditional GANs. The initial evaluation was performed on RGB images of different kinds, ranging from clothes to landscapes. The authors showed how the network can than specialize in performing distinct tasks like image in painting, grayscale to color conversion, and sketch images to realistic photos. Nonetheless, this initial evaluation found successful applications also in medical imaging [77]. Some key examples of these applications are shown later in this section.

3.5 Deep perceptual losses

In the initial image-to-image transformation networks [86], rather structural loss functions have been used to describe the quality of reconstructed images. To name but a few, these have mostly been the peak signal to noise ratio, the structural similarity index, the L1 and the L2 loss. The rather geometrical definition of these metrics does not always match the human understanding of image similarity [87]. This has recently led to the investigation of alternative methodologies, which can better mimic the perceptual understanding of the human brain [30,88]. This led to the definition of distance metrics defined in the different latent spaces defined by the convolutional layers of a trained neural network [87]. Instead of measuring the, for example, L2 distance between the generated output and the relative ground truth, recent literature suggests to measure the L2 distance between the outputs, or weight activations, of a trained CNN when executed with the generated image and when executed with the ground truth image. This approach is rather like the feature matching loss which we previously discussed for the improved training of GANs. Strong of their popularity, pretrained VGG networks have been widely used for the calculation of the deep metric [87,88]. Nonetheless, Zhang et al. [87] showed how the final accuracy depends only marginally on the selection of the pretrained network. This finding is of interest for the application of deep perceptual losses in medical imaging where it is less simple to retrieve pretrained networks for 3D vision and image generation.

3.6 Applications of generative adversarial networks in maxillofacial imaging

Deep learning was a breakthrough for medical image analysis, despite the costly requirement for large, annotated datasets [89], which led to the recommendation of common guidelines for the collection and preparation of medical data for machine learning applications [90]. Some studies tried to limit the need for manual processing: Gsaxner et al. [43] replaced manual tumor annotations with the peak regions of PET images from combined PET/CT datasets. Lindner et al. [91] added artificial glioblastomas in brain MRI images to augment regular datasets of healthy patients. Alternatively, Chen et al. [92] exploited the role of GAN and suggested a one-shot adversarial learning approach for the segmentation of maxillofacial bony structures in MRI. Following the approach of Gsaxner et al. [43], bone information in MRI images could be retrieved from paired MRI/CT datasets. A side effect is the patient's exposure to harmful radiations. Instead, Chen et al. [92] leveraged one-shot and adversarial learning strategies to use unpaired MRI and CT images and only one MRI/CT pair. This was achieved by training two separate cross-modality generators—CT-to-MRI and MRI-to-CT—on 3D patches of size 32×32×32 voxels. The authors also showed how the generation of MRI from CT images is more difficult than MRI to CT. It is interesting how, in their results, the proposed method can outperform the better-known U-Net [36]. Another common application for GAN in medical imaging is denoising and artifact reduction [77]. For example, Nakao et al. [93] recently applied regularized 3D GAN for metal artifact reduction in head and neck CT images. Following the architecture of Chen et al. [92], Nakao et al. [93] used to adversarial generators, one to generate artifact-free images from CT images with metal artifacts and one computing the opposite task. In their tests, the authors showed how the 3D information is extremely important in artifact reduction. These applications are extremely helpful in the dental area where different metal implants can be present.

3.7 Applications of deep perceptual losses in maxillofacial imaging

Initial studies based on GAN used common loss functions for training convergence such as the mean squared error (L2) and the mean absolute error (L1) [77]. The innovation brought by deep perceptual losses [88] had a tangible impact also on medical image reconstruction. For example, Gjesteby et al. [94] also targeted the problem of metal streak artifact reduction in CT images. In particular, unlike Nakao et al. [93], they used a residual convolutional

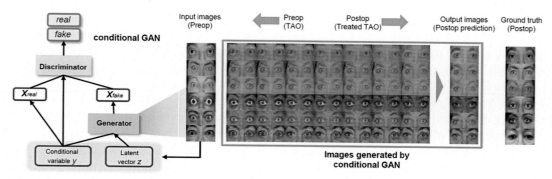

FIGURE 3.7 Application of a generative adversarial network and deep perceptual losses for the prediction of postoperative appearance after orbital decompression surgery for thyroid eye disease [97] .

neural network with a deep perceptual loss computed on the feature maps of a pre-trained VGG network [95]. A comparison between the two approaches is not yet available, but Gjesteby et al. [94] showed the performance increase brought by the deep perceptual loss with respect to the more common mean squared error. Yang et al. [96] applied a perceptual loss to the training of a Wasserstein GAN for low-dose CT image denoising. The authors did not focus on the maxillofacial region, but their approach did not show any specific limitation, which would hinder this process. The suggested approach consisted of a generative network and two parallel discriminative networks: An adversarial discriminator and a VGG network on which the perceptual loss is computed. Also in this case, the authors reported a significant increase in performance with the introduction of a deep perceptual loss. In particular, performances were measured using the peak signal/noise ratio and the structural similarity index. Although it is rather related to ophthalmology, Yoo et al. [97] used a GAN to predict the postoperative appearance after orbital decompression surgery (Fig. 3.7). The authors applied a conditional GAN to transform the original preoperative images. An interesting outcome of their study is that the synthetized postoperative images can be used to increase the performance of a classifier. In their work, two different GAN architectures, Pix2Pix and CycleGAN, were trained with a composite loss function based on the deep perceptual loss. The feature maps where calculated over both a pretrained VGG and a pretrained InceptionNet. Some limitations of their study included the low resolution, of only 64×64 pixels, and the need for a larger data collection.

4 Uncertainty quantification in deep learning

Convolutional neural networks have found a number of different applications in medical image analysis [39,77,98]. Yet, the related data and model uncertainties have been less intensively investigated in the field of biomedical imaging, although there is a clear need for uncertainty awareness [99]. Kendall et al. [100] evaluated the impact of data and model uncertainty in computer vision applications for Bayesian neural networks. The authors showed how model uncertainty is less relevant compared to data uncertainty when a model is trained on large data collections. Model uncertainty is instead critical when the model is trained on small collections. Classic neural networks do not directly provide a quantification of model uncertainty, and Bayesian neural networks, can be harder to train, especially in 3D medical imaging where data are usually scarce, and also have higher computational costs [101]. Bayesian neural networks describe the weight parameters as distributions over the parameters [100]: The nodes and connections of the network, (n_i, c_j) are not only described by their bias b_k but also by a variance σ_k over a Gaussian distribution. The presence of σ_k doubles the number of network parameters. An alternative is to train K models independently: Given the data pairs $(\mathbf{x}, \mathbf{y})$ and the weights' distribution $\mathcal{D}$, the output distribution of the model $p(\mathbf{y}|\mathbf{x}, \mathcal{D})$ can then be represented, empirically, as the mean and variance of the K independent predictions. This can be achieved, for example, by training the K models using bootstrapping and adversarial training [102]. A different approach was proposed by Gal et al. [101] called Monte Carlo dropout sampling (MCDS). The particularity of this approach lies in the application of dropout, a regularization technique generally used only during the training phase [103], also during test executions. The dropout regularization deactivates a random subset of neurons, thus implicitly generating a collection of different models. Leibig et al. [13] were among the first to apply MCDS in medical image analysis. They compared a Bayesian convolutional neural network, a Gaussian process, and MCDS on the detection of diabetic retinopathy in fundus images. In their evaluation, MCDS reported the highest improvement when observing the receiver-operating characteristic curves. Eaton-Rosen et al. [12] used Bayesian convolutional neural networks for image-to-image transformation tasks. The authors particularly addressed the problem of brain tumor segmentation. The suggested approach provided an estimation of the overall uncertainty, although the authors argumented on how this quantification only partially models the actual underlying uncertainty.

Nair et al. [104] recently applied MCDS for the detection of multiple sclerosis lesions (Fig. 3.8). These initial applications demonstrate the important role of uncertainty quantification in computer-aided medical image analysis, but also show the limitations of the current

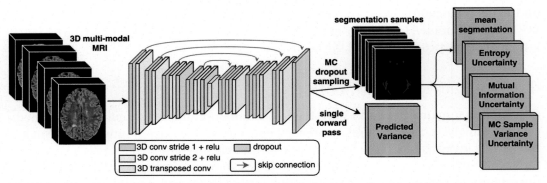

FIGURE 3.8 The figure shows the CNN architecture evaluated by Nair et al. [104] for an uncertainty-aware detection of multiple sclerosis lesions in 3D brain MRI images.

approaches: Bayesian convolutional neural networks, bootstrapping and MCDS, all intro-duce a non-negligible, computational overhead compared to the classical convolutional neu-ral networks. In particular, for MCDS the overhead is mostly proportional to the amount of executions we perform during the Monte Carlo sampling. Postel et al. [105] recently suggested a sampling-free approach for model uncertainty quantification of deep neural networks for 2D visual tasks. The authors approximate the model uncertainty using error propagation and noise injection at training time. To the best of our knowledge, the benefits of similar, sam-pling-free approaches have not been investigated in 3D medical image analysis, yet.

5 Outline and future directions

Deep learning methods have considerably influenced the way medical image analysis tasks are automated, showing state-of-the-art accuracy [7,28,36]. Bone or tumor segmen-tation tasks, which were previously performed manually or semi-automatically with com-mercial software [35], can now be fully automated with a final quality that can outclass that of a trained user [7,35,39,77,92]. Automatic landmark detection approaches have also been suggested for the detection of points of interest, which are essential during sur-gery planning [57,58,60,61]. Leveraging this information, or with alternative end-to-end approaches, deep learning was successfully applied in clinical decision support tasks such as the detection of dental pathologies [67] or the automatic scoring of oral lesions for can-cer-related risk [68]. A non-negligible noise is present in a high number of head CT images, due to the metallic material used for dental implants. An important milestone was also set by deep generative methods, which allow, for example, to automatically reduce the amount of noise in CT images [94].

Although the initial applications were positively received by the community, these also faced some strong limitations. The original deep learning methods were conceived to be trained over large training sets [7,77]. This resulted in a *hunger* for high-quality manual annotations, which are often difficult and costly to acquire [106]. This due to legal require-ments, such as internal review board (IRB) approval, and manual annotations, which are generally performed by highly trained personnel during their working hours. For example, Hahn et al. [106] evaluated that an experienced radiologist requires about two hours to seg-ment one single dissected aorta. For this reason, initial one- or few-shot approaches were suggested [92], showing that the state of the art can be reached with a smaller amount of manual annotations. Furthermore, none of the initial studies considered prediction uncer-tainty. Although cancer-related risk prediction is highly important in maxillofacial surgery [68], a prediction may be wrong and some of the Bayesian approaches should be consid-ered [100,101,107]. Another important limitation to be considered is that, although genera-tive networks provided state- of-the-art quality in image denoising [93,94], these methods usually regenerate the original image using trained kernels, which were previously learnt during the training phase. For this, a thorough evaluation would be necessary before apply-ing the methods in clinical practice. Small abnormalities or pathologies, which might be absent in the training data, could be recognized as noise and therefore removed. These automatically denoised images are nonetheless extremely helpful: the segmentation task can be performed on the denoised version, so that noisy images do not need to be included in the training set. Additionally, these images can help physicians and surgeons in evaluating the overall shape of a bone or organ. Following this idea, some studies even tried to reconstruct the image content before the formation of a disease [108–110]. Furthermore, the application of Bayesian approaches could be investigated: areas with higher uncertainty could relate to important information, which was possibly classified as noise and removed.

6   Conclusion

In this chapter, we provided a general introduction to deep learning, generative adversarial networks, and deep perceptual losses, with an emphasis on their applications in medical image analysis for oral and maxillofacial surgery. We provided a general overview of how these techniques can be applied to the field. In particular, we discussed how these approaches were successfully applied to image segmentation, anatomical landmark detection, image reconstruction and denoising. To reduce the annotation cost, we analyzed how few- or one-shot approaches can reduce the amount of required training data while still preserving state-of-the-art accuracy. Additionally, we discussed uncertainty quantification methods, such as Bayesian neural networks and Monte Carlo dropout sampling approaches, and why they should be considered for prediction tasks, where a single prediction might provide insufficient information. Although these methods were not yet widely applied in the field of oral and maxillofacial image analysis, they already showed their potential in other areas of medical image analysis.

Acknowledgment

This chapter was financially supported by the TU Graz LEAD Project *Mechanics, Modeling and Simulation of Aortic Dissection* (https://biomechaorta.tugraz.at), the Austrian Science Fund (FWF) KLI 678-B31 *"enFaced: Virtual and Augmented Reality Training and Navigation Module for 3D-Printed Facial Defect Reconstructions,"* and by CAMed (COMET K-Project 871132), which is funded by the Austrian Federal Ministry of Transport, Innovation and Technology (BMVIT), and the Austrian Federal Ministry for Digital and Economic Affairs (BMDW) and the Styrian Business Promotion Agency (SFG). Finally, we want to point out to our web-based medical image analysis framework, Studierfenster (www.studierfenster.at): in this framework, the reader can interactively try to perform tasks of image segmentation [111], vessel and skull reconstruction [110,112], or anatomical landmark detection [113] with the support of a deep neural network. Visual guides are available on YouTube at: https://www.youtube.com/channel/UCSe-q1nicDVwC550dngQT2w.

References

[1] T. Ching, D.S. Himmelstein, B.K. Beaulieu-Jones, A.A. Kalinin, G.P. Way, E. Ferrero, et al. Opportunities and obstacles for deep learning in biology and medicine, J. R. Soc. Interf. 15 (141) (2018) 1–47.

[2] S.J. Russel, P. Norvig, Artificial Intelligence: A Modern Approach, 3rd ed, Pearson College Div, (2010).

[3] K. Fukushima, Neocognitron: a self-organizing neural network model for a mechanism of pattern recognition unaffected by shift in position, Biol. Cybernet. 36 (4) (1980) 193–202.

[4] Y. LeCun, L. Bottou, Y. Bengio, P. Haffner, Gradient-based learning applied to document recognition, Proc. IEEE 86 (1998) 2278–2324.

[5] A. Krizhevsky, I. Sutskever, G. Hinton, Imagenet classification with deep convolutional neural networks, Advances in Neural Information Processing Systems 25 (2012) 1097–1105.

[6] G. Litjens, T. Kooi, B.E. Bejnordi, A.A.A. Setio, F. Ciompi, M. Ghafoorian, et al. A survey on deep learning in medical image analysis, Med. Image Anal. 42 (2017) 60–88.

[7] D. Shen, G. Wu, H.-I. Suk, Deep learning in medical image analysis, Ann. Rev. Biomed. Eng. 19 (2017) 221–248.

[8] S. Shanmuganathan, Artificial neural network modelling: An introduction, Artificial Neural Network Modelling, Springer, Cham, 2016, pp. 1–14.

[9] J.A.K. Suykens, J.P.L. Vandewalle, B.L.De Moor, Springer Science and Business Media (2012).

[10] J. Li, A. Pepe, C. Gsaxner, G. von Campe, J. Egger, A baseline approach for autoimplant: the miccai 2020 cranial implant design challenge, Multimodal Learning for Clinical Decision Support and Clinical Image-Based Procedures, Springer, 2020, pp. 75–84.

[11] A. Brunetti, L. Carnimeo, G.F. Trotta, V. Bevilacqua, Computer-assisted frameworks for classification of liver, breast and blood neoplasias via neural networks: A survey based on medical images, Neurocomputing 335 (2019) 274–298.

[12] Z. Eaton-Rosen, F. Bragman, S. Bisdas, et al. Towards safe deep learning: Accurately quan- tifying biomarker uncertainty in neural network predictions. In: Proceedings of International Conference on Medical Image Computing and Computer-Assisted Intervention, vol. 11070, pp. 691–669 (2018).

[13] C. Leibig, V. Allken, M.S. Ayhan, et al. Leveraging uncertainty information from deep neural networks for disease detection, Sci. Rep. 7 (17816) (2017) 1–14.

[14] W. McCulloch, W. Pitts, A logical calculus of the ideas immanent in nervous activity, Bull. Math. Biophys. 5 (1943) 115–133.

[15] A. Krenker, A. Kos, J. Bešter, Introduction to the Artificial Neural Networks, INTECH Open Access Publisher, (2011).

[16] M. Minsky, S.A. Papert. MIT Press, 1969.

[17] E.L. Kinney, Medical expert systems. Who needs them? Chest 91 (1) (1987) 3–4.

[18] G.D. Sanders, E.A. Lyons, The potential use of expert systems to enable physicians to order more cost-effective diagnostic imaging examinations, J. Digital Imaging 4 (2) (1991) 112–122.

[19] J. Hopfield, Neural networks and physical systems with emergent collective computational abilities, Proc. Natl. Acad. Sci. USA 79 (2006) 2554–2558.

[20] T. Kohonen, Visual Explorations in Finance with Self-Organizing Maps, Springer, London, (1998).

[21] C.E. Rasmussen, Z. Ghahramani. Occam's Razor. In: Proceedings of Advances in Neural Information Processing Systems (2001).

[22] C.M. Bishop, Pattern recognition, Mach. Learn. 128 (2006) 1–58.

[23] S.K. Zhou, H. Greenspan, D. Shen, Deep Learning for Medical Image Analysis, Academic Press, (2017).

[24] Y.A. LeCun, L. Bottou, G.B. Orr, K.-R. Müller, Efficient backprop, Neural Networks: Tricks of the Trade, Springer, 2012, pp. 9–48.

[25] D.E. Rumelhart, G.E. Hinton, R.J. Williams, Learning representations by back-propagating errors, Cognitive Model. 5 (3) (1988) 533–536.

[26] Y. LeCun, Y. Bengio, et al. Convolutional networks for images, speech, and time series, The Handbook of Brain Theory and Neural Networks Vol. 3361 (10), MIT Press, 1998, pp. 255–258.

[27] A. Fourcade, R.H. Khonsari, Deep learning in medical image analysis: A third eye for doctors, J. Stomatol. Oral Maxillofac. Surgery 120 (4) (2019) 279–288.

[28] J.-J. Hwang, Y.-H. Jung, B.-H. Cho, M.-S. Heo, An overview of deep learning in the field of dentistry, Imaging Sci. Dentistry 49 (1) (2019) 1–7.

[29] M. Codari, A. Pepe, G. Mistelbauer, D. Mastrodicasa, S. Walters, M.J. Willemink, et al. Deep reinforcement learning for localization of the aortic annulus in patients with aortic dissection. In: Proc MICCAI International Workshop on Thoracic Image Analysis, Springer, 2020.

[30] Q. Wu, C. Fan, Y. Li, Y. Li, J. Hu, A novel perceptual loss function for single image super-resolution, Multimed. Tools Appl. 79 (2020) 21265–21278.

[31] J. Egger, B. Pfarrkirchner, C. Gsaxner, L. Lindner, D.J. Wallner. Schmalstieg, Fully convolutional mandible segmentation on a valid ground- truth dataset, In: Proc. of Annual International Conference of the IEEE Engineering in Medicine and Biology Society (2018).

[32] M. Murata, Y. Ariji, Y. Ohashi, T. Kawai, M. Fukuda, T. Funakoshi, et al. Deep-learning classification using convolutional neural network for evaluation of maxillary sinusitis on panoramic radiography, Oral Radiol. 35 (2019) 301–307.

[33] A. Morais, J.V. Alves. Egger, Automated computer-aided design of cranial implants using a deep volumetric convolutional denoising autoencoder, In: Proc. of World Conference on Information Systems and Technologies, (2019), pp. 151–160.

[34] M. Kass, A. Witkin, D. Terzopoulos, Snakes: Active contour models, Int. J. Comput. Vision 1 (4) (1988) 321–331.

[35] J. Wallner, M. Schwaiger, K. Hochegger, C. Gsaxner, W. Zemann, J. Egger, A review on multiplatform evaluations of semi-automatic open-source based image segmentation for cranio-maxillofacial surgery, Comput. Methods Program. Biomed. 182 (105102) (2019) 1–23.

[36] O. Ronneberger, P. Fischer, T. Brox, U-Net: convolutional networks for biomedical image segmentation, Proc. Med Image Comput Comput. Assist. Interven. 9351 (2015) 234–241.

[37] Özgün Çiçek, A. Abdulkadir, S.S. Lienkamp, T. Brox, O. Ronneberger. 3D U-Net: Learning Dense Volumetric Segmentation from Sparse Annotation. In: Proceedings of Medical Image Computing and Computer-Assisted Intervention, 2016

[38] C.M. Deniz, S. Xiang, R.S. Hallyburton, A. Welbeck, J.S. Babb, S. Honig, et al. Segmentation of the proximal femur from MR images using deep convolutional neural networks, Sci. Rep. 8 (16485) (2018) 1–14.

[39] A. Pepe, J. Li, M. Rolf-Pissarczyk, et al. Detection, segmentation, simulation and visualization of aortic dissections: A review, Med. Image Anal. 64 (101773) (2020) 1–16.

[40] B. Qiu, J. Guo, J. Kraeima, H.H. Glas, R.J.H. Borra, M.J.H. Witjes, et al. Automatic segmentation of the mandible from computed tomography scans for 3D virtual surgical planning using the convolutional neural network, Comput. Methods Progr. Biomed. 64 (19) (2019) 1–13.

[41] S. Tian, N. Dai, B. Zhang, F. Yuan, Q. Yu, X. Cheng, Automatic classification and segmentation of teeth on 3D dental model using hierarchical deep learning networks, IEEE Access 7 (2019) 84817–84828.

[42] J. Wallner, I. Mischak, J. Egger, Computed tomography data collection of the complete human mandible and valid clinical ground truth models, Sci. Data 6 (190003) (2019) 1–14.

[43] C. Gsaxner, B. Pfarrkirchner, L. Lindner, A. Pepe, P.M. Roth, J. Wallner et al. PET-Train: automatic ground truth generation from PET acquisitions for urinary bladder segmentation in CT images using deep learning. In: Proceedings of IEEE BioMedical Engineering International Conference, pp. 1–5, 2018.

[44] A. Pepe, G.F. Trotta, C. Gsaxner, D. Schmalstieg, J. Wallner, J. Egger, et al. Pattern recognition and mixed reality for computer-aided maxillofacial surgery and oncological assessment. In: Proceedings of IEEE 11th Biomedical Engineering International Conference, 2018.

[45] A. Pepe, G.F. Trotta, P. Mohr-Ziak, C. Gsaxner, J. Wallner, V. Bevilacqua, et al. A marker-less registration approach for mixed reality–aided maxillofacial surgery: a pilot evaluation, J. Digital Imaging 32 (2019) 1008–1018.

[46] J. Egger, T. Lüddemann, R. Schwarzenberg, B. Freisleben, C. Nimsky, Interactive-cut: Real-time feedback segmentation for translational research, Comput. Med. Imaging Graph. 38 (4) (2014) 285–295.

[47] A. Pepe, R. Schussnig, J. Li, C. Gsaxner, X. Chen, T.-P. Fries et al. IRIS: interactive real-time feedback image segmentation with deep learning. In: Proceedings of SPIE Medical Imaging 2020: Biomedical Applications in Molecular, Structural, and Functional Imaging, 2020

[48] C. Gsaxner, A. Pepe, J. Wallner, D.J. Egger. Schmalstieg, Markerless image-to-face registration for untethered augmented reality in head and neck surgery, International Conference on Medical Image Computing and Computer-Assisted Intervention, Springer, 2019, pp. 236–244.

[49] G.H. Kwak, E.-J. Kwak, J.M. Song, H.R. Park, Y.-H. Jung, B.-H. Cho, et al. Automatic mandibular canal detection using a deep convolutional neural network, Sci. Rep. 10 (5711) (2020) 1–8.

[50] V. Badrinarayanan, A. Kendall, R. Cipolla, A deep convolutional encoder-decoder architecture for image segmentation, IEEE Trans. Pattern Anal. Mach. Intell. 39 (2020) 2481–2495.

[51] S. Ioffe, C. Szegedy. Batch normalization: accelerating deep network training by reducing internal covariate shift. In: Proceedings of International Conference on Machine Learning, 2015.

[52] J. Xu, S. Wang, Z. Zhou, J. Liu, X. Jiang, X. Chen, Automatic CT image segmentation of maxillary sinus based on VGG network and improved V-Net, Int. J. Comput. Assist. Radiol.Surgery 15 (2020) 1457–1465.

[53] F. Milletari, N. Navab, S. Ahmadi. V-net: Fully convolutional neural networks for volumetric medical image segmentation. In: Proceedings of International Conference on 3D Vision, 2016.

[54] G.R. Swennen, F.A. Schutyser, J.-E. Hausamen, Three-Dimensional Cephalometry: A Color Atlas and Manual, Springer Science & Business Media, 2005.

[55] B. Bier, M. Unberath, J.-N. Zaech, J. Fotouhi, M. Armand, G. Osgood, et al. X-ray-transform invariant anatomical landmark detection for pelvic trauma surgery. International Conference on Medical Image Computing and Computer-Assisted Intervention, pp. 55–63, Springer, 2018.

[56] Y. Zheng, D. Liu, B. Georgescu, H. Nguyen, D. Comaniciu. 3D deep learning for efficient and robust landmark detection in volumetric data. International Conference on Medical Image Computing and Computer-Assisted Intervention, pp. 565–572, Springer, 2015.

[57] F.C. Ghesu, B. Georgescu, T. Mansi, D. Neumann, J. Hornegger, D. Comaniciu, An artificial agent for anatomical landmark detection in medical images, International Conference on Medical Image Computing and Computer-Assisted Intervention, Springer, 2016, pp. 229–237.

[58] C. Payer, D. Štern, H. Bischof, M. Urschler, Regressing heatmaps for multiple landmark localization using cnns, International Conference on Medical Image Computing and Computer-Assisted Intervention, Springer, 2016, pp. 230–238.

[59] J. Zhang, M. Liu, D. Shen, Detecting anatomical landmarks from limited medical imaging data using two-stage task-oriented deep neural networks, IEEE Trans. Image Process. 26 (10) (2017) 4753–4764.

[60] Q. Ma, E. Kobayashi, B. Fan, K. Nakagawa, I. Sakuma, K. Masamune, et al. Automatic 3d landmarking model using patch-based deep neural networks for CT image of oral and maxillofacial surgery, Int. J. Med. Robot. Comput. Assist. Surgery 16 (3) (2020) e2093.

[61] Y. Li, J. Cheng, H. Mei, H. Ma, Z. Chen, and Y. Li. Clpnet: Cleft lip and palate surgery support with deep learning. In: 2019 41st Annual International Conference of the IEEE Engineering in Medicine and Biology Society (EMBC), pp. 3666–3672, 2019.

[62] A. Newell, K. Yang, J. Deng, Stacked Hourglass Networks for Human Pose Estimation, in: J. Leibe, N. Matas, M. Sebe, Welling (Eds.), European Conference on Computer Vision (ECCV), Springer International Publishing, Cham, 2016, pp. 483–499.

[63] J. Lee, D. Kim, S. Jeong, Diagnosis of cystic lesions using panoramic and cone beam computed tomographic images based on deep learning neural network, Oral Dis. 26 (1) (2019) 152–158.

[64] C. Szegedy, W. Liu, Y. Jia, P. Sermanet, S. Reed, D. Anguelov, et al. Going deeper with convolutions. In: Proceedings of IEEE/CVF Conference on Computer Vision and Pattern Recognition, 2015.

[65] O. Kwon, T.-H. Yong, S.-R. Kang, J.-E. Kim, K.-H. Huh, M.-S. Heo, et al. Automatic diagnosis for cysts and tumors of both jaws on panoramic radiographs using a deep convolution neural network, Dentomaxillofac. Radiol. 49 (20200185) (2020).

[66] J. Redmon, A. Farhadi, Yolov3: An incremental improvement, arXiv:1804.02767 (2018).

[67] A. Laishram, K. Thongam. Detection and classification of dental pathologies using faster-RCNN in orthopantomogram radiography image. In: Proceedings of IEEE International Conference on Signal Processing and Integrated Networks (SPIN), 2020.

[68] R.A. Welikala, P. Remagnino, J.H. Lim, C.S. Chan, S.R.T.G. Kallarakkal, R.B. Zain, et al. Automated detection and classification of oral lesions using deep learning for early detection of oral cancer, IEEE Access 8 (2020) 132677–132693.

[69] D.W. Kim, S. Lee, S. Kwon, W. Nam, I.-H. Cha, H.J. Kim, Deep learning-based survival prediction of oral cancer patients, Sci. Rep. 9 (6994) (2019) 1–10.

[70] E. Wang, H. Shi, Y. Sun, C. Politis, L. Lan, X. Chen, Computer-aided porous implant design for cranio-maxillofacial defect restoration, Int. J. Med. Robot. Comput. Assist. Surgery 16 (2020) e2134.

[71] M.A. Fuessinger, S. Schwarz, C.-P. Cornelius, M.C. Metzger, E. Ellis, F. Probst, et al. Planning of skull reconstruction based on a statistical shape model combined with geometric morphometrics, Int. J. Comput. Assist. Radiol. Surgery 13 (4) (2018) 519–529.

[72] A. Sharma, O. Grau, M. Fritz, Vconv-dae: Deep volumetric shape learning without object labels, in: Proceedings of European Conference on Computer Vision, Springer, 2016, pp. 236–250.

[73] I. Sumida, T. Magome, H. Kitamori, I.J. Das, H. Yamaguchi, H. Kizaki, et al. Deep convolutional neural network for reduction of contrast-enhanced region on CT images, J. Radiat. Res. 60 (5) (2019) 586–594.

[74] S. Chen, D. Shi, M. Sadiq, X. Cheng, Image denoising with generative adversarial networks and its application to cell image enhancement, IEEE Access 8 (2020) 82819–82831.

[75] J. Agnese, J. Herrera, H. Tao, A survey and taxonomy of adversarial neural networks for text-to-image synthesis. WIREs Data Mining and Knowledge, Discovery 10 (4) (2020) e1345.

[76] L. Gonog, Y. Zhou. A review: generative adversarial networks. In: 14th IEEE Conference on Industrial Electronics and Applications (ICIEA), 2019.

[77] X. Yi, E. Walia, P. Babyn, Generative adversarial network in medical imaging: A review, Med. Image Anal. 58 (2019) 101552.

[78] I. J. Goodfellow, J. Pouget-Abadie, M. Mirza, B. Xu, D. Warde-Farley, S. Ozair, et al. Generative Adversarial Nets. In: Advances in Neural Information Processing Systems (NIPS), pp. 1–9, 2014.

[79] A. Radford, L. Metz, S. Chintala. Unsupervised representation learning with deep convolutional generative adversarial networks. In: International Conference on Learning Representations, 2016.

[80] T. Salimans, I. Goodfellow, W. Zaremba, V. Cheung, A. Radford, and X. Chen. Improved Techniques for Training GANs. In: 30th Conference on Neural Information Processing Systems (NIPS), 2016.

[81] M. Arjovsky, S. Chintala, L. Bottou. Wasserstein Generative Adversarial Networks. In: Proceedings of the 34th International Conference on Machine Learning, 2017.

[82] I. Gulrajani, F. Ahmed, M. Arjovksy, V. Dumoulin, Improved Training of Wasserstein GANs, Advances in Neural Information Processing Systems, NIPS, 2017.

[83] X. Wei, B. Gong, Z. Liu, W. Lu, L. Wang. Improving the improved training of Wasserstein GANs: A consistency term and its dual effect. In: Proceedings of International Conference on Learning Representations, 2018.

[84] J. Adler, S. Lunz. Banach Wasserstein GAN. In: 32nd Conference on Neural Information Processing Systems (NIPS), 2018.

[85] T. Miyato, T. Kataoka, M. Koyama, Y. Yoshida. Spectral normalization for generative adversarial networks. In: Proceedings of International Conference on Learning Representations, 2018.

[86] P. Isola, J.-Y. Zhu, T. Zhou, A.A. Efros. Image to image translation with conditional generative adversarial networks. In: Proceedings of IEEE/CVF Conference on Computer Vision and Pattern Recognition, 2017.

[87] R. Zhang, P. Isola, A.A. Efros, E. Schechtman, O. Wang. The unreasonable effectiveness of deep features as a perceptual metric. In: Proceedings of IEEE/CVF Conference on Computer Vision and Pattern Recognition, 2018.

[88] J. Johnson, A. Alahi, L. Fei-Fei. Perceptual losses for real-time style transfer and super-resolution. In: European Conference on Computer Vision, 2016.

[89] A.S. Lundervold, A. Lundervold, An overview of deep learning in medical imaging focusing on MRI, Zeitschrift für Medizinische Physik 29 (2) (2019) 102–127.

[90] M.J. Willemink, W.A. Koszek, C. Hardell, J. Wu, D. Fleischmann, H. Harvey, et al. Preparing medical imaging data for machine learning, Radiology 295 (1) (2020) 4–5.

[91] L. Lindner, D. Narnhofer, M. Weber, C. Gsaxner, M. Kolodziej, J. Egger. Using synthetic training data for deep learning-based GBM segmentation. In: Proceedings of Annual International Conference of the IEEE Engineering in Medicine and Biology Society (EMBC), pp. 6724–6729, 2019.

[92] X. Chen, C. Lian, L. Wang, H. Deng, S.H. Fung, D. Nie, et al. One-shot generative adversarial learning for MRI segmentation of craniomaxillofacial bony structures, IEEE Trans. Med. Imaging 39 (3) (2020) 787–796.

[93] M. Nakao, K. Imanishi, N. Ueda, Y. Imai, T. Kirita, T. Matsuda, Regularized three-dimensional generative adversarial nets for unsupervised metal artifact reduction in head and neck CT images, IEEE Access 8 (2020) 109453–109465.

[94] L. Gjesteby, H. Shan, Q. Yang, Y. Xi, Y. Jin, D. Giantsoudi, et al. A dual-stream deep convolutional network for reducing metal streak artifacts in CT images, Phys. Med. Biol. 64 (235003) (2019) 1–11.

[95] K. Simonyan, A. Zisserman. Very deep convolutional networks for large-scale image recognition. In: Proc. International Conference on Learning Representations (ICLR), 2015.

[96] Q. Yang, P. Yan, Y. Zhang, H. Yu, Y. Shi, X. Mou, et al. Low-dose CT Image denoising using a generative adversarial network with Wasserstein distance and perceptual loss, IEEE Trans. Medical Imaging 37 (6) (2018) 1348–1357.

[97] T.K. Yoo, J.Y. Choi, H.K. Kim, A generative adversarial network approach to predicting postoperative appearance after orbital decompression surgery for thyroid eye disease, Comput. Biol. Med. 118 (103628) (2020).

[98] Y. Xie, F. Xing, X. Kong, et al. Beyond classification: Structured regression for robust cell detection using convolutional neural network. In: Proceedings of International Conference on Medical Image Computing and Computer-Assisted Intervention, 9351, pp. 358–365, 2015.

[99] T. Vercauteren, M. Unberath, N. Padoy, N. Navab, CAI4CAI: The rise of contextual artificial intelligence in computer-assisted interventions, Proc. IEEE 108 (1) (2020) 198–214.

[100] A. Kendall, Y. Gall. What uncertainties do we need in Bayesian deep learning for computer vision? In: Proceedings of Conference on Neural Information Processing Systems, pp. 5580–5590, 2017.

[101] Y. Gal, Z. Ghahramani, Dropout as a bayesian approximation: Representing model uncertainty in deep learning, Proc. Int. Conf. Mach. Learn. 48 (2016) 1050–1059.

[102] B. Lakshminarayanan, A. Pritzel, C. Blundell. Simple and scalable predictive uncertainty estimation using deep ensembles. In: Proceedings of Conference on Neural Information Processing Systems, pp. 1–12, 2017.

[103] N. Srivastava, G. Hinton, A. Krizhevsky, I. Sutskever, R. Salakhutdinov, Dropout: A simple way to prevent neural networks from overfitting, J. Mach. Learn. Res. 15 (56) (2014) 1929–1958.

[104] T. Nair, D. Precup, D.L. Arnold, T. Arbel, Exploring uncertainty measures in deep networks for multiple sclerosis lesion detection and segmentation, Med. Image Anal. 59 (101557) (2020) 1–10.

[105] J. Postels, F. Ferroni, H. Coskun, N. Navab, F. Tombari. Sampling-free epistemic uncertainty estimation using approximated variance propagation. In: Proceedings of International Conference on Computer Vision, 2019.

[106] L.D. Hahn, G. Mistelbauer, K. Higashigaito, et al. Ct-based true- and false-lumen segmenta- tion in type B aortic dissection using machine learning, Radiology: Cardiothoracic Imaging 2 (3) (2020) 1–10.

[107] Y. Gal, J. Hron, A. Kendall. Concrete dropout. In: Proceedings of Conference on Neural Information Processing Systems, 2017.

[108] Y. Mirsky, T. Mahler, I. Shelef, Y. Elovici. Ct-gan: Malicious tampering of 3d medical imagery using deep learning. In: Proceedings of the 28th USENIX Security Symposium, 2019.

[109] A. Pepe, G. Mistelbauer, C. Schwarz-Gsaxner, J. Li, D. Fleischmann, D. Schmalstieg, et al. Semi-supervised virtual regression of aortic dissections using 3D generative in painting. In: Proceedings of The Second International Workshop on Thoracic Image Analysis, 2020.

[110] A. Prutsch, A. Pepe, J. Egger. Design and development of a web-based tool for inpainting of dissected aortae in angiography images. In: Proceedings of Central European Seminar on Computer Graphics, pp. 1–8, 2020.

[111] D. Wild, M. Weber, J. Wallner, J. Egger. Client/server based online environment for manual segmentation of medical images. CoRR, abs/1904.08610, 2019.

[112] J. Li, A. Pepe, C. Gsaxner, J. Egger, An online platform for automatic skull defect restoration and cranial implant design, In: Proc. Multimodal Learning for Clinical Decision Support and Clinical Image-Based Procedures (2020).

[113] A. Pepe, D. Fleischmann, D. Schmalstieg, J. Egger, Visual Computing of Dissected Aortae, Austrian Marshall Plan Foundation Scholarship, 2019.

Radiomics in head and neck cancer

Maria Gonçalves[a,b,c], Christina Gsaxner[a,b,d], Jan Egger[a,b,d], Victor Alves[c]

[a]INSTITUTE OF COMPUTER GRAPHICS AND VISION, GRAZ UNIVERSITY OF TECHNOLOGY, GRAZ, AUSTRIA; [b]COMPUTER ALGORITHMS FOR MEDICINE LABORATORY, GRAZ, AUSTRIA; [c]CENTRE ALGORITMI, UNIVERSITY OF MINHO, BRAGA, PORTUGAL; [d]DEPARTMENT OF ORAL AND MAXILLOFACIAL SURGERY, MEDICAL UNIVERSITY OF GRAZ, GRAZ, AUSTRIA

1 Introduction

W.C. Röntgen discovered the X-rays in 1895, and since then, medical imaging has been a focal point for advances in medicine. It includes all the techniques to visualize the body for investigating the anatomy, metabolic processes and structures, which cannot be seen through the skin [1,2].

Nowadays, medical imaging is one of the major factors informing medical science and treatment in the field of oncology, as it has the capability to visualize and assess, noninvasively, the characteristics of human tissue and exhibits the strong phenotypic differences in human cancer before, during, and after treatment [3,4].

Among all cancers in Europe, head and neck cancers are the 6th type with the highest incidence rate. Worldwide, they account for more than 650,000 patients diagnosed and 330,000 deaths every year [5,6]. This type of cancer is a complex disease developing in different structures (oral cavity, pharynx, larynx, nasal cavity, and salivary glands) and presents challenging diagnostic and treatment selection tasks, including the complexity of regional anatomy, the minute scale of critical structures, the variable manifestation of tumors (both primary and recurrent), high intratumoral heterogeneity and the significant anatomic changes related to tumor response to the therapy [7].

Depending on the location of the tumor, there are a variety of presentations and clinical outcomes and, therefore, several strategies for treatment, which may include surgery, radiotherapy, chemotherapy or a combination of different treatments [8,9]. Even among tumors of the same pathological type (the same primary site and tumor staging), it is possible to observe a tumor heterogeneity, whose existence is strongly related to a high risk of resistance to treatment, progression, metastasis and recurrence [9,10].

Precision cancer medicine is the medical area, which studies the clinical condition of a single patient in depth, in order to conduct a personalized cancer therapy, that is, to be able to decide, individually, the best treatment for each patient. Its aim is to improve the patient's outcome, for example, the response to treatment and survival without disease progression [11,12].

Computer-Aided Oral and Maxillofacial Surgery. http://dx.doi.org/10.1016/B978-0-12-823299-6.00004-3

The term radiomics refers to a process of quantitative extraction of large and minable data from medical imaging for further analysis and production of prognostic values, which is the most advantageous way of complementing, facilitating, and accelerating the advance toward precision cancer medicine [7,10].

Radiomics applies a set of innovative computational methodologies to medical imaging data to convert them into quantitative oncological tissue descriptors. In this context, unlike biopsies, radiomics can help to extract information in a non-invasive way from medical images, providing information of the whole tumor. This process allows the characterization of the tumor's phenotype. From a single lesion, it is possible to simultaneously generate/extract hundreds of features. The translation of radiomics analysis into standard cancer care to support treatment decision-making involves the development of prediction models, integrating clinical information that can assess the risk of specific tumor outcomes [13,14].

2 Head and neck cancer

This section is dedicated to head and neck cancer, providing an overview of the anatomy and clinical presentation, epidemiology and risk factors, diagnosis, staging evaluation, and treatments.

2.1 Anatomy and clinical presentation

Head and neck cancer generally begins as squamous cell carcinomas of the head and neck (HNSCC), as they first appear in the squamous cells that align the moist and mucous surfaces of this area, such as the inside of the mouth, nose, and throat. However, this type of cancer can also occur in other areas of the head and neck region and it is categorized according to the area from which it first arises [15–17]. Fig. 4.1 illustrates the five main

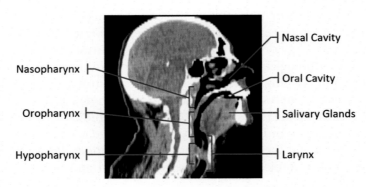

FIGURE 4.1 Illustration of the five basic head and neck cancer regions and their subdivisions.

Table 4.1   Clinical presentations of HNSCC.

Primary site	Clinical presentation
Oral cavity	Sores, ulcers, pain.
Nasopharynx	Otitis media unresponsive to antibiotics, unilateral nasal airway obstruction, epistaxis, and cranial nerve palsies.
Oropharynx	Sore throat, chronic dysphagia, odynophagia, otalgia.
Hypopharynx	Soreness, dysphagia, otalgia, and hoarseness.
Larynx	Persistent hoarseness, shortness of breath.
Unknown	Neck mass.

Adapted from Ref. [15].

basic areas of head and neck cancer (oral cavity, pharynx, larynx, nasal cavity, and salivary glands) and their subdivisions, which will be described further:

- Oral cavity: includes the lips, anterior tongue, floor of the mouth, upper and lower gingiva, buccal mucosa, hard palate, and retromolar trigone.
- Pharynx: contains the nasopharynx (the top of the larynx, is the narrow tubular orifice behind the oral cavity), the oropharynx (the middle part that includes the tongue base, tonsils, uvula, soft palate, and posterior and lateral pharyngeal wall), and the hypopharynx (the bottom part of the larynx, it embraces the piriform sinus, the lateral and posterior hypopharyngeal, and the postcricoid area).
- Larynx: incorporates the vocal cord and epiglottis. It is separated into three anatomic regions: the supraglottic, glottic, and subglottic larynx.
- Nasal cavity and paranasal sinuses: comprise the maxillary, ethmoid, sphenoid, and frontal sinuses.
- Salivary glands: can be distinguished between major salivary glands and minor salivary glands.

Head and neck cancer can also have an unknown primary site (metastatic squamous neck cancer with unknown primary), this happens when squamous cells are found in the lymph nodes of the upper or mid-cervical area and there are no vestiges of tumors in other parts [15,17].

Depending on the primary site of the head and neck cancer, the patient has distinct clinical manifestations and functional considerations. Table 4.1 summarizes the different clinical presentations according to the anatomic location of HNSCC.

In general, head and neck cancer includes the whole area of the head and neck; however, cancers of the brain, eye, esophagus, thyroid gland, scalp, and skin, muscles and bones of that area are categorized separately and not considered as head and neck cancer.

2.2 Epidemiology and risk factors

Head and neck cancer present significant differences according to the geography of the person, which shows that in addition to behavioral risk factors, ethnic and genetic risk factors also contribute [8,15–18].

Behavioral risks are understood as those related to the decisions and behaviors of the patient, such as the consumption of tobacco and alcohol, and the poor oral hygiene [15,17,18].

Regarding ethnic risk factors, that is, those comprising cultural factors, the following behaviors can be highlighted: radiation and other environmental and occupational exposures (e.g., paint fumes and plastic by-products), infection with human papillomavirus (HPV) or Epstein-Barr virus, the use of marijuana, and dietary factors. Several studies have linked vitamin deficiency with this type of cancer (e.g., vitamin A deficiency with oral and pharyngeal cancer) and the inclusion of carcinogenic foods such as betel nut, characteristic of Asia and East Africa [8,15–18].

Lastly, genetic factors refer to the hereditary predisposition of each person to suffer from cancer and it can be aggravated with the risk factors mentioned earlier [15,17,18].

2.3 Diagnosis, staging evaluation, and treatments

To make an accurate and precise diagnosis, the physician has to evaluate the patient according to his symptoms, based on his clinical and hereditary history and a combination of tests. The exams and tests performed may vary according to the patient's complaints, however; in general, the initial evaluation consists of a combination of an inspection test, palpation, indirect mirror examination and direct endoscopy. Under suspicion of the presence of cancer, it is necessary to perform a biopsy, that is, an invasive procedure in which a tissue sample is collected for later microscopic analysis [16,17].

Medical imaging studies, namely computerized tomography (CT), magnetic resonance imaging (MRI), positron emission tomography (PET) and PET/CT combination, have an important role in tumor diagnosis as they allow its visualization and evaluation.

For an initial evaluation, all patients usually perform a CT or MRI. Patients considered having a high metastatic risk and/or secondary malignant tumors should also perform a PET examination. The PET examination can be used both for an initial assessment (e.g., locating primary tumors of unknown site) and for re-assessment after treatment as it allows the identification of persistent tumors, that is, tumor recurrences. The PET/CT combination has been highly used for tumor detection and therapeutic planning and monitoring. Technological advances in medical imaging have contributed to the oncologic advance, however, these methods still lack valuable information in the evaluation of tumor progress and involvement [15,16].

The knowledge of the stage of the disease is paramount for the physician to plan the best treatment. Currently, oncologists use the tumor-node-metastasis (TMN) classification system developed by the American Joint Committee on Cancer and the Union for International Cancer Control. The T indicates the size and extent of the primary tumor and invasive characteristics. The N evaluates the spread of regional lymph nodes. Finally, the M reveals the presence or absence of distant metastasis. In opposition to the T and M classification systems, which are independent of the site of occurrence, the N classification system differs if the tumor has developed in the nasopharynx [8,15,16,18,19].

Patients with the same tumor location and classified with the same stage may present different responses to the same treatment and, consequently, present disparate clinical results. Thus, the choice of the best and most appropriate treatment for each case takes into consideration not only the tumor location and its stage, but also specific factors of the patient (e.g., his clinical status and comorbidities). The decision is made jointly by oncologists and surgeons, radiation oncologists, dentists, as well as nutritionists and rehabilitation therapists and the treatment possibilities are currently surgery, radiation therapy, chemotherapy, or a combination of them [2,15,18].

3 Radiomics: the concept and workflow

This section focuses on the concept of radiomics, addressing its origin, cancer-related applications, the workflow of the entire process for radiomics analysis from medical imaging to the evaluation of the final models, and finally, a brief description of the different categories of radiomic features is given.

3.1 The concept

Medical imaging is routinely used in clinical practice for cancer diagnosis, treatment guidance and monitoring [3]. In case of suspected cancer, diagnosis is typically reached by means of several medical tests, for instance biopsy and diagnostic imaging [20]. Despite biopsy can be very informative, it is an invasive way to focally access the tumor. As tumors are spatially and temporally heterogeneous, this technique is limited [3,20]. In contrast, diagnostic imaging is not invasive and contains information regarding the entire tumor. It provides information on the tumor's overall shape, growth over time, and heterogeneity, which is considered a crucial factor in tumor characterization in cancer prognosis and treatment [3,20,21].

Progress in medical imaging technologies has led to a large amount of three dimensional, high-quality digital data [22]. However, tumor staging based on medical imaging is, in clinical practice, usually performed using only one-dimensional descriptors of tumor size, as recommended by the Response Evaluation Criteria In Solid Tumors (RECIST), or two-dimensional descriptors of tumor size, as suggested by the World Health Organization (WHO) [3,21,23]. The response to therapy can be slow, which decreases the efficacy of this procedure by giving clinicians a reduced margin to tailor the treatment. Consequently, the development of automatic and reproducible methodologies to obtain more information from medical images is a necessity [21].

Radiomics is an emerging and relatively new research field that can address these problems by extracting quantitative, measurable, and mineable features from the region of interest of medical images. The term "radiomics" was first introduced by Lambin et al. [14] in 2012, describing the automatic determination of distinctive features in cancer imaging data. The ultimate goal is to associate radiomics-based data with biological and clinical endpoints, to provide a clinical decision-making, improving diagnostic, prognostic and predictive accuracy and consequently, enabling a personalized therapy and response assessment. It consists of algorithms that decompose input images into basic and abstract mathematical features, generally not detectable by the human eye that may be used to decipher the image, such as edges, gradients, shapes, signal intensity, wavelength, and textures [3,13,14,20–22,24,25].

3.2 Applications

In recent years, radiomics has been widely applied in various specialties in the health field, presenting promising results. In the area of neurology, studies have shown that it allows the diagnosis and prognosis of Amyotrophic Lateral Sclerosis (ALS) [26], Alzheimer's disease [27], and Parkinson's disease [28]. In obstetrics and gynecology, it allows Placenta Accreta Spectrum disorder (PAS) assessment to identify women who need cesarean hysterectomy [29]. It is also promising in the area of cardiology, as it allows the analysis of cardiac alterations in patients with hypertension [30] and the identification of coronary plaques [31].

Among all the areas of application of radiomics, the one with the greatest focus has been oncology. Several studies on lung cancer [3], head and neck cancer [10], breast cancer [32] and esophageal and gastric cancer [33], among others, have shown that radiomics can successfully be applied in (1) cancer diagnosis and tissue identification, (2) tumor classification, (3) cancer staging, and (4) prediction of treatment response and outcomes [20,34].

1. **Cancer diagnosis and tissue identification:** This application concerns the confirmation of the presence of cancer. This is one of the most crucial and delicate processes, because the earlier its presence is detected, the greater the probability of treatment success and, consequently, survival rate. Depending on the tumor's location and patient's symptoms, it may or may not be easy to detect a tumor. The radiomic analysis can help to improve the efficacy of early diagnosis since, on one hand, through radiomic features it is possible to distinguish different tissue types, for example, brain tumor tissue, edema, cerebrospinal fluid, white matter, and gray matter in brain cancer. On the other hand, it allows to find the exact location of cancerous cells, improving the selection and performance of treatment. For instance, radiotherapy and drug delivery are processes that require accurate information.
2. **Tumor classification:** Tumor classification refers to the stipulation of the type of tumor, that is, whether the tumor is benign or malignant. Benign tumors are not considered cancer and grow only in one place; they do not spread or invade other parts of the body. However, they need to be monitored because they can grow out of control and need to be removed or become malignant tumors, which are harmful to health and can spread to various organs of the body. Concerning malignant tumors, one can distinguish primary malignant tumors and metastatic malignant tumors. In some cases, such as breast cancer and pulmonary nodule, these two types of tumor are very difficult to distinguish, but through the analysis of radiomic features it is possible to differentiate them with non-invasive methods, since it allows a better understanding of the characteristics (shape, size, texture, tumor contours, among

others), while different types of tumor are associated with different properties and behaviors.

3. **Cancer staging:** Cancer can be diagnosed both in an early or advanced stage. Stage prediction is a relevant factor, since early stage cancer detection helps the physicians to better stratify the patients, leading to a greater impact on the selection of the best individual treatment. In most tumors, the staging is determined invasively (biopsy or surgery), emphasizing the importance of radiomic analysis.

4. **Prediction of treatment response and outcomes:** Through the analysis of imaging properties, tumor characteristics, clinical data and/or genetic information, it is possible to make predictions about the response to treatment and different outcomes (survival, recurrence, and metastasis). Radiomics have been shown to be valuable in these predictions, which are important for both the physician and the patient, as they allow decisions to be made for the selection of the best treatment and choices to improve the quality of life.

3.3 Radiomic workflow

The radiomic workflow is essentially composed of four phases: (1) image acquisition and pre-processing, (2) segmentation of the region of interest, (3) feature extraction, and (4) feature selection. Fig. 4.2 shows a representation of the earlier-mentioned steps.

1. **Image acquisition and pre-processing**
   Routine clinical imaging includes a variety of techniques, which can be employed in the radiomic analysis, such as Magnetic Resonance Imaging (MRI), Computed Tomography (CT), and Positron Emission Tomography (PET). The selection of an

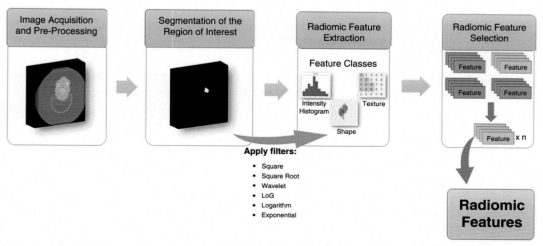

FIGURE 4.2 Radiomic workflow. Generally, the acquisition of radiomic features consists of four steps: image acquisition and pre-processing, segmentation of the region of interest, feature extraction by applying several mathematical filters, and feature selection.

appropriate imaging modality is essential for the successful extraction of radiomic features, as this technique depends on comparability. It is, therefore, important to use images which are to some extend normalized, to ensure correlation between different examinations, patients, imaging devices and manufacturers.

MRI imaging is a high-resolution, advanced technique, which, through the impact of magnet strength, provides better tissue discrimination, multiple views and spectrography information that facilitates the provision of information on cancer prognosis [24]. It is worth highlighting that for a given sequence, even under exactly the same conditions (scanner, patient, position), signal intensity may change, whereas tissue contrast remains unchanged. Since radiomic feature analysis depends on the numeric value of voxel intensity, MRI studies could lose significance. To overcome this problem, one possible way is to normalize the data before performing quantitative image analysis; or focusing texture analysis quantifying the relationship between voxel intensities in which numerical values are independent of the individual voxel intensity [13]. It is important to note that technical compatibility issues, for instance, magnetic field strength, image spatial resolution, slice thickness, administration of contrast agents and manufacturer's settings affect image properties (noise and texture), and consequently, the value of radiomic features. As a result, imaging data frequently requires pre-processing before analysis, which typically includes image smoothing and image enhancement techniques [13,20,24].

CT imaging is commonly used to diagnose, stage, and follow cancer; hence, a significant volume of this imaging data is available [13,24]. CT scanning is a high-resolution imaging procedure in which a narrow beam of X-rays revolves around the patient, generating signals that are processed by the CT scanner's computer to produce cross-sectional images (slices) of the body. It is necessary to take into consideration the clinical variables of the patient since the presence of metal prostheses causes artifacts in the image. Similarly, it is important to note that the quality of images greatly depends on the protocol used, for example (1) a decrease in slice thickness, that is, the distance between two slices (in mm), reduces the photon statistics within each slice, increasing the noise, (2) the axial field of view and the size of the reconstruction matrix determine the pixel size, affecting heterogeneity, (3) maintaining the rest of the parameters unaltered, the decrease in pixel size increases noise and spatial resolution, (4) the density expressed in Hounsfield Units may vary with the reconstruction and/or calibration algorithm of the equipment [13,20]. Shafiq-ul-hassan et al. [35] have found that some radiomic features depend on voxel size and gray level discretization. This dependence can be minimized by introducing standardized definitions. Thus, voxel size re-sampling is a pre-processing step capable of obtaining more reproducible CT features in acquired image data sets whose voxel sizes are variable.

PET scans can reveal functional information about tumor metabolism, hypoxia, and spread. However, this modality is obtained less frequently and has relatively poor resolution compared to CT, because of low accuracy in describing the spatial distribution of voxel intensity, which radiomic features aim to quantify [13,24]. Of note, the voxel intensity, expressed in terms of Standardized Uptake Value (SUV) can depend on the scanner and, for the same scanner model, SUV (and, subsequently, the radiomic features) can vary due to the acquisition at different times post injection, patient blood glucose level, and presence of inflammation [13].

2. Segmentation of the region of interest (ROI)

Segmentation, or delineation, of the target structure is a crucial and challenging step within the radiomics process since features are obtained from the segmented volumes and various tissues/tumors show unclear borders. At present, the tumor volume is mostly delineated manually by physicians using specialized software, such as Pinnacle; however, this method is laborious, time-consuming and sensitive to interobserver variability. As radiomics analysis requires very large data sets, the high workload for physicians is not always feasible [13,20,24].

As segmentation is a crucial step in many medical image processing and analysis tasks, during the last few decades, the pursuit to develop advanced automatic and semi-automatic segmentation approaches has increased. The goal is to develop algorithms with a maximal automaticity, minimal operator interaction, high accuracy, and boundary reproducibility. Automatic and semi-automatic segmentation techniques can be either conventional or Deep Learning based, applying, respectively, pre-defined features or deep networks to classify image pixels/voxels as tumor or non-tumor [13,20,36].

The conventional techniques can further be divided into three categories: intensity-based, where the main distinguishing feature is the pixel or voxel value; model-based, which proposes to improve an initial contour by optimizing an energy function; and Machine Learning methods which apply models such as Support Vector Machine (SVM), K-Nearest Neighbor (KNN), and Decision Tree to classify the pixels, using as inputs a set of extracted features (including intensity and gradient). Nevertheless, the conventional techniques present some issues that require extra attention, for instance, the intensity is not a good discriminator since the intensity of a tumor can, sometimes, be similar to other tissues. On the other hand, in the model-based segmentation, the formulation of the energy function may involve a large number of parameters, which makes optimization of this function difficult and time-consuming [13,36].

Alternatively, Deep Learning methods are capable of automatically learning features that can best distinguish tumors and non-tumor pixels and models can be trained in an end-to-end manner. Currently, the Deep Learning approaches commonly used for medical image segmentation are different variations of U-Net, DenseNet and Hybrid Dilated Convolutions (HDC) [2,13].

While Deep Learning approaches have achieved remarkable accuracy for specific data sets and tasks, no universal algorithm, working for all kinds of data and applications, exists. Therefore, segmentation usually still requires human interaction, while new algorithms are constantly under evaluation.

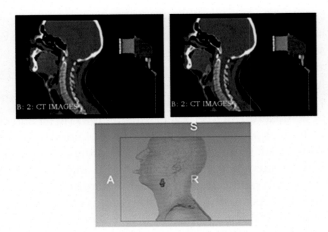

FIGURE 4.3 Tumour segmentation in CT image using a semi-automated algorithm. Top Left: CT slice of head and neck with tumor. Top Right: Tumor outlined in *blue* by a radiologist in a CT slice. Down: 3D view of the head and neck and the segmented tumor.

The most important metric for evaluating a segmentation method is to calculate the accuracy according to the ground truth. However, this is controversial, since there is no consensual search for both ground truth and the reproducibility of segmentation, and for this reason, despite the great interrelated variability, most authors consider the manual segmentation by expert readers to be the ground truth [13,20].

In Fig. 4.3, a CT image where the tumor (in Head and Neck cancer) was segmented using a semi-automatic method and a representation of the segmentation in three dimensions is presented.

3. **Feature extraction**

Regarding feature extraction, quantitative features are extracted from the tumor region explained in the previous step. Features can be determined in the original images or in filtered images. This process can be achieved through a range of commercial and open-source software programs, for example, the PyRadiomics platform or 3D Slicer. There is a wide choice of commonly used filters, including simple filters, such as square, square root, logarithm, and exponential filters as well as more complex filters, like Wavelet and Laplacian of Gaussian (LoG) [37,38].

4. **Feature selection**

To better understand this step, it is essential to differentiate the extraction of features and the selection of features. Whereas the feature extraction generates a wide range of parameters that deeply describe the region of interest, in the feature selection, the aim is to reduce this number of parameters to the minimum possible by grouping them in a robust way to identify hidden information in the data. Therefore, this process is at present the main method for establishing a radiomic signature [24].

Table 4.2   Feature selection methods more used within the radiomics literature.

Category	Sub-category	Methods
Supervised	Filters (Univariate)	Fisher Score (FSCR), Wilcoxon rank sum test, Gini index (GINI), Mutual information feature selection (MIFS), Minimum redundancy maximum relevance (mRMR), and Student *t*-test.
	Wrappers (Multivariate)	Greedy forward selection, and Greedy backward elimination.
Unsupervised	Linear	Principle component analysis (PCA) and multidimensional scaling (MDS).
	Nonlinear	Isometric mapping (Isomap) and locally linear embedding (LLE).

Adapted from Ref. [20].

Feature selection, also called feature reduction, is a critical step when analyzing radiomics, as most of the large amount of features extracted are highly correlated, irrelevant for a specific task and/or can lead to over-fitting of the model (making it highly sensitive to noise) [20,21]. Feature selection methods used in radiomics can be divided into supervised and unsupervised categories as shown in Table 4.2.

Supervised techniques consider the relationship of features with their associated class labels. Features are selected mainly on the basis of their contribution to distinguishing classes, taking into account the discriminatory capacity of the features and favoring features that can better distinguish data based on a predefined class [20]. They can, in turn, be subdivided into filters and wrappers. Filters search for relations between the feature and the target attribute and ranks the features one by one according to their relation. However, filtering methods have the downside of ignoring the relationships between features, which has led to the development of wrapper techniques that do an exhaustive search to look for the set of features that provides the highest predictive performance of a subset of features, and the score is a weighted based on both relevance and redundancy [20,21].

Unsupervised approaches attempt to reduce the spatial dimensionality of features by removing redundant features (those that are highly correlated and do not provide any additional information to the model). Although these methods are not susceptible to over-fitting, they are not guaranteed to result in the optimum space of features. Unsupervised methods can also be divided into two sub-categories: linear and non-linear methods, where features have linear correlations or features are not assumed to be lying in a linear space, respectively [20].

3.4 Modeling workflow

Once the radiomic features are selected, the next step is to build predictive models on top of them. These models should be able to forecast important diagnostic parameters, such as tumor staging or response to a certain therapy, from unseen images and their respective features. As illustrated in Fig. 4.4, the modeling workflow can generally be divided into two steps: (1) model development, and (2) model evaluation.

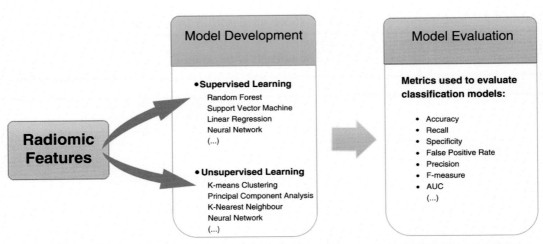

FIGURE 4.4 Modeling workflow. Building a predictive model on top of selected radiomic features generally consist of model development and model evaluation. These steps are usually iteratively applied, until the best possible outcome is achieved.

1. Model development

Model development refers to utilizing the selected radiomic features to create models which are able to predict valuable information, such as cancer diagnosis, tumor stage classification or survivability, among others as described in Section 3.2. The extracted features are used to train machine-learning algorithms, which should later predict an outcome from new data. Machine learning is a branch of artificial intelligence that combines essential concepts of computer science with the knowledge of statistics, probability, and optimization. Its purpose is to find patterns in massive amounts of data to build a model capable of predicting and/or classifying a given scenario. Machine learning models can, in general, follow a supervised or unsupervised learning approach.

An unsupervised learning approach comprises a set of unlabelled data and a learning algorithm, which learns some sort of structure within the data. A basic approach to analyzing the radiomic features is to perform a cluster analysis, which aims to create groups of similar features (clusters) with high intra-cluster redundancy and low inter-cluster correlation, and to look for associations between these clusters and clinical outcomes. Patients belonging to the same cluster can be expected to have a similar diagnosis or treatment response pattern. In radiomics, hierarchical clustering is most commonly used. However, unsupervised techniques are not suitable for target prediction purposes, which require the use of tools that are specially trained based on a predefined class label [13,20,21].

Differently, in supervised learning, the training set includes a set of features matched with a corresponding class label, such as the survival rate or rate of tumor growth. Supervised algorithms learn the patterns between features and labels in order to assign the right label given a new set of features. Depending on the purpose of the study and the category of the result, there are different analysis approaches from statistical methods to data mining/machine learning approaches, such as Random Forest (RF), Support Vector Machine (SVM), Neural Networks (NN) and Deep Learning, Linear Regression, and Cox Proportional Hazards Regression Model (PHM) [13,20,21,24].

2. Model evaluation

To generate the best possible results, the best combination of reduced and selected features, as well as predictive model, have to be chosen. The model needs to be evaluated in terms of its generalization capacity, as far as possible, with an independent, unseen data set. If an independent data set is not available, the available data should be divided into a training set to train the model and a test set to assess its performance. In some cases, the training set is further split into training and validation data. The validation data is not used for training, but instead, its main purpose is to evaluate and monitor the performance of the model during the training phase, by passing this data through the model after a pre-defined number of training iterations. Consequently, adjustments in the training process (e.g., hyperparameter tuning, early stop) can be made. It is imperative that the test set remains untouched until the final model is created, allowing its generalization capability to be fairly evaluated [21].

Several measures can be used to evaluate the predictive performance of a rating model. Most of these measures were developed for binary classification tasks; however, they can be easily adjusted for multiclass tasks. The main classification metrics are based on the so-called confusion matrix, which shows for a set of objects how many were correctly classified and poorly classified. In Fig. 4.5 a representation of such a confusion matrix, in which the two columns represent the correct classes, whereas the two rows represent the predicted classes, is shown. The main diagonal holds the correct predictions, that is, True Positives (TP) and True Negatives (TN), while the incorrect predictions are included in the secondary diagonal, that is, False Positives (FP) and False Negatives (FN) [39].

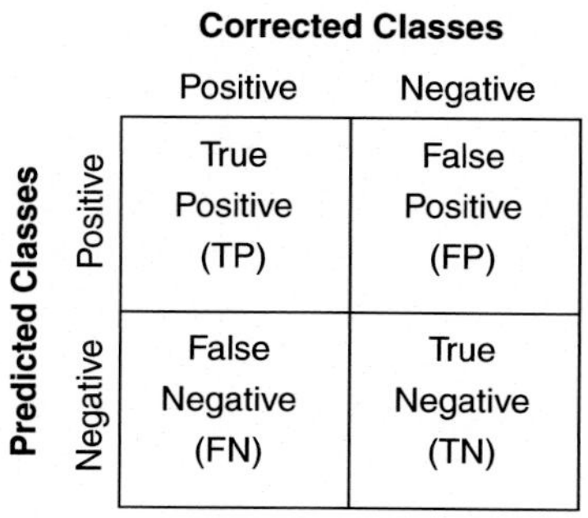

Corrected Classes

	Positive	Negative
Predicted Classes Positive	True Positive (TP)	False Positive (FP)
Predicted Classes Negative	False Negative (FN)	True Negative (TN)

FIGURE 4.5 Confusion matrix for a binary classification task.

From these four simple measures, a variety of metrics can be extracted to comprehensively describe the predictive power of a model. In (Eqs. 4.1–4.6), different metrics used and their definition, are shown.

- Accuracy: returns the ratio of correctly predicted observation to the total observations.

$$Accuracy = \frac{TP+TN}{TP+TN+FP+FN} \tag{4.1}$$

- Recall: provides the percentage of objects that are correctly classified as positive by model, among all those that have been classified as positive. Also called as true positive rate.

$$Recall = \frac{TP}{TP+FN} \tag{4.2}$$

- Specificity: is the equivalent of recall, but in relation to the negative class. The same as true negative rate.

$$Specificity = \frac{TN}{TN+FP} \tag{4.3}$$

- False positive rate: as the name suggests, is the complement to the specificity.

$$False\,positive\,rate = \frac{FP}{TN+FP} \tag{4.4}$$

- Precision: returns the percentage of objects classified as positive among all objects that are truly positive.

$$Precision = \frac{TP}{TP+FP} \tag{4.5}$$

- F-measure: the balance between precision and recall, which is an important metric, especially in problems of class imbalance.

$$F-measure = 2\times\frac{Precision\times Recall}{Precision+Recall} \tag{4.6}$$

Finally, the area under the curve (AUC) is also a good estimator of the predictive performance of a classifier, since, for most classifiers, different threshold values to decide the class of a new object result in different performances, and AUC takes into account the performance of the classifier at different threshold values by calculating the area under the receiver operating characteristic curve (ROC), which makes it possible to investigate the impact of different decision thresholds on PF and FN rates.

3.5 Radiomic features description

During the extraction of radiomic features, it is possible to discern a wide variety of features that define the tumor's region of interest. For a better understanding of the results obtained, it is fundamental to understand the meaning of each feature extracted, which according to its complexity are generally classified into three main categories: intensity histogram-based features (first-order statistics), morphological features (shape-based features), and texture-based features (higher-order statistics).

A succinct description of each category will be provided in this section, following the definitions presented in Refs. [20,21,40,41].

3.5.1 Intensity histogram-based features (first-order statistics)

First order statistical features are also known as intensity histogram-based features, since they describe the distribution of the intensities of the voxels, turning the tumor region of multidimensional interest into a histogram. It is important to note that, although it allows the interpretation of hidden information at the voxel level (which helps in the analysis of subtle changes in tumors), the histogram analysis does not contain any spatial information.

It is possible to investigate, among other properties, the sharpness, dispersion and asymmetry of the tumor voxels through intensity features such as mean, median, standard deviation, kurtosis, skewness, energy, entropy and uniformity, where the last two mentioned are the most frequently employed in radiomics. Entropy calculates the degree of disorder in the system of the intensities of the voxels, presenting a maximum value when all the intensities occur with the same probability (complete disorder). In contrast, uniformity evaluates the consistency of the intensities, being its maximum value when all the voxels have the same value.

3.5.2 Morphological features (shape-based features)

Shape-based features, also referred as morphological features or semantic features, describe the geometry of the tumor, and can be extracted from both 2D and 3D structures, characterizing it in terms of shape and volume. There is a wide variety of shape-based features, however, the most commonly used in radiomic analysis are volume, surface area, surface to volume ratio, sphericity, compactness, diameter, and flatness.

Morphological features are traditionally used by physicians due to the fact that they are easily evaluated visually, however, the goal is to quantify them with computer assistance since they have high predictive capacity for issues such as malignancy of the tumor and response to treatment. For instance, the surface area totally measures the surface of the tumor; the volume is the three-dimensional measurement that consists of the space occupied by the tumor, while the sphericity measures the degree of roundness of the volume/region of interest. These parameters are especially advantageous for predicting the malignancy of the tumor, since a lower surface to volume ratio represents a rounder and smoother tumor, while a higher ratio represents an acute and irregular tumor, and the majority of benign tumors are more spherical than the malignant ones.

In Fig. 4.6, a representation of tumors with different surface to volume ratio and, consequently, different shapes.

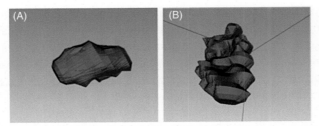

FIGURE 4.6 A representation of tumors with different surface to volume ratio. (A) Low ratio showing a round tumor, which is more likely to be benign. (B) High ratio showing an acute tumor, which is more likely to be malignant.

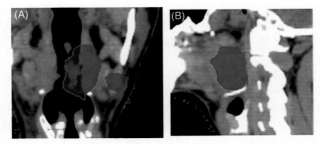

FIGURE 4.7 A representation of tumors with different textures. (A) More heterogeneous and (B) more homogeneous.

3.5.3 Texture-based features (higher-order statistics)

The features based on the texture of the tumor's region of interest, also called higher order statistics, are able to capture the spatial relationships between pixels, playing an important role in the evaluation of tissue heterogeneity. Fig. 4.7 illustrates tumors with different texture properties.

In Radiomics, the texture features are extracted by taking advantage of descriptive matrices: gray level co-occurrence matrix (GLCM), gray level run length matrix (GLRLM), gray level size zone matrix, (GLSZM), gray-level dependence matrix (GLDM) and neighborhood gray tone difference matrix (NGTDM). Each of these matrices can be further divided into radiomic features as shown in Table 4.3.

4 Radiomics in head and neck cancer—literature review

In this section, recent studies of the application of radiomics for the construction of predictive models related to head and neck cancer will be analyzed, whereby their prediction target is explained and a brief description of the workflow is given. The studies are presented according to their final objective. Finally, Table 4.4 contains a summary of the studies, where the most relevant and distinctive factors are focused on.

4.1 Distant metastasis

Zhang et al. [42] employed data from 176 patients with nasopharyngeal, nonmetastatic carcinoma to develop a predictive model of distant metastasis, the main cause of

Table 4.3 Different radiomic features depending on the descriptive matrices.

Higher-order statistics	Radiomic features
GLCM	Autocorrelation, Joint Average, Cluster Prominence, Cluster Shade, Cluster Tendency, Contrast, Correlation, Difference Average, Difference Entropy, Difference Variance, Joint Energy, Joint Entropy, Imc1, Imc2, Idm, Idmn, Id, Idn, Inverse Variance, MCC, Maximum Probability, Sum Average, Sum Entropy, Sum Squares.
GLRLM	Gray Level Non Uniformity, Gray Level Non Uniformity Normalized, Gray Level Variance, High Gray Level Run Emphasis, Long Run Emphasis, Long Run High Gray Level Emphasis, Long Run Low Gray Level Emphasis, Low Gray Level Run Emphasis, Run Entropy, Run Length Non Uniformity, Run Length Non Uniformity Normalized, Run Percentage, Run Variance, Short Run Emphasis, Short Run High Gray Level Emphasis, Short Run Low Gray Level Emphasis.
GLSZM	Gray Level Non Uniformity, Gray Level Non Uniformity Normalized, Gray Level Variance, High Gray Level Zone Emphasis, Large Area Emphasis, Large Area High Gray Level Emphasis, Large Area Low Gray Level Emphasis, Low Gray Level Zone Emphasis, Size Zone Non Uniformity, Size Zone Non Uniformity Normalized, Small Area Emphasis, Small Area High Gray Level Emphasis, Small Area Low Gray Level Emphasis, Zone Entropy, Zone Percentage, Zone Variance.
GLDM	Dependence Entropy, Dependence Non Uniformity, Dependence Non Uniformity Normalized, Dependence Variance, Gray Level Non Uniformity, Gray Level Variance, High Gray Level Emphasis, Large Dependence Emphasis, Large Dependence High Gray Level Emphasis, Large Dependence Low Gray Level Emphasis, Low Gray Level Emphasis, Small Dependence Emphasis, Small Dependence High Gray Level Emphasis, Small Dependence Low Gray Level Emphasis.
NGTDM	Busyness, Coarseness, Complexity, Contrast, Strength.

Table 4.4 Summary table of the most recent studies on the use of radiomics to construct predictive models for head and neck cancer.

Study	Publication date	Modality	Number of patients	Anatomic site (if specified)	Endpoint/ prediction target	Statistical method	Performance
Vallières et al. [10]	Aug 2017	CT, PET	300	—	DM, R, and OS	Kaplan-Meier	AUC(DM): 0.86 AUC (R): 0.69 AUC (OS): 0.74
Yu et al. [44]	Nov 2017	CT	315	Oropharynx	HPV status	GLM	AUC: 0.91549
Li et al. [43]	Dec 2018	CT, MRI, PET/CT	306	Nasopharynx	In field recurrence	ANN	AUC: 0.812
Zhang et al. [42]	Jan 2019	MRI	176	Nasopharynx	DMMM	LR	AUC: 0.827
Diamant et al. [9]	Feb 2019	CT	300	—	DM	CNN de novo	AUC: 0.92

ANN, Artificial Neural Network; CNN, Convolutional Neural Network; DM, Distant Metastasis; DMMM, Distant Metastasis MRI-Based Model; GLM, Generalized Linear Model; KNN, K-Nearest Neighbor; LDA, Linear Discriminant Analysis; LR, Logistic Regression; OS, Overall Survival; R, Recurrences.

therapeutic failure in this type of cancer. The study included clinical and biological data of patients, as well as pre-treatment MRI data. The data were divided into 123 cohorts for training and 53 cohorts for validation. In order to try to decrease the error rate, the segmentation was done manually by two radiologists with vast experience, and the process was repeated and evaluated by both. Regarding feature extraction, this phase was achieved through the PyRadiomics platform. In total, a set of 2803 radiomic features was obtained, which were subject to several stages for their reduction. The first step in the feature selection was the calculation of the interclass correlation coefficient (ICC), eliminating the features with ICC < 0.75. Clinical variables were then added to complete the dataset and univariate analyses were made for survival in which Mann-Whitney U and χ^2 tests were applied, keeping the features with $p < 0.05$. The minimum redundancy maximum relevance (mRMR) and the least absolute shrinkage and selection operator (LASSO) algorithms were also performed. After the selection, the logistic regression-based model was built and trained to evaluate whether patients have high or low risk of developing distant metastasis. The AUC values for the training and validation cohorts were, respectively, 0.827 and 0.792. Patients considered at high risk of developing distant metastases by the model had a 5-year survival rate of 12%, which is 14% lower than the survival rate of patients categorized as low risk (26%). Despite the lower values in the validation cohort, which indicate that overfitting might have occurred, the model is promising, showing that it is able to predict the risk of the appearance of distant metastasis.

4.2 Distant metastasis, locoregional recurrence, and overall survival

Vallières et al. [10] developed a study whose main objective was to build prediction models using machine learning algorithms to assess the risk of the appearance of distant metastasis (DM), locoregional recurrence (LR) before radiotherapy and overall survival (OS). For the study, data from 4 different institutions of 300 patients diagnosed with head and neck cancer were available. All patients underwent an FDG-PET/CT scan before treatment. The tumor segmentation was done manually by professional and experienced radiation oncologists. From the tumor region composed of the gross volume of the primary tumor and lymph nodes, a total of 1615 PET scan radiomics, 1615 CT scan radiomics and a set combining the PET and CT scan radiomics were calculated. The process of reducing features was divided into 25 experiments. For each of these experiments, an "initial feature" was defined, and all possible logistic regression models of order 2 (i.e., combination of 2 variables) were created by combining this feature with each of the remaining features of the reduced set still available for that specific experiment. Bootstrap re-sampling (100 samples) was performed for each of these models in order to calculate the AUC 0.632+ bootstrap. Then, the remaining feature that maximizes the AUC of 0.632+ bootstrap when combined with the initial feature was selected, and the process was repeated until an ideal model was found. The prediction models combined radiomics and clinical variables of the patients (age, tumor type, stage, among others) through random forest classifiers. The best models varied according to the endpoint, for DM, the best model included CT radiomics + clinical variables, for LR, PET/CT radiomics + clinical variables achieved the best results, and for OS, clinical variables only lead to the best prediction. AUC values were, respectively, 0.86, 0.69, and 0.74.

Based on the above-mentioned reference study, Diamant et al. [9] proposed a new approach in which they used an end-to-end convolutional neural network (CNN) designed de novo to build the DM, LR and OS models. The goal of this new approach is to realize whether a CNN can achieve improved results, compared to traditional machine learning approaches, for example, the random forest classifiers. To accomplish that, the same data set as in the previous study was used, however, Diamant et al. opted to use only the data from CT scans. In contrast to the benchmark study in which the total gross volumes of the primary tumor and lymph nodes were used, in this study, training and evaluation was done only on the central slide of the tumor, that is, on the slide with a greatest number of tumor pixels. To ensure that the choice of the central slide of the tumor was made correctly and in order to assess the robustness of the model, the slides directly above and below were also included in the training and evaluation. However, they observed that the values were very similar and significantly improve predictive accuracy. The best AUC values for DM, LR, and OS were 0.88, 0.65, and 0.70, respectively. Only the model for DM was significantly better than the benchmark study. The final output of the DM CNN model was then combined with the reference model, and the AUC value increased to 0.92. This study revealed some limitations of current approaches, however, it showed quite promising results when it comes to oncology related predictive models.

4.3 Type of recurrence

Regarding to recurrences, radiomics is able not only to predict the overall risk, but also to distinguish between the type of recurrence, specifically locoregional or distant metastasis. Li et al. [43] developed a predictive model to determine the type of recurrence (in field, out of field or marginal). The study included a range of inclusion criteria such as presenting biopsy evidence of nasopharyngeal carcinoma, absence of metastasis, CT and/or MRI/PET performed before and after radiotherapy, among others. Therefore, from the initial set of 306 patients, only 20 patients met the criteria. The radiomic features were generated from the original images and after the application of the Laplacian of Gaussian (LoG) and Wavelet filters. As a result, using the PyRadiomics platform, a total of 1117 features were obtained (13 shape-based, 18 1st order-based, 74 texture-based, 276 LoG-based and 734 Wavelet-based). The extracted features were evaluated using the interclass correlation coefficient (ICC) and were selected based on a classification as poor (ICC < 0.40), moderate ($0.40 \leq$ ICC < 0.60), good ($0.60 \leq$ ICC < 0.80), or excellent (ICC $\geq$ 0.80). Before the construction of the model, the correlations of features classified as excellent were furthermore evaluated through the Pearson correlation coefficient (PCC). Finally, three predictive models were built through supervised machine learning algorithms: Artificial Neural Network (ANN), K-Nearest Neighbor (KNN), and Support Vector Machine (SVM). ANN was the model with the best accuracy value (0.812), compared to KNN and SVM whose values are 0.775 and 0.732, respectively. This study shows that, using the same set of radiomic features, deep learning algorithms can result in more expressive, accurate predictive models than traditional machine learning methods.

4.4 HPV status

The presence of HPV is one of the risk factors for head and neck cancer, so knowing its status is essential for accurate prognosis [8,15,16]. Yu et al. [44] used a data set of 315 oropharyngeal cancer patients to develop a model for predicting HPV status. In this study, the gross volumes of primary and nodal tumors were analyzed, and their segmentation was done manually by professionals. The extraction process resulted in a total of 1683 features, which were subject to selection criteria. Thus, to reduce the initial number of radiomic features, following exclusion criteria were applied: (1) features with heterogeneity between the training and validation cohorts, (2) features without any relevance for the distinction between positive and negative HPV, (3) features whose absolute biserial correlation between each feature and HPV status was less than 0.3. As a next step in the statistical analysis of features, the remaining features were classified by calculating the AUC (obtained by random division and repeating the process 10 times). Then, several machine learning models were trained and evaluated (e.g., random forest and support vector machine), keeping only the 10 main features whose AUC values were highest. Finally, the final features were selected by forward selection where one by one features were added until the AUC value was unchanged (no more increases). To select the best final model, they resorted to a public challenge. Among all the models and features tested, the model that showed the best AUC results was the general linear model (GLM) and the most important features were Mean Breadth and Spherical Disproportion that measure, respectively, the width of the tumor and the disproportion compared to the surface of a sphere. The models were tested on data from a public hospital, which resulted in an AUC = 0.86667 for predicting HPV status, and a private hospital, resulting in AUC = 0.91549 for the prediction.

5 Conclusion

Head and neck cancer is a type of cancer with high regional anatomical complexity, presenting several tumor manifestations and high intratumoral heterogeneity, which leads to a high failure rate in response to therapy.

Radiomics is a relatively new technique that provides the ability to extract hundreds of medical imaging features that quantify the phenotypic characteristics of the tumor. Several studies have demonstrated the discriminant capacity of radiomic features for several clinical outcomes (e.g., occurrence of distant metastases, overall survival, tumor recurrence, HPV status) as well as for tumor classification and tissue identification, among others.

For radiomics analysis, machine learning has proven to be a crucial tool [45,46]. Recent studies have shown that deep learning models, such as CNNs, can have superior predictive capabilities when trained with radiomic features compared to traditional machine learning algorithms, as for example, SVMs or RFs.

In summary, a variety of research works showed great potential and promising results by combining radiomics and machine learning to aid in the diagnosis, prediction, and treatment of head and neck cancers.

Acknowledgments

This works was supported by the Erasmus+ Programme from the European Union (EU) and the Austrian Science Fund (FWF) KLI 678-B31: "enFaced: Virtual and Augmented Reality Training and Navigation Module for 3D-Printed Facial Defect Reconstructions." Furthermore, this work was supported by CAMed (COMET K-Project 871132), which is funded by the Austrian Federal Ministry of Transport, Innovation and Technology (BMVIT), and the Austrian Federal Ministry for Digital and Economic Affairs (BMDW), and the Styrian Business Promotion Agency (SFG). Moreover, the work was supported by TU Graz Lead Project (Mechanics, Modeling and Simulation of Aortic Dissection) and by FCT – Fundação para a Ciência e Tecnologia within the R&D Units Project Scope: UIDB/00319/2020.

References

[1] K. Doi, Diagnostic imaging over the last 50 years: Research and development in medical imaging science and technology, Phys. Med. Biol. 51 (2006) R5.

[2] V. Fink, *Head and neck tumor segmentation from combined PET/CT scans using deep learning* [Unpublished bachelor's thesis], Institute of Computer Graphics and Vision Graz University of Technology (2019).

[3] H.J.W.L. Aerts, E.R. Velazquez, R.T.H. Leijenaar, C. Parmar, B. Haibe-kains, P. Grossmann, et al. Decoding tumour phenotype by noninvasive imaging using a quantitative radiomics approach, Nat. Commun. 5 (2014) 4006.

[4] X.A. Li, Radiomic machine-learning classifiers for prognostic biomarkers of head and neck cancer, Front. Oncol. 5 (2015) 272.

[5] K.M. Stenson, Epidemiology and risk factors for head and neck cancer [Internet], 2019. Available from: https://www.uptodate.com/contents/epidemiology-and-risk-factors-for-head-and-neck-cancer.

[6] Head & Neck Cancers, 2019. Available from: http://www.ecpc.org/activities/policy-and-advocacy/policy-initiatives/head-neck-cancer-make-sense-campaign.

[7] A.J. Wong, A. Kanwar, A.S. Mohamed, C.D. Fuller, Radiomics in head and neck cancer: from exploration to application, Transl. Cancer Res. 5 (4) (2016) 371–382.

[8] L. Mao, W.K. Hong, V.A. Papadimitrakopoulou, Focus on head and neck cancer, Cancer Cell. 5 (2004) 311–316.

[9] A. Diamant, A. Chatterjee, M. Vallières, G. Shenouda, J. Seuntjens, Deep learning in head & neck cancer outcome prediction, Sci. Rep. 9 (2019) 2764.

[10] M. Vallières, E. Kay-rivest, L.J. Perrin, X. Liem, C. Furstoss, H.J.W.L. Aerts, et al. Radiomics strategies for risk assessment of tumour failure in head-and-neck cancer, Sci. Rep. 7 (2017) 10117.

[11] M. Morash, H. Mitchell, H. Beltran, O. Elemento, J. Pathak. The role of next-generation sequencing in precision medicine: a review of outcomes in oncology. J. Pers. Med. 8(3) (2018) 30.

[12] L. Oakden-rayner, G. Carneiro, T. Bessen, J.C. Nascimento, P. Andrew, L.J. Palmer, Precision radiology: Predicting longevity using feature engineering and deep learning methods in a radiomics framework, Sci. Rep. 7 (2017) 1648. Available from: http://dx.doi.org/10.1038/s41598-017-01931-w.

[13] S. Rizzo, F. Botta, S. Raimondi, D. Origgi, C. Fanciullo, A.G. Morganti, et al. Radiomics: the facts and the challenges of image analysis, Eur. Radiol. Exp. 2 (1) (2018) 36.

[14] P. Lambin, E. Rios-velazquez, R. Leijenaar, Radiomics: extracting more information from medical images using advanced feature analysis, Eur. J. Cancer 48 (2012) 441–446.

[15] S. On, Head and neck cancer: changing epidemiology, Diagn. Treat. 83 (2008) 489–501.

[16] A.C.S. Poon, K.M. Stenson, Overview of the diagnosis and staging of head and neck cancer, In: Post, TW (Ed). UpToDate, Waltham, MA, 2020. (2020).

[17] N.C. Institute. Head and neck cancers, 2017. Available from: https://www.cancer.gov/types/head-and-neck/head-neck-fact-sheet.

[18] A.B.E. Brockstein, K.M. Stenson, S. Song. Overview of treatment for head and neck cancer, 2020.

[19] J.A. Brennan, D. Sidransky, Molecular staging of head and neck squamous carcinoma, Cancer Metastasis Rev. 15 (1996) 3–10.

[20] P. Afshar, S. Member, A. Mohammadi, S. Member, N. Konstantinos. From hand-crafted to deep learning-based cancer radiomics : challenges and opportunities. IEEE Sig. Process. Mag. 36 (219) 132–160.

[21] C.M.F. Dias, (2019). *Radiomics: tumour genotype prediction* (Identificador TID: 202390713) [Master dissertation, FEUP- Faculdade de Engenharia da Universidade do Porto]. FEUP - Dissertação.

[22] A.F. Leite, K.D.F. Vasconcelos, H. Willems, R. Jacobs, Radiomics and machine learning in oral healthcare, Proteomics Clin. Appl. 14 (2020) e1900040.

[23] E.A. Eisenhauer, P. Therasse, J. Bogaerts, L.H. Schwartz, D. Sargent, R. Ford, et al. New response evaluation criteria in solid tumours: Revised RECIST guideline (version 1. 1), Eur. J. Cancer 45 (2) (2008) 228–247. Available from: http://dx.doi.org/10.1016/j.ejca.2008.10.026.

[24] A. Vial, D. Stirling, M. Field, C. Ritz, M. Carolan, A.A. Miller, The role of deep learning and radiomic feature extraction in cancer-specific predictive modelling : a review, Transl. Cancer Res. 7 (3) (2018) 803–816.

[25] M. Bogowicz, O. Riesterer, L.S. Stark, G. Studer, M. Guckenberger, S. Tanadini-lang, et al. Comparison of PET and CT radiomics for prediction of local tumor control in head and neck squamous cell carcinoma, Acta Oncol. 56 (11) (2017) 1531–1536. Available from: https://doi.org/10.1080/028418 6X.2017.1346382.

[26] M. Mazón, J. Francisco, V. Costa, A. Ten-esteve, L. Martí-bonmatí, C. Salvatore, Imaging biomarkers for the diagnosis and prognosis of neurodegenerative diseases. The example of amyotrophic lateral sclerosis, Front. Neurosci. 12 (2018) 784.

[27] K. Zhao, Y. Ding, Y. Han, Y. Fan, A.F. Alexander-bloch, T. Han, et al. Independent and reproducible hippocampal radiomic biomarkers for multisite Alzheimer's disease: diagnosis, longitudinal progress and biological basis, Sci. Bull. 65 (13) (2020) 1103–1113. Available from: https://doi.org/10.1016/j.scib.2020.04.003.

[28] P. Liu, H. Wang, S. Zheng, F. Zhang, X. Zhang, Parkinson's disease diagnosis using neostriatum radiomic features based on T2-weighted magnetic resonance imaging, Front. Neurol. 11 (2020) 248.

[29] Q.N. Do, M.A. Lewis, Y. Xi, A.J. Madhuranthakam, S.K. Happe, J.S. Dashe, et al. MRI of the placenta accreta spectrum (PAS) disorder : radiomics analysis correlates with surgical and pathological outcome, J. Magn. Reson. Imaging 51 (2019) 1–11.

[30] I. Cetin, S.E. Petersen, S. Napel, K. Lekadir, BCN MedTech, Universitat Pompeu Fabra, Barcelona, Spain Catalan Institution for Research and Advanced Studies (ICREA), Barcelona, Spain William Harvey Research Institute, Queen Mary University of London, London, UK Department of Radiology, School of Medicine, Stanford University, Stanford, USA, 2019, pp. 640–643.

[31] M. Kolossváry, J. Karády, B. Szilveszter, P. Kitslaar, Radiomic features are superior to conventional quantitative computed tomographic metrics to identify coronary plaques with napkin-ring sign, Circ. Cardiovasc. Imaging 10 (2017) e006843.

[32] A. Stefano, M. Piana, D. Schenone, R. Lai, A. Maria, N. Houssami, Overview of radiomics in breast cancer diagnosis and prognostication, Breast 49 (2020) 74–80.

[33] B. Sah, K. Owczarczyk, M. Siddique, G.J.R. Cook, V. Goh, Radiomics in esophageal and gastric cancer, Abdom. Radiol. 44 (2018) 2048–2058. Available from: https://doi.org/10.1007/s00261-018-1724-8.

[34] S.S.F Yip, H.J.W.L. Aerts. Applications and limitations of radiomics. Phys. Med. Biol. 150, R150. Available from: http://dx.doi.org/10.1088/0031-9155/61/13/R150.

[35] M. Shafiq-ul-hassan, G.G. Zhang, K. Latifi, G. Ullah, C. Dylan, D. Mackin, et al. Intrinsic dependencies of CT radiomic features on voxel size and number of gray levels, Med. Phys. 44 (2017) 1050–1062.

[36] Z. Guo, N. Guo, K. Gong, S. Zhong, Q. Li, Gross tumor volume segmentation for head and neck cancer radiotherapy using deep dense multi-modality network Gross tumor volume segmentation for head and neck cancer radiotherapy using deep dense multi-modality network, Phys. Med. Biol. 64 (2019) 205015.

[37] J.J.M. Griethuysen, Van, A. Fedorov, C. Parmar, A. Hosny, N. Aucoin, V. Narayan, et al. Computational radiomics system to decode the radiographic phenotype, Cancer Res. 77 (21) (2017) 104–108.

[38] L.E. Court, X. Fave, D. Mackin, J. Lee, J. Yang, L. Zhang, Computational resources for radiomics, Transl. Cancer Res. 5 (4) (2016) 340–348.

[39] J. Moreira, A.C.P.L. Ferreira, T. Horvath, in: J.W. Sons (Ed.), A general introduction to data analytics, 2018, p. 352.

[40] V. Kumar, Y. Gu, S. Basu, A. Berglund, S.A. Eschrich, M.B. Schabath, et al. Radiomics : the process and the challenges, Magn. Reson. Imaging 30 (9) (2012) 1234–1248. Available from: http://dx.doi.org/10.1016/j.mri.2012.06.010.

[41] G. Lee, H.Y. Lee, H. Park, M.L. Schiebler, E.J.R. Beek, Van, Y. Ohno, et al. biomarkers and clinical management : State of the art, Eur. J. Radiol. (2016). Available from: http://dx.doi.org/10.1016/j.ejrad.2016.09.005.

[42] L. Zhang, D. Dong, H. Li, J. Tian, F. Ouyang, X. Mo, et al. EBioMedicine development and validation of a magnetic resonance imaging-based model for the prediction of distant metastasis before initial treatment of nasopharyngeal carcinoma: A retrospective cohort study, EBioMedicine 40 (106) (2019) 327–335. Available from: https://doi.org/10.1016/j.ebiom.2019.01.013.

[43] S. Li, K. Wang, Z. Hou, J. Yang, W. Ren, S. Gao, Use of radiomics combined with machine learning method in the recurrence patterns after intensity-modulated radiotherapy for nasopharyngeal carcinoma: a preliminary study, Front. Oncol. 8 (2018) 648.

[44] K. Yu, Y. Zhang, Y. Yu, C. Huang, R. Liu, T. Li, et al. Clinical and translational radiation oncology radiomic analysis in prediction of human papilloma virus status, Clin. Transl. Radiat. Oncol. 7 (2017) 49–54. Available from: https://doi.org/10.1016/j.ctro.2017.10.001.

[45] P. Giraud, P. Giraud, A. Gasnier, R.El Ayachy, S. Kreps, J. Foy, et al. Radiomics and machine learning for radiotherapy in head and neck cancers, Front. Oncol. 9 (2019) 174.

[46] K. Hao, What is machine learning?, 2018. Available from: https://www.technologyreview.com/2018/11/17/103781/what-is-machine-learning-we-drew-you-another-flowchart/.

5

Augmented reality in oral and maxillofacial surgery

Christina Gsaxner[a,b,c], Ulrich Eck[d], Dieter Schmalstieg[a], Nassir Navab[d,e], Jan Egger[a,b,c]

[a]INSTITUTE OF COMPUTER GRAPHICS AND VISION, GRAZ UNIVERSITY OF TECHNOLOGY, GRAZ, AUSTRIA; [b]COMPUTER ALGORITHMS FOR MEDICINE LABORATORY, GRAZ, AUSTRIA; [c]DEPARTMENT OF ORAL AND MAXILLOFACIAL SURGERY, MEDICAL UNIVERSITY OF GRAZ, GRAZ, AUSTRIA; [d]COMPUTER AIDED MEDICAL PROCEDURES & AUGMENTED REALITY, TECHNICAL UNIVERSITY OF MUNICH, GARCHING, GERMANY; [e]WHITING SCHOOL OF ENGINEERING, JOHNS HOPKINS UNIVERSITY, BALTIMORE, MD, UNITED STATES

1 Introduction

Augmented reality (AR) is a technology which links the real and virtual world, extending the user's reality with virtual information. With the advancement of mobile computing, AR applications have been implemented in a wide range of fields, such as gaming and industry. Medicine has always been an area of great potential for AR, with a first system introduced as early as 1986 by Roberts et al. [1], and several works following in the early 1990s [2–4]. The appeal of medical AR goes back to the notion of "X-ray" vision, the ability to effectively see through objects. In medicine, where an inside view of the patient's body is usually readily available through medical imaging, such as X-ray, computed tomography (CT), or magnetic resonance imaging (MRI), this information can be merged into the same physical space as the patient to permit *in situ visualization*.

This new visualization paradigm offers several benefits over the traditional method of viewing medical imaging data on a separate 2D monitor. First, AR visualization eliminates the need for physicians to mentally transform imaging data to the patient. This is beneficial in many scenarios, such as physical examination of the patient or treatment planning but is especially helpful during image-guided interventions. In current practice, navigation information is displayed on one or several monitors placed around the surgical site, which is a challenging task itself due to constraints resulting from insufficient space or line-of-sight requirements. The physician is consequently forced to divide his attention between navigation and the patient, while coordinating the manipulation of surgical tools. By using in situ visualization, this attention disruption becomes unnecessary, resulting in improved hand-eye coordination for the physician and therefore, facilitating the surgeon's performance in terms of accuracy and time efficiency [5]. A comparison between traditional image guidance and guidance using AR is illustrated in Fig. 5.1. A second important

Computer-Aided Oral and Maxillofacial Surgery. http://dx.doi.org/10.1016/B978-0-12-823299-6.00005-5

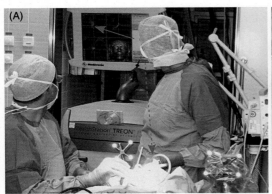

FIGURE 5.1 Comparison between traditional image-guided surgery and augmented reality (AR) guided surgery. (A) With conventional navigation systems, the surgeon is forced to divide his attention between navigation information and the surgical site. (B) AR systems supporting in-situ visualization allow surgeons to focus on the patient only, while viewing navigation information directly overlaid with the patient in their view.

benefit of medical AR is an improved perception of imaging data in support of the physician's decision-making process. Modern AR displays enable stereoscopic visualization of volumetric data, resulting in a true three-dimensional (3D) view. This implicitly results in perceptual cues such as binocular disparity and motion parallax, which lead to a stronger spatial understanding of structures [6]. Furthermore, automatically aligning the viewpoint of real and virtual objects aids in 3D inspection of data, by making the adjustment of the viewpoint more natural [5].

Oral and cranio-maxillofacial surgery (OCMS) was among the first specialities investigated in the context of medical AR, pioneered in 1995 by Wagner et al. [4]. This was presumably caused by the fact that OCMS is a surgical speciality working with a particularly complex anatomy, were image guidance has a high potential. The oral and cranial region is home to delicate structures like the larynx, oral cavity and a rich nervous system, which, if damaged during surgery or treatment, might leave the patient unable to speak, swallow or seriously disfigured [7]. Only highly accurate procedures can guarantee a surgical outcome, which is both functionally and aesthetically adequate and preserves the patient's quality of life as much as possible. Therefore, AR has found its application in OCMS implantology, orthognathic surgery, trauma, and oncology [8].

2 Augmented reality: concepts and technology

2.1 Definition of augmented reality

A term often used interchangeable with augmented reality is mixed reality (MR). According to the popular definition of the "virtuality continuum" by Milgram and Kishino [9] (Fig. 5.2), MR describes all combinations of real and virtual between real environment and virtual reality (VR). While VR completely immerses the user within a virtual world, AR contains mainly real elements, enhanced with some virtual content. However, a simple

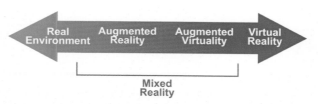

FIGURE 5.2 Virtuality continuum by Milgram and Kishino [9]. Mixed reality describes all combinations between the real environment (a direct view of reality) and virtual reality (an immersion in a fully digital environment). Augmented reality usually refers to the overlay of virtual objects over the real-world environment, while augmented virtuality describes real objects, projected, and controlled in a virtual world.

blend of virtual and real objects does not yet constitute an AR system. According to Azuma [10], AR is defined by the following characteristics: it (1) combines real and virtual, (2) is interactive in real-time, and (3) is registered in 3D. Traditional special effects in movies or TV overlays in news or sports broadcasts don't fall into this characterization of AR, since they are not interactive or not registered three-dimensionally, respectively.

2.2 Augmented reality displays

In principle, three concepts for visual AR displays can be distinguished. **Video see-through** (VST) displays capture the observed scene with a camera and combine the resulting image digitally with virtual information. They have the advantage of a flexible, arbitrary merging between virtual and real images, which allows a depiction of fully opaque virtual objects with correct colours. Furthermore, by delaying the real view, relative lag between reality and virtuality can be minimized [5]. On the downside, VST displays are limited in their resolution and image quality by the capturing optics, both for real and virtual content. **Optical see-through** (OST) displays, on the other hand, do not require a camera to capture the real world. Instead, virtual imagery is directly overlaid with reality using an optical combiner. Compared to VST, OST displays have the advantage of not blocking the user's vision, not falsifying the real view by non-ideal capturing optics of a camera [11], and the visualization quality of real content is not limited by the resolution of the viewing camera or display. However, for correct alignment of virtual content with the reality, the relation of the user's eyes to the display must be known to achieve a synchronization between real and virtual viewing parameters. This is typically accomplished by display calibration, often involving manual calibration steps [12]. A limitation of OST displays is that virtual content is usually perceived as an overlay over real content. Accurate perception of structures located within real objects is difficult to achieve, since the reality cannot be manipulated, contrary to VST modalities. Finally, **spatial** displays use a projector to cast images directly onto real world objects, which they usually capture using a camera. Even though modern projectors have high resolution, refresh rates, and often support stereo projection, image quality is rather low compared to state-of-the art OST or VST displays. This shortcoming is amplified when projecting onto irregular surfaces or using the system in environments with bright natural lighting. Furthermore, spatial displays suffer from the same constraint on depth perception as OST displays do. Fig. 5.3 provides an overview over display types in AR.

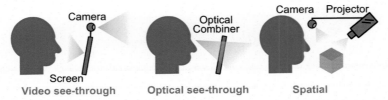

FIGURE 5.3 Different AR display types. Video see-through displays capture the reality with a camera and digitally combine real and virtual images before displaying them on a screen. Optical see-through displays, on the other hand, overlay virtual content directly with reality using an optical combiner. Finally, spatial displays project images directly onto real objects, which are usually captured by a camera.

According to Schmalstieg and Höllerer [13], AR displays can further be categorized according to the distance between eyes and display. In head space, **head-mounted displays** (HMDs) show information directly in front of the user's eyes. Such wearable displays allow a natural synchronization of real world, virtual content and the user's perspective and actions, while keeping the hands of the user free [14]. VST-HMDs, OST-HMDs, and projector-based HMDs have been proposed in the past. Moving further away from the eyes to the body space, **hand-held displays**, in particular smartphones and tablets, are prevalent AR devices. Since an estimation of the relation between eyes and display is increasingly more difficult with a larger distance, VST or, in some cases, spatial systems are more common in this space. Lastly, **world space displays** are stationary placed within the environment, independent of the user. They can enable VST AR using monitors and cameras, OST AR by employing fixed optical combiners or virtual content projected on real objects using non-movable projector.

2.3 Registration and tracking

While the display takes care of *combining* real and virtual content, registration is needed for *aligning* real and virtual coordinate systems and therefore, correlating computer-generated content with the real scene. For applications where some sort of X-ray vision is desired, accurate 3D registration is important to not ruin the perception of real and virtual world coexisting. For medical applications, demands are even higher—a misalignment between a virtual interventional target and the patient may cause the entire procedure to fail, leading to a possibly serious medical accident [15].

Accurate registration in the user's perspective relies on continuous tracking of the viewing camera within the environment. Tracking is integral in any AR system to synchronize the viewpoint of virtual content with the viewpoint of the real scene. For full tracking, both position and orientation need to be determined, resulting in six degrees of freedom (6DOF) describing the pose of the device.

2.3.1 Tracking paradigms and sensors

One can distinguish between **outside-in** and **inside-out** approaches for tracking, depending on the location of the tracking sensors. For outside-in methods, external tracking

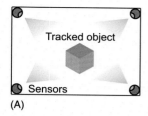
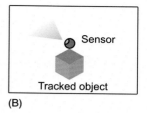

FIGURE 5.4 **Tracking paradigms in AR.** In (A) outside-in tracking, the sensors a stationary mounted in the environment and observe the tracked object within a fixed volume. Meanwhile, (B) inside-out tracking places the sensors on the tracked object itself. The sensor localizes itself by relating itself to stationary features, either artificial or natural, within the environment.

infrastructure (e.g., a camera) needs to be stationary mounted and the position and orientation of the tracked object, which can move within a limited tracked volume, in relation to the sensor, can be calculated. In inside-out tracking, the sensor is located on or within the device, which then moves around the environment, tracking itself. Static references need to be observable by the tracker, such that the pose of the device in relation to them can be determined, however, the tracking sensors are mobile. Inside-out approaches have recently exploited the fact that AR devices are equipped with increasingly powerful hardware, promoting the integration of advanced computer vision algorithms for detection and tracking of the environment from images captured by a high-resolution camera, integrated into the device. The difference between these two paradigms is visualized in Fig. 5.4. When selecting a tracking modality, one is often confronted with a trade-off between accuracy, usability and reliability [16]. While outside-in approaches are considered to be more accurate and reliable, they come at the cost of additional system components and line of sight constraints. Inside-out approaches work in an unprepared environment, but their accuracy and reliability often does not meet the requirements of high precision applications, such as medicine [5].

In principle, tracking can be accomplished with different kinds of sensors, such as mechanical, haptic devices, electromagnetic fields, or global positioning systems (GPS). However, vision-based sensors, such as visible light cameras or infrared (IR) sensors are by far the most active area of research and will therefore be the focus of the following chapter [17].

2.3.2 Marker-based systems

Optical registration and tracking can be accomplished with marker-based approaches, which rely on artificial indicators rigidly attached to real world objects. A fast and cheap method is to track known image patterns (fiducials) with standard red-green-blue (RGB) visible light cameras. However, such approaches are sensitive to uneven, non-controllable lighting conditions. The tracking of retro-reflective spheres with infrared (IR) cameras has been shown to be a more robust alternative [16]. This principle is used by many commercial tracking and motion capturing solutions, such as OptiTrack (Natural Point, Inc., Corvallis, Oregon, USA) or Vicon (Vicon Motion Systems Ltd, UK), which operate in an outside-in fashion. Marker-based approaches have the advantage of providing a solution for both tracking and registration in one go. For an accurate marker-based registration, markers and real objects are usually rigidly calibrated to each other, so that tracking of the markers allows a precise, 6DOF pose estimation of the real object to which the markers are attached. Stationary markers can also serve as easy to detect references for inside-out tracking. The obvious disadvantage of marker-based systems is that they require a meticulously prepared environment, were markers and real-world counterparts need to be calibrated, line-of-sight constraints must be adhered to, and lighting conditions must be adjusted.

2.3.3 Marker-free systems

Markerless registration and tracking is an approach which exploits natural features observable by the tracking device within the environment. One of the most noteworthy techniques for markerless, model-free tracking is simultaneous localization and mapping (SLAM) [18]. As the name suggests, SLAM algorithms build a map of the environment from information gathered from a variety of sensors within a device and simultaneously locate this device within this map. Other markerless tracking approaches are based on models or templates, where a 3D model of parts of the observed scene is available and compared with the camera images to estimate it's 6DOF pose as a 3D to 2D matching problem [13,17]. As an alternative, some AR systems integrate 3D surface information of the scene directly, in example by capturing the scene with stereo cameras, structured light or time-of-flight (TOF) depth sensors. The so acquired surfaces can directly be registered with a 3D model of the target. However, these additional sensors must be dynamically calibrated with the remaining system components, which generally results in complicated setups.

Finally, registration can be performed manually or semi-manually. For example, the pose of the real object to be annotated with augmented content can be digitized by capturing some known points on its surface with a tracked tool. Then, the virtual model can be registered to it using a point-based registration. Alternatively, the pose of a virtual object can be adjusted in a purely manual way, by using controls supported by the AR application, such as touch buttons or gestures. The major drawback of manual approaches is that the registration is not dynamic—in case the real object moves, coherence is lost, and the procedure must be repeated. This is why such registration strategies are often combined with marker-based systems, were manual user input is only required for initial calibration, and real-time tracking is thereafter accomplished with the aid of fiducials.

2.4 Visualization and visual coherence

Even after real and virtual objects have been correctly aligned, there are still some important factors influencing the perception of the virtual content in AR, which can be related to visualization. To obtain an actual impression of location and characteristics of virtual objects, they need to be blended with the reality in a visually coherent, non-obstructive way.

A naïve opaque overlay of virtual graphics may occlude important information in the real scene and even semi-transparent overlays might be distracting and falsifying real information. Furthermore, basic image fusion techniques such as overlays suffer from their lack of depth cues, which is especially problematic for X-ray visualization, where the user should percept augmented content as lying within real objects.

One particularly important depth cue is **occlusion** [19]. In a basic overlay, only virtual content can occlude the real scene, and not vice versa, which might lead to the impression of virtual objects floating on top of the environment. A deeper understanding of the observed scene is required to properly handle occlusions. For example, phantom rendering, first introduced by Breen et al. [20], and similar techniques register an invisible model of the real occluder to the object and use it to inhibit the rendering of virtual objects where they would be occluded by reality. The idea of phantom rendering can be extended by texturing phantom objects using the information captured by the camera and fusing real and virtual information in these overlapping regions in a way that enhances the inference of spatial relations. Widespread techniques in that regard are cutaways, Focus-and-Context (F + C) visualization, and ghosting. Cutaways can easily be realized by cutting a hole into the phantom object and displaying this hole with the virtual object within. In F + C, the virtual focus objects are partially occluded by key features, such as edges, from real context objects [21]. Ghosting, on the other hand, renders the phantom object transparently on top of the virtual object. In the process, the transparency of the occluder is determined by its important salient video image features, such as their curvature [22].

While occlusion offers information about the ordering of objects within the scene, it does not provide information about the distance of objects. **Motion parallax** and **stereo disparity** are cues that deliver information about this relative and absolute distance. With stereoscopic head-mounted displays, both of these cues can be intuitively realized.

Illumination and **shadowing** are other important factors in visual coherence. Aside from providing a sense of depth, these cues are also important for correctly perceiving the shape of objects. By approximating the light sources in the reality, for example using light probes, virtual objects can be illuminated accordingly, and virtual shadows can be correctly cast on real objects.

2.5 Current augmented reality hardware

Advances in mobile displays, graphics processing units (GPUs) and tracking technology have recently resulted in a large choice of enabling technologies for AR, apart from standard monitor and camera setups. First and foremost, low cost smartphones and tablet computers have made VST AR accessible to a broad range of users and developers. Smartphones can be integrated into affordable head mounted devices containing simple optics, such as the Google Cardboard (Google, Mountain View, CA, United States) or the Samsung Gear VR (Samsung, Seoul, South Korea), to create a more immersive experience. Easy to use development platforms such as ARCore (Google, Mountain View, CA, United States) and ARKit (Apple Inc., Cupertino, CA, United States) provide out-of-the-box solutions for environmental understanding and device tracking. Due to limited computing power, reliability and accuracy, such setups are, however, more suitable for entertainment purposes than for serious applications with high precision requirements.

Tethered VST-HMDs, which require a connection to a PC, overcome these limitations at the expense of reduced mobility and higher cost for the consumer. Noteworthy examples of such displays include the HTC Vive (HTC Corporation, New Taipei City, China) or the Oculus Rift (Oculus VR, Menlo Park, CA). For accurate tracking, these devices use a combination of sensors, such as inertial measurement units (IMU) and outside-in cameras.

OST display solutions have only recently been commercialized, with the Google Glass (Google, Mountain View, CA, United States) released in 2013 being one of the most prominent examples. Currently, the Microsoft HoloLens (Microsoft Corporation, Redmond, WA, United States), released in 2016, is the most popular hardware choice in the category of OST-HMDs. The HoloLens uses several sensor types (TOF sensor, visible light cameras, IMU) for inside-out tracking. Virtual images are projected onto a pair of transparent combiner lenses, allowing for a true, stereoscopic 3D visualization of content.

3 Augmented reality in medicine: current practice and challenges

3.1 Applications of AR in medicine

Medical AR has become a very broad topic, with applications ranging from medical education to image guided surgery, and employment in a wide variety of medical fields. According to recent surveys by Eckert et al. [23] and Chen et al. [15], the largest body of research focuses on clinical applications, with the majority of research going toward surgery or intervention, followed by applications in therapy and rehabilitation. A considerable amount of studies also explores AR in medical education and training. Examples for these diverse fields of applications are displayed in Fig. 5.5.

3.1.1 Education and training

In an educational context, AR can aid learners by visualizing complicated spatial relationships, animating complex phenomena, and facilitating interactive learning through real-time interaction and feedback [24]. Furthermore, new technologies, such as AR, potentially enhance the attractiveness and appeal of traditional educational interfaces such as books or lectures, increasing the students' motivation to learn [25]. A prime example of AR-supported education in medicine is anatomy learning, where textbook images or anatomical models can be annotated with virtual information and made interactive. AR-supported anatomy learning has been shown to reduce the cognitive load for students [26] and increase their motivation to study [27]. Commercial applications for AR supported anatomy learning, such as the Human Anatomy Atlas by VisibleBody (Argosy Publishing Inc, Newton, MA, United States) or Complete Anatomy by 3D4Medical (Elsevier,

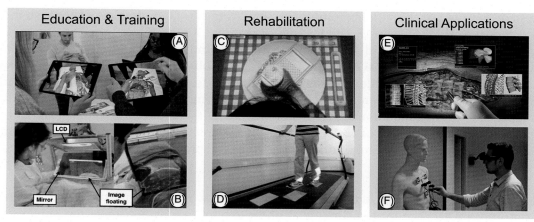

FIGURE 5.5 Examples for the different fields of applications of medical AR. (A) A handheld, video see-through AR system used for anatomy learning. (B) The Perk Station is employed for training percutaneous surgical procedures using a world-localized optical see-through system. (C) A projector-based AR application is used to aid stroke patients in regaining their ability to perform day-to-day tasks. (D) A similar application is employed for helping patients in walking adaptability therapy. (E) A mock-up showing AR assisted, image-guided spine surgery. (F) Using a head-worn AR display for aiding untrained people in performing electrocardiography. *Part A: (Image courtesy of 3D4Medical by Elsevier); Part B: Image adopted from Ref. [32]; Part C: Image adopted from Ref. [37], published under CC BY 4.0 license; Part D: Image adopted from Ref. [36], published under CC BY 4.0 license; Part E: Image adopted from Ref. [45]; Part F: Image adopted from [56], published under CC BY 4.0 license.*

Amsterdam, Netherlands), as shown in Fig. 5.5A, are now internationally used by universities and clinics.

AR also has a place in medical training, where the overall goal is not the studying of theoretical concepts, but the acquisition of technical skills. By using specialized phantoms or simulators, medical students and residents can improve their ability to perform tasks with a high perceptual, cognitive, and sensorimotor workload, without the instrumentation of the patient [28]. Such training systems can be enhanced using AR, by providing image guidance or instant feedback to the trainee. Several commercial training tools using AR technology exist and have been evaluated in the literature [29], in example the ProMIS system for laparoscopic tasks (Haptica, Inc., Dublin, Ireland), or the CAE Vimedix (CAE Healthcare, Inc., Montreal, Canada) for training ultrasound examinations. Experimental systems have, in example, also been applied to train the insertion of needles [30–32], as seen in Fig. 5.5B, and neurosurgical procedures [32]. These studies show that AR in medical training can improve the accuracy and speed of carrying out a simulated task, however, how well skills acquired in these mixed environments translate to skills needed to perform actual clinical interventions still remains questionable.

3.1.2 Rehabilitation

In rehabilitation, medical AR can help patients in the recovery from mental or physical conditions, either in their homes or in specialized rehabilitation centers. An area of particularly high research interest is the rehabilitation of deficiencies of the musculoskeletal system, of which stroke patients commonly suffer from [33–37]. Examples of such systems are shown in Fig. 5.5C and D. These studies show that AR interfaces have the potential to make repetitive tasks and activities, which usually must be performed during rehab, more engaging. Furthermore, AR systems allow a more objective evaluation of the therapy progress, also remotely. Aside from sensorimotor defects, successful implementations of AR rehab systems have been reported for the management of chronic pain [38,39]. AR applications for rehabilitation are facilitated by the fact that affordable, mobile technologies, such as smartphones or tablets, can easily be deployed in the patients' homes and additionally enable remote monitoring of activities and progress.

3.1.3 Clinical applications

Most AR systems for usage in hospitals and clinics focus on applications within the operating room (OR). The overreaching goal of these applications is usually the enhancement of conventional image-guided surgical navigation. Image-guided surgery (IGS) has helped surgeons to perform safer, less invasive interventions for almost 30 years [40], by aiding physicians in localizing and reaching target regions more quickly and accurately, while reducing the risk of harming critical structures during the procedure. In IGS, a preprocessed dataset of the patient (e.g., containing imaging data and planning information) is accurately registered to him or her within the OR, and a navigation system is used to track instruments in relation to this data. Commercial surgical navigation systems, in example manufactured by Brainlab (Brainlab AG, Feldkirchen, Germany) or Medtronic (Medtronic, Minneapolis, MN, United States), provide imaging, planning, and tracking information on a separate monitor. It is evident that AR interfaces have the potential to greatly simplify such procedures by providing in situ visualization, for example, fusing navigation information directly with the patient. This allows the surgeons to focus their attention on the patient and the surgical site alone, and they do not have to mentally map information between two different sites. Several experimental AR systems to support complex interventions have been experimentally trailed, in example for tumor resection [41–44], pedicle screw placement [45–47] (as shown exemplary in Fig. 5.5E), and surgical drilling [48,49]. Even though IGS is the most common procedure supported by medical AR, it is also the most challenging. Navigated surgical procedures usually have highest demands in terms of accuracy and reliability. Furthermore, cumbersome and bulky setups or distracting visualizations have to be avoided to assure acceptance and usability. The currently very restricted usage of AR within the OR shows that most developmental AR systems fail to deliver some of these requirements so far. However, medical technology companies are slowly starting to open up to the integration of AR into their navigation systems.

Interventions outside of the OR have also been subject of interest for AR research. In example, support for radiation therapy [50], the placement of catheters [51,52] or other needle interventions [53] have been explored. Furthermore, AR has the potential to aid novice health care workers or untrained personnel in performing and interpreting complex examinations such as ultrasound [54,55] or electrocardiography [56] (Fig. 5.5F).

Clinical application of AR in these scenarios is usually less critical than within the OR, since they are more tolerant of errors caused by device or system failures. Nonetheless, for procedures where guidance is not absolutely necessary, the benefits of AR must outweigh the cost of additional hardware components and work steps AR systems usually come with. Therefore, their contribution to the clinical routine has yet to be validated [15].

3.2 Medical AR displays

The type of display used for medical AR applications does not only determine the way augmented data is presented to the user, but also has a major influence on precision and practicality of a system. An exemplary overview of medical display choices is shown in Fig. 5.6.

3.2.1 World space displays

World localized VST displays in the form of stationary monitors with additional tracked cameras have long been the most widely used technology in medical AR [23]. Aside from using a conventional camera to capture the scene, live images from tracked medical devices can be augmented directly. A notable example is the Camera Augmented Mobile C-arm (CamC) introduced in 1999 by Navab et al. [57]. Their first system allows the overlay of X-ray images from a mobile C-arm and optical images from a camera in real-time. CamC has since been extended by numerous capabilities and is one of the few AR systems,

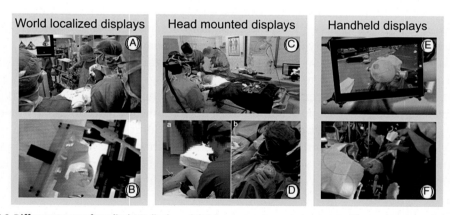

FIGURE 5.6 Different types of medical AR displays. (A) A laparoscopic surgery supported by a conventional world localized AR system using a 2D monitor. The laparoscopic video is augmented with pre-surgical planning data but still, the surgeons must look away from the patient for navigation. (B) An optical see-through, world localized display shows a surface rendering of an anatomical structure directly overlaid with the patient. (C) A tethered head-worn display is used during orthopaedic surgery. (D) The HoloLens, an optical see-through HMD, is emerging as a popular display choice for medical applications, as shown here for vascular surgery. (E) A handheld tablet computer is used for pre-operative visualization of a brain tumor, and (F) A handheld projector, developed by Gavaghan et al. [80], displays navigation information directly on the patient's skin surface. *Part A: Image adapted from Ref. [61]; Part B: Image adopted from Ref. [135], published under CC BY 4.0 license; Part C: Image adopted from Ref. [15]; Part D: Image adopted from Ref. [71], published under CC BY 4.0 license; Part E: Image adopted from Ref. [79]; Part F: Image courtesy of Kate Gerber, University of Bern.*

which have successfully translated into clinical practice [48]. In another example, the Intraoperative Brain Imaging System (IBIS) by Drouin et al. [58] allows the augmentation of traditional navigation information with ultrasound images captured by a tracked probe and a live video from the surgical site, fusing all information within one view [59]. In particular, minimally invasive procedures, such as laparoscopy or endoscopy have been an active focus of AR research, as the loss of direct vision inherent to these interventions can be partially compensated by augmenting the camera images with pre-interventional planning. For examples, the reader is referred to reviews by Bernhardt et al. [23] or Linte et al. [61]. AR-supported laparoscopy tools are also commercially available, for example, the NeoChord system (NeoChord, Minnetonka, MN, United States). However, all these set-ups have the common limitation of not offering immersive in situ visualization. Virtual data, even though fused with the reality captured by a camera, is displayed on external monitors, and therefore, is still diverting the physician's attention away from the patient. Moreover, conventional monitors do not support stereoscopic vision, reducing the visualization possibilities to 2D. An example is given in Fig. 5.6A.

World localized OST solutions do not have this limitation. Such so called AR windows typically use half-silvered mirrors for an overlay of imaging with the live patient. For example, an integral videography (IV) device for medical applications, as shown in Fig. 5.6B), was developed by Liao et al. [62]. IV systems reconstruct points stereoscopically in space using a micro convex lens array. Recent applications of IV overlay devices are reported by Ma et al. [47,63], where CT imaging is fused with the patient in support of pedicle screw and dental implant placement. Such systems usually suffer from inferior image quality in comparison to other displays and require bulky stationary infrastructure directly between physician and patient, possibly blocking the interventional site.

Similarly, projector-based systems enable situ visualization directly on the patient, but without a device amidst patient and doctor. An advantage of projector-based displays is that virtual content can be seen by multiple people at once, allowing for easy collaboration. However, projector-based AR suffers from limitations in terms of image quality, and generally only works in darker environments, which is often not realizable in a medical context. Furthermore, projecting data on irregular, deformable tissue, such as a patient's outer anatomy, is challenging since it requires dynamic adjustment of the data to avoid distortions.

3.2.2 Head mounted displays

Compared to world space displays, HMDs have the advantage of not cluttering the complex medical environment with too many additional components and not blocking the physician's access to the patient in any way. Head-worn operating binoculars, a special case of OST-HMDs, were amongst the first medical AR displays explored by Roberts et al. in the late 1980s [1]. Their system enabled the superimposition of planning data with the optical imagery as seen through the binoculars. The augmentation of the surgeon's view through operating binoculars or microscopes has since found its way into commercial surgical microscopes, such as the Zeiss Kinevo (Carl Zeiss AG, Oberkochen, Germany) or the Leica ARveo (Leica Camera AG, Wetzlar, Germany). Such systems are now routinely used, especially in the fields of neurosurgery, dentistry, and otorhinolaryngology, just to name a few. Augmented operating microscopes, therefore, present an example of a successful integration of AR into the clinical routine. Nonetheless, their field of application is limited to microsurgical procedures.

One of the first VST-HMDs, designed specifically for medical purposes, was the "Reality Augmentation for Medical Procedures" (RAMP) system introduced by Sauer et al. in the early 2000s [64,65]. Aside from two stereoscopic color cameras, the RAMP VST-HMD included a separate IR camera, which was able to detect retro-reflective markers for inside-out tracking and registration. Originally proposed for needle guidance, RAMP has found its way into many experimental applications in the medical domain and was used to study perceptual and visualization difficulties in medical AR [66–68].

With the recent improvements in mobile computing, consumer-grade HMDs have gained considerable popularity in the medical domain. State-of-the-art VST displays, such as the Oculus Rift, are still used in medicine [69], however, the focus has shifted towards OST-HMDs. This shift was largely caused by the introduction of the HoloLens in 2016. Since then, numerous experimental systems for the HoloLens have been described in a large range of medical specialties. Examples include orthopedics [46,70], angiology [51,71] (see also Fig. 5.6D), neurosurgery [72,73], pathology [74], and critical care [75], just to name a few. Furthermore, the HoloLens found its application in commercial medical solutions such as OpenSight (Novarad, American Fork, UT, United States), which has recently been FDA approved [76]. OST-HMDs are usually preferred to VST-HMDs in medical scenarios, since the physician wearing it is not completely separated from his or her real surroundings and thus, can still safely navigate within the environment in case of device failures. In a safety critical environment, such as the operating room, this is of utmost importance. Unfortunately, current OST-HMDs still provide insufficient precision and latency for many interesting clinical applications such as IGS [15]. Furthermore, limited rendering capabilities result in restrictions to the level of detail of virtual content, which is also detrimental for medical applications, were small details can have a large impact on decision-making. Promising hardware such as the HoloLens 2 or specifically developed displays for the medical sector, such as Augmedics xvision (Augmedics, Arlington Heights, IL, United States), might overcome these limitations in the future, affirming the status of OST-HMDs as the new gold standard for medical AR.

3.2.3 Handheld displays

Handheld AR systems are less popular in the medical domain, since they occupy the hands of the user, impeding the physician's interaction with the patient or with interventional tools. Therefore, it's applications are focused on training and education [77], the evaluation of surgical outcomes [78] or pre-operative visualization [79], mostly using tablet computers as displays, as exemplary shown in Fig. 5.6E. A handheld, portable projector system for medical applications was developed by Gavaghan et al. [80] (Fig. 5.6F), and a similar system was employed for neurosurgical navigation by Tabrizi et al. [81].

3.3 Registration and tracking in medical AR

The choice of registration and tracking technique plays a fundamental role in medical AR. Obviously, many medical procedures, such as image-guided interventions, have very high demands in terms of accuracy and are not tolerant to lag or loss of tracking. For convincing in situ visualization, accurate image-to-patient registration is absolutely necessary to profit from its potential benefits. At the same time, the tracking modality should be simple enough to not add undue technical complexity to already complicated workflows.

Marker-based AR systems are still dominating in current research, as they are more straightforward to implement and usually more precise than marker-less systems. Outside-in tracking of retro-reflective IR markers is a very popular technique applicable to both registration and tracking. It integrates well with all display types, as demonstrated in example for IV displays [47], world space monitor setups [58], handheld devices [79] and HMDs [82]. The obvious advantage of this method is that the same technology for tracking is used in the majority of commercial navigation systems, such as the Brainlab Curve or the Medtronic Stealth Station. Since such systems are already well integrated in the clinical routine, repurposing them for AR might ease the translation of such systems from research to the clinic. A drawback of this tracking modality is, however, that a constant line of sight between the tracking camera and the tracked objects needs to be maintained. Especially for complex setups with multiple tracked targets (e.g., the patient, the AR device, and surgical instruments), this constraint restricts the freedom of movement of the physician. Surgical navigation systems using electromagnetic tracking instead of IR do not suffer from this limitation but have proven to be less reliable due to interferences from ferromagnetic or conductive objects within the OR.

Inside-out tracking of markers alleviates the line-of-sight constraint by eliminating the need to track the AR device. Most often, it is performed by tracking planar fiducials using standard visible light cameras integrated in mobile devices such as smartphones and tablets [83,84] or HMDs [45,75,85,86]. A shortcoming of all marker-based approaches for registration is that the attachment of a marker or fiducial to the patient usually requires an invasive procedure, since they need to be fixed on rigid tissue such as bone to avoid unwanted shifts caused by tissue deformation. To enable in situ visualization, the markers need to be also visible in the virtual imaging data, and their position in relation to the patient's anatomy needs to be calibrated manually. This requires time and human as well as technical resources while limiting usability, therefore making the usage of such systems only justifiable for complex surgical procedures, were accurate image-guided navigation is absolutely necessary.

An alternative to using fiducial markers for registration is the utilization of natural anatomical landmarks. During anatomy education, medical students learn to identify a large variety of such landmarks in all parts of the body and in corresponding medical imaging, which allows for a point-based matching to achieve registration. However, since the automatic detection of such points is difficult, this registration strategy usually requires manual input, in example by digitizing the landmarks through touching them with tracked tools [51,87–89]. A progression of this technique are surface-based registration methods, where instead of a few points, parts of the patients' skin surface are captured and registered to the skin surface extracted from pre-interventional imaging through standard surface registration algorithms, such as Iterative Closest Point (ICP) [90]. Brainlab has commercialized this technique with their z-touch, a laser pointer which can be used to capture the patients' outer anatomy. In research, other setups to capture the 3D representation of the patient have been explored, for example, TOF depth sensors [91–93] or stereo cameras [94–96]. A common drawback of surface-based methods is that they only provide a solution for registration, not racking. The devices which capture the 3D representation and the AR device need to be calibrated to a common reference frame to achieve a dynamic overlay, which usually, again, requires the introduction of markers and/or navigation systems. This results in a quite substantial technical setup, which furthermore requires manual calibration steps, which is an important impeding factor when it comes to clinical usability and acceptance.

All approaches described earlier perform rigid registration, that is, estimate the 6DOF pose of the real object (e.g., the patient) to transform the virtual content accordingly. In the medical domain, the target anatomy can only be considered as rigid in some areas, while in others, one is usually confronted with soft tissue. This tissue is subject to deformation and movement from physiological sources such as breathing and heartbeat, the interventional or surgical procedure itself, or gravity. Tissue deformation needs to be considered in image-to-patient registration for many applications, especially endoscopic and laparoscopic interventions [60]. Non-rigid registration algorithms usually rely on intraoperatively captured data, either for using it directly for augmentation [59], or for updating a 3D patient model with the acquired data [97]. However, more research in the area of real-time online 3D modeling is needed to fully address this challenge [15].

3.4 Visualization of medical data in AR

The overarching goal of an AR visualization of medical data is to support the physicians' decision-making process, without overwhelming them. Clinicians are usually accustomed to conventional radiographs presented on 2D monitors, where medical data is visualized in 2D, in the form of orthogonal slices through the image volume (axial, sagittal, and coronal planes), or, sometimes, oblique reformats, so called multi-planar reformations. In the case of AR visualization, they are confronted with a more complex 3D situation. Furthermore, the visualization of virtual content must not occlude the real view too much and should not distract from the patient.

To preserve the clinically established 2D view, slice rendering has also been employed in medical AR systems [98,99]. This technique has, of course, the drawback that data is only shown in selected planes. Hence, given an AR display, 3D visualization is becoming more widely used, mostly in the form of 3D surface rendering. For surface rendering, tissue has to be segmented and converted to polygons prior to visualization, making it more complicated to establish a workflow. These polygons can be visualized as dense surfaces, but other representations, such as wireframes or contours, can be derived from them. In contrast, direct volume rendering offers superior image quality and does not require surface extraction before visualization [68]. However, performance requirements of volume rendering can still not be easily addressed with mobile hardware, such as HMDs.

Aside from the form of data representation, the technique to fuse real and virtual plays a large role in the visualization of medical data in AR. In a complex medical context, the implementation of advanced visualization effects such as lightning and shadows might not be feasible, but depth cues from correct occlusion handling and context-aware visualization can have a large influence on the perception of medical data [68]. Depth perception is especially important to infer information about spatial relations between anatomic and pathologic landmarks, obtain a size estimate of or a path to target structures. Phantom rendering-based occlusion handling for medical AR was already described in very early work by State et al. [2,100], where cutaway visualization is used for AR-supported, ultrasound-guided needle biopsies. Pauly et al. [101] developed a learning-based method for identifying objects in the surgical scene and medical imaging data and building a fused image based on the physician's preferences, as seen in Fig. 5.7A. Bichlmeier et al. described the first F + C visualization specifically for medical applications [67], which is shown in Fig. 5.7B). They enumerate several conditions for effective in situ visualization, including a non-restricted view of the target anatomy, concealing occluding anatomy and focusing on the region of interest, and an integration of virtual content, which allows an intuitive perception of spatial relations. Their approach was later extended for volume rendering using stereoscopic visualization on an HMD [68] (Fig. 5.7C). The same group also studied the concept of "Magic Mirrors" for medical AR visualization, a technique which allows the physician to use a virtual mirror to look at target anatomy from different perspectives [102]. Lerotic et al. [103] proposed an "inverse realism" technique similar to F + C, by superimposing strong features of the AR occluded surface with the virtual content, displayed in Fig. 5.7D). Hansen et al. [104] utilized illustrative contour rendering techniques to create a sense of perspective on a 2D display.

FIGURE 5.7 Different strategies for improving depth perception in medical AR. (A) By identifying relevant objects in the scene and combining them in a meaningful way, occlusions can be handled correctly [101]. (B) Focus and context visualization as introduced by Bichlmeier et al. [67]. (C) The technique was also implemented on a head worn display [68]. (D) Inverse realism accentuates strong features of the real object, while still focusing on the virtual content to obtain depth cues [103].

3.5 Requirements and challenges

In this chapter, we have shown that the feasibility of AR within a medical environment has been studied by a considerable number of research projects. However, it is also evident that few AR systems have successfully been implemented in actual clinical practice, and even fewer systems are commercially available. Demanding requirements and unique challenges still preclude the adoption of AR systems in medicine.

3.5.1 Accuracy and reliability of tracking and registration

Even though remarkable technological advances were made in the past years, the implementation of medical AR systems still faces major technical challenges. In particular, the demands in accuracy and reliability of calibration, registration and tracking are still not straightforward to address. While medical applications have the advantage of usually being carried out in a relatively small, closed, and controlled environment, they still have unique demands in terms of lightning and arrangement of devices, which can have an adverse influence on visual tracking. Consequently, within a clinical setting, one is often confronted with a trade-off between accuracy, invasiveness, and usability [5].

Surgical navigation systems already deliver sub-millimeter precision and real-time interactivity, and therefore, many research projects focus on integrating AR solutions with these already well-established devices. However, a typical AR system requires the addition of several components, such as image capturing devices and displays, which have to seamlessly integrate with the tracking technology. Evidently, each system component contributes to the overall error and latency. This chain of components influencing each other also convolutes the calculation of the overall error and reliability of the system. It is desirable to perform an online computation of the current system error, so the physician is always aware of the accuracy of the information currently presented to him [5]. Aside from that, multi-component systems might require lengthy set up times and manual calibration procedures, which require additional time and human resources. It is, therefore, desirable to develop systems requiring minimal components and minimal technical knowledge to set up, while still preserving the tracking and registration accuracy delivered by high-end devices.

Although advances in mobile computing have made wearable and handheld devices more powerful, current state-of-the-art hardware is often still not able to meet the high demands medical AR has in tracking and registration. The HoloLens, which we have already shown to be one of the most popular devices for medical AR right now, still has deficiencies in terms of robustness and latency of its built-in SLAM tracking [105,106] or in the stability of registered virtual content [107]. Even after accurate registration, virtual content can be misaligned because of these shortcomings, hampering the implementation of the HoloLens within the OR for a real clinical application.

3.5.2 Visualization and representation

While the effective, natural visualization of medical data in AR was quite actively studied in the past, recently, research focus has shifted again towards tracking and registration issues. Nevertheless, the visualization problem has not yet been fully solved.

We summarized a number of strategies to overcome the problem of incorrect depth perception in medical AR. However, most of the discussed visualization techniques can only be applied to VST displays in a straightforward way, because they usually require a manipulation of the reality, as captured as images by a video camera. Since for OST and projector displays the appearance of the real scene cannot be altered, producing depth cues or realistic lightning and shadows through visualization techniques is much more difficult. In this regard, more research into display technology itself might be necessary to achieve the desired effects

But not only the "how" is important when thinking about medical data visualization, also the "what" and "when" should be prime concerns, as pointed out by Kersten-Oertel et al. [108]. To determine what content is required by the physicians in the current situation, without overwhelming them with redundant information, some sort of context aware augmentation is necessary [109]. Ideally, an AR system would automatically recognize the situation the physician is in and adapt the virtual content accordingly. Current advances in machine learning, especially deep neural networks for action recognition and object detection, will be invaluable aids to realize such systems in the future.

3.5.3 Acceptance and usability in the clinic
The acceptance, usability, and interoperability of medical AR systems within the clinic are, unfortunately, often overlooked by researchers, even though they are arguably among the most important factors in clinical translation [110].

Proposed systems often come with overburdened setups, lengthy calibration, and unintuitive user interfaces and data representations, which cause health care professionals to reject those new technologies. The actual clinical benefit and utility are often insufficiently addressed in research projects. Most studies focus on a validation of their system in terms of objective measurements, such as accuracy or latency, usually performed ex vivo or on phantoms. However, such metrics alone do not guarantee a clinical benefit to the physician or to the patient. A closer collaboration between engineers and medical staff is required to transition medical AR systems from proof-of-concept prototypes to medical devices, by taking into account clinical needs and constrains enforced by the clinical routine [111].

4 Augmented reality in oral and cranio-maxillofacial surgery
4.1 Traditional CAS procedures and their limitations

The concept of computer-assisted surgeries in the head and neck area were first described in the late 1980s [112]. Since then, surgical navigation systems have been implemented in the clinical routine in different subspecialties of OCMS, such as trauma surgery, foreign body removal, tumor resection, reconstructive surgery and orthognathic surgery [113]. The oral and cranio-maxillofacial complex houses delicate anatomy and critical organs, such as the brain, eyes, larynx, and oral cavity. Surgical interventions in this region have, therefore, high demands in precision, to guarantee an outcome for the patient, which is both functionally and aesthetically optimal. With a technical system accuracy in the

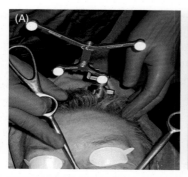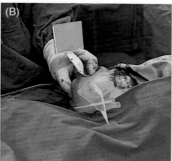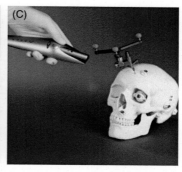

FIGURE 5.8 Image-to-patient registration strategies in OCMS. (A) In traditional navigated OCMS, a skull-fixed marker, here using retro-reflective spheres for tracking with an infrared sensor, are used for registration. (B) Alternatively, using patient-specific occlusal splints for non-invasive marker fixation has been proposed. (C) Markerless registration, for example, using a laser scanner to capture the outer anatomy of the patient has also been suggested. However, to track the movement of the patient, a marker is still required. *Part B: Image adapted from Ref. [141]; Part C: Image adapted from Refs. [117].*

sub-millimeter range and an average intra-operative error of maximal two millimeters [113], current navigation systems can satisfy this demanding criteria, making OCMS more precise and predictable and leading to a more optimized workflow for the surgeon, and an improved outcome for the patient. In terms of tracking technology, both optical and electromagnetic navigation systems are still commonly used in OCMS clinics [114].

The benefits of IGS do, however, come at a cost. Conventional navigation increases the complexity of a surgery. The first challenge is image-to-patient registration. Most often, navigated OCMS requires the fixation of fiducial markers to the skull as seen in Fig. 5.8A, which is invasive. Alternatively, the non-invasive usage of an occlusal dental splint to hold reference markers has been proposed [115], see Fig. 5.8B, which is, however, much more prone to error due to the movable temporomandibular joints and the small operating field. Additionally, as patient-specific dental casts have to be prepared for the surgery, it increases planning and preparation time. After marker placement, specialized pre-operative scans must be acquired, which will later be referenced with the patient in the OR and used for image guidance. This process requires time and human resources and therefore, must be planned several days in advance. At the same time, in case of CT scanning which is the most commonly used imaging modality in OCMS [116], increases radiation dose for the patient in a critical area. Marker-less methods, for example, using a laser scanner to digitize the patients skin surface as in Fig. 5.8C, have been evaluated as an alternative [117], but require the patient to remain stationary and are, therefore, only applicable to selected applications. Since AR systems usually require the addition of displays and capturing devices to the setup, making them even more complex, registration is still an interesting area of research in IGS in general and AR-guided IGS in particular. Reliable, precise registration and tracking of the patient, which does not involve invasiveness and limits manual interaction to a minimum, would be most desirable.

Another limitation arises from the fact that IGS systems usually render medical imaging and planning data in 2D on an external monitor, while the anatomical structures and surgical interactions themselves are three-dimensional. This forces the surgeon to divide his attention between navigation system and operation site, and furthermore requires complex hand-eye coordination, which can only be acquired during years of training. In situ visualization using AR technology could alleviate this problem by transferring imaging data directly in the same reference space as the patient, improving the spatial perception of targeted anatomies and the coordination of 3D interactions.

4.2 History and state of the art of AR in OCMS

The work in AR for OCMS was pioneered by the group of Wagner et al. from the University of Vienna in the mid-1990s. They used the ARTMA Virtual Patient system (ARTMA Biomedical, Vienna, Austria), an AR system based on a VST-HMD for capturing and augmenting the surgical scene, and a tracking system based on electromagnetic sensors, fixed on the craniofacial bone or an occlusal splint, for image-to-patient registration and tracking. The ARTMA system supported several means of visualizing medical data, such as surface renderings of anatomical structures, task-oriented geometrical primitives, and numerical information. They published several case studies of different OCMS procedures, including foreign body removal and dental implant placement [118], intra-oral tumor resection [4], osteotomy [119], and temporomandibular joint movement measurement [120]. Furthermore, they tested the feasibility of their system for teleassistance and telenavigation [121]. While their system was reported to increase the perceived safety of the procedures by surgeons and, in some cases, reduced the operative time, pre-operative planning, and preparation time was increased significantly. Although they did not provide measures about system accuracy, they state that the tracking and registration methodology did not meet the requirements in precision and reliability for some procedures, and their system can, therefore, only be used for selected cases.

Birkfeller et al. [122] designed both an augmented, head-mounted operating microscope called Varioscope AR, as well as a navigation system specifically designed for implantology [123], which is based on optical tracking of active infrared light-emitting diodes (LEDs). They combined their devices to create an AR system for the support of skull-base surgery [124], by attaching LED markers to the HMD, the patient, and tracked tools. In their study, they showed that surgeons were able to localize target structures with high accuracy when supported with a rendering of pre-operative planning data. A challenge their system is confronted with is the relatively low refresh rate of 15–50 Hz and the precondition of a complicated, manual calibration procedure. Nonetheless, since they integrated their system into an already well-accepted device, they report superior clinical agreement of physicians as to comparable systems.

Around the same time, Salb et al. developed Intraoperative Presentation of Surgical Planning and Simulation Results (INPRES) [125], using a stereoscopic, see-through HMD, at the Universities of Karlsruhe and Heidelberg. Similar to previously described systems, it is based on the combination of an HMD, at that time the commercially available Sony Glasstron LDI (Sony Corporation, Tokyo, Japan) and an optical infrared tracking system for outside-in tracking. Image-to-patient registration is realized by digitizing landmarks, marked by titanium screws implanted in the patient's head or on a dental splint, using a tracked pointing device. Although their system showed promising results in terms of tracking and registration accuracy, they report some limitations in terms of hardware, especially concerning the resolution and image quality of the HMD. Manual display calibration and registration are other drawbacks of their approach.

The same group of collaborators between Karlsruhe and Heidelberg later presented an alternative system, which was the first to use surface-based registration for AR in OCMS [126,127]. More precisely, a structured light-based surface scanner was used to capture the patient's outer anatomy prior to intervention, and this 3D model was registered with pre-operative CT or MRI for an initial registration. Still, skull-attached IR markers and a corresponding navigation system were used to track the patient's movement during surgery. One advantage of this registration scheme is that a pre-operative scan showing the IR fiducials is not necessary, therefore, they need to be placed only during the primary surgery and radiation dose for the patient is confined. Instead of displaying data on an HMD, a projector-based display modality was used to show task-oriented geometrical primitives, such as osteotomy lines and tumor margins. The group reported on the successful application of their system in selected cases of tumor resection and reconstructive surgery in the oral-craniomaxillofacial complex and quantify the system error with around one mm. A notable limitation is the deformation of projected images on non-rigid, irregular soft tissue during the surgery.

Mischkowski et al. first described the clinical use of X-Scope (Brainlab, Heimstetten, Germany), which their group co-developed, in 2006 [128]. X-Scope is based on a handheld VST, integrated with an IR-based navigation system for tracking. Registration is accomplished point-based through anatomical landmarks and a tracked pointer. The system supports the visualization of surface renderings and was used in orthognathic surgery, specifically the translocation of bony segments, in five cases. With an average deviation of 9.7 mm between real and virtual objects, X-Scope was not precise enough for IGS, however, authors attribute usability as a control device to their system. The same setup was used for 46 orthognathic interventions by Zinser et al., reported in comparison to several conventional techniques in 2013 [129,130]. They also experimented with stereotactic image-to-patient registration but found that skull-fixed fiducials were more reliable. System accuracy was improved to around 1.7 mm. Overall, by usage of the AR system, operating time was 60 min longer than conventionally, but the technique using AR navigation was described to be superior to conventional protocols for specific clinical requirements, leading to favorable outcomes for the patients.

At the University of Tokyo, an IV-based display modality using a half-silvered mirror for medical augmented reality was developed [131]. This display was first integrated into an AR system for oral surgery by Tran et al. [132], where it was combined with an optical navigation system for instrument and patient tracking. They experimented with the overlay of geometric information, such as surgical paths and instrument positions, as well as textual information for situations where small differences are difficult to perceive trough pure visualization. Their system was evaluated in a hole-drilling task on a phantom and sub-millimeter accuracy between planning and outcome was reported. Geometric primitives were rendered 10 frames per second (fps). The stationary setup between physician and patient might, however, limit the workspace of the surgeons, and the response time of the system was still an area of improvement. The same setup was later used by Suenaga et al. [49] for displaying surface renderings of the maxillary and mandibular jaw on a human volunteer.

The same group from the University of Tokyo developed a tracking methodology based on a stereo camera setup for markerless image-to-patient registration in dental implantology [133]. Their principle is based on tracking the 3D contour of the patients' teeth and matching it to a pre-operatively acquired teeth model using an ICP algorithm. Wang and Suenaga combined this tracking and registration paradigm with the previously described IV display [134,135]. Further improvements in terms of rendering and implementation were realized, resulting in an average system accuracy of 0.9–1.1 mm and a rendering frame rate of 50–60 fps. This system is the first AR system for OCMS which performs marker-free, real-time registration, and tracking. Per contra, since the teeth contours of the patient must be fully visible for this tracking strategy, its applications are limited to dental surgery. Later, Wang et al. adapted their tracking and registration paradigm based on the teeth contour to work with monoscopic cameras, using a method by Ulrich et al. [136] for initial registration and an ICP for refinement, and implemented both the stereoscopic and monoscopic version in a VST AR application for implantology [137,138].

Zhu et al. based their registration strategy for AR in orthognathic surgery on a non-invasively placed occlusal dental splint fixed on the mandible [139]. They used an image-based marker, trackable with the ARToolKit software (ARToolworks, Seattle, WA, United States) and a standard visible light camera. The system supported 15 interventions by displaying pre-operatively planned osteotomy lines and a surface model of the mandible in relation to the patient anatomy. Unfortunately, they do not report on the used display modality or system performance. The setup was subsequently used for surgical navigation in orbital hypertelorism surgery [140], were they report an average deviation of 2.2 mm between pre-operative design and actual osteotomy outcome. Qu et al., from the same university, describe a similar approach for the treatment of hemifacial microsomia in 10 cases [141], but achieve a smaller deviation of around 1.4 mm between the pre-operative plan and actual outcome. They conclude that AR can aid in mandibular distraction osteogenesis to generate an aesthetic outcome for the patient. Nonetheless, they also report on deficiencies of the system in terms of user friendliness. Han et al. also report the application of this system in synostotic plagiocephaly surgery of seven patients in 2019 and report sufficient accordance between the pre-surgical plan and the surgical outcome [142].

In 2016 and 2017, this group reported the integration of their dental splint-based registration strategy with a head worn AR display, performing drilling tasks during mandibular angle split osteotomies, a robot-assisted surgery [143,144], and to display inferior alveolar nerve bundles during orthognathic surgeries [145]. All these works have the common drawback of being heavily reliant of the manufacture and rigid fixation of an occlusal splint, which is reliant on stable occlusal relations and excludes edentulous patients from a treatment with these systems, and prolongs preparation time for the interventions.

Another projector-based AR system was introduced in 2012 by Gavaghan et al. [146]. Their contribution is the usage of a portable projector device, which should reduce overhead and intrusiveness, while increasing workspace flexibility, compared to stationary projector systems. Once again, an IR-based tracking system is used to establish a correspondence between target and projector, as well as target and imaging data by using a point matching-based registration strategy. They used their overlay device to project a tumor, the facial nerve, and the mandible onto the patient for guidance during mandible tumor resection. An accuracy evaluation revealed a mean projection accuracy of 1.3 mm, while a refresh rate of 50–60 Hz could be maintained for surface rendering of anatomical structures.

A markerless VST system, using a stationary stereo camera setup, together with a movable camera, and a conventional monitor as a display, was introduced by Lee et al. in 2012 [94]. Similar to other surface-based registration strategies, they reconstruct the patients' skin surface from matching stereo frames and use an ICP-based algorithm to register it with pre-interventional imaging. After initial registration, the patient needs to remain stationary. The movable camera is tracked using an ARToolKit marker. The proposed system is capable of rendering surface data and orthogonal CT planes with an average target registration error of 3.3 mm. Later, they replaced the stereo camera in their system with a TOF depth sensor, the Kinect (Microsoft Corporation, Redmond, WA, United States) [99]. However, the system accuracy did not improve significantly, and a clinical application of the system has not yet been demonstrated.

In 2014, a VST-HMD-based system for LeFort 1 orthognathic surgery was introduced by Badiali et al. [147]. As a registration and tracking strategy, they implemented an inside-out paradigm with a set of visible markers implanted into the skull of a phantom and point-based registration. Therefore, they do not require external infrastructure for tracking. Overall, a mean system error of 1.7 mm was determined in vitro using a phantom.

Another VST-HMD application, this time for implantology, was proposed by Lin et al. [148]. Similar to other groups, they use an occlusal splint with an ARToolkit marker, tracked inside-out with a conventional visible light camera mounted on top of the headset, as a registration strategy. They projected pre-operational planning data for dental implant surgery within the field of view of the surgeons and achieved a sub-millimeter accuracy between planning data and outcome in an in vitro experiment.

Profeta et al. experimented with the application of AR to guide freehand Single Photon Emission Computed Tomography (SPECT) in sentinel lymph node biopsy of head and neck cancer patients [149]. A conventional monitor and camera setup, as well as outside-in IR-based optical tracking for co-referencing the SPECT probe and patient, were used to overlay textual elements and 3D surface renderings showing SPECT hotspots on the patient. The same principles were later evaluated for navigated surgery of head and neck tumors [150].

A case report of the usage of an augmented operating microscope for intra-orbital tumor resection was reported by Scolozzi and Bijlenga in 2017 [151]. An IR-based navigation system was used to track the microscope, and the microscope itself served as a reference coordinate system correlating the surgical site and the pre-operative plan. A surface rendering of the tumor was overlaid within the microscope to grant a better insight into its deep extension.

Wang et al. performed a cadaver study using AR to guide temporomandibular joint arthrocentesis [152]. A projector-camera system and an image-based registration method based on the homography between camera and projector were employed. The entire system is stationary, thus no inside-out or outside-in tracking was implemented. Another drawback is the manual calibration procedure between camera and projector image, which is time intensive and error prone. It is unclear whether the reported accuracy of an average of 3.5 mm is sufficient for a clinical application of the system.

Recently, Ahn et al. presented a system for Le Fort 1 osteotomy using a stationary monitor based VST modality. Their system uses image markers, an intermediate splint for attaching a marker cube to the patient and a stereo camera for outside-in optical tracking. By using this stereo setup, they were able to achieve high system accuracy with registration errors below 0.5 mm, making it comparable to commercial navigation solutions. However, since their visualization is still based on a monitor, it does not alleviate the problem of the surgeon having to divert his attention between surgical site and navigation information.

Pietruski et al. described a proof of concept study of an OST-HMD based system for mandibular resection in 2019 [153]. They use the well-established, outside-in tracked configuration with an IR tracking camera and rigidly fixed markers on the HMD and the patient. In their study, they performed an in vitro comparison between AR-guided osteotomies and the conventional procedure using cutting guides, and found that both varieties lead to similar outcomes, however, improved hand-eye coordination and orientation within the operating field were reported by surgeons using the AR system.

Finally, our group, in cooperation between the Medical and Technical Universities of Graz, started to develop an AR system for OCMS in 2018. We were the first to use the HoloLens for supporting OCMS for the immersive visualization of imaging data from head and neck cancer patients. Our main idea is to develop an AR system which is comfortable for both the patient and the surgeon, thus neither requiring invasive markers, nor excessive hardware infrastructure or complicated manual calibrations. Pepe et al. described an initial approach using facial landmark detection to determine the orientation and the HoloLens' built-in spatial mapping module and ray casting to estimate the 3D position of the patient, in order to overlay pre-interventional imaging data accurately with him [154,155]. However, due to the coarseness of the spatial map built by the HoloLens, the registration error was high, especially in the back-front dimension, and the procedure required some manual adjustments of the imaging data. In a second approach by Gsaxner et al., we therefore utilize the HoloLens' TOF depth sensor to reconstruct a more accurate, finer representation of the patients face, and relate it with information from its self-localization capabilities for improved image-to-patient registration [44]. Our current system supports rendering of surface meshes and orthogonal 2D imaging data, to support clinicians in target localization during surgery planning (a video is available under [156]). To facilitate the development of AR solutions for OCMS, we furthermore published our dataset including PET-CT scans and 3D models of 12 head and neck cancer patients, which can be used for low-cost phantom creation and the implementation and evaluation of AR systems [157].

Acknowledgments

This work was supported by the Austrian Science Fund (FWF) KLI 678-B31: "enFaced: Virtual and Augmented Reality Training and Navigation Module for 3D-Printed Facial Defect Reconstructions." Furthermore, this work was supported by CAMed (COMET K-Project 871132), which is funded by the Austrian Federal Ministry of Transport, Innovation and Technology (BMVIT), and the Austrian Federal Ministry for Digital and Economic Affairs (BMDW), and the Styrian Business Promotion Agency (SFG). Moreover, the work was supported by TU Graz Lead Project (Mechanics, Modeling and Simulation of Aortic Dissection).

References

[1] D.W. Roberts, J.W. Strohbehn, J.F. Hatch, W. Murray, H. Kettenberger, A frameless stereotaxic integration of computerized tomographic imaging and the operating microscope, J. Neurosurg. 65 (4) (1986) 545–549.

[2] A. State, et al. Case study: observing a volume rendered fetus within a pregnant patient, Proc. Visual. (1994) 364–368.

[3] H. Fuchs, et al. Towards performing ultrasound-guided needle biopsies from within a head-mounted display,, Visual. Biomed. Comput. 1131 (1996) 591–600.

[4] A. Wagner, O. Ploder, G. Enislidis, M. Truppe, R. Ewers, Virtual image guided navigation in tumor surgery - technical innovation, J. Cranio-Maxillofac. Surg. 23 (5) (1995) 271–273.

[5] T. Sielhorst, M. Feuerstein, N. Navab, Advanced medical displays: A literature review of augmented reality, J. Disp. Technol. 4 (4) (2008) 451–467.

[6] M.A. Livingston, A. Dey, C. Sandor, B.H. Thomas, , Pursuit of 'X-Ray Vision' for Augmented Reality in Human Factors in Augmented Reality Environments, Springer, New York, 2013, pp. 67–107.

[7] M. Al-Sarraf, Treatment of locally advanced head and neck cancer: Historical and critical review, Cancer Control, vol. 9, SAGE Publications Inc, 2002, pp. 387–399 5.

[8] A.D. Nijmeh, N.M. Goodger, D. Hawkes, P.J. Edwards, M. McGurk, Image-guided navigation in oral and maxillofacial surgery, Br. J. Oral Maxillofac. Surg. 43 (4) (2005) 294–302.

[9] P. Milgram, F. Kishino, Taxonomy of mixed reality visual displays, IEICE Trans. Inf. Syst. E77-D (12) (1994) 1321–1329.

[10] R.T. Azuma, A survey of augmented reality (1997).

[11] L. Qian, A. Plopski, N. Navab, P. Kazanzides, Restoring the awareness in the occluded visual field for optical see-through head-mounted displays, IEEE Trans. Vis. Comput. Graph. 24 (11) (2018) 2936–2946.

[12] J. Grubert, Y. Itoh, K. Moser, J.E. Swan, A survey of calibration methods for optical see-through head-mounted displays, IEEE Trans. Vis. Comput. Graph. 24 (9) (2018) 2649–2662.

[13] D. Schmalstieg, T. Hollerer, Augmented Reality: Principles and Practice. Addison-Wesley Professional, 2016.

[14] M. Queisner, Medical screen operations: how head-mounted displays transform action and perception in surgical practice, MediaTropes 6 (1) (2016) 30–51.

[15] L. Chen, T.W. Day, W. Tang, N.W. John, Recent developments and future challenges in medical mixed reality, in: Proceedings of the International Symposium on Mixed and Augmented Reality (ISMAR), 2017, pp. 123–135.

[16] G. Badiali, et al. Review on augmented reality in oral and cranio-maxillofacial surgery: towards 'surgery-specific' head-up displays, IEEE Access. 8 (2020) 9015–59028.

[17] F. Zhou, H.B.L. Dun, M. Billinghurst, Trends in augmented reality tracking, interaction and display: A review of ten years of ISMAR, in: Proceedings of the International Symposium on Mixed and Augmented Reality (ISMAR), 2008, pp. 193–202.

[18] H. Durrant-Whyte, T. Bailey, Simultaneous localization and mapping: Part I, IEEE Robot. Autom. Mag. 13 (2) (2006) 99–108.

[19] J.E. Cutting, P.M. Vishton, Perceiving Layout and Knowing Distances in Perception of Space and Motion, Academic Press, 1995, pp. 69–117.

[20] D.E. Breen, R.T. Whitaker, E. Rose, M. Tuceryan, Interactive occlusion and automatic object placement for augmented reality, Comput. Graph. Forum 15 (3) (1996) 11–22.

[21] D. Kalkofen, E. Mendez, D. Schmalstieg, Interactive focus and context visualization for augmented reality, in: Proceedings of the International Symposium on Mixed and Augmented Reality (ISMAR), 2007, pp. 191–201.

[22] J. Krüger, J. Schneider, R. Westermann, ClearView: An interactive context preserving hotspot visualization technique, Trans. Vis. Comput. Graph. 12 (5) (2006) 941–948.

[23] M. Eckert, J.S. Volmerg, C.M. Friedrich, Augmented reality in medicine: Systematic and bibliographic review, J. Med. Internet Res. 21 (4) (2019).

[24] H.K. Wu, S.W.Y. Lee, H.Y. Chang, J.C. Liang, Current status, opportunities and challenges of augmented reality in education, Comput. Educ. 62 (2013) 41–49.

[25] K. Lee, Augmented reality in education and training, TechTrends 56 (2) (2012) 13–21 Springer.

[26] S. Küçük, S. Kapakin, Y. Göktaş, Learning anatomy via mobile augmented reality: Effects on achievement and cognitive load, Anat. Sci. Educ. 9 (5) (2016) 411–421.

[27] S.S. Jamali, M.F. Shiratuddin, K.W. Wong, C.L. Oskam, Utilising mobile-augmented reality for learning human anatomy, Procedia Soc. Behav. Sci. 197 (2015) 659–668.

[28] T. Nomura, et al. Characteristics predicting laparoscopic skill in medical students: nine years' experience in a single center, Surg. Endosc. 32 (1) (2018) 96–104.

[29] E.Z. Barsom, M. Graafland, M.P. Schijven, Systematic review on the effectiveness of augmented reality applications in medical training, Surg. Endosc. 30 (10) (2016) 4174–4183.

[30] L.R. Rochlen, R. Levine, A.R. Tait, First-person point-of-view-augmented reality for central line insertion training: a usability and feasibility study, Simul. Healthc. 12 (1) (2017) 57–62.

[31] C.T. Yeo, T. Ungi, A U-Thainual, R.C. Lasso, McGraw, G. Fichtinger, The effect of augmented reality training on percutaneous needle placement in spinal facet joint injections, Trans. Biomed. Eng. 58 (7) (2011) 2031–2037.

[32] S. Vikal, P U-Thainual, J.A. Carrino, I. Iordachita, G.S. Fischer, G. Fichtinger, Perk station-percutaneous surgery training and performance measurement platform, Comput. Med. Imaging Graph. 34 (1) (2010) 19–32.

[33] S. Hoermann, et al. Computerised mirror therapy with augmented reflection technology for early stroke rehabilitation: clinical feasibility and integration as an adjunct therapy, Disabil. Rehabil. 39 (15) (2017) 1503–1514.

[34] H.M. Hondori, M. Khademi, L. Dodakian, S.C. Cramer, C.V. Lopes, A spatial augmented reality rehab system for post-stroke hand rehabilitation, Stud. Health Technol. Inform. 184 (2013) 279–285.

[35] H. Mousavi Hondori, M. Khademi, L. Dodakian, A. McKenzie, C.V. Lopes, S.C. Cramer, Choice of human-computer interaction mode in stroke rehabilitation, Neurorehabil. Neural Repair 30 (3) (2016) 258–265.

[36] C. Timmermans, M. Roerdink, M.W. van Ooijen, C.G. Meskers, T.W. Janssen, P.J. Beek, Walking adaptability therapy after stroke: Study protocol for a randomized controlled trial, Trials 17 (1) (2016) 425.

[37] C. Colomer, R. Llorens, E. Noé, M. Alcañiz, Effect of a mixed reality-based intervention on arm, hand, and finger function on chronic stroke, J. Neuroeng. Rehabil. 13 (2016) 45.

[38] M. Ortiz-Catalan, N. Sander, M.B. Kristoffersen, B. Håkansson, R. Brånemark, Treatment of phantom limb pain (PLP) based on augmented reality and gaming controlled by myoelectric pattern recognition: A case study of a chronic PLP patient, Front. Neurosci. 8 (24) (2014).

[39] D. Mouraux, et al. 3D augmented reality mirror visual feedback therapy applied to the treatment of persistent, unilateral upper extremity neuropathic pain: a preliminary study, J. Man. Manip. Ther. 25 (3) (2017) 137–143.

[40] U. Mezger, C. Jendrewski, M. Bartels, Navigation in surgery, Langenbeck's Arch. Surgery 398 (4) (2013) 501–514.

[41] M. Kersten-Oertel, I.J. Gerard, S. Drouin, K. Petrecca, J.A. Hall, D.L. Collins, Towards augmented reality guided craniotomy planning in tumour resections. Lecture Notes Comput. Sci. 9805 (2016) 163–174.

[42] K. Abhari et al., Use of a mixed-reality system to improve the planning of brain tumour resections: Preliminary results. Lecture Notes Comput. Sci. 2013 (7815) 55–66.

[43] K.B. Soulami, E. Ghribi, Y. Labyed, M.N. Saidi, A. Tamtaoui, and N. Kaabouch, Mixed-reality aided system for glioblastoma resection surgery using microsoft hololens. IEEE Int. Conf. Electro Inf. Technol. 2019 (2019) 079–084.

[44] C. Gsaxner, A. Pepe, J. Wallner, D. Schmalstieg, J. Egger, Markerless image-to-face registration for untethered augmented reality, Head Neck Surgery (2019) 236–244.

[45] F. Müller, S. Roner, F. Liebmann, J.M. Spirig, P. Fürnstahl, M. Farshad, Augmented reality navigation for spinal pedicle screw instrumentation using intraoperative 3D imaging, Spine J. 20 (2019) 621–628.

[46] J.T. Gibby, S.A. Swenson, S. Cvetko, R. Rao, R. Javan, Head-mounted display augmented reality to guide pedicle screw placement utilizing computed tomography, Int. J. Comput. Assist. Radiol. Surgery 14 (3) (2019) 525–535 Springer International Publishing.

[47] L. Ma, Z. Zhao, F. Chen, B. Zhang, L. Fu, H. Liao, Augmented reality surgical navigation with ultrasound-assisted registration for pedicle screw placement: a pilot study, Int. J. Comput. Assist. Radiol. Surg. 12 (12) (2017) 2205–2215.

[48] N. Navab, S.-M. Heining, J. Traub, Camera augmented mobile C-Arm (CAMC): calibration, accuracy study, and clinical applications, IEEE Trans. Med. Imaging 29 (7) (2010).

[49] H. Suenaga, et al. Real-time in situ three-dimensional integral videography and surgical navigation using augmented reality: A pilot study, Int. J. Oral Sci. 5 (2) (2013) 98–102.

[50] F. Cosentino, N.W. John, J. Vaarkamp, An overview of augmented and virtual reality applications in radiotherapy and future developments enabled by modern tablet devices, J. Radiother. Pract. 13 (3.) (2014) 350–364 Cambridge University Press.

[51] I. Kuhlemann, M. Kleemann, P. Jauer, A. Schweikard, F. Ernst, Towards X-ray free endovascular interventions - using HoloLens for on-line holographic visualisation, Healthc. Technol. Lett. 4 (5) (2017) 184–187.

[52] S. Fumagalli, et al. Effects of a new device to guide venous puncture in elderly critically ill patients: results of a pilot randomized study, Aging Clin. Exp. Res. 29 (2) (2017) 335–339.

[53] Z. Baum, T. Ungi, A. Lasso, G. Fichtinger, Usability of a real-time tracked augmented reality display system in musculoskeletal injections, Medical Imaging 2017: Image-Guided Procedures, Robotic Interventions, and Modeling 10135 (2017) 101352T.

[54] Y. Xiao, et al. An augmented-reality system prototype for guiding transcranial Doppler ultrasound examination, Multimed. Tools Appl. 77 (21) (2018) 27789–27805.

[55] S. Tano et al., Simple augmented reality system for 3D ultrasonic image by see-through HMD and single camera and marker combination, in: Proceedings - IEEE-EMBS International Conference on Biomedical and Health Informatics: Global Grand Challenge of Health Informatics, BHI 2012, 2012, pp. 464–467.

[56] P. Bifulco, F. Narducci, R. Vertucci, P. Ambruosi, M. Cesarelli, M. Romano, Telemedicine supported by augmented reality: An interactive guide for untrained people in performing an ECG test, Biomed. Eng. Online 13 (1) (2014) 153.

[57] N. Navab, A. Bani-Kashemi, M. Mitschke, Merging visible and invisible: Two Camera-Augmented Mobile C-arm (CAMC) applications, in: Proceedings - 2nd IEEE and ACM International Workshop on Augmented Reality, IWAR 1999, 1999, pp. 134–141.

[58] S. Drouin, et al. IBIS: an OR ready open-source platform for image-guided neurosurgery, Int. J. Comput. Assist. Radiol. Surg. 12 (3) (2017) 363–378.

[59] I.J. Gerard, et al. Combining intraoperative ultrasound brain shift correction and augmented reality visualizations: a pilot study of eight cases, J. Med. Imag. 5 (2) (2018) 21210.

[60] S. Bernhardt, S.A. Nicolau, L. Soler, C. Doignon, The status of augmented reality in laparoscopic surgery as of 2016, Med. Image Anal. (2017).

[61] C.A. Linte, et al. On mixed reality environments for minimally invasive therapy guidance: Systems architecture, successes and challenges in their implementation from laboratory to clinic, Comput. Med. Imaging Graph. 37 (2) (2013) 83–97.

[62] H. Liao, N. Hata, S. Nakajima, M. Iwahara, I. Sakuma, T. Dohi, Surgical navigation by autostereoscopic image overlay of integral videography, IEEE Trans. Inf. Technol. Biomed. 8 (2) (2004) 114–121.

[63] L. Ma, et al. Augmented reality surgical navigation with accurate CBCT-patient registration for dental implant placement, Med. Biol. Eng. Comput. 57 (1) (2019) 47–57.

[64] F. Sauer, A. Khamene, B. Bascle, G.J. Rubino, A head-mounted display system for augmented reality image guidance: Towards clinical evaluation for iMRI-guided neurosurgery, Lect. Notes Comput. Sci. 2208 (2001) 707–716.

[65] F. Sauer, A. Khamene, S. Vogt, An augmented reality navigation system with a single-camera tracker: System design and needle biopsy phantom trial, Lect. Notes Comput. Sci. 2489 (2002) 116–124.

[66] J. Traub et al., Hybrid navigation interface for orthopedic and trauma surgery. Lect. Notes Comput. Sci. 4190 (2006) 373–380.

[67] C. Bichlmeier, F. Wimmer, S.M. Heining, N. Navab, Contextual anatomic mimesis: Hybrid in-situ visualization method for improving multi-sensory depth perception in medical augmented reality, in: 2007 6th IEEE and ACM International Symposium on Mixed and Augmented Reality, ISMAR, 2007.

[68] O. Kutter, et al. Real-time volume rendering for high quality visualization in augmented reality, Int. Work. Augment Environ. Med. Imaging Incl. Augment. Real. Comput. Surgeryncluding Augment. Real. Comput. Surg. (2008) 104–113.

[69] J. Jayender et al., A novel mixed reality navigation system for laparoscopy surgery. Lect. Notes Comput. Sci. 11073 (2018) 72–80.

[70] S. Andress, et al. On-the-fly augmented reality for orthopedic surgery using a multimodal fiducial, J. Med. Imaging 5 (02) (2018) 1.

[71] P. Pratt, et al. Through the HoloLens™ looking glass: augmented reality for extremity reconstruction surgery using 3D vascular models with perforating vessels, Eur. Radiol. Exp. 2 (1) (2018) 1–7.

[72] C. Karmonik, et al. Augmented reality with virtual cerebral aneurysms: a feasibility study, World Neurosurg. 119 (2018) e617–e622.

[73] F. Incekara, M. Smits, C. Dirven, A. Vincent, Clinical feasibility of a wearable mixed-reality device in neurosurgery, World Neurosurg. 118 (2018) e422–e427.

[74] M.G. Hanna, Augmented reality technology using microsoft hololens in anatomic pathology, Arch. Pathol. Lab. Med. 142 (2018) 638–644.

[75] E. Azimi et al., Evaluation of optical see-through head-mounted displays in training for critical care and trauma, in: 25th IEEE Conference on Virtual Reality and 3D User Interfaces, VR 2018 - Proceedings, 2018, pp. 511–512.

[76] Novarad's OpenSight Augmented Reality System is the First Solution for Microsoft HoloLens 510(k) Cleared by the FDA for Medical Use, Busines Wire, 2018.

[77] P.M. O'Shea, Augmented reality in education, Int. J. Gaming Comput. Simul. 3 (1) (2011) 91–93.

[78] H. Ogawa, S. Hasegawa, S. Tsukada, M. Matsubara, A pilot study of augmented reality technology applied to the acetabular cup placement during total hip arthroplasty, J. Arthroplast. 33 (6) (2018) 1833–1837.

[79] E. Watanabe, M. Satoh, T. Konno, M. Hirai, T. Yamaguchi, The trans-visible navigator: a see-through neuronavigation system using augmented reality, World Neurosurg. 87 (2016) 399–405.

[80] K.A. Gavaghan, M. Peterhans, T. Oliveira-Santos, S. Weber, A portable image overlay projection device for computer-aided open liver surgery, IEEE Trans. Biomed. Eng. 58 (6) (2011) 1855–1864.

[81] L.B. Tabrizi, M. Mahvash, Augmented reality–guided neurosurgery: accuracy and intraoperative application of an image projection technique, J. Neurosurg. 123 (2015) 206–211.

[82] H. El-Hariri, P. Pandey, A.J. Hodgson, R. Garbi, Augmented reality visualisation for orthopaedic surgical guidance with pre- and intra-operative multimodal image data fusion, Healthc. Technol. Lett. 5 (5) (2018) 189–193.

[83] R. Hecht, et al. Smartphone augmented reality CT-based platform for needle insertion guidance: a phantom study, Cardiovasc. Intervent. Radiol. 43 (2020) 756–764.

[84] H.G. Kenngott, et al. Mobile, real-time, and point-of-care augmented reality is robust, accurate, and feasible: a prospective pilot study, Surg. Endosc. 32 (6) (2018) 2958–2967.

[85] N. Kalavakonda, L. Sekhar, B. Hannaford, Augmented reality application for aiding tumor resection in skull-base surgery, in: 2019 International Symposium on Medical Robotics, ISMR 2019 (2019).

[86] R. Moreta-Martinez, D. García-Mato, M. García-Sevilla, R. Pérez-Mañanes, J. Calvo-Haro, J. Pascau, Augmented reality in computer-assisted interventions based on patient-specific 3D printed reference, Healthc. Technol. Lett. 5 (5) (2018) 162–166.

[87] F. Liebmann, et al. Pedicle screw navigation using surface digitization on the Microsoft HoloLens, Int. J. Comput. Assist. Radiol. Surg. 14 (7) (2019) 1157–1165.

[88] T.P.C. Van Doormaal, J.A.M. Van Doormaal, T. Mensink, Clinical accuracy of holographic navigation using point-based registration on augmented-reality glasses, Oper. Neurosurg. 17 (6) (2019) 588–593.

[89] N. Mahmoud, et al. On=-patient see-through augmented reality based on visual SLAM, Int. J. Comput. Assist. Radiol. Surg. 12 (1) (2017) 1–11.

[90] P.J. Besl, N.D. McKay, A method for registration of 3-D shapes, IEEE Trans. Pattern Anal. Mach. Intell. 14 (2) (1992) 239–256.

[91] J.C. Chien, Y.R. Tsai, C.T. Wu, J. Der Lee, Hololens-based AR system with a robust point set registration algorithm, Sensors (Switzerland) 19 (16) (2019).

[92] M.L. Wu, J.C. Chien, C.T. Wu, J. Der Lee, An augmented reality system using improved-iterative closest point algorithm for on-patient medical image visualization, Sensors (Switzerland) 18 (8) (2018).

[93] A. Seitel, et al. Towards markerless navigation for percutaneous needle insertions, Int. J. Comput. Assist. Radiol. Surg. 11 (1) (2016) 107–117.

[94] J. Der Lee, C.H. Huang, T.C. Huang, H.Y. Hsieh, S.T. Lee, Medical augment reality using a markerless registration framework, Expert Syst. Appl. 39 (5) (2012) 5286–5294.

[95] A. Elmi-Terander, et al. Surgical navigation technology based on augmented reality and integrated 3D intraoperative imaging a spine cadaveric feasibility and accuracy study, Spine (Phila. Pa. 1976). 41 (21) (2016) E1303–E1311.

[96] Y. Zhang, X. Shen, Y. Hu, Face registration and surgical instrument tracking for image-guided surgical navigation, in: Proceedings of 2016 International Conference on Virtual Reality and Visualization, ICVRV 2016 (2017) pp. 65–71.

[97] R. Modrzejewski, T. Collins, A. Bartoli, A. Hostettler, J. Marescaux, Soft-body registration of pre-operative 3D models to intra-operative RGBD partial body scans. Lect. Notes Comput. Sci. 11073 (2018) 39–46.

[98] T.-C. Chang, et al. Interactive medical augmented reality system for remote surgical assistance, Appl. Math. Inf. Sci. 9 (1L) (2015) 97–104.

[99] C. Hsieh, J.-D. Lee, C. Wu, J.-D. Lee, A kinect-based medical augmented reality system for craniofacial applications using image-to-patient registration, Neuropsychiatry (London) 7 (6) (2017) 927–939.

[100] A. State et al. Technologies for augmented reality systems: Realizing ultrasound-guided needle biopsies, in: Proceedings of the 23rd Annual Conference on Computer Graphics and Interactive Techniques, SIGGRAPH 1996 (1996) pp. 439–446.

[101] O. Pauly, A. Katouzian, A. Eslami, P. Fallavollita, N. Navab, Supervised classification for customized intraoperative augmented reality visualization, in: ISMAR 2012-11th IEEE International Symposium on Mixed and Augmented Reality 2012, Science and Technology Papers, 2012, pp. 311–312.

[102] C. Bichlmeier, E. Euler, T. Blum, N. Navab, Evaluation of the virtual mirror as a navigational aid for augmented reality driven minimally invasive procedures, in: 9th IEEE International Symposium on Mixed and Augmented Reality 2010: Science and Technology, ISMAR 2010 - Proceedings, 2010, pp. 91–97.

[103] M. Lerotic, A.J. Chung, G. Mylonas, G.Z. Yang, Pq-space based non-photorealistic rendering for augmented reality. Lect. Notes Comput. Sci. 4792 (no. PART 2) (2007) 102–109.

[104] C. Hansen, J. Wieferich, F. Ritter, C. Rieder, H.O. Peitgen, Illustrative visualization of 3D planning models for augmented reality in liver surgery, Int. J. Comput. Assist. Radiol. Surg. 5 (2) (2010) 133–141.

[105] M.E. de Oliveira, H.G. Debarba, A. Lädermann, S. Chagué, C. Charbonnier, A hand-eye calibration method for augmented reality applied to computer-assisted orthopedic surgery, Int. J. Med. Robot. Comput. Assist. Surg. 15 (2) (2019) e1969.

[106] T. Frantz, B. Jansen, J. Duerinck, J. Vandemeulebroucke, Augmenting Microsoft's Hololens with vuforia tracking for neuronavigation, Healthc. Technol. Lett. 5 (5) (2018) 221–225.

[107] R. Vassallo, A. Rankin, E.C.S. Chen, T.M. Peters, Hologram stability evaluation for Microsoft HoloLens, Med. Imaging Image Percep. Observ. Perform. Technol. Assess. (10136) (2017) 1013614.

[108] M. Kersten-Oertel, P. Jannin, D.L. Collins, The state of the art of visualization in mixed reality image guided surgery, Comput. Med. Imaging Graph. 37 (2) (2013) 98–112.

[109] N. Navab, J. Traub, T. Sielhorst, M. Feuerstein, C. Bichlmeier, Action- and workflow-driven augmented reality for computer-aided medical procedures, IEEE Comput. Graph. Appl. 27 (5) (2007) 10–14.

[110] K. Cleary, T.M. Peters, Image-guided interventions: technology review and clinical applications, Annu. Rev. Biomed. Eng. 12 (1) (2010) 119–142.

[111] M. Kersten-Oertel, P. Jannin, D.L. Collins, DVV: A taxonomy for mixed reality visualization in image guided surgery, IEEE Trans. Vis. Comput. Graph. 18 (2) (2012) 332–352.

[112] G. Schlöndorff, R. Mösges, D. Meyer-Ebrecht, W. Krybus, L. Adams, CAS (computer assisted surgery). A new procedure in head and neck surgery, HNO 37 (5) (1989) 187–190.

[113] I. Azarmehr, K. Stokbro, R. Bryan Bell, T. Thygesen, Surgical navigation: a systematic review of indications, treatments, and outcomes in oral and maxillofacial surgery, J. Oral Maxillofac. Surg. 75 (2017) 1987–2005.

[114] S. Sukegawa, T. Kanno, Y. Furuki, Application of computer-assisted navigation systems in oral and maxillofacial surgery, Jpn. Dental Sci. Rev. 54 (3) (2018) 139–149 Elsevier Ltd.

[115] A. Schramm, et al. Intraoperative accuracy of non-invasive registration in computer assisted cranio–maxillofacial surgery, Int. Congr. Ser. 1230 (2001) 1239–1240.

[116] G. Orentlicher, D. Goldsmith, A. Horowitz, Applications of 3-dimensional virtual computerized tomography technology in oral and maxillofacial surgery: Current therapy, J. Oral Maxillofac. Surg. 68 (8) (2010) 1933–1959.

[117] J. Hoffmann, C. Westendorff, C. Leitner, D. Bartz, S. Reinert, Validation of 3D-laser surface registration for image-guided cranio-maxillofacial surgery, J. Cranio-Maxillofac. Surg. 33 (1) (2005) 13–18.

[118] A. Wagner, O. Ploder, G. Enislidis, M. Truppe, R. Ewers, Image-guided surgery, Int. J. Oral Maxillofac. Surg. 25 (2) (1996) 147–151.

[119] A. Wagner, M. Rasse, W. Millesi, R. Ewers, Virtual reality for orthognathic surgery: The augmented reality environment concept, J. Oral Maxillofac. Surg. 55 (5) (1997) 456–462.

[120] A. Wagner, O. Ploder, J. Zuniga, G. Undt, R. Ewers, Augmented reality environment for temporomandibular joint motion analysis, Int. J. Adult Orthodon. Orthognath. Surg. 11 (2) (1996) 127–136.

[121] A. Wagner, et al. Clinical experience with interactive teleconsultation and teleassistance in craniomaxillofacial surgical procedures, J. Oral Maxillofac. Surg. 57 (12) (1999) 1413–1418.

[122] W. Birkfellner, et al. A head-mounted operating binocular for augmented reality visualization in medicine—Design and initial evaluation, IEEE Trans. Med. Imaging 21 (8) (2002) 991–997.

[123] W. Birkfellner, et al. A modular software system for computer-aided surgery and its first application in oral implantology, IEEE Trans. Med. Imaging 19 (6) (2000) 616–620.

[124] W. Birkfellner, et al. Computer-enchanced stereoscopic vision in a head-mounted operating binocular, Phys. Med. Biol. 48 (3) (2003) 49–57.

[125] T. Salb, J. Brief, O. Burgert, S. Hassfeld, R. Dillmann, Intraoperative presentation of surgical planning and simulation results using a stereoscopic see-through head-mounted display, Stereosc. Displays Virtual Real. Syst. VII 3957 (2000) 68.

[126] R. Marmulla, H. Hoppe, J. Mühling, G. Eggers, An augmented reality system for image-guided surgery, Int. J. Oral Maxillofac. Surg. 34 (6) (2005) 594–596.

[127] R. Marmulla, H. Hoppe, J. Mühling, S. Hassfeld, New augmented reality concepts for craniofacial surgical procedures, Plast. Reconstr. Surg. 115 (4) (2005) 1124–1128.

[128] R.A. Mischkowski, M.J. Zinser, A.C. Kübler, B. Krug, U. Seifert, J.E. Zöller, Application of an augmented reality tool for maxillary positioning in orthognathic surgery—A feasibility study, J. Cranio-Maxillofacial Surg. 34 (8) (2006) 478–483.

[129] M.J. Zinser, R.A. Mischkowski, T. Dreiseidler, O.C. Thamm, D. Rothamel, J.E. Zöller, Computer-assisted orthognathic surgery: Waferless maxillary positioning, versatility, and accuracy of an image-guided visualisation display, Br. J. Oral Maxillofac. Surg. 51 (8) (2013) 827–833.

[130] M.J. Zinser, H.F. Sailer, L. Ritter, B. Braumann, M. Maegele, J.E. Zöller, A paradigm shift in orthognathic surgery? A comparison of navigation, computer-aided designed/computer-aided manufactured splints, and 'classic' intermaxillary splints to surgical transfer of virtual orthognathic planning, J. Oral Maxillofac. Surg. 71 (12) (2013) 2151e1–2151e21.

[131] H. Liao, M. Iwahara, N. Hata, T. Dohi, High-quality integral videography using a multiprojector, 2004.

[132] H.H. Tran et al., Augmented reality system for oral surgery using 3D auto stereoscopic visualization. Lect. Notes Comput. Sci. 6891 (2011) 81–88.

[133] J. Wang et al., Real-time marker-free patient registration and image-based navigation using stereovision for dental surgery. Lect. Notes Comput. Sci. 8090 (2013) 9–18.

[134] J. Wang, et al. Augmented reality navigation with automatic marker-free image registration using 3-d image overlay for dental surgery, IEEE Trans. Biomed. Eng. 61 (4) (2014) 1295–1304.

[135] H. Suenaga, et al. Vision-based markerless registration using stereo vision and an augmented reality surgical navigation system: A pilot study, BMC Med. Imaging 15 (1) (2015) 51.

[136] M. Ulrich, C. Wiedemann, C. Steger, Combining scale-space and similarity-based aspect graphs for fast 3D object recognition, IEEE Trans. Pattern Anal. Mach. Intell. 34 (10) (2012) 1902–1914.

[137] J. Wang, H. Suenaga, L. Yang, E. Kobayashi, I. Sakuma, Video see-through augmented reality for oral and maxillofacial surgery, Int. J. Med. Robot. Comput. Assist. Surg. 13 (2) (2017) e1754.

[138] J. Wang, Y. Shen, S. Yang, A practical marker-less image registration method for augmented reality oral and maxillofacial surgery, Int. J. Comput. Assist. Radiol. Surg. 14 (5) (2019) 763–773.

[139] M. Zhu, G. Chai, Y. Zhang, X. Ma, J. Gan, Registration strategy using occlusal splint based on augmented reality for mandibular angle oblique split osteotomy, J. Craniofac. Surg. 22 (5) (2011) 1806–1809.

[140] M. Zhu, et al. Effectiveness of a novel augmented reality-based navigation system in treatment of orbital hypertelorism, Ann. Plast. Surg. 77 (6) (2016) 662–668.

[141] M. Qu, et al. Precise positioning of an intraoral distractor using augmented reality in patients with hemifacial microsomia, J. Cranio-Maxillofacial Surg. 43 (1) (2015) 106–112.

[142] W. Han, et al. A new method for cranial vault reconstruction: Augmented reality in synostotic plagiocephaly surgery, J. Cranio-Maxillofacial Surg. 47 (8) (2019) 1280–1284.

[143] L. Lin, et al. Mandibular angle split osteotomy based on a novel augmented reality navigation using specialized robot-assisted arms - A feasibility study, J. Cranio-Maxillofacial Surg. 44 (2) (2016) 215–223.

[144] C. Zhou, et al. Robot-assisted surgery for mandibular angle split osteotomy using augmented reality: preliminary results on clinical animal experiment, Aesthetic Plast. Surg. 41 (5) (2017) 1228–1236.

[145] M. Zhu, et al. A novel augmented reality system for displaying inferior alveolar nerve bundles in maxillofacial surgery, Sci. Rep. 7 (1) (2017) 1–11.

[146] K. Gavaghan, et al. , Evaluation of a portable image overlay projector for the visualisation of surgical navigation data: phantom studies, Int. J. CARS 7 (2012) 547–556.

[147] G. Badiali, et al. Augmented reality as an aid in maxillofacial surgery: Validation of a wearable system allowing maxillary repositioning, J. Cranio-Maxillofac. Surg. 42 (8) (2014) 1970–1976.

[148] Y.K. Lin, H.T. Yau, I.C. Wang, C. Zheng, K.H. Chung, A novel dental implant guided surgery based on integration of surgical template and augmented reality, Clin. Implant Dent. Relat. Res. 17 (3) (2015) 543–553.

[149] A.C. Profeta, C. Schilling, M. McGurk, Augmented reality visualization in head and neck surgery: an overview of recent findings in sentinel node biopsy and future perspectives, Br. J. Oral Maxillofac. Surg. 54 (6) (2016) 694–696.

[150] M. Chand, D.S. Keller, L. Devoto, M. McGurk, Furthering precision in sentinel node navigational surgery for oral cancer: a novel triple targeting system, J. Fluoresc. 28 (2) (2018) 483–486.

[151] P. Scolozzi, P. Bijlenga, Removal of recurrent intraorbital tumour using a system of augmented reality, Br. J. Oral Maxillofac. Surg. 55 (9) (2017) 962–964.

[152] Y.Y. Wang, H.P. Liu, F.L. Hsiao, A. Kumar, Augmented reality for temporomandibular joint arthrocentesis: a cadaver study, Int. J. Oral Maxillofac. Surg. 48 (8) (2019) 1084–1087.

[153] P. Pietruski, et al. Supporting mandibular resection with intraoperative navigation utilizing augmented reality technology—A proof of concept study, J. Cranio-Maxillofacial Surg. 47 (6) (2019) 854–859.

[154] A. Pepe, et al. A marker-less registration approach for mixed reality-aided maxillofacial surgery: a pilot evaluation, J. Digit. Imaging 32 (6) (2019) 1008–1018.

[155] A. Pepe et al., Pattern recognition and mixed reality for computer-aided maxillofacial surgery and oncological assessment, in: BMEiCON 2018-11th Biomedical Engineering International Conference, 2019.

[156] C. Gsaxner, J. Egger, Markerless augmented reality in head and neck surgery, Youtube, 2019. Available: https://www.youtube.com/watch?v=7zVP0KCSrpw.

[157] C. Gsaxner, J. Wallner, X. Chen, W. Zemann, J. Egger, Facial model collection for medical augmented reality in oncologic cranio-maxillofacial surgery, Sci. Data 6 (1) (2019) 310.

Haptics and virtual reality for oral and maxillofacial surgery

Qiong Wang, Xiangyun Liao, Yinling Qian, Ping Liu

SHENZHEN INSTITUTE OF ADVANCED TECHNOLOGY, CHINESE ACADEMY OF SCIENCES, SHENZHEN, CHINA

1 Introduction

With the continuous improvement of science and technology, clinical surgery has gradually developed from open surgery to minimally invasive surgery [1]. However, the development of new clinical procedures has also brought higher requirements for physician training and the risk of surgery has always been high [2]. Long physician training cycle can hardly meet people's increasing demand for high-quality medical services. With the rapid explosion of virtual reality technology and computer hardware, virtual surgery training systems came into being.

According to the complexity of the operation, virtual surgery systems can be divided into three categories: simulators for needle based procedure, simulators for minimally invasive surgery and simulators for open surgery [3]. Simulators in the early stage mainly focuses on procedure using instruments like needles, catheters and guidewires. Ursino et al. [4] developed The Immersion Medical CathSim Vascular Access Simulator which is targeting for training nursing students to start an intravenous line in the proper way. A haptic interface device is developed to simulate the needle and catheter with three degrees of freedom haptic feedback. With the same hardware configuration, Liu et al. [5,6] developed a simulator for needle-based trauma procedures, such as pericardiocentesis and diagnostic peritoneal lavage. Minimally invasive surgery uses tiny cuts in the skin rather than the large cuts which is often needed in traditional surgery. Due to its benefits of less pain, shorter hospital stay, and fewer complications, it has become the first choice for the treatment of many diseases. Many mature commercial virtual surgery systems are developed for minimally invasive surgery training. Among the most famous ones are the series of virtual operation systems developed by Simbionix [7] which is an Israel company. The system provides training for laparoscopy, gastrointestinal endoscopy, and arthroscopy surgeries [8,9]. The company SimSurgery [10] designed a laparoscopic training simulator named SEP series realizing the simulation of laparoscopic surgery such as cholecystectomy, minimally invasive surgery for ectopic pregnancy, and ovarian cystectomy. Open surgery is more difficult to simulate because the visual field, range of haptic feedback, and freedom of motion are considerably larger compared to minimally invasive procedures. Bielser et al. [11] proposed a simulator for simulating incisions and skin retractions. Canadian Avionics Corporation developed the NeuroVR virtual surgery system [12] for neurosurgery training. So far, high fidelity open surgery training remains a challenge problem in virtual surgery simulation.

In order to apply virtual reality technology to surgical training, the virtual surgery system builds three-dimensional models of human tissue from medical images, models the deformation of human tissue under the interaction of surgical tools, and finally displays the simulation results to the doctor through three-dimensional rendering technology [3]. At the same time, it has to provide a high fidelity human–computer interface for doctors to perform virtual surgical operations [13]. Simulation technology has demonstrated its value and effectiveness in clinical education [14,15] and virtual surgery systems provide numerous advantages over traditional surgical education [16]. The three main advantages are as follows: first, virtual surgical simulators can provide unlimited training opportunities and this is the best guarantee of a lasting training effect; second, surgical simulators can help to assess and evaluate the performance of the trainees with the simulation progress made; besides, simulators can provide tasks with complexity and difficulty scaled to the skills and experience of the trainee. With these advantages, personalized training program can be scheduled thus to greatly shorten the training cycle of doctors.

2 Haptics in virtual surgery

Haptic is the one of the five known senses of human and it's an important channel for humans to perceive information about the external environment, including objects' shape, size, temperature, and the surface texture [17]. Based on various types of haptic information, human beings can smoothly interact with the environment. In order to build a more natural way of human–computer interaction, haptics is playing an increasingly important role in the last few decades [18,19]. Haptic interaction technology has a wide range of application prospects including virtual surgery, product design, entertainment and somatosensory games, etc. [20,21].

Driven by the advent of the Phantom force feedback device invented by Massie et al. [22], it has set off a research boom in force generation algorithms for desktop force feedback devices. The mainstream of early research was the three-degree-of-freedom (3-DoF) force generation algorithm. The principle was to represent the virtual space avatar of the handheld device as a point, which has three-dimensional motion and can contact and interact with objects in the virtual environment and generates a three-dimensional force. Then the 3D force is fed back to the operator through a force-sensing interactive device [23]. Obviously, the 3-DoF force generation algorithm cannot simulate the multi-point contact feeling between objects. In 1999, Mcneely et al. [24] first proposed the concept of six-degree-of-freedom (6-DoF) force along with the advent of desktop six-degree-of-freedom force feedback equipment [25,26]. Its goal is to solve the multi-point and multi-region non-penetrating contact interaction simulation of complex shapes and the six-dimensional force of rigid body interaction. Until today, the 6-DoF force generation algorithm is still a research focus. Due to the growth of the computing power of smartphones and the demand for entertainment applications, how to enable users to touch mobile terminals, such as virtual objects on the screen of mobile phones, has become a research hotspot in recent years [27,28]. Several typical surface textures of objects are successfully simulated by using techniques of high frequency piezoelectric vibration [27] and electrostatic adsorption effect [28]. At the same time, some researchers focus on combing the feelings of force and tactile feedback, thus to develop an integrated device for both feedbacks [29]. Most recently, mid-air devices appear as a good solution for touchless interactions and ultrasonic/ultrasound haptic devices are the most distinguishable mid-air devices and they have been studied in many related works [30]. Hoshi et al. [31] presented a hologram with tactile reactions. The tactile display produces force on user's bare hand without any contact by using radiation pressure of airborne ultrasound. Hoshi et al. [32] proposed Ultra-Haptics which can provide multi-point haptic feedback above an interactive surface. Laser provides another mid-air approach and it has advantages such as accuracy and precision of the deployed systems. Lee et al. [33] extended a laser device with an orientation control platform and a magnetic tracker so that it can elicit tapping and stroking sensations to a user's palm from a distance. By fusing femtosecond-laser light fields and ultrasonic acoustic fields, Ochiai et al. [34] presented a method of rendering aerial haptic images which benefits such as multi-resolution haptic images and a synergistic effect on haptic perception.

The research of haptic technology involves computer science, psychology, cognitive science, neuroscience, mechanics and control, computers, and other disciplines. Although it has received intensive research over the last few decades, it is still a great challenge today [35] and the continuous demand for the fidelity of force tactile interaction will continuously promote the progress of haptic interaction technology.

3 Surgical simulation for the oral and maxillofacial surgery

3.1 Data acquisition and analysis

The advancement of medical imaging technology enables visualization of the volumetric information of patient. Computed tomography (CT) is a commonly used imaging modality in oral and maxillofacial fields. In addition, cone-beam computed tomography (CBCT) is another 3D imaging method of better choice, thanks to its high accuracy in detecting bone characteristics at lower risk of radiation exposure compared to CT. There are two most common diseases in oral and maxillofacial surgery, that is, tumors and fractures. CBCT imaging is the gold standard for diagnosis and surgical treatment for fractures, and is also commonly used for locating the lesion and recognizing the lesion type.

Medical image segmentation is the process of identifying the pixels of organs or lesions from background medical images such as CT or CBCT images. As for oral and maxillofacial surgery, the aim is to extract head organs and structures such as skull, mandible, dentition, inferior alveolar nerve, and a pathological lesions or fractured bone fragments in head medical images. Accurate segmentation of these organs and structures is a key step for medical three-dimensional visualization, diagnosis or surgery planning and guidance, especially in complex oral and maxillofacial surgery cases. Clinically, they are usually segmented manually or semi-automatically with a certain kind of image segmentation software, such as the Mimics software (Materialise, Leuven, Belgium), Invesalius (Centro de Tecnologia da Informação Renato Archer, Campinas, SP, Brazil), Slicer 3D and ITK-Snap. In manual segmentation, the operator outlines the object contour slice by slice, distinguishing the object from adjacent tissues [36,37]. Though with great accuracy when operated by experts, full manual segmentation process is time-consuming and of limited reproducibility [36].

Conversely, semiautomatic or automatic image segmentation is not only efficient and reliable, but also would reduce the workload of operators [38]. The semiautomatic segmentation is a hybrid approach where the operator sets a few parameters for the segmentation software, and the software generates initial segmentation. Then the initial segmentation is checked and refined by the operator manually. For example, the operator sets the threshold interval (Hounsfield units) interactively which guides the automatic 3D reconstruction procedure [39] for bone tissue segmentation from CT or CBCT images. Binary threshold-based algorithm [40,41] and region growing algorithm are usually used in semi-automatic segmentation software. In binary threshold-based method, the operator sets the region of interest (ROI) with specific tools to remove structures outside the ROI, while in the region growing method the user sets specific seed-points on different slices that grows or expands based on the image features. Xi et al. [42] proposed a condyles segmentation protocol by combining 3D region growing and local thresholding algorithms for CBCT segmentation, while Méndez-Manjón et al. [43] selected a gray-scale cut-off value to define the volume of interest, and manual refined the condylar contours generated automatically. Subsequently, condylar contours were refined manually. Recently, Wallner et al [44] assessed the quality and accuracy of six segmentation methods (GrowCut, Robust Statistics Segmenter, Region Growing 3D, Otsu & Picking, Canny Segmentation and Geodesic Segmenter) for semi-automatic mandible segmentation on the open-source platforms 3D Slicer, MITK and MeVisLab. GrowCut and the Canny segmentation method obtain the highest segmentation accuracy with Dice Score Coefficient (DSC) 85.6%, the Hausdorff Distance (HD) 33.5 voxel) and DSC 82.1%, HD 8.5 voxel, respectively. Similarly, Lo et al. [45] evaluated the accuracy of segmentation of the mandibular condylar region by different semi-automatic segmentation approaches using three open-source software (Invesalius, ITK-Snap, Slicer 3D) and one commercially available software Dolphin 3D (Dolphin Imaging, version 11.0, Chatsworth, CA, United States). The manually segmented results of Mimics were set as ground truth. Although they obtained excellent reliability from intra-observer and inter-observer, they suggested that further evidence was needed to validate accurate definition of a condylar region through semi-automatic segmentation.

Compared with semiautomatic segmentation, automatic oral and maxillofacial structures segmentation is more efficient and reliable. However, it is more challenging because of the complicated and varied anatomical structure. This is more difficult for CBCT images for its lower contrast and higher sensitivity to noise comparing to CT. Due to these challenges, most study just focuses on automatic mandible segmentation. Conventional methods for mandible segmentation including statistical shape model [46], 3D gradient-based fuzzy connectedness algorithm [47], multi-atlas methods [48], active appearance models (AAM) [49], and a multi-atlas method combined with an active shape model (ASM) [50]. However, the conventional approaches are often sensitive to the noise and metal artifacts in the CT images, resulting inaccurate segmentation of the mandible with weak and false edges.

In recent years, deep learning techniques, especially convolutional neural networks (CNNs), have become achieved state-of-the-art performance in many image segmentation tasks [51–55]. There are two typical structures for image segmentation, fully convolutional networks (FCN) [51] and UNet [52]. As a variant of CNN, FCN is a quite popular choice for image segmentation not only in computer vision but also in medical image fields. It trains neural networks end-to end by learning feature layers directly from data, making it outperform the conventional methods, which consider the feature learning and segmentation separately. UNet takes a symmetric encoder-decoder structure with skip connections to learn multi-scale features with jump connections and performs well in many medical image segmentation tasks. Its latest improved structure nnUNet [56] achieved great success across 10 different medical image datasets. For oral and maxillofacial structures segmentation, Ibragimov et al. [57] first used CNN to segment organs-at-risks in head and neck CT images. Zhu et al. [58] presented AnatomyNet based on 3D U-net architecture by introducing residual blocks in the encoding layers and a loss function combining Dice score and focal loss to train the network. Lei et al. [59] utilized a 3D Faster R-CNN to automatically locate the head and neck OARs, then used an attention U-Net to segment the multiple OARs from MR images. Zhao et al. [60] proposed Deep-supGAN for automatic bony structures segmentation with one block to generate a high-quality CT image from an MRI and a second block to segment bony structures from the generated CT image and MRI. Qiu et al. [61] adopted the U-Net structure and combined the resulting 2D segmentations from three orthogonal planes into a 3D segmentation to segment mandible automatically in CT scans.

3.2 3D modeling

Three-dimensional (3D) reconstruction of maxillofacial structures with CBCT or CT has been widely used in oral and maxillofacial surgery in orthodontics [62] and oral and maxillofacial surgery [63,64]. It plays an important role in the process of diagnosis, preoperative planning, surgical simulation and precise intraoperative operations. It can also provide more accurate anatomical evaluations for postoperative curative effects and prognosis. 3D reconstruction technology refers to converting multiple 2D medical image slices to a 3D anatomical model. It facilitates accurate display of the spatial position, size, geometric shape of the anatomical structure and the lesion, as well as their spatial relationship with the surrounding tissues. The reconstructed 3D model can be dynamically displayed on the computer screen with different brightness, transparency, color, wire frame and reflectivity, and can be rotated, cut, reconstructed, and measured from any angle. The doctors can also selectively reconstruct the area of interest in three dimensions. By enlarging and rotating the local details, it can improve the three-dimensional visual effect. With all these functions, 3D reconstruction technology provides accurate and quantitative evaluations of disease and facilitates the development and application of more precise and accurate surgical procedures [65–67]. For a patient with an ameloblastoma on the right mandible, the patient's skull, the tumor, nerve, dentition, bone, and other tissue structures around the lesion area are segmented and reconstructed. In the 3D visualization model, the tumor size can be accurately measured, and the position of the tumor and the spatial adjacent relationship between the tumor and the surrounding tissue can be accurately located. The mandibular osteotomy line can be accurately planned according to the 3D model. The doctor could simulate the operation before actual surgery.

Currently, there are two main rendering algorithms in computer graphics for 3D visualization, that is, surface rendering and direct volume rendering (DVR) [68,69]. Surface rendering is a commonly used visualization technique to render vasculature and skeletal structures. It generates a geometrical surface representation of structure according to the segmentation of the image volume by extracting the segmented contours with surface tiling techniques. This kind of techniques for volume data operates by fitting polygons to an isosurface in the volume by using the marching cubes algorithm, contour tracking, opaque cubes etc., and then rendering the polygonal model with conventional polygon rendering techniques. The surface-fitting process needs to make binary decisions, that is, the volume must be thresholded to generate regions that are either inside or outside the isosurface. Thus, segmentation of the image volume is usually required as a preproces for surface rendering. The marching-cubes (MC) algorithm [70] is one of the most famous surface-rendering algorithm and there are various improvements for different applications. However, as previously described, accurate automatic segmentation is difficult and manual or automatic segmentation is more often clinically. Because of this issue, there are no interactive capabilities to change the surface in surface rendering. Compared with surface rendering, DVR has two advantages. First, it is able to render the entire volume. Second, there is no need to threshold the volume data for DVR. These make DVR the dominant rendering technique for biomedical images visualization. The idea of DVR is to obtain a 3D representation of the volume data directly, by assigning a color and an opacity to each voxel in the 3D volume data, projecting the voxels onto an image plane, and then blending the projected voxels. The volume data is considered as a semi-transparent light-emitting medium, while DVR is an approximate simulation of the propagation of light through the medium. Some backward or forward methods are used to implement the assignment. Detailed computing pipeline of DVR please refer to [71]. DVR visualization is also feasible to combine surface rendering with a region of interest (ROI) segmentation, providing "focus-and-context" to the volume data [72,73]. It also offers a selective view of ROIs in the interior of the volume with volume clipping allows by omitting other extraneous details [74].

3D reconstruction process relies on hardware with powerful computing capability. Modern graphics processing units make fast 3D reconstruction possible. In addition to hardware advancement, developments in software also play an important role for the advancement of research in medical image visualization. There are a few open-source visualization platforms or libraries, such as Volume rendering engine (Voreen), visualization toolkit (VTK), and MeVisLab. These platforms provide data visualization frameworks and advanced 3D modeling techniques. They are also freely available for use, modification, and redistribution [75]. A lot of medical image processing software with 3D reconstruction function (Mimics, Slicer 3D, ITK-Snap, Mango, ProPlan, Simplant, iPlan, etc.) are developed taking advantage of them. The reconstructed 3D model quality depends both on the quality of volume images obtained by CBCT or CT and the reconstruction method, affecting the accuracy of volumetric measurements. For 3D model obtained by surface rendering, the choice of HU thresholds on segmentation of the volume data is important [39]. If the threshold is too low, it is easy to introduce soft tissue artifacts and noise. If the threshold is too high, it is easy to lose real data and cause errors. It is generally recommended that the reconstruction threshold (lower limit) of the mandible is set to 500 Hu, and the upper jaw threshold is set to 250 Hu. Special situations require special attention. If a bone surface support guide is required, the cortical bone edge must be accurately reconstructed, which can be carefully identified through the image magnification function.

The structures of the dentition, maxillofacial bone tissue and the facial tissue can be reconstructed from CBCT or CT, without color and texture. However, due to the presence of silver amalgam fillings and metal artifacts around the teeth, the dentition surface obtained by CT is not accurate enough. Accurate surface data can be obtained by scanning the plaster model with a laser scanner, which is suitable for the analysis and reconstruction of the fine structure of the tooth surface and the facial soft tissue. In addition, to obtain facial color and texture data, three-dimensional photography technology is required. The accuracy of optical scanning is much higher than that of CT images, which overcomes the shortcomings of CBCT's unclear display of occlusal surfaces and avoids radiation, but this also requires special optical scanning instruments and supporting software to match CT data with optical scanning data. Different modalities can be fused by software to form an enhanced virtual head model [76]. There are three types of registration methods that can realize the fusion of CT image data, laser scan data and 3D photography data, that is, point-based registration (PBM), surface-based registration (SBM), and surface-based registration (VBM).

3.3 Oral and maxillofacial surgical simulation platform

Maxillofacial surgery is a surgical specialty which specializing in the treatment of lesions in the jaw, mouth, head, face, and neck [44]. Common maxillofacial surgery includes maxillary fractures, benign, and malignant tumors, and orthognathic surgery. With the development of science and technology, computer-assistant medical techniques, such virtual reality (VR) and augmented reality (AR), play an important role in the diagnosis and treatment of maxillofacial surgery [77,88].

3.3.1 VR maxillofacial surgical platform

VR maxillofacial surgical platform mainly focus on 3D modeling and visualization as the fundamental issues, which facilitates the preoperative planning and training by analyzing the complex three-dimensional anatomy of the face. In recent years, several VR maxillofacial surgical platforms were developed for the surgical training and planning and navigation. Wu et al. developed a virtual training system for maxillofacial surgery using advanced haptic feedback and immersive workbench [79]. They reconstructed virtual models of anatomical structures with the CT data and laser scanning, and proposed a simulation algorithm to calculate the tactile force feedback based on the regression equation, thereby realizing a virtual maxillofacial surgery training system. Similarly, a simulation system based on arthroscopy was implemented for training [80], which improved doctors' skills in performing surgery in real surgery.

VR maxillofacial surgical platform is also a promising tool to accurately plan the maxillofacial surgery. Landmarking is a common method in cephalometric analysis, which can identify the patient's anatomical features for evaluation and surgical planning. In [81], the CT images from 66 patients with maxillofacial surgery were landmarked by using MIMICS. Then the CT slices were used as images to recreate the 3D volume. By adopting a principal component analysis (PCA) method, further processed coordinate data of landmarks were used to train a patch-based deep neural network model with a three-layer convolutional neural network to obtain landmarks from CT images. This study shows a very meaningful work, which not only facilitates the surgical training, but also reduces the dependence on experience in OMS landmarking. What's more, a maxillofacial surgical planning platform requires the ability to customize the implants to more accurately replace the damaged maxillofacial anatomical structures. A study in [82] established a system called EasyImplant that can easily and efficiently design customized maxillofacial implant with porous structure. This system uses the skull model on the healthy side to obtain the initial implant model on the defective side by mirroring method, and then the original model can be adjusted and repaired according to the curvature of the undamaged surface, so as to design a complete porous implant model.

The increasing development of 3D modeling and visualization greatly promotes the application of the navigation in maxillofacial surgery. An earlier virtual maxillofacial surgery navigation system, shown in [83], proposed a new method to transfer patients' personalized surgical plan in the operating room by using navigation system, and then confirmed that this simulation-guided navigation would be a helpful procedure during maxillofacial surgery. In a recent research [84], experiments have proved the effectiveness of the maxillofacial surgery navigation system in maxillofacial trauma surgery including complex mid-facial fractures, orbital trauma reconstruction, and orthognathic surgery. Besides, a patient-specific surgical planning and navigation software system was demonstrated [85], as shown in Fig. 6.1, which developed a semi-automated segmentation pipeline that can perform accurate and time-saving 3D modeling for patients based on CT, simulate facial

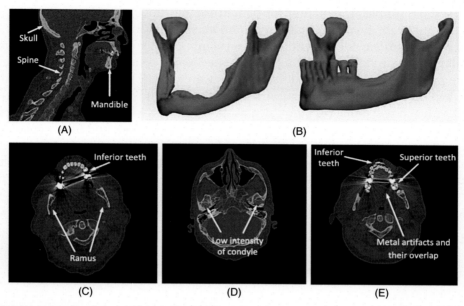

FIGURE 6.1 Examples of typical cases that challenge the accurate mandible segmentation in CT scans [61]. (A) Various bone-structured organs in the head and neck CT, such as the skull and the spine. (B) Large variation of mandibles between individuals. (C) Metal artifacts and noises in the teeth. (D) Lower intensity in the condyles. (E) Metal artifacts and the presence of inferior and superior teeth in the same slice.

soft tissues and guide the surgical operations. Besides, the navigation system has a novel user-friendly interface, which improves the surgical accuracy and efficiency.

3.3.2 AR maxillofacial surgical platform

Augmented reality (AR) is a new technology that allows the merging of data from the real environment and virtual information, which is often used in maxillofacial surgery platforms to improve the surgical experience and accuracy. A recent study [86] designed a stereo camera-based AR navigation system, and then investigated the tracking accuracy during repositioning of the surgery. The experiments have proved its reliability after comparing the tracking accuracy with an existing infrared-based optical tracking system. At the same time, the maxillofacial AR surgery platform requires high geometric accuracy. The system in [87], which consists of a rotation matrix and translation vector algorithm, was proposed to obtain high accuracy of the navigation. Two stereo cameras and a semi-transparent mirror are installed in the operating room to reduce geometric errors and improve depth perception. Experiments have proved that it provides an acceptable accuracy range in a short operation time and provides a smooth operation process for surgeons. Researchers have developed pre-operative and intraoperative registration method to obtain accurate positioning and navigation [88,89], thus a virtual 3D model can be successfully merged with the intraoperative surgical scene in the manner of video see-through overlay to achieve interactive 3D navigation for the surgery. Moreover, in [90], a video perspective AR system is developed. The system consists of a camera and a data processing workstation, and the physical setup is simple. By matching the patient's dental model with the camera image, the system automatically performs image registration, superimposes the results of the surgical plan on the camera video, identifies key structures, and guides the surgical operation. Fig. 6.2 illustrates the video see-through augmented reality system for maxillofacial surgery.

In the past 2 decades, VR and AR techniques were usually integrated to the maxillofacial surgical robotic system, as an automatic tool to treat the diseases like head and neck tumors. With the assistance of surgical robotic systems, maxillofacial surgery performs with fewer complications, less bleeding, shorter recovery period, and better cosmetic results than the open surgery [91]. A maxillofacial surgery robotic system is developed [92], in which the researchers seamlessly integrated the marker-less navigation module and the compact maxillofacial surgery robot into one system, as shown in Fig. 6.3, so that it

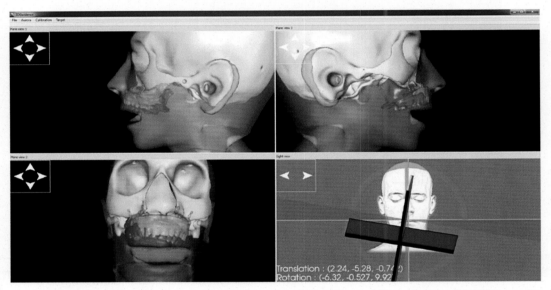

FIGURE 6.2 GUI of the software. On the 3D views in the top part and the bottom left, the target position of the maxilla is colored in *cyan*, whereas its real-time tracked position is in *red*. The bottom right part displays the colored crosshair matching the real-time tracked position of the maxilla.

FIGURE 6.3 Video see-through augmented reality for maxillofacial surgery.

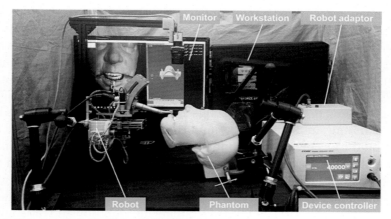

FIGURE 6.4 Surgical robot platform for AR maxillofacial surgery.

can successfully guide the robot to complete the operation regardless of the pose of the mandible and effectively reduce the operation risk during the surgery. Similarly, a surgical robot is proposed in [93], which can automatically execute the planned surgical plan with the help of the surgeons, thereby significantly reducing their workload (Fig. 6.4).

3.4 Haptic rendering method

Surgical simulator with visual feedback can provide surgeons an intuitive inception of the three dimensional body of the patient, furthermore allowing them to interact with the virtual body and planning the procedure. However, haptic clue is a crucial key that could provide the surgeon more feedback and information. In the oral and maxillofacial surgery, vision is always blocked because of the limited operating region, the sense of the touch is the only way that the surgeon relies on to accomplish the steps. For example, during the bone drilling and sawing, surgeon catches the imperceptible force changes to judge the drill head moving from cortex of bone to the cancellous bone; similarly, in the dental surgery, surgeon feel the drilling force turning to tough to make sure that all the corrupted part has been removed. In order to cooperate with this vital information, haptic rendering is widely studied and developed in the virtual oral and maxillofacial surgical simulation. The haptic rendering is greatly relying on the hardware that exhibits the force. Some of the research used the commercial device, such as Geometric Touch; the other parties concentrate to develop more flexible force feedback device, or haptic device with more degree of freedom.

For the haptic rendering of oral and maxillofacial surgery, operating on bone with various drills or saws is very common. However, the bone drilling and sawing force has a very special vibration feeling and is a little difficult to emulate. This vibration fore is caused by the frequent rigid contacts between the drill and the bone, combining with the small pieces of material being cut down. It is a complex process. Mohammadreza et al. [94] have developed a general physics-based haptic model to simulate the bone machining force. The structure of the drill is discretized into a small part with an element of a cutting edge. The interaction of the elemental cutting edge with the bone is analyzed. It holds an assumption obtained from the experiment, that the energy required to remove a unit volume of bone is a constant for every particular bone material. With this assumption, the whole problem becomes to estimate the volume removed by the elemental cutting edge, then all the forces generated on every cutting edge are summed. This method has been tested on a dental machining simulator with Omni PHANToM device. This method is a general method that could transfer a physical model of bone machining to an estimated model that could be realized in the computer. However, the accuracy of the method is highly related to the volume resolution of the 3D data, low resolution would have a large difference between the simulated force and the real collected force. Qiong et al. [95,96] developed an impulse-based haptic rendering method to simulate the vibration and resistance fore during the bone drilling and sawing. The translational velocity and the high-speed rotational velocity of burrs have been considered as the input that will infect the resistance force. Otherwise, this method includes the material parameters of both the drill and the bone, is able to mimic more complex interaction situations. The sawing simulation based on the impulse-based method has been tested in a real-time mandibular angle reduction surgical simulation application. Wang et al. [97] have constructed an iDental simulator, providing 6-Dof haptic feedback to the trainers. Mohammadreza et al. [98] introduces a haptic rendering method to simulate the bone machining process. The method is an improvement of voxmap point-shell method and developed a data-parallel framework allowing quick visit of voxel-point pairs. The computational efficiency is greatly improved. Due to the inherent mechanical friction, inertia, and limited workspace, current haptic devices usually fail to provide natural haptic interaction in virtual surgery. Some of the work [99] designs a magnetic levitation haptic device based on electromagnetic principles to augment the tissue stiffness perception. It proposes the viewpoint that the effective magnetic field is closely related to the coil attitude for the first time. Probability clouds are designed to describe the requirement of interactive applications, which facilitates the calculation of the best coil attitude. Moreover, it designs a control interface circuit and present a self-adaptive fuzzy PID algorithm to precisely control the coil current for obtaining desired haptic perception. This haptic device has advantages of none mechanical friction, easy expansibility, high accuracy and low power consumption. So, the investigation of how to achieve the spatial and temporal consistency between visual and haptic display is still a problem, so as to provide users with more immersive haptic feedback.

Also, soft tissue cutting is one of the indispensable steps in a lot of maxillofacial procedures. Correspondingly, virtual cutting is at the core of virtual surgical simulators [100]. With the rapid development of computer graphics, virtual cutting has also made great progress in the past 2 decades. Due to its high simulation accuracy [101], the finite element method (FEM) is currently the most commonly used method for virtual cutting simulation. These methods discretize the cutting simulation domain into small finite elements, such as tetrahedron and hexahedron, and then the kinetic equations bound to these basic elements govern the global motion of the simulation domain [102]. Most early research methods employ tetrahedral meshes and model cuts by splitting elements or/ and snapping element vertices onto the cutting surfaces [103–106]. Unfortunately, these procedures are prone to producing ill-shaped elements and easily lead to numerical unstable problem. Current mainstream methods using hexahedral elements for simulation without having to worry about ill-shaped elements [107,108]. These methods model cutting by determining the element faces lying on the cutting surface and always combine a separate surface representation to compensate the jagged simulation domain boundary resulting from the hexahedral discretization. Dick et al. [107] embed an adaptive element refinements and topological changes of the simulation grid into a geometric multigrid solver thus to offer high computational efficiency and physical accuracy. Wu et al. [108] present an efficient collision detection method for composite finite elements (CFEs) simulation of cuts, which can significantly reduce the number of simulation degrees of freedom and support interactive applications. With the same simulation framework, Jia et al. [109] designed a real-time interactive cutting simulation framework of deformable objects by taking advantage of parallel processing capabilities of CPUs and GPUs. In their further work, they employ a pseudo voxel octree to accelerate collision between a cutting tool and deformable objects, which is modeled as voxels connected by links [110].

References

[1] R.K. Sethi, A.J. Henry, N.D. Hevelone, S.R. Lipsitz, M. Belkin, Nguyen LL, Impact of hospital market competition on endovascular aneurysm repair adoption and outcomes", J. Vasc. Surg. 58 (3) (2013) 596–606.

[2] J.E. Davis, The use of simulation in causal analysis of sentinel events in healthcare. Ph.D. thesis, University of Pennsylvania, 2016.

[3] A. Liu, F. Tendick, K. Cleary, et al. A survey of surgical simulation: applications, technology, and education, PTVE 12 (6) (2003) 599–614.

[4] M. Ursino, P.D.J.L. Tasto, B.H. Nguyen, R. Cunningham, G.L. Merril, CathSim: An intravascular catheterization simulator on a PC. Medicine Meets Virtual Reality: The Convergence of Physical and Informational Technologies: Options for a New Era in Healthcare, pp. 360–366, 1999.

[5] A. Liu, C. Kaufmann, T. Ritchie, A Computer-Based Simulator for Diagnostic Peritoneal Lavage, in: J.D. Westwood, et al. (Ed.), Medicine Meets Virtual RealityIOS Press, Amsterdam, 2001, pp. 279–285.

[6] A. Liu, C. Kaufmann, D. Tanaka, An architecture for simulating needle-based surgical procedures, MICCAI 2001 (2001) 1137–1144.

[7] A.D. Koch, S.N. Buzink, J. Heemskerk, et al. Expert and construct validity of the Simbionix GI Mentor II endoscopy simulator for colonoscopy, Surg. Endoscop. 22 (1) (2008) 158–162.

[8] T. Wang, D. Zhang, L. Da, Remote-controlled vascular interventional surgery robot, Int. J. Med. Robot. Comput. Assist. Surg. 6 (2) (2010) 194–201.

[9] D.C. Kelly, A.C. Margules, C.R. Kundavaram, et al. Face, content, and construct validation of the da Vinci Skills Simulator, Urology 79 (5) (2012) 1068–1072.

[10] S.N. Buzink, R.H. Goossens, H.D. Ridder, et al. Training of basic laparoscopy skills on SimSurgery SEP, MITAT 19 (1) (2010) 35–41.

[11] D. Bielser, M.H. Gross, Open surgery simulation, Studies in health technology and informatics 85 (2002) 57–63.

[12] G. Riva, A. Gaggioli, D. Villani, et al. NeuroVR: an open source virtual reality platform for clinical psychology and behavioral neurosciences, Stud. Health Technol. Inform. 125 (1) (2007) 394–399.

[13] Hamza-Lup, G. Felix, Bogdan, M. Crenguta, Popovici, M. Dorin, Costea, D. Ovidiu, A survey of visuo-haptic simulation in surgical training, arXiv preprint (2019).

[14] N.E. Seymour, A.G. Gallagher, S.A. Roman, et al. Virtual reality training improves operating room performance: results of a randomized, double-blinded study, Ann. Surg. 236 (2002) 458–463 discussion 463–464.

[15] T.P. Grantcharov, V.B. Kristiansen, J. Bendix, BardramL, J. Rosenberg, Randomized clinical trial of virtual reality simulation for laparoscopic skills training, Br. J. Surg. 91 (2004) 146–150.

[16] Hiten R.H. Patel, Bijen P. Patel, Virtual reality surgical simulation in training, Exp. Rev. Anticancer Ther. 12 (4) (2012) 417–420.

[17] R. Stilla, K. Sathian, Selective visuo-haptic processing of shape and texture[J], Human Brain Mapping 29 (10) (2008) 1123–1138.

[18] C. Cameron, J.K. Park, D. Beim, Human-computer interaction experiments in an immersive virtual reality environment for elearning applications, Shanxi Arch. 93 (5) (2014) 1820–1870.

[19] K.H. Englmeier, C. Krapichler, M. Haubner, et al. Virtual reality and multimedia human-computer interaction in medicine. Proceedings of the 2nd IEEE International Workshop on Multimedia Signal. IEEE Computer Society Press, Los Alamitos (1998), 193–202.

[20] B.D. Varalakshmi, J. Thriveni, K.R. Venugopal, L.M. Patnaik, Haptics: state of the art survey, Int. J. Comput. Sci. Issues 9 (3) (2012) 234–244.

[21] B. Buxton, V. Hayward, I. Pearson, et al. Big data: the next google, Nature 455 (2008) 8–9.

[22] T.H. Massie, J.K. Salisbury, The PHANToM Haptic Interface: a device for probing virtual objects. Proceedings of IEEE Symposium on Haptic Interfaces for Virtual Environment and Teleoperator Systems. IEEE Computer Society Press, Los Alamitos (1994) 295–301.

[23] M.A. Srinivasan, C. Basdogan, Haptics in virtual environments: taxonomy, research status, and challenges, Comput. Graphic. 21 (4) (1997) 393–404.

[24] W. Mcneely, K. Puterbaugh, J., Six degrees-of-freedom haptic rendering using voxel sampling. Computer Graphics Proceedings, Annual Conference Series, ACM SIGGRAPH. ACM Press, New York (1999) 401–408.

[25] Geomagic. Control geomagic touch & haptics. http://www.geomagic.com/zh/.

[26] Haptic device. Force dimension-home. http://www.forcedimension.com/.

[27] N.D. Marchuk, J.E. Colgate, M.A. Peshkin, Friction measurements on a large area TpaD. Proceedings of IEEE Haptics Symposium. IEEE Computer Society Press, Los Alamitos (2010) 317–320.

[28] J. Mullenbach, C. Shultz, A.M. Piper, et al. Surface haptic interactions with a TPad tablet. Proceedings of the Adjunct Publication of the 26th Annual ACM Symposium on User Interface Software and Technology. ACM Press, New York (2013) 7–8.

[29] A.G. Perez, D. Lobo, F. Chinello, et al. Soft finger tactile rendering for wearable haptics. Proceedings of IEEE World Haptics Conference. IEEE Computer Society Press, Los Alamitos (2015) 327–332.

[30] C. Bermejo, P. Hui, A survey on haptic technologies for mobile augmented reality, arXiv:1709 00698 (2017).

[31] T. Hoshi, D. Abe, H. Shinoda, Adding tactile reaction to hologram. Robot and Human Interactive Communication, 2009. RO-MAN 2009. The 18th IEEE International Symposium on IEEE (2009) 7–11.

[32] T. Carter, S.A. Seah, B. Long, B. Drinkwater, S. Subramanian, UltraHaptics : Multi-Point Mid-Air Haptic Feedback for Touch Surfaces. In: Proceedings of the 26th annual ACM symposium on User interface software and technology (UIST '13). Association for Computing Machinery, New York, NY, USA, (2013) 505–514.

[33] H. Lee, H. Cha, J. Park, S. Choi, H.S. Kim, S.C. Chung . LaserStroke. Proceedings of the 29th Annual Symposium on User Interface Software and Technology - UIST 16 Adjunct (2016) 73–74.

[34] Y. Ochiai, K. Kumagai, T. Hoshi, S. Hasegawa, Y. Hayasaki, Cross-field aerial haptics : rendering haptic feedback in air with light and acoustic fields, Chi 16 (2016) 3238–3247.

[35] W. Dangxiao, S. Meng, N. Afzal, Z. Yukai, X. Weiliang, Z. Yuru, Toward whole-hand kinesthetic feedback: a survey of force feedback gloves, IEEE Trans. Haptics 12 (2) (2019) 189–204.

[36] J.J. Kim, H. Nam, N.R. Kaipatur, P.W. Major, C. Flores-Mir, M.O. Lagravere, D.L. Romanyk, Reliability and accuracy of segmentation of mandibular condyles from different three-dimensional imaging modalities: A systematic review, Dentomaxillofac. Radiol. 49 (2019) 20190150.

[37] M. Bayram, S. Kayipmaz, O.S. Sezgin, M. Küçük, Volumetric analysis of the mandibular condyle using cone beam computed tomography, Eur. J. Radiol. 81 (2012,) 1812–1816.

[38] T.J. Huff, P.E. Ludwig, J.M. Zuniga, The potential for machine learning algorithms to improve and reduce the cost of 3-dimensional printing for surgical planning Expert Rev, Med. Dev. 15 (2018) 349–356.

[39] T. Dong, L. Xia, C. Cai, L. Yuan, N. Ye, B. Fang, Accuracy of in vitro mandibular volumetric measurements from cbct of different voxel sizes with different segmentation threshold settings, BMC Oral Health 19 (2019) 206.

[40] W.P. Engelbrecht, Z. Fourie, J. Damstra, P.O. Gerrits, Y. Ren, The influence of the segmentation process on 3d measurements from cone beam computed tomography-derived surface models, Clin. Oral Invest. 17 (2013) 1919–1927.

[41] Z. Fourie, J. Damstra, R.H. Schepers, P.O. Gerrits, Y. Ren, Segmentation process significantly influences the accuracy of 3d surface models derived from cone beam computed tomography, Eur. J. Radiol. 81 (2012) e524–e530.

[42] T. Xi, R. Schreurs, W.. Heerink, et al. A novel region-growing based semi-automatic segmentation protocol for three-dimensional condylar reconstruction using cone beam computed tomography (CBCT)[J], PloS One 9 (11) (2014) e111126.

[43] I. Méndez-Manjón, O.L. Haas Jr., R. Guijarro-Martínez, et al. Semi-automated three-dimensional condylar reconstruction, J. Craniofac. Surgery 30 (8) (2019) 2555–2559.

[44] J. Wallner, M. Schwaiger, K. Hochegger, et al. A review on multiplatform evaluations of semi-automatic open-source based image segmentation for cranio-maxillofacial surgery[J], Comput. Methods Prog. Biomed. 182 (2019) 105102.

[45] A. Lo Giudice, V. Quinzi, V. Ronsivalle, et al. Evaluation of imaging software accuracy for 3-dimensional analysis of the mandibular condyle a comparative study using a surface-to-surface matching technique, Int. J. Environ. Res. Public Health 17 (13) (2020) 4789.

[46] S.T. Gollmer, T.M. Buzug, Fully automatic shape constrained mandible segmentation from cone-beam CT data. Ninth IEEE International Symposium on Biomedical Imaging (IEEE) (2012), 272–275.

[47] N. Torosdagli, D.K. Liberton, P. Verma, M. Sincan, J. Lee, S. Pattanaik, et al., Robust and fully automated segmentation of mandible from CT scans. IEEE Fourteenth International Symposium on Biomedical Imaging (IEEE) (2017) 1209–1212.

[48] A. Chen, B. Dawant, A multi-atlas approach for the automatic segmentation of multiple structures in head and neck CT images. Head and Neck Auto-Segmentation Challenge, Munich, 2015.

[49] R. Mannion-Haworth, M. Bowes, A. Ashman, G. Guillard, A. Brett, G. Vincent, Fully automatic segmentation of head and neck organs using active appearance models. MIDAS J. (2015).

[50] T. Albrecht, T. Gass, C. Langguth, M. Lüthi, Multi atlas segmentation with active shape model refinement for multi-organ segmentation in head and neck cancer radiotherapy planning. Head and Neck Auto-Segmentation Challenge, Munich, 2015.

[51] J. Long, E. Shelhamer, T Darrell, Fully convolutional networks for semantic segmentation, Proc. IEEE Conf. Comput. Vision Pattern Recog. (2015) 3431–3440.

[52] O. Ronneberger, P. Fischer, T. Brox. U-net: Convolutional networks for biomedical image segmentation. International Conference on Medical image computing and computer-assisted intervention. Springer, Cham, 2015, 234–241.

[53] L. Yu et al., Volumetric convnets with mixed residual connections for automated prostate segmentation from 3d MR images, AAAI, 2017.

[54] J. Minnema, M. van Eijnatten, W. Kouw, F. Diblen, A. Mendrik, J. Wolff, Ct image segmentation of bone for medical additive manufacturing using a convolutional neural network, Comput. Biol. Med. 103 (2018) 130–139.

[55] T. Pan, B. Wang, G. Ding, J.H. Yong, Fully convolutional neural networks with full-scale-features for semantic segmentation, 2017.

[56] F. Isensee, J. Petersen, A. Klein, et al. nnu-net: Self-adapting framework for u-net-based medical image segmentation, arXiv preprint 1809 (2018) 10486.

[57] B. Ibragimov, Xing L, Segmentation of organs-at-risks in head and neck CT images using convolutional neural networks, Med. Phys. 44 (2017) 547–557.

[58] W. Zhu, Y. Huang, H. Tang, Z. Qian, N. Du, W. Fan, et al., Anatomynet: deep 3D squeeze-and-excitation U-Nets for fast and fully automated whole-volume anatomical segmentation. arXiv:1808.05238 (2018).

[59] Y. Lei, J. Zhou, X. Dong, et al., Multi-organ segmentation in head and neck MRI using U-Faster-RCNN. Proceedings of SPIE, Medical Imaging 2020: Image Processing. International Society for Optics and Photonics 11313 (2020) 113133A.

[60] M. Zhao, L. Wang, J. Chen, et al., Craniomaxillofacial bony structures segmentation from MRI with deep-supervision adversarial learning. International Conference on Medical Image Computing and Computer-Assisted Intervention. Springer, Cham, 2018, 720–727.

[61] B. Qiu, J. Guo, J. Kraeima, et al. Automatic segmentation of the mandible from computed tomography scans for 3D virtual surgical planning using the convolutional neural network, Phys. Med. Biol. 64 (17) (2019) 175020.

[62] B.S. Almaqrami, M.S. Alhammadi, B. Cao, Three dimensional reliability analyses of currently used methods for assessment of sagittal jaw discrepancy, J. Clin. Exp. Dent. 10 (4) (2018) e352–e360.

[63] S. Pelo, P. Correra, G. Gasparini, T.M. Marianetti, D. Cervelli, C. Grippaudo, et al. Three-dimensional analysis and treatment planning of hemimandibular hyperplasia, J Craniofac Surg. 22 (6) (2011) 2227–2234.

[64] N. Mathew, S. Gandhi, I. Singh, et al. 3D models revolutionizing surgical outcomes in oral and maxillofacial surgery: experience at our center, J. Maxillofac. Oral Surgery (2019) 1–9.

[65] J. Montúfar, M. Romero, R.J. Scougall-Vilchis, Automatic 3-dimensional cephalometric landmarking based on active shape models in related projections, Am. J. Orthod. Dentofac. Orthop. 153 (3) (2018) 449.

[66] D. Jaffray, P. Kupelian, T. Djemil, R.M. Macklis, Review of image-guided radiation therapy, Exp. Rev. Anticancer Ther. 7 (2007) 89–103.

[67] M. Kersten-Oertel, P. Jannin, D.L. Collins, The state of the art of visualization in mixed reality image guided surgery, Comput. Med. Imaging Graphic. 37 (2013) 98–112.

[68] J.K. Udupa, H.M. Hung, K.S. Chuang, Surface and volume rendering in three-dimensional imaging: a comparison, J. Digital Imaging 4 (3) (1991) 159.

[69] R. Shahidi, B. Lorensen, R. Kikinis, et al. Surface rendering versus volume rendering in medical imaging: techniques and applications, Visual. Conf. IEEE (1996) 439–440.

[70] W. Lorensen, H. Cline, Marching cubes: a high resolution 3D surface construction algorithm, ACM Comput. Graphic. 21 (4) (1987).

[71] J. Kim, Y. Jung, D.D. Feng, et al. Biomedical image visualization and display technologies, Biomedical Information TechnologyAcademic Press, 2020, pp. 561–583.

[72] C. Tominski, S. Gladisch, U. Kister, R. Dachselt, SchumannF H., Interactive lenses for visualization: an extended survey, Comput. Graphic. Forum (2017) 173–200.

[73] S. Takahashi, I. Fujishiro, Y. Takeshima, T. Nishita, A feature-driven approach to locating optimal viewpoints for volume visualization, VIS 05. IEEE (2005) 495–502.

[74] U.D. Bordoloi, H.-W. Shen, View selection for volume rendering, VIS 05. IEEE (2005) 487–494.

[75] J.J. Caban, A. Joshi, P. Nagy, Rapid development of medical imaging tools with open-source libraries, J. Digital Imaging 20 (2007) 83–93.

[76] S. Rasteau, N. Sigaux, A. Louvrier, et al. Three-dimensional acquisition technologies for facial soft tissues–Applications and prospects in orthognathic surgery, J. Stomatol. Oral Maxillofac. Surg. 121 (6) (2020) 721–728.

[77] G. Badiali, L. Cercenelli, S. Battaglia, E. Marcelli, C. Marchetti, V. Ferrari, F. Cutolo, Review on augmented reality in oral and cranio-maxillofacial surgery: toward "surgery-specific" head-up displays, IEEE Access 8 (2020) 59015–59028.

[78] A.R. Memon, E. Wang, J. Hu, J. Egger, X. Chen, A review on computer-aided design and manufacturing of patient-specific maxillofacial implants, Exp. Rev. Med. Device. 17 (4) (2020) 345–356.

[79] F. Wu, X. Chen, Y. Lin, C. Wanf, X. Wang, G. Shen, J. Qin, P.A.S. Heng, A virtual training system for maxillofacial surgery using advanced haptic feedback and immersive workbench, Int. J. Med. Robot. 10 (1) (2014) 78–87.

[80] P. Peserico-DalFarra, A.F. Gagliardi-Lugo, Training simulation for oral and maxillofacial surgeons based on the techniques of arthroscopy in the temporomandibular joint, Br. J. Oral Maxillofac. Surg. 57 (9) (2019) 929–931.

[81] Q. Ma, E. Kobayashi, B. Fan, K. Nakagawa, I. Sakuma, K. Masamune, H. Suenaga, Automatic 3D landmarking model using patch-based deep neural networks for CT image of oral and maxillofacial surgery, Int. J. Med. Robot. Comput. Assist. Surg. 16 (3) (2020) e2093.

[82] E. Wang, H. Shi, Y. Sun, C. Politis, L. Lan, X. Chen, Computer-aided porous implant design for cranio-maxillofacial defect restoration, Int. J. Med. Robot. Comput. Assist. Surg. (2020) e2134.

[83] S. Mazzoni, G. Badiali, L. Lancellotti, L. Babbi, A. Bianchi, C. Marchetti, Simulation-guided navigation: a new approach to improve intraoperative three-dimensional reproducibility during orthognathic surgery, J. Craniofac. Surg. 21 (6) (2010) 1698–1705.

[84] S. Sukegawa, T. Kanno, Y. Furuki, Application of computer-assisted navigation systems in oral and maxillofacial surgery, Jpn. Dental Sci. Rev. 54 (3) (2018) 139–149.

[85] J.C. Lutz, A. Hostettler, V. Agnus, S. Nicolau, D. George, L. Soler, Y. Rémond, A new software suite in orthognathic surgery: patient specific modeling, simulation and navigation, Surg. Innov. 26 (1) (2019) 5–20.

[86] J. Ahn, H. Choi, J. Hong, J. Hong, Tracking accuracy of a stereo camera-based augmented reality navigation system for orthognathic surgery, J. Oral Maxillofac. Surg. 77 (5) (2019) 1070.e1–1070.e11.

[87] Y.P. Murugesan, A. Alsadoon, P. Manoranjan, P.W.C. Prasad, A novel rotational matrix and translation vector algorithm: Geometric accuracy for augmented reality in oral and maxillofacial surgeries, Int. J. Med. Robot. Comput. Assist. Surg. 14 (3) (2018) e1889.

[88] J. Wang, Y. Shen, S. Yang, A practical marker-less image registration method for augmented reality oral and maxillofacial surgery, Int. J. Comput. Assist. Radiol. Surg. 14 (5) (2019) 763–773.

[89] Nysjö, J., Interactive 3D image analysis for cranio-maxillofacial surgery planning and orthopedic applications (Doctoral dissertation, Acta Universitatis Upsaliensis), 2016.

[90] J. Wang, H. Suenaga, L. Yang, E. Kobayashi, I. Sakuma, Video see-through augmented reality for oral and maxillofacial surgery, Int. J. Med. Robot. Comput. Assist. Surg. 13 (2) (2016) e1754.

[91] H.H. Liu, L.J. Li, B. Shi, C.W. Xu, E. Luo, Robotic surgical systems in maxillofacial surgery: a review, Int. J. Oral Sci. 9 (2) (2017) 63–73.

[92] Q. Ma, E. Kobayashi, J. Wang, K. Hara, H. Suenaga, I. Sakuma, K. Masamune, Development and preliminary evaluation of an autonomous surgical system for oral and maxillofacial surgery, Int. J. Med. Robot. Comput. Assist. Surg. 15 (4) (2019) e1997.

[93] Q. Ma, E. Kobayashi, H. Suenaga, K. Hara, J. Wang, K. Nakagawa, K. Masamune, Autonomous surgical robot with camera-based markerless navigation for oral and maxillofacial surgery, IEEE/ASME Trans. Mech. 25 (2) (2020) 1084–1094.

[94] M. Arbabtafti, M. Moghaddam, A. Nahvi, M. Mahvash, B. Richardson, B. Shirinzadeh, Physics-based haptic simulation of bone machining, IEEE Trans. Haptics 4 (1) (2011) 39–50.

[95] Q. Wang, H. Chen, W. Wu, H.Y. Jin, P.A. Heng, Real-time mandibular angle reduction surgical simulation with haptic rendering, IEEE Trans. Inform. Technol. Biomed. 16 (6) (2012) 1105–1114.

[96] Q. Wang, H. Chen, W. Wu, J. Qin, P.A. Heng, Impulse-based rendering methods for haptic simulation of bone-burring, IEEE Trans. Haptics 5 (4) (2012) 344–355.

[97] W. Dangxiao, Z. Yuru, H. Jianxia, W. Yong, L. Peijun, C. Yonggang, Z. Hui, iDental: a haptic-based dental simulator and its preliminary user evaluation, IEEE Trans. Haptics 5 (4) (2012) 332–343.

[98] S. Mohammadreza Faieghi, O. Farokh Atashzar, Remus Tutunea-Fatan, Roy Eagleson, Parallel haptic rendering for orthopedic surgery simulators, IEEE Robot. Automat. Lett. 5 (4) (2020) 6388–6395.

[99] T. Qianqian, Y. Zhiyong, L. Xiangyun, Z. Mianlun, Y. Tianchen, Z. Jianhui, Magnetic levitation haptic augmentation for virtual tissue stiffness perception, IEEE Trans. Visual. Comput. Graphic. 24 (12) (2018) 3123–3136.

[100] W. Jun, W. Rudiger, D. Christian, A survey of physically based simulation of cuts in deformable bodies, Comput. Graphic. Forum 34 (6) (2015) 161–187.

[101] M. Moumnassi, S. Belouettar, E.B Bechet, S.P Ordas, D Quoirin, Y.M. Potier-Ferr, Finite element analysis on implicitly defined domains: An accurate representation based on arbitrary parametric surfaces, Comput. Methods Appl. Mech. Eng. 200 (5–8) (2011) 774–796.

[102] A. Hrennikoff, Solution of problems of elasticity by the framework method, J. Appl. Mech. 8 (4) (1941) 169–175.

[103] J.F. O'brien, J.K. Hodgins, Graphical modeling and animation of brittle fracture, in: Proceedings of SIGGRAPH, ACM Press/Addison-Wesley Publishing Co., Los Angeles, CA, United States (1999) 137–146.

[104] S. Cotin, H. Delingette, N. Ayache, A hybrid elastic model for real-time cutting, deformations, and force feedback for surgery training and simulation, Visual Comput. 16 (8) (2000) 437–452.

[105] A.B. Mor, T. Kanade, Modifying soft tissue models: Progressive cutting with minimal new element creation, in: MICCAI '00: Proceedings of the Third International Conference on Medical Image Computing and Computer-Assisted Intervention, Springer-Verlag, Berlin, Heidelberg (2000) 598–607.

[106] J.F. O'brien, A.W. Bargteil, J.K. Hodgins, Graphical modeling and animation of ductile fracture, ACM Trans. Graphic. 21 (3) (2002) 291–294.

[107] C. Dick, J. Georgii, R. Westermann, A hexahedral multigrid approach for simulating cuts in deformable objects, IEEE Trans. Visual. Comput. Graphic. 17 (11) (2011) 1663–1675.

[108] J. Wu, C. Dick, R. Westermann, Efficient collision detection for composite finite element simulation of cuts in deformable bodies, Visual Comput. 29 (6–8) (2013) 739–749.

[109] J. Shiyu, Z. Weizhong, Y. Xiaokang, P. Zhenkuan, CPU–GPU parallel framework for real-time interactive cutting of adaptive octree-based deformable objects, Comput. Graphic. Forum 37 (1) (2018) 45–59.

[110] J. Shiyu, Z. Weizhong, P. Zhenkuan, W. Guodong, Y. Xiaokang, Using pseudo voxel octree to accelerate collision between cutting tool and deformable objects modeled as linked voxels, Visual Comput. 36 (2020) 1017–1028.

Surgical navigation

Wang Manning[a,b], Song Zhijian[a,b]

[a]*DIGITAL MEDICAL RESEARCH CENTER, SCHOOL OF BASIC MEDICAL SCIENCES, FUDAN UNIVERSITY, SHANGHAI, CHINA;* [b]*SHANGHAI KEY LABORATORY OF MEDICAL IMAGE COMPUTING AND COMPUTER ASSISTED INTERVENTION, SHANGHAI, CHINA*

Surgical navigation is an analogy of Global Positioning System (GPS) used on your car. The core function of GPS is to locate your car on an electronic map, so as to help you drive to the destination rapidly and safely. Similarly, the core function of a surgical navigation system is to locate surgical tools on an electronic map of the human anatomical structure, so as to help surgeons perform operation rapidly and safely. There are two key elements for the GPS to fulfill its function: First, it needs an accurate electronic map of the place where you want to go; second, it is able to track the position of your car and draw it on the correct position of the map in real time. Similarly, there are also two key elements for a surgical navigation system to fulfill its function: First, it needs an accurate map of the human anatomical structure, which is usually established by radiological images of the patient to be operated on; second, it needs to track the position of surgical tools relative to the patient and visualize the tools on the map. The working principle and some technical details of surgical navigation will be first introduced in this chapter, followed by a brief introduction of its clinical application in oral and craniomaxillofacial (OCMF) surgery and several latest technical progress.

1 From stereotaxy to surgical navigation

It has always been the focus of surgical operation to accurately locate the patient's normal anatomical structures and lesions. With the fast development of several medical imaging techniques in 1980s, such as computed tomography (CT) and magnetic resonance imaging (MRI), for the first time, surgeons have an accurate three dimensional (3D) map of a patient's body, which can help them to locate the normal structures and lesions. At the beginning, the medical images are printed on radiographic films or displayed on a computer screen, and surgeons can only memorize the patient's anatomical structures and the location of the lesions to guide their operation and the images cannot be used directly to locate the surgical tools. This process is just like that you drive your car on the road with a paper map in your pocket. Though this kind of indirect use of medical images is very helpful for surgeons, directly using the images to guide operation is more desirable.

The first technique that accomplishes direct locating anatomical structure and lesions with medical images is stereotaxy used in neurosurgery, as illustrated in Fig. 7.1. In stereotactic

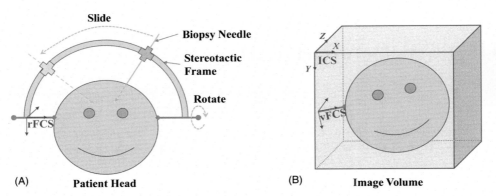

FIGURE 7.1 Illustration of the working principle of stereotactic neurosurgery.

neurosurgery, a frame is first fixed onto the patient's skull firmly with several bone screws. The patient undergoes medical imaging with the frame on his head so that the frame itself is visible on the images. A 3D medical image volume is shown in Fig. 7.1B, in which we can see both the patient's head and some parts of the frame that can be imaged. There is a coordinate system associated with the image volume and we denote it as image coordinate system (ICS), and for each voxel in the volume there is a coordinate in the ICS. The next step of stereotactic neurosurgery is to make surgical plans in a planning workstation. The images are loaded into the workstation and the visible parts of the frame are segmented out, based on which a local coordinate system is established, and we denote it as virtual frame coordinate system (vFCS). There is a coordinate system associated with the real frame and it is denoted as real frame coordinate system (rFCS). The stereotactic frame is specially designed so that the visible parts in the images has a fixed coordinate in rFCS, and in the surgical planning workstation, the vFCS is defined on a pre-defined position and orientation relative to the visible parts of the frame. In this way, the coordinate transformation between vFCS and rFCS can be calculated directly from their definition. The transformation from vFCS to rFCS is denoted as Tvr, which usually consists of a 3D rotation and a 3D translation. The simplest Tvr is that 3D rotation is an identity matrix and 3D translation is a zero vector, which means that the vFCS and rFCS are identical. If the rFCS and vFCS are defined on different position or with different orientation relative to the frame, there will be a rotation and/or a translation between them. Furthermore, there may also be some anisotropic scaling along each axis.

With the coordinate transformation between vFCS and rFCS calculated by using the stereotactic frame, a spatial correspondence is established between the real patient's anatomical structure and the images, which is the prerequisite of direct using images to locate surgical tools. One major application of stereotactic frames in neurosurgery is biopsy, where a needle is inserted into the brain precisely to a pre-planned position to take a tissue sample. The biopsy target is identified on the images in the surgical planning workstation and its coordinate in vFCS is recorded, which is then transformed into rFCS by applying Tvr, so that the coordinate of the biopsy target in rFCS is obtained. The stereotactic frame is designed so that it can be adjusted to guide the biopsy needle to reach a pre-defined position. For example, in Fig. 7.1A, the biopsy needle can be adjusted to an arbitrary direction by rotating the arc-shaped frame and sliding the rod along the frame. The insertion depth of the needle can be controlled according to scale lines on the needle.

With the stereotactic frame system, very high biopsy accuracy can be achieved and this kind of system is still widely used nowadays in neurosurgery with high accuracy requirements, such as stereotactic function neurosurgery. However, the limitations of the stereotactic frame system are also very obvious. First, the frame needs to be fixed to the patient's head before surgery and the patient has to keep the frame on his head until the surgery is finished, including during the process of medical imaging. The fixation of the frame and the long period of time with the frame on head is not only invasive but also bring big psychological pressure to the patient. Second, the system can only be used to guide the insertion of a needle to a predefined position, and cannot be used to guide other surgical tools that move freely during surgery. Third, during the process of adjusting the needle orientation and inserting the needle, no feedback of the position of the needle relative to the patient's anatomical structure is provided. Finally, the frame is usually bulky and hinders surgical operation.

Surgical navigation borrows ideas from stereotactic system while extends its application and avoid its shortcomings by applying new technology. Surgical navigation was first used in neurosurgery in 1980s and at early times, it is usually called frameless stereotactic system. The basic objective of surgical navigation is the same as that of stereotactic system, that is, to locate surgical tools with images. The first idea that surgical navigation borrows from stereotactic system is the image coordinate system, and it is also denoted as ICS in surgical navigation. In surgical navigation, ICS is also defined on an image volume, which is composed of a series of sectional images. The second concept borrowed is the definition of a real world coordinate system and the efforts to establish correspondence between it and ICS. In stereotactic system, the real world coordinate system is defined on the stereotactic frame and the transformation between real world coordinate system and ICS is achieved by imaging the frame together with the patient. However, in surgical navigation, the frame is removed, so some new techniques must be adopted to define a new real world coordinate system and map it to ICS. In the next section, the working principle of surgical navigation system will be introduced and focus will be placed on how surgical navigation establishes a real world coordinate system and how it is mapped to ICS.

The essence of surgical navigation is to use images to guide surgery, so it is also called image-guided surgery in some literature. In almost all circumstances, surgical navigation, frameless stereotactic system, and image-guide surgery can be regarded as identical terms, and the term of surgical navigation is used in this book.

2 Working principle of surgical navigation

Similar to stereotactic system, surgical navigation also establishes a correspondence between a real world coordinate system and an image coordinate system so that the images can be used to locate the position of surgical tools in the real world. Surgical

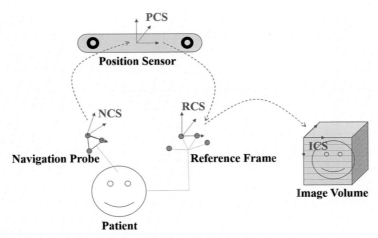

FIGURE 7.2 Illustration of the working principle of surgical navigation.

navigation defines ICS in the same way as stereotactic surgery, but the real world coordinate systems are different because no frame is used in surgical navigation.

The working principle of surgical navigation is shown in Fig. 7.2, where a position sensor is used to help establish the real world coordinate system and calculate transformation between the real world coordinate system and the ICS [1]. The position sensor tracks specially designed tools in real time, which are called tracked tools. The tracking is done in the following way. There is a coordinate system defined on the position sensor and it is denoted as position-sensor coordinate system (PCS). For each tracked tool, there is a coordinate system defined on the tool. There are two tracked tools in Fig. 7.2, the navigation probe and the reference frame, and the two coordinate systems defined on the two tracked tools are denoted as navigation-probe coordinate system (NCS) and reference-frame coordinate system (RCS). The position sensor is designed to track the tools and calculate a spatial transformation between the tool's local coordinate system and the PCS. In Fig. 7.2, the spatial transformation from NCS to PCS and from PCS to RCS is denoted as Tnp and Tpr, respectively. Please note that the spatial transformation is invertible. For example, the inverse of Tnp is the spatial transformation from PCS to NCS. There are mainly two types of position sensors used in surgical navigation, optical sensors, and electromagnetic sensors, and the working principle of each type and the corresponding pros and cons will be discussed in the next section.

In surgical navigation performed on the head, a reference frame is firmly fixed to the head. Therefore, the position of the patient in the RCS keeps unchanged during the whole process of surgery. The reference frame helps define the real world coordinate system where the patient anatomy resides in, and its function is similar to the stereotactic frame in stereotactic surgery. The difference is that the reference frame is fixed to the patient's head just before the surgery and the patient does not need undertake medical imaging with the reference frame on his head. As a result, the reference frame does not exist in the images and the method used in stereotactic surgery to establish correspondence between the real world and the images cannot be used in surgical navigation. On the contrary, surgical navigation utilizes a different technique to obtain this spatial transformation, and the technique is called spatial registration. Concretely, surgical navigation uses spatial registration to calculate a spatial transformation between RCS and ICS. Spatial registration is done by aligning corresponding structures existing in the two coordinate systems to be registered. In surgical navigation, the structures aligned include fiducial points [2] and head surface [3]. Here, we introduce the process of spatial registration and real-time navigation in the scenario of spatial registration with fiducial points.

In fiducial point based spatial registration, surgeons first identify several fiducial points on the images and record their coordinates in ICS. The points that can serve as fiducial points should be easily accessible and can be precisely located both in the real world and on the images. The fiducial points can be anatomical landmarks, such as nose tip, inner canthus, outer canthus, and so on [4]. Alternatively, some artificial fiducial points can be used such as adhesive markers or bone screws, which need to be fixed on the patient's head before medical imaging so that they exist in the image volume [2]. Usually, four to eight fiducial points are recorded in the ICS. Then, for each fiducial point, the surgeon records the coordinates of its corresponding point in RCS by putting the tip of the navigation probe to the point. At the same time, the position sensor tracks the navigation probe and the reference frame simultaneously and obtains the spatial transformation from NCS to PCS and from PCS to RCS, which are denoted as Tnp and Tpr, respectively. The coordinates of the tip of the navigation probe in NCS is known from tool designing, so its coordinate in RCS when pointing to a fiducial point can be calculated by applying Tnp and Tpr sequentially to its original coordinate in NCS. Therefore, by pointing the navigation probe to a fiducial point and tracking the navigation probe and the reference frame at the same time, the fiducial point's coordinates in RCS can be recorded. After recording the coordinates in RCS for all the fiducial points, together with their coordinates in ICS, some analytical algorithm can be used to calculate an optimal spatial transformation between RCS and ICS [5], and we denote the transformation from RCS to ICS as Tri.

After calculating Tri from spatial registration, real time navigation can be done during the whole period of surgery by applying Tnp, Tpr, and Tri. When the surgeon points the navigation probe to the patient's head, the position sensor tracks the tool and the reference frame at the same time so as to obtain Tnp and Tpr, which transform the coordinates of the tip of the navigation probe from NCS to PCS and from PCS to RCS, respectively. Then by applying Tri, the coordinates of the probe tip are transformed into ICS so that it can be displayed on the corresponding point on the images. The relative position of the probe tip to the images is the same as the relative position of the tool tip to the patient's anatomical structure in the real world. When the surgeon moves the navigation probe to a different position, its coordinates in RCS changes and this change is captured in real time by the position sensor and it is reflected in the changes of Tnp. The patient may also move in the real world and this movement is captured by the position sensor tracking the reference frame and it is reflected in the changes of Tpr. The transformation Tri keeps unchanged during the whole process of surgery and it is effective as long as the patient's position keeps unchanged in RCS.

We explore the images and the ICS here in more detail. In Fig. 7.2, ICS is defined on a series of axial images of head. Concretely, the origin is put on the lower left corner of the first (upper most) slice, and X- and Z-axis are defined to be along the two edge of the first slice. The Y-axis is defined to be vertical to the slice and pointing to the lower slices. In different systems, the origin may be defined on different positions in the image volume and the axes may point to different directions, though in most cases the axes align with the volume edges. There is one thing that we should pay attention to, which is that the inter-pixel resolution within each slice is usually different from the inter-slice resolution. If we simply stack every slice together to get the image volume, its resolution in different directions may be different. Conceptually, we establish an ICS in the volume and maintain a transformation between the coordinates expressed in ICS and the voxel index in the volume, which corresponds to the slice index in the series and pixel index in the slice. We can define the ICS in a specific position and orientation and then resample the volume to make the voxel index the same as the voxel's coordinates in ICS. No matter if the image volume is resampled to align with the ICS, once we obtain a coordinate in ICS, we can always identify the corresponding position in the image volume.

3 Technical details of surgical navigation used in OCMF surgery

Surgical navigation was first used in neurosurgery and it is widely used in many different disciplines nowadays, such as neurosurgery, orthopedic surgery, spinal surgery, ENT surgery, and so on. In addition, many systems for new application have also been developed, such as for prostate biopsy and bronchoscopy biopsy. Though the basic idea of using medical images to locate surgical tools is the same in different systems, the technical details in different systems may be different. A general description of techniques and applications of surgical navigation can be found in recent reviews [6,7]. In this section, we introduce the technical details of surgical navigation used in OCMF surgery.

3.1 Image processing in the ICS

The purpose of using surgical navigation is to use medical images in ICS to guide the surgical operation, so the more information the ICS contains the more helpful the navigation system will be. Therefore, medical image processing in the ICS plays an important role in the application of surgical navigation. A typical interface window of a surgical navigation system consists of four sub-windows, in which three sub-windows are used to display the axial, coronal, and sagittal images of the volume and the fourth sub-window is used to display the 3D model. Three commonly used image-processing techniques will be introduced in this subsection.

1. **Three dimensional reconstruction and visualization**

   In surgical navigation, surgeons mainly depend on 2D images to locate the position of a surgical tool relative to the patient's structures, but the 3D model of the patient's anatomical structure is also essential, because they are used in identifying fiducial points or doing surgical planning. Displaying the 3D anatomical structures contained in original 2D slices is called visualization, and the commonly used visualization algorithms can be divided into two categories: direct visualization and indirect visualization [8]. Direct visualization means that an image of the 3D structure is directly generated from the original 2D slices without intermediate processing, such as ray casting. Indirect visualization means an intermediate process is used to extract the surface of the 3D structure, which is also called reconstruction of the 3D model of the structure, and then the 3D model is visualized by using dedicated surface visualizing algorithms. Sophisticated direct and indirect visualization algorithms exist in literature, and the readers are referred to [8] for more details. Generally speaking, the advantage of direct visualization is that no intermediate processing is needed and richer information is usually contained in the 3D images. The disadvantage of direct visualization is that there is not an explicit 3D model of the visualized structure, which makes it difficult to do complex surgical planning. Segmentation of the structure that we want to visualize is an essential step for indirect visualization, and the error in segmentation will result in the error in the 3D model. For some structures in medical images, segmentation itself might be a demanding task. It should be noted that direct visualization can also visualize the surface of an organ only if a segmentation is done. When using a surgical navigation system, surgeons usually need not know what techniques are used for visualization. In OCMF surgery, skin and craniomaxillofacial bone are usually visualized. Some other structures may be visualized for different purposes.

2. **Image segmentation**

   Segmentation is to assign a label to a subset of voxels in the image volume to designate that the labeled voxels belong to a specific structure, such as skull, lesion, and so on. In most surgical navigation systems, segmentation of some structures is a prerequisite of 3D visualization and surgical planning. The simplest medical image segmentation method is threshold segmentation, and it can produce reliable results when the image intensity of the structure of interest is different from surrounding structures. For example, in both CT and MRI images, threshold segmentation can successfully segment out the human anatomy from background so as to visualize the skin of a patient. In CT images, the intensity of bone is higher than the intensity of surrounding soft tissue, so it is usually easy to accurately segment out and visualize bone in CT images.

   In some more complex scenarios, it may be difficult to segment out the structure of interest by simply using an intensity threshold. For example, for some patients with lesions, it may be difficult to segment out the lesion from surrounding organs because of the heterogeneity of lesion intensity. In patients with fracture, the intensity of different bone fragments is similar to each other so we cannot segment out each bone fragment simply by an intensity threshold. In addition, if MRI images are used, the intensity distribution of different organs and lesions in MRI images are more complicated and segmentation is usually more difficult. Medical image segmentation has always been a hot research topic in the field of medical image analysis, and a great deal of algorithms have been developed for different applications, including surgical navigation. A comprehensive discussion of medical image segmentation is out of the scope of this book, and the readers are referred to latest reviews on conventional [9] and deep learning based [10] medical image segmentation approaches. Because of the difficulty of medical image segmentation, no one algorithm can meet all different requirements in different applications. In many systems, manual or interactive segmentation tools are provided as the final solution when automatic algorithms fail.

3. **Image registration**

In the working principle shown in Fig. 7.2, there is only one image volume and the ICS is defined on it. In OCMF surgical navigation, the most widely used images are CT images, but in some cases, images of other modalities, such as MRI images are also needed to provide complementary information. For example, the bone can be clearly seen in CT images but at the same time, we may need MRI images to view lesions. In this scenario, we need to locate navigation tools on different image volumes. Surgical navigation does not register the RCS to different ICSs, but instead registers different image volumes and transform all image volumes into the same ICS. Medical image registration is also a hot research topic in the field of medical image analysis, and in surgical navigation, we often perform a rigid registration of images of different modalities, in which a rigid transformation is calculated between the two image volumes so that when the two volumes are transformed into the same ICS, corresponding anatomical structures align with each other. A comprehensive review of medical image registration method can be found in Refs. [11,12] .

In surgical navigation, two image registration algorithms are often used: fiducial point based registration and image volume based registration. The algorithm and workflow of fiducial point based medical image registration is the same as fiducial point based spatial registration, which is briefly introduced in Section 2 and will be further discussed in detail in the next section. When registering two image volumes, a set of corresponding fiducial points are recorded in both image volumes and then an analytical algorithm is used to calculate the rigid transformation between the two volumes. Fiducial point based registration is stable and in the cases that the fiducial points can be precisely located in both image volumes, such as in CT and MRI T1 image volumes, high registration accuracy can be achieved. However, some medical images have low resolution and the image itself is very blurry, such as MRI DWI, fMRI, and MRS images, and in these kinds of images, it is impossible to precisely locate a fiducial point. In registering these blurry and low-resolution images with other images, volume based registration methods can be explored, and the most widely used one of them is maximization of mutual information (MMI) [13].

The two volumes to be registered is called reference volume and floating volume, and the objective of MMI is to calculate a rigid transformation from the floating volume to the reference volume so that the mutual information between the two image volumes are maximized. MMI iteratively optimizes the transformation, which usually consists of a 3D rotation and a 3D translation to gradually maximize the mutual information. The rationale behind MMI registration is that though the intensity of the same organ is different in different images, they tend to be the same in the same image, so when two image volumes are registered and the same organ in different image volumes are aligned, the joint intensity distribution tends to concentrate together. On the contrary, when the two volumes are not aligned correctly, an organ in one image volume may overlap with several different organs with different intensities in the other image, which makes the joint intensity distribution disperse. MMI iteratively maximizes the mutual information between two image volumes and aligns them at the same time. Two things need to be pointed out about MMI based image registration. First, it can also be used to register high-resolution images, such as CT and MRI T1, T2 images. Second, MMI is an iterative algorithm and can only converge to a local optimum, so a good initialization is needed for it to return a good registration result. Initialization can be achieved by manually aligning the two volumes roughly or by a coarse fiducial point registration.

3.2 Spatial registration

In surgical navigation, spatial registration is to calculate a spatial transformation between RCS and ICS by matching corresponding structures in the real world and in the image volumes. Two types of structures are commonly used for spatial registration, fiducial points [2] and head surfaces [3]. In this section, spatial registration using these two types of structures will be introduced first and then the metrics used to evaluate spatial registration will discussed.

1. **Fiducial point based spatial registration.**
   In fiducial point based registration, the coordinates of a set of corresponding points are first recorded in both ICS and RCS, and then an analytical algorithm is used to calculate the optimal rigid transformation between the ICS and the RCS. There are three basic requirements on the fiducial points: First, they should be easily recognizable and can be precisely located both in the real world and in the image volume; second, there should be at least four points recorded in each coordinate system to perform registration; third, there should be one-to-one correspondence between the fiducial points in the two coordinate systems. In OCMF surgical navigation, four kinds of points can serve as fiducial points:
   a. **Anatomical landmarks.** Anatomical landmarks, such as nose tip, inner canthus, and outer canthus, can serve as fiducial points. The advantage of using anatomical

landmarks is that they are naturally applicable and no artificial point is needed, which means that a medical imaging dedicated for surgical navigation may not be needed. On the contrary, all the other three kinds of fiducial points need some artificial object attached to the patient's head and a dedicated medical imaging after the attachment is needed to make the attached objects visible in the image volume. The disadvantage of anatomical landmarks is that the accuracy of locating anatomical landmarks is usually low in both ICS and RCS, and several millimeters of error may exist in locating an anatomical landmark.

b. **Adhesive markers.** Adhesive markers are the most commonly used fiducial points in surgical navigation because it achieves a good balance between invasiveness and accuracy. Adhesive markers are adhered to the patient's head and then the patient undergoes a medical imaging to obtain images for navigation. The markers will be on the patient's head until spatial registration is finished in the operation room. The markers are non-invasive to the patient and the use of markers is flexible since the number and distribution of the markers can be decided according to the surgical requirement. Adhesive markers are made of special material so that it can be easily recognized in the image. It has a special shape and a point on it can be precisely located both in the image and in the real world. Generally speaking, the accuracy of locating fiducial markers is higher than that of locating anatomical landmarks, but there still may be some locating error because of the sliding or sinking of the patient's skin when the marker is touched by a probe.

c. **Bone screws.** Bone screws provide the highest accuracy for fiducial point based spatial registration. The workflow of using bone screws is the same as using adhesive markers. The screws are inserted into the patient's bone, which may be skull, maxilla or mandible, and then the patient undergoes CT imaging with the screws in the bone. Bone screws can be easily and accurately located in CT images and in the real world, and it won't move as the adhesive marker does. Therefore, bone screws provide the highest accuracy for spatial registration, which is its major advantage. Comparing to adhesive markers, the major disadvantage of bone screws is its invasiveness.

d. **Oral splint.** In OCMF surgical navigation, oral splint provides another option of adopting fiducial points. Some artificial markers can be installed in an oral splint, and the patient can undergo CT scanning with the splint in his mouth. The splint can be removed after image scanning and be put on again during the process of spatial registration so that the surgeon can record the coordinates of the fiducial points in RCS. Splint can tightly fit with the teeth so that there is little movement of the fiducial points between image scanning and spatial registration, so the accuracy of registration using oral splint are comparable to or even higher than using adhesive markers. Comparing to bone screws, oral splint is almost non-invasive. The disadvantage of oral splint is that a dedicated splint needs to be manufactured for each patient, which increases the cost of the operation and the time needed for preparing the operation.

After recording the coordinates of all fiducial points in each coordinate system, they are first stack into a 3-by-N matrix, where N is the number of fiducial points, and each column of the matrix is the 3D coordinates of a fiducial point. Let the matrix containing fiducial points' coordinates in RCS and ICS are denoted by X and Y, respectively. Let x_1 and y_1 are column vectors representing a fiducial point in RCS and ICS, respectively, where $i \in \{1,2,...N\}$. The transformation from RCS to ICS, which consists of a 3D rotation and a 3D translation, is calculated by the following three steps [5]:

a. **Demean the fiducial points.** The mean position of the fiducial points in each coordinate system is first subtracted from the fiducial point's coordinate to eliminate the influence of translation so that the relative rotation can be first calculated. Let $\tilde{x}$ and $\tilde{y}$ are the mean position of the fiducial points in RCS and ICS, respectively. A pair of new matrices $\tilde{X}$ and $\tilde{Y}$ are calculated by subtracting $\tilde{x}$ and $\tilde{y}$ from each column of X and Y, respectively.

b. **Calculate relative rotation**. Calculate the SVD decomposition of the matrix $\tilde{X}\tilde{Y}^t$, and let $U \wedge V^t = \tilde{X}\tilde{Y}^t$. Then the rotation matrix is $R = VDU^t$, where

$$D = \begin{bmatrix} 1 & 0 & 0 \\ 0 & 1 & 0 \\ 0 & 0 & \det(VU) \end{bmatrix}$$

c. **Calculate relative translation**. After obtaining the rotation matrix R, the translation vector t can be calculated as follows

$$t = \tilde{Y} - R\tilde{X}$$

2. **Surface based spatial registration**

   Comparing to fiducial point based registration, surface based registration is relatively new. In surface based registration, the transformation between RCS and ICS is calculated by aligning a common surface in both coordinate systems, which is a part of the head surface in OCMF surgical navigation. Usually, the aligned surface is represented by point sets, and spatial registration is formulated as a point set registration problem. In ICS, the point set representing head surface can be obtained by simple image processing, and the point set of head surface in RCS can be obtained in the following three ways.

   a. **Navigation probe.** Navigation probe is the most widely used tool for surgical navigation. When it points to the patient, its tip is displayed in ICS so that the surgeon can view the relative position of the probe tip and the patient's anatomical structures in ICS. Navigation probe is used to record fiducial points' coordinates in RCS for fiducial point based spatial registration, and it can also be used to record head surface point set in RCS for surface registration [14]. With the navigation probe and the reference frame tracked by the position sensor, the surgeon slides the probe tip on the head surface and the navigation system will be able to record a set of coordinates of the probe tip in RCS as the head surface point set.

b. **Laser pointer.** The skin may deform when we put the navigation probe on it, so the point set obtained by using navigation probe may have some deformation, which will have negative effects on registration accuracy. To solve this problem, some surgical navigation systems provide laser pointer for surface point set collection in RCS [15]. A dedicated laser pointer is used to cast a laser point on the head surface, and together with the laser there is light spectrum that can be tracked by the position sensor. The position sensor tracks the laser point on the head surface and calculates its coordinates in PCS and then uses the transformation from PCS to RCS to obtain the laser point's coordinates in RCS. Obviously, this way of collecting head surface point set can only be used with optical position sensor. The advantage of using a laser pointer is that it need not to touch the head surface so it will not cause skin deformation. One limitation is that because of the viewing angle restriction of the position sensor, the area where surface points can be collected by laser pointer are usually limited, and it has some restriction on the positioning of the patient and the navigation system in the operation room.

c. **3D laser scanner.** 3D laser scanner is also used for head surface point set collection in RCS for spatial registration [16,17]. Comparing to navigation probe and laser pointer, 3D laser scanner can collect a denser point set in a larger region, which is helpful to improve registration accuracy and stability. In using a laser scanner, there are two approaches to calculate the point sets' coordinates in RCS, as shown in Fig. 7.3A. The laser scanner has its own coordinate system, and we denote it as SCS. The traditional way is to use a tracked tool, which is called adapter, to track the laser scanner, and the coordinate system defined on the adapter is denoted as ACS [16]. Calibration is done before using the scanner to calculate a spatial transformation from SCS to ACS. During scanning, both the adapter and the reference frame are tracked by the position sensor and the point set coordinates are first transformed

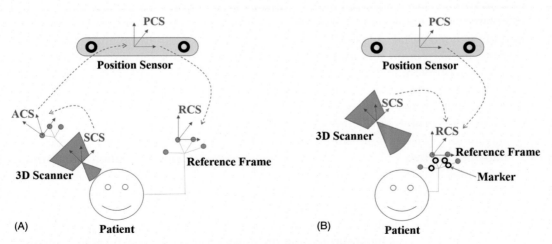

FIGURE 7.3 Two approaches of using 3D scanning for surface based spatial registration.

from SCS to ACS by using the calibration results and then transformed from ACS to PCS and RCS by using the position sensor. A new approach is proposed in Ref. [17] for neurosurgical navigation, as shown in Fig. 7.3B, and conceptually it can also be used in OCMF surgical navigation. In this approach, the scanner needs not to be tracked. Instead, several markers that can be recognized by the scanner are placed on the reference frame. The markers' coordinates in RCS are recorded before registration. When the scanner is used to collect head surface points, these markers are also scanned and their coordinates in SCS can be calculated automatically by the scanner. With the coordinates of the makers both in SCS and RCS, a spatial transformation between SCS and RCS can be obtained directly, and it is used to transform the scanned point set's coordinates from SCS to RCS. In the traditional approach, the scanner must not move when scanning from one direction because the corresponding transformation from SCS to PCS could not change. Of course, scanning can be done from several different directions but the scanning area is still restricted because the adapter needs to be tracked by the position sensor when scanning. On the contrary, a freehand scanning scheme can be easily applied in the new approach because the scanner need not to be tracked during scanning, which makes it possible to scan a larger area of head surface.

After obtaining point set coordinates in both RCS and ICS, spatial registration can be done by point set registration, which is also a fundamental problem in the field of computer vision. One thing needs to be pointed out is that, in point set registration, the correspondence between the points in the two sets is unknown in prior. A comprehensive review of point set registration methods can be found in Refs. [18,19], and here we introduce the most widely used algorithm, Iterative Closest Point (ICP) [20]. Let $X = \{x_i\}_{i=1}^{M}$ and $Y = \{y_i\}_{j=1}^{N}$ be the two point sets on the head surface in RCS and ICS, respectively. Here, M and N are the number of points in X and Y, and they may be different. The original ICP algorithm is composed of the following steps:

1. Given the point set X in RCS and point set Y in ICS, and an initial transformation T_0 from RCS to ICS.
2. Transform X into ICS using the current transformation, and the transformed point set is denoted as X'. Then, for each point in X', find its closest point in Y as its corresponding point, and all the corresponding points form a new set Y'.
3. In the previous step, two corresponding point sets X and Y' are found, and a new transformation T is calculated by using fiducial point based registration method on X and Y'.
4. Terminate if some predefined condition is met and return to step (2) otherwise. The termination condition may be a limit on iteration number, a threshold on fiducial point based registration accuracy, a threshold on accuracy increment over previous iteration, and so on.

After the introduction of the original ICP algorithm, a series of variants have been proposed to improve its speed, accuracy, and robustness [21]. Despite all these improvements, ICP and most of its variants can only converge to a local optimum near the initial transformation and a good initialization is needed to achieve an accurate registration. In surgical navigation, the initialization is often done by fiducial point based registration using three or four anatomical landmarks. If dense point set is collected in RCS, a rough registration by key points extraction and feature matching can be used as the initialization [22]. Recently, several global point set registration methods have been proposed [23,24], and these algorithms can find the globally optimal transformation without initialization, but they tend to be slow and have not been used in surgical navigation.

3. Accuracy metrics of spatial registration

Three metrics are often used in evaluating the accuracy of spatial registration: Target Registration Error (TRE), Fiducial Registration Error (FRE), and Surface Registration Error (SRE). TRE can be used in any kinds of spatial registration, while FRE and SRE are used to evaluate the registration accuracy of fiducial point based registration and surface based registration, respectively.

TRE. When a transformation T is calculated from spatial registration, TRE reflects how accurately an arbitrary point is transformed from RCS to ICS. For any point x in RCS, which is called a target point, there is a true corresponding point y in ICS, and the TRE at point x is

$$\text{TRE}(x) = \|y - \text{T}(x)\|$$

Though TRE reflects the actual registration accuracy at an arbitrary point, surgical navigation systems cannot calculate TRE or report it to the user, because the exact true corresponding point is unknown in real spatial registration. What are really reported to users are usually FRE or SRE.

FRE. FRE is used in fiducial point registration to reflect how the fiducial points are aligned with each other. FRE is the root mean square distance of the fiducial points after registration. It should be noted that FRE is different from TRE, and a smaller FRE does not necessarily mean a smaller TRE at an arbitrary point. After fiducial point based registration is finished, FRE is a definite value and it won't change. However, TRE is a function of the position of the target point, which means that under the same registration, the TRE at different positions may also be different. Fitzpatrick et al. [25] derive an equation to calculate the expectation of TRE at point x from FRE and fiducial points coordinates.

$$E[\text{TRE}^2(x)] \approx \frac{E[\text{FRE}^2]}{N-2}\left(1 + \frac{1}{3}\sum_{k=1}^{3}\frac{d_k^2}{f_k^2}\right)$$

Where $E[\cdot]$ is the expectation of a random variable, $d_k(k=1,2,3)$ is the distance from x to the kth axis of the coordinate system whose center is at the center of the fiducial points and whose axes align with the principle axes of the fiducial point set, and f_k^2 is the sum of squares of the distance from each fiducial point to the kth axis of the same coordinate system. Intuitively, for a fixed distribution of the fiducial points, which means f_k^2 is fixed, a smaller FRE will result in a smaller expectation of TRE at any point. Therefore, it is reasonable to minimize FRE by adjusting the position of fiducial points in RCS during registration. Furthermore, for a fixed distribution of fiducial points and a fixed FRE, the TRE at different position is different. A simple rule is that TRE tends to be small near the center of the fiducial points and increase when it moves away from the center. In addition, if the fiducial points distribute nearly in a plane, the TRE increase rapidly when the target point moves away in the direction vertical to the plane. From another perspective, the TRE at a point depends on both FRE and the distribution of the fiducial points used in spatial registration, so if we want to achieve a small TRE at a specific target point, such as at the lesion or the surgical site, we should distribute the fiducial points around the target to make the target near the center of the fiducial points. At the same time, we should avoid making all fiducial points reside on a plane. Some surgical navigation system can return the expectation of TRE at an arbitrary point, or draw TRE iso-surfaces on the 2D and 3D images to give more information about registration accuracy besides FRE.

SRE. SRE is used to evaluate how accurately two surfaces are registered. When surface registration is formulated as point set registration, and the two point sets to be registered are X and Y, SRE can be calculated as the mean square root distance between every point in X to its closest point in Y after transforming X into the same coordinate system with Y. Obviously, SRE is very sensitive to outliers in X, which are the points that do not have correspondence in Y, and if we change the order of X and Y, the SRE will also be different. SRE is the objective that many point set registration algorithms try to minimize, but in different algorithm the definition of SRE may have subtle difference. In addition, a large number of other point set registration methods define other objectives instead of SRE to optimize. Anyway, most surgical navigation systems use ICP variants for surface based spatial registration, and return a SRE as an indication of registration accuracy. A smaller SRE usually means a more accurate surface registration, but there is still one thing that the user should pay attention to, that SRE is different from TRE, and a small SRE can be obtained from a totally wrong registration.

FRE and SRE are the two parameters that surgical navigation systems usually report to users, but both parameters do not exactly reflect the registration accuracy at a target point. What's more serious is that TRE can be very large due to poor distribution of the fiducial points even if the FRE is small in fiducial point registration, and the TRE can also be very large due to local convergence of ICP even if the SRE is very small in surface based registration. Therefore, it is a good practice to visually check the registration accuracy after spatial registration. This can be done by simply use the navigation probe to point to several anatomical landmarks on the head surface in the real world and visually check if the probe points to the correct position on the image.

3.3 Position sensor

From the working principle shown in Fig. 7.2 we can see that the position sensor plays a crucial role in surgical navigation. Currently, position sensors used in surgical navigation can be divided into two categories: optical sensor and electromagnetic sensor.

Optical position sensor tracks objects by stereo vision, and according to the light used to generate vision, it can be further divided into two sub-categories: visible light sensor and infrared light sensor. The optical position sensors of Northern Digital Inc., which is currently the leading position sensor provider for surgical navigation worldwide, belong to infrared light sensors. In this kind of sensors, an infrared emitter is used to emit infrared light to the viewing range of the sensor, and the reflected infrared light by a special-designed sphere is captured by two cameras on the sensor. The sphere is the minimal unit that can be tracked by the sensor. The position of the sphere in PCS is calculated from stereo-vision. Tracked tools are designed with several spheres on it and the spheres on each tool have a unique geometry. When the two cameras of the sensor locate multiple spheres in PCS, it matches the loaded tools' geometry to the tracked spheres and a tracked tool is found when its sphere geometry is matched. The transformation from the tool's local coordinate system defined on the spheres to PCS is calculated according to the spheres' coordinates in the tool coordinate system and that in PCS. In infrared light position sensor, an infrared light emitting diode can be used to replace spheres. In this scenario, the sensor tracked the diode according to the light emitted from it and no light emission is needed from the sensor. This kind of tools is usually called active tools, and accordingly the tools using spheres are called passive tools. Besides infrared position sensor, there are optical position sensors that use visible light to track tools. The unit to be tracked by this kind of sensor is a specially designed marker, which is usually composed of crossed black and white checks. The marker's role is the same as the sphere in infrared sensor, and the tracked tools are designed to contain several markers with a unique geometry.

The latest version of infrared position sensor from Northern Digital Inc., Polaris Vega®, has a root mean square tracking error of as low as 0.12 mm in tracking a single sphere. Commercially available sensors all have a root mean square tracking error of around 0.20 mm, which is enough for surgical navigation. It should be noted that what we really care about in surgical navigation is how accurately a tool instead of a sphere or a marker is tracked. Studies shows that if the tracked tools are properly designed and manufactured, its tracking accuracy is at the same level with tracking a single sphere [26]. In using a surgical navigation system, we should be careful not to destroy the geometry of the tracked tools. If the geometry of the part of a tool with spheres or diodes is destroyed, the tool may become untrackable or the tracking error will increase. On the other hand, if geometry of the part without the spheres or diodes on a tracked tool is destroyed, this may bring big error to the tracked interest point on the tool. For example, if the tip of a navigation probe is banded, it can still be tracked normally but the tracked probe tip is no longer the real tip of the tool and this will be very misleading to the users. For this reason, many surgical navigation systems have a step to verify the tip of the navigation tool before it is used. One last word about infrared position sensor is that the tracking accuracy of active and passive tools is equivalent [26].

Electromagnetic position sensor uses different physical principle to track tools and have different working condition from optical position sensors. It generates an electromagnetic field in front of field generator, and a small tool is placed in the electromagnetic field so that small currents are induced by the electromagnetic field, which varies in a designed pattern. The current depends on the relative position and direction between the tool and the electromagnetic field so that its position and orientation can be calculated from the current signals.

Generally speaking, the tracking error of electromagnetic position sensors is higher than that of optical position sensors, but it is also acceptable for most surgical navigation applications. The biggest advantage of electromagnetic position sensor is that it needs not directly see the tracked tools, which means that the sensor won't be occluded only when it resides in the electromagnetic field. On the contrary, optical position sensors must directly see the spheres or diodes on a tracked tool, and otherwise the tool will be lost. The limitation of electromagnetic position sensor is that it needs a precisely controlled electromagnetic field and any objects that may interfere with the electromagnetic field, such as some metal surgical tools or electronic equipments are not allowed in the electromagnetic field.

3.4 Dynamic referencing

As shown in Fig. 7.2, surgical navigation uses a reference frame to establish a coordinate system for the real world where the patient resides in. The reference frame is firmly fixed to the patient's head, and there are three kinds of reference frames commonly used in OCMF surgical navigation.

1. **Reference frame attached to head clamp.** As in neurosurgery, in some OCMF surgery, the patient's head needs to be fixed by a head clamp. In this case, the reference frame can be attached to the head clamp and indirectly attached to the patient's head.
2. **Reference frame directly attached to the patient's head.** In some OCMF surgery, a head clamp is not used because it is fairly invasive. In this case, the reference frame can be directly attached to the patient's head by using a head belt or skull screws.
3. **Oral splint.** As introduced in Section 3.2, fiducial points used in spatial registration can be set on oral splint, and similarly, reference frame can also be set on an oral splint.

Besides the three ways of attaching reference frame to the patient's head discussed earlier, there is another thing that needs to be mentioned. In OCMF surgery, the mandible may have movement relative to the skull. When the operation happens on mandible, the surgeon must make sure that mandible and maxilla are fixed together if the reference frame is attached to the skull. Otherwise, the reference frame should be fixed to the mandible directly.

4 Clinical application of surgical navigation in OCMF surgery

Since 1990s, surgical navigation systems have been more and more used in OCMF surgery. Two meta-analysis are introduced here to demonstrate the clinical application of surgical navigation systems in OCMF surgery [27,28]. The readers are referred to the original meta-analysis and its references for more details.

In 2019, Michael R. Delong et al. published a review about the surgical navigation in craniofacial surgery [27]. They did preferred reporting items for systematic reviews and meta-analysis (PRISMA) systematic review on terms related to image-guided navigation and craniofacial surgery published before March of 2017. With inclusion criteria of clinical study and written in English, and exclusion criteria of case reports, reviews, and animal study, 104 articles were finally included in the analysis. In all the studies, the three leading categories of surgery are orbit (36), maxillary (19), and orthogmathic (17). There are nine articles with mixed surgical categories. Other articles are tumor resection/reconstruction (9), pediatric (7), zygoma (4), and foreign body (3). Most of the studies provide subjectively satisfactory results, but at the same time, only 14 of them included some comparison and analysis.

In 2020, Marzieh Jamali et al. published a PRISMA review on studies with more than five patients that are randomized controlled trials studies, controlled clinical trials, or prospective/retrospective cohort investigations [28]. Nine studies with total 182 patients of maxillofacial trauma surgery were included, and the risk ratio of meta-analysis is 0.187 (95% CI:0.16–0.21). Five studies with total 112 patients of reconstructive surgery were included, and the risk ratio of meta-analysis is 0.26 (95% CI: 0.22–0.31). Five studies with total 46 patients of orthognathic surgery were included, and the risk ratio of meta-analysis is 0.10 (95% CI: 0.08–0.14). These studies demonstrated that surgical navigation is a great tool for these surgeries.

5 New techniques used in OCMF surgical navigation

Since the introduction of the first surgical navigation system about 40 years ago, the basic idea of surgical navigation remains the same: track the position of a surgical tool in the real world and display it onto the images of the patient so as to use its position relative to the images to demonstrate its position relative to the patient in the real world. The last 40 years have witnessed rapid development of many techniques, and some of them have also been introduced into surgical navigation. Here, we introduce three relative new techniques in the field of OCMF surgical navigation. There are some proof-of-concept studies or preliminary clinical studies on these new techniques, but they are not widely used yet.

5.1 Augmented reality (AR)

In most surgical navigation systems, the images are displayed on a screen and the surgeon needs to watch the screen to view the position of a navigation probe relative to the patient's image. In this traditional way of navigation, the surgeon needs to switch its view between the screen and the surgical site frequently, which interrupts and slows down the operation. In addition, it is a little difficult to transform the relative position displayed on the screen to the real surgical site. For example, on the 2D axial section, we may see that the surgical target is to the front left of the probe tip, but in the real surgical site, it is difficult to know exactly which direction corresponds to the "front left" shown on screen. All these issues are caused by the separation of the navigation information and the real surgical site, and the solution is to apply AR technology.

The essence of AR is to fuse the display of virtual and real scenes. In surgical navigation, the objective is to fuse the display of virtual anatomical models and the display of real surgical site. Therefore, it needs a device to capture the video of the surgical site and display it in real time. Several devices have been used in surgical navigation for this purpose, such as head-mounted display [29], tablet [30], and surgical microscope [31]. Most of these devices use a video camera to capture the video and display it on a screen. Another thing needs to do for AR is to display the virtual model on the screen of the AR device and make the virtual model align with its real counterpart shown in the video. This process involves a series of spatial transformation, most of which already exist in surgical navigation. Usually, an adapter is attached to the video camera to track its position, and calibration is done to calculate a transformation from the adapter's coordinate system to the displaying screen so that an object in the adapter's coordinate system can be displayed at proper position on the screen to align with its counterpart in the real world. Then, during navigation, the virtual model is transformed from ICS to RCS, PCS and the adapter's coordinate system by using the spatial transformation obtained from spatial registration and the tracking of the position sensor. Finally, it is projected onto the screen by using the calibration results. There have been several clinical studies of AR in OCMF surgical navigation, and the readers are referred to a latest review for more details [32].

5.2 Intraoperative imaging

Most surgical navigation system uses medical images taken preoperatively to construct the image volume for navigation and establish ICS on it. Recently, several surgical navigation systems have been integrated with intraoperative CT, especially in spinal and orthopedic surgical navigation. In Ref. [33], two cases are reported to use intraoperative imaging with mobile cone-beam CT in navigation of maxillofacial surgery. When using intraoperative image for navigation, the process of establishing ICS, tracking the patient's movement, establishing RCS with a reference frame, and transforming a navigation tools position into ICS are all the same with traditional surgical navigation system using preoperative images. However, the registration between RCS and ICS is different. Since the images are taken in the operation room, the imaging device can be calibrated in prior and be tracked by the position sensor of the navigation system, so that a spatial transformation between RCS and ICS can be calculated automatically during imaging. Therefore, in the application of surgical navigation system with intraoperative imaging, there may not be an explicit procedure of spatial registration.

5.3 Robot

Surgical navigation systems can guide operation but the operation has to be done by surgeons. With the success of the Da Vinci® surgical robot from Intuitive Inc., a lot of different surgical robots used in different kinds of surgeries have been developed, including in

OCMF surgery. A proof-of-concept study of using robot in OCMF surgery is presented in Ref. [34], where an automatic robot can perform drilling according to surgical planning. The system is tested on five 3D-printed mandible models and high accuracy was achieved on the phantoms. There is still a lot of work to do before the surgical robot can be clinically used.

References

[1] M. Wang, Z. Song, Classification and analysis of the errors in neuronavigation, Neurosurgery 68 (4) (2011) 1131–1143.

[2] Wang Manning, Song Zhijian, Improving target registration accuracy in image-guided neurosurgery by optimizing the distribution of fiducial points, The International Journal of Medical Robotics and Computer Assisted Surgery 5 (1) (2009) 26–31.

[3] Fan Yifeng, Jiang Dongsheng, Wang Manning, Song Zhijian, A new markerless patient-to-image registration method using a portable 3D scanner, Medical Physics 41 (10) (2014), doi: 10.1118/1.4895847 101910.

[4] Omara Akram, Wang Manning, Fan Yifeng, Song Zhijian, Anatomical landmarks for point-matching registration in image-guided neurosurgery, The International Journal of Medical Robotics and Computer Assisted Surgery 10 (1) (2014) 55–64.

[5] D.W. Eggert, A. Lorusso, R.B. Fischer, Estimating 3-D rigid body transformations: A comparison of four major algorithms, Mach. Vision Appl. 9 (5–6) (1997) 272–290.

[6] K. Cleary, T.M. Peters, Image-guided interventions: technology review and clinical applications, Ann. Rev. Biomed. Eng. 12 (2010) 119–142.

[7] I. Azarmehr, K. Stokbro, R.B. Bell, T. Thygesen, Surgical navigation: a systematic review of indications, treatments, and outcomes in oral and maxillofacial surgery, J. Oral Maxillofac. Surg. 75 (9) (2017) 1987–2005.

[8] Q. Zhang, R. Eagleson, T.M. Peters, Volume visualization: a technical overview with a focus on medical applications, J. Digit. Imaging 24 (4) (2011) 640–664.

[9] W. Khan, Image segmentation techniques: a survey, J. Image Graph. 1 (4) (2013) 166–170.

[10] N. Tajbakhsh, L. Jeyaseelan, Q. Li, J. Chiang, Z. Wu, X. Ding, Embracing imperfect datasets: A review of deep learning solutions for medical image segmentation, Med. Image Anal. Vol. 63 (2020) 101693.

[11] J.B.A. Maintz, M.A. Viergever, A survey of medical image registration, Med. Image Anal. 2 (1) (1998) 1–36.

[12] G. Haskins, U. Kruger, P. Yan, Deep learning in medical image registration: a survey, Mach. Vision Appl. 31 (2020) Article number: 8.

[13] F. Maes, A. Collignon, D. Vandermeulen, G. Marchal, P. Suetens, Multimodality image registration by maximization of mutual information, IEEE Trans. Med. Imaging 16 (2) (1997) 187–198.

[14] D. Ji, Y. Dong, M. Wang, Z. Song, Accuracy analysis of line-based registration for image guided neurosurgery at different operating areas–a phantom study, Comput. Assist. Surg. 22 (Suppl. 1) (2017) 148–156.

[15] J. Schlaier, J. Warnat, A. Brawanski, Registration accuracy and practicability of laser-directed surface matching, Comput. Aided Surg. 7 (5) (2002) 284–290.

[16] D. Troitzsch, J. Hoffmann, F. Dammann, D. Bartz, S. Reinert, Registration using three-dimensional laser surface scanning for navigation in oral and craniomaxillofacial surgery, Zentralbl Chir 128 (7) (2003) 551–556.

[17] Y. Fan, D. Jiang, M. Wang, Z. Song, A new markerless patient-to-image registration method using a portable 3D scanner, Med. Phys. 41 (10) (2014) Article number: 101910.

[18] B. Bellekens, V. Spruyt, R. Berkvens, et al. A benchmark survey of rigid 3D point cloud registration algorithms, Int. J. Adv. Intell. Syst. 8 (1&2) (2015) 118–127.

[19] G. Tam, Z. Cheng, Y. Lai, et al. Registration of 3D point clouds and meshes: survey from rigid to nonrigid, IEEE Trans. Visual. Comput. Graph. 19 (7) (2013) 1199–1217.

[20] P. Besl, N. Mckay, A method for registration of 3-D shapes, IEEE Trans. Pattern Anal. Mach. Intell. 14 (2) (1992) 239–256.

[21] F. Pomerleau, F. Colas, R. Siegwart, S. Magnenat, Comparing ICP variants on real-world data sets, Auton. Robots 34 (3) (2013) 133–148.

[22] Y. Liu, Z. Song, M. Wang, A new robust markerless method for automatic image-to-patient registration in image-guided neurosurgery system, Comput. Assist. Surg. 22 (Suppl. 1) (2014) 319–325.

[23] J. Yang, H. Li, Y. Jia, Go-ICP: Solving 3D registration efficiently and globally optimally, In: Proceeding International Conference of Computer Vision, Sydney, NSW, Australia, 2013.

[24] Y. Liu, C. Wang, Z. Song, M. Wang, Efficient global point cloud registration by matching rotation invariant features through translation search, European Conference on Computer Vision, 2018.

[25] J.M. Fitzpatrick, J.B. West, The distribution of target registration error in rigid-body point-based registration, IEEE Trans. Med. Imaging 20 (9) (2001) 917–927.

[26] A.D. Wiles, D.G. Thompson, D.D. Frantza, Accuracy assessment and interpretation for optical tracking systems, In: Medical Imaging 2004 Proc. 5367, Visualization, Image-Guided Procedures, and Display.

[27] M.R. DeLong, B.M. Gandolfi, M.L. Barr, N. Datta, T.D. Willson, R. Jarrahy, Intraoperative image-guided navigation in craniofacial surgery: review and grading of the current literature, J. Craniofac. Surg. 30 (2) (2019) 465–472.

[28] M. Jamali, J. Jamali, M.G. Vojoodi, H. Ahmadizadeh, Assessment of therapeutic indications of surgical navigation in maxillofacial surgery: a systematic review and meta-analysis, Int. J. Sci. Res. Dent. Med. Sci. 2 (2020) 29–36.

[29] G. Badiali, V. Ferrari, F. Cutolo, C. Freschi, D. Caramella, A. Bianchi, et al. Augmented reality as an aid in maxillofacial surgery: Validation of a wearable system allowing maxillary repositioning, J. Cranio-Maxillofac. Surg. 42 (8) (2014) 1970–1976.

[30] W. Deng, F. Li, M. Wang, Z. Song, Easy-to-use augmented reality neuronavigation using a wireless tablet PC, Stereotactic and functional neurosurgery 92 (1) (2014) 17–24.

[31] R. Vassallo, H. Kasuya, B.W.Y. Lo, T. Peters, Y. Xiao, Augmented reality guidance in cerebrovascular surgery using microscopic video enhancement, Healthcare Technol. Lett. 5 (5) (2018) 158–161.

[32] G. Badiali, L. Cercenelli, S. Battagli, E. Marcelli, C. Marchetti, V. Ferrari, et al. Review on augmented reality in oral and cranio-maxillofacial surgery: toward surgery-specific head-up displays, IEEE Access 8 (2020) 59015–59028.

[33] Q. Goguet, S.H. Lee, J. Longis, P. Corre, H. Bertin, Intraoperative imaging and navigation with mobile cone-beam CT in maxillofacial surgery, Oral Maxillofac. Surg. 23 (2019) 487–491.

[34] Q. Ma, E. Kobayashi, H. Suenaga, K. Hara, J. Wang, K. Nakagawa, et al. Autonomous surgical robot with camera-based markerless navigation for oral and maxillofacial surgery, IEEE/ASME Trans. Mechatron. 25 (2) (2020) 1084–1094.

8

3D printing and 3D printed scaffolds

Yifei Gu[a], Jeroen Van Dessel[a,b], Constantinus Politis[a,b], Yi Sun[a,b]

[a]DEPARTMENT OF IMAGING AND PATHOLOGY, OMFS IMPATH RESEARCH GROUP, KU LEUVEN, LEUVEN, BELGIUM; [b]DEPARTMENT OF ORAL AND MAXILLOFACIAL SURGERY/ FACULTY OF MEDICINE, KU LEUVEN, UNIVERSITY HOSPITALS, LEUVEN, BELGIUM

1 Introduction of 3D printing

Three-dimensional (3D) printing or additive manufacturing (AM) technique, enables the fabrication a wide range of 3D structures and complex geometries from a patient's own 3D model data, which is extracted from medical images such as computed axial tomography (CAT) and magnetic resonance imaging (MRI). This process is based on the principle of successive printing of materials, which overlapped each other layer by layer. It was first introduced in the 1980s and has become one of the most efficient methods which brings new possibilities for building bionic tissue or organs and transform the manufacturing processes.

In 1986, a process known as stereolithography (SLA) was developed by Charles Hull, and subsequent developments such as fused deposition modeling (FDM), powder bed fusion, inkjet printing, etc. have come into use later. Nowadays, 3D printing has evolved over the years and has become a leading manufacturing technique in different industries, including construction, prototyping, and biomechanical. Novel materials and methods are continuously being developed, and the 3D printing industry has exploded due to the increased accessibility and manufacturing speed of 3D printers. A wide range of applications, including dentistry, tissue engineering, and regenerative medicine, engineered tissue models, medical devices, anatomical models, and drug formulation, have involved the use of 3D printing techniques.

Traditional fabrication methods, including molding, casting, leaching and electrospinning, could not produce complexed constructs which are custom-designed and patient-specific [1]. Compared to these, AM technology is able to fabricate interconnected porous structures with predictable and predetermined units. The size and shape of the pores are predetermined, and the pore morphology shows a regular arrangement rather than a random distribution. 3D printing provides commercially available medical products and a platform for emerging research areas including tissue and organ printing. Meanwhile, it enables the production of anatomically matched and patient-specific devices

Computer-Aided Oral and Maxillofacial Surgery. http://dx.doi.org/10.1016/B978-0-12-823299-6.00008-0

and constructs with high tunability and complexity. For example, in bone reconstruction, since the porosity affects the compressive strength and elastic modulus of the implant, the mechanical properties of the implant can be altered to approximate the mechanical properties of the human bone. Therefore, the stress shielding effect after implantation can be avoided by precisely controlling the porosity of the implant [2]. In addition, the porous structure can also provide space for migration and proliferation of osteoblasts and mesenchymal stem cells, and also allow extramedullary tissue to grow into the implant, which enhances bone–implant interface enhances osseointegration.

3D printing enables on-demand fabrication of medical products from CT-imaged tissue replicas, making it potentially attractive for in-house production as well as fabrication in remote areas [3]. Meanwhile, it is also specifically useful in the healthcare industry, where unique patient-customized products are required. Today, 3D printing is widely used in the biomedical and academic field. It is currently employed in a large variety of medical applications, including medical devices, surgical instruments, tissue models, tissue engineering scaffolds, drug formulation as well as anatomical models, etc. [4,5]. Personalized surgical instruments are necessary to ensure accuracy and improve efficiency [6]. Since AM technique enables the production of relatively small-sized and patient-specific medical products, it is especially popular in the dental market and hearing aid industry. 3D printing technology has also been applied to develop personalized-dose medicines in the pharmaceutical field [5]. Besides, more and more focus has been given to the application of 3D printing for tissues and organs in the fields of tissue engineering and regenerative medicine. In addition, 3D bio-printing of pre-clinical, patient-specific tissue, and disease models for drug testing and high-throughput screening is promising for the development of patient-tailored drugs and reducing the use of animal models [7].

2 Methods of 3D printing

AM technologies mean to meet the demand of printing complex structures at satisfying resolutions. The most popular 3D printing methods include fused deposition modeling (FDM), selective laser sintering (SLS), selective laser melting (SLM), or liquid binding in three-dimensional printing (3DP), etc. Different methods and their suitable materials will be briefly introduced further, and their benefits and drawbacks will be discussed. Generally, AM technologies can be classified into four main groups: vat polymerization-based printing, powder-based printing, droplet-based printing, and extrusion-based printing.

2.1 Vat polymerization-based printing

In vat photopolymerization printing, light of a specific wavelength is directed to a vat of photocurable resin to locally cure the resin one layer at a time. This technology includes stereolithography (SLA), direct or digital light processing (DLP) and continuous direct light processing (CDLP), also known as continuous liquid interface production (CLIP).

SLA is one of the earliest methods of AM technology, which was developed by Chuck Hull in 1986. It was first applied in an alloplastic implant surgery in 1994 [8]. In this technique, a UV beam (or electron beam) is used to initiate a chain reaction on a resin layer. The monomers are UV-active and are instantly turned into polymer chains after UV activation (radicalization). After polymerization, a platform lifts up the solidified layer allowing a fresh layer of resin to flow beneath the cured layer. The unnecessary resin will be removed after the printing process. The post-treatment of SLA process includes heating or photocuring for a finer structure and more satisfying mechanical property. A final accuracy of 10 μm can be reached in SLA. In addition to many advantages, the application of SLA is limited due to the high price, limited available materials and slow speed of production. Besides, since the entire printing process is controlled by the light source, the curing reaction is relatively unstable. DLP is similar to SLA, but uses a shallower vat of resin and a digital light projector located beneath the resin bath, which cures each entire layer once. DLP is, therefore, a much faster process and requires less material [9]. CDLP (or CLIP) is very similar to DLP, but the build plate moves continuously in the Z-direction leading to faster print times [10]. In vat polymerization printing, printed constructs are usually exposed to light post-printing to enhance the stability and mechanical properties.

2.2 Powder-based printing

Powder-based printing technologies include selective laser sintering (SLS), direct metal laser sintering (DMLS), selective laser melting (SLM), and electron beam melting (EBM) [11]. SLM and EBM have been selected to be the preferred scaffolds fabrication methods in many researches because of their good controllability and high precision. Sintering means a relatively rougher surface since the powders are not fully melted, while in melting process the powders are consolidated, thus creates products with higher mechanical properties [12]. Powder-based printing technologies all rely on localized heating to fuse the powdered materials, yet differ in the energy source and powder materials [13].

SLS uses laser source directed by mirrors to sinter powder layer by layer according to the CAD file. No support or post-processing is needed for SLS process. However, SLS needs heat treatment and material infiltration, and the relatively rough surfaces of productions can be an obvious drawback. SLS can use a wide range of materials, including polymer, ceramic-based powders, and metal powders. DMLS is essentially the same process as SLS, but exclusively utilizes metal alloys. SLM also utilizes laser beams directed by mirrors, and thin layers of atomized fine metal powders are evenly distributed on substrate plate. The 2D slices of part geometry are fused by selectively melting the powder, and the process is repeated layer after layer until the part is complete. SLM is capable of fully melting the powder materials, producing fully dense near net-shaped components without the need for post-processing, and a high precision of 10 μm can be achieved in SLM process. EBM uses a high-energy electron beam precisely directed by electromagnetic coils, and the powder layers are melted successively, which require vacuum conditions thus increasing the production cost. A lower thermal stress can be acquired due to the kinetic energy transfer and the metal does not oxidize easily because of the vacuum environment. In addition, one major advantage of the melting process is that it is capable of producing nearly fully dense parts, thus eliminating lengthy post-processing steps such as thermal treatments or infiltration, which is usually required for the SLS (or DMLS)-printed products.

2.3 Droplet-based printing

Droplet-based (or inkjet-based) printing is one of the main methods for the additive manufacturing of ceramics. It utilizes precise jetting of liquid droplets onto a substrate in a layer-by-layer manner. It is used for printing complex structures like scaffolds for tissue engineering, droplet-based technologies include multi-jet modeling (MJM), wax deposition modeling (WDM), laser-induced forward transfer (LIFT), and binder jetting (BJ). In MJM technology, the print head selectively deposit the materials on a platform. The droplets include photopolymers as well as supporting materials such as wax. At the next step, an ultraviolet light solidifies the photopolymer material to shape the cured parts. At the final pass, the planerizer levels the material to create a nice flat surface. In WDM, molten wax is deposited onto a build platform, where it solidifies as it cools. LIFT does not require a printhead, but utilizes laser light instead [14]. LIFT was initially used with metals but has recently been applied to cell-laden hydrogels: a layer of hydrogel-cell mixture is deposited onto a gold-coated glass substrate, which is used as a donor slide. The transfer process is initiated by a pulsed laser beam focused through the donor slide onto the laser-absorbing gold layer, which is then locally vaporized. BJ, or 3DPTM [15], could also be considered as a powder-based technology. In this technique, a liquid binding agent (adhesive) is jetted from the printhead to bind the powder particles, including ceramics, polymers, and metals.

2.4 Extrusion-based printing

The extrusion-based technologies include fused deposition modeling (FDM) and direct ink writing (DIW), also referred to as bioplotter, pressure-assisted microsyringe, or pressure-assisted printing. The FDM method involves the melt extrusion of filament materials through a heated nozzle and deposition as thin solid layers on a platform. The nozzle is positioned on the surface of a build platform at the start of fabrication. It is part of the extruder head (FDM head), which also encloses a liquefier to melt the filament material fed through two counter-rotating rollers. DIW utilizes a pneumatic or mechanical (piston- or screwdriven) dispensing system to extrude solutions, suspensions, gels or molten materials through a nozzle or a syringe. DIW is the most common technique for bioprinting cell suspensions, cell-laden hydrogels, and extracellular matrix based-solutions.

3 Introduction of 3D printed scaffolds

Orofacial cancer is one of the most common tumors worldwide, and it is often necessary to remove the bone tissue that may be affected by the tumor during the surgery. Orofacial bone defects caused by tumor resection can cause serious aesthetic problems and dysfunction, including difficulties in speech, chewing, and swallowing. These defects impede the patients' quality of life, so most patients with orofacial deformities need to be reconstructed after tumor surgery. Due to the complex three-dimensional (3D) structural features of the cranial and maxillofacial bones, as well as the aesthetic and functional requirements of the patients, orofacial reconstruction has proven to be a significant challenge for maxillofacial surgeons [16].

Methods commonly used in oral bone reconstruction surgery have evolved from autologous or allogeneic transplantations to allogeneic transplantations. Autografts are still considered the "gold standard" for large bone defects because they have the advantages of osteogenic potential, without the risk of antigenic reactions and cross-contamination. However, autografts have limitations, including restricted availability of donor sites and additional trauma caused by surgical harvesting procedure. For these reasons, the use of other bone graft biomaterials (i.e., xenogeneic or allogeneic) has increased. However, these biological materials have defects: poor vascularization, limited mechanical properties, and incomplete osseointegration with surrounding natural bone. Therefore, these biological materials have a high failure rate. These deficiencies have led to the development of innovative technologies, including bone tissue engineering (BTE), which have great potential for optimal bone healing in difficult cases while circumventing the drawbacks associated with conventional treatments. Tissue engineered scaffolds are the most important component in tissue engineering as they manipulate cell function, provide the structural support for cells to attach, migrate, proliferate, and guide the formation of new organs and tissues [17,18].

The goal of tissue engineering is to repair tissue defects, which are difficult or even impossible to treat by conventional methods. Successful implementation of tissue engineering lies in the perfection of porous 3D scaffolds, which provide 3D frameworks for delivering reparative cells or regenerative factors in an organized manner to repair or regenerate damaged tissues.

Ideally, scaffolds for tissue engineering should meet several design criteria: biocompatible, bioactive, mechanically strong, porous with high pore interconnectivity to allow cell diffusion and nutrient transportation. In addition, it needs to be biodegradable and eventually eliminated [19,20]. The conventional fabrication methods, such as porogen leaching, freeze-drying, molding, and electrospinning, have been widely used to produce tissue-engineering scaffolds. However, due to their inability to create spatially tunable properties, including porosity, architecture, mechanics, bioactivity, and distribution of cells, they are not the best options for creating tissue mimicking constructs. Over the past 15 years, AM has attracted widespread interest as an alternative manufacturing technique as it offers many advantages, including precise control of overall size and shape, structural architecture (porosity and pore distribution), material composition and chemistry (i.e., mechanics and degradation), and multi-cellular composition in 3D space [21]. In addition, custom design, on-demand fabrication, high reproducibility, and high throughput are other advantages as compared with conventional techniques.

In general, an AM approach for tissue engineered scaffolds requires cells to be incorporated either post printing by seeding the cells into the scaffold or pre-printing by

FIGURE 8.1 An example of 3D printed scaffold made for bone tissue engineering.

encapsulating the cells into the ink formulation. The most commonly used printing methods for creating scaffolds described in the first approach are FDM, SLS/DMLS, BJ, and vat polymerization. A number of 3D porous scaffolds fabricated from various kinds of materials have been developed and used for tissue engineering (Fig. 8.1).

3.1 Material of 3D-printed scaffolds

Suitable materials for the manufacture of metallic scaffolds shall include the following characteristics: high strength; high fatigue, corrosion, and wear resistance; suitable elastic modulus; ideal surface characteristics; no hypersensitivity and cytotoxicity [22]. Currently, porous 3D scaffolds are categorized into four major categories based on the material: natural polymers, synthetic polymers, metallic materials, and inorganic materials such as ceramics and bioactive glass [23]. Apart from these materials, multi-component systems can be designed to produce composites with enhanced properties [24].

The polyesters such as poly(glycolic acid) (PGA), poly(lactic acid) (PLA), and their copolymer of poly[lactic-co-(glycolic acid)] (PLGA) are most commonly used fort issue engineering. Among the four groups, natural polymers, such as collagen and glycosaminoglycan, alginic acid, chitosan, and polypeptides, have the advantage of having natural biological functions, but due to their low mechanical strength, they have a small advantage in bone reconstruction. The main biodegradable synthetic polymers include polyesters, polyanhydride, polyorthoester, polycaprolactone, and polycarbonate. Polyesters are most commonly used for tissue engineering, and their mechanical properties can be precisely controlled; however, cell adhesion in synthetic polymers is poor.

Bio-ceramics have been used for over 20 years and are known to enhance and promote biomineralization, but they are highly brittle and have low toughness, so they are mostly only suitable in combination with other materials and in form of composites [23].

Metallic scaffolds are often used as implant materials in dental and orthopedic surgery to replace damaged bone or provide support for bone healing or bone defects. Compared with other biomaterials mentioned above, metallic scaffolds are more promising for bone reconstruction after tumor resection, mainly because of their excellent mechanical properties. Mechanical properties are particularly important in scaffolds for bone tissue because the scaffold must also interact with its physiological environment to deliver mechanical signals to the cells and modulate cellular behavior (i.e., differentiation, motility, and contractility). The stiffness of the scaffold can act at the transcriptional level, determining whether stem cells are determined to be as diverse as osteoblasts [23]. The main disadvantages of metal biomaterials is the lack of biometric recognition on the surface of the material, and the difference in mechanical properties between the metal material and the natural bone, causing stress shielding and eventually loosening of the implant. To overcome these limitations, advances in surface modification and bioprinting techniques are necessary. Surface modification or surface coating provides a means of maintaining the mechanical properties of established biocompatible metals, improving surface biocompatibility. Furthermore, in order to enhance communication between cells and promote their organization within the porous scaffold, it is desirable to integrate cell recognizable ligands and signaling growth factors on the scaffold surface. Furthermore, the mismatch in mechanical properties can be corrected by a low modulus porous network of additive manufacturing. This can cause bone tissue ingrowth, resulting in a stable interface between the scaffold and the host tissue [25].

Titanium and titanium alloys have low density, high strength, good biocompatibility, and corrosion resistance, as well as strong bone integration capability. The mechanical properties of these alloys, including fatigue strength and tensile strength, can be improved by thermomechanical processing. Furthermore, during the early stages of corrosion, a thin, protective oxide film can be formed due to their biocompatibility, and this layer can be rebuilt immediately after damaged because of its thermodynamic stability. It acts as a barrier against the diffusion of metal ions from the bulk metal into the surrounding, effectively limiting the uniform corrosion rate. Therefore, the improved cell/tissue response results in very little adverse tissue reaction, and close apposition between the bone and implant is established.

Since 1970s, Ti and titanium alloys have been widely used in the manufacture of biomedical implant devices to replace damaged hard tissues. Cp Ti (98.8–99.6 wt% Ti) and Ti–6Al–4V (89.0–91.0 wt% Ti, 5.5–6.5 wt% Al, and 3.5–4.5 wt% V) are currently the most commonly used materials in the fabrication of biomedical implants. CP-Ti is highly resistant to corrosion and is regarded as the biocompatible metal due to the stable and inert oxide layer formed when it is exposed to oxidizing media. However, the strength of CP-Ti is lower to Ti-64, which is the most popular titanium alloy used in biomedical implants due to its high strength [26].

Although Ti and its alloys have many of the advantages already mentioned earlier, they have some disadvantages: they are soft and have low wear resistance, and problem of vanadium contained in Ti-64 alloy. Vanadium is concerned as cytotoxic, which means the alloy is limited to certain suitable applications and devices. In addition, although very rare, patients have been reported to be allergic to titanium [27]. Another disadvantage is the mismatch in the modulus of elasticity (or Young's) between the implant and the bone. Titanium has an elastic modulus of about 114 GPa, while cancellous and cortical bones have an elastic modulus ranging from 0.5 GPa to a maximum of 20 GPa [28]. Low modulus of elasticity is required in implants because it helps to avoid stress shielding and associated bone resorption. One solution to this high titanium modulus of elasticity problem is to use advanced manufacturing processes such as selective laser melting (SLM) to make highly porous titanium structures. These porous structures can be tailored to have excellent mechanical properties similar to human bone and are typically designed to promote bone ingrowth, and it has been shown that the elastic modulus of porous titanium decreases with increasing pore size under a compressive force [28].

4 3D-printed scaffolds used in bone reconstruction

In this section, we focus on the use of 3D printed scaffolds in bone reconstruction, which is a great market and shows promising research prospects in tissue engineering. The ideal features for porous 3D scaffolds in bone tissue engineering include strength, desired architecture, resistance to corrosion/degradation, good biocompatibility and good wear resistance [25]. For any type of scaffold to be successful and achieve good longevity, osseointegration is required. Osteointegration is an establishment of a rigid connection between the scaffold and the bone. It means a direct bone anchorage, without forming an intervening fibrous tissue layer, which enhances the load-bearing capacity of the implant.

The main advantage of AM technology over conventional methods is the ability to fabricate interconnected porous structures with predictable and predetermined units. Therefore, the mismatch between the implant and the host bone is prevented [29]; the size and shape of the pores are predetermined, and the pore morphology shows a regular arrangement rather than a random distribution. In addition, since the porosity affects the compressive strength and elastic modulus of the implant, the mechanical properties of the implant can be altered to approximate the mechanical properties of the human bone. Therefore, the stress shielding effect after implantation can be avoided by precisely controlling the porosity of the implant. In addition, the porous structure can also provide space for migration and proliferation of osteoblasts and mesenchymal stem cells, and also allow extramedullary tissue to grow into the implant. Strong bone–implant interface enhances osseointegration (Fig. 8.2).

In recent years, the porous Ti alloy scaffold produced by AM is a hot topic in research, among which Ti6Al4V is dominant. Key features in the design of porous metal implants

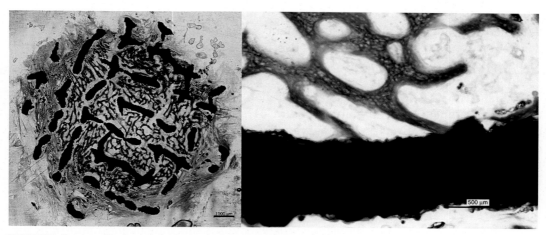

FIGURE 8.2 An example of new-born bone tissue found inside the 3D-printed porous scaffold.

include careful selection of porosity, pore size, and pore interconnects for satisfactory clinical results. These porous structural parameters can be controlled by AM technology and they have a profound effect on the mechanical and biological properties of metal implants.

In order to enhance osseointegration between the metallic scaffold and the host bone, the scaffold should include the following features: (1) biocompatible with surrounding tissues; (2) non-allergic and non-carcinogenic; (3) easy to shape or mold, perfectly conforming to bone defects; (4) mechanical properties meeting the requirements of surrounding tissues; (5) suitable for cell attachment, proliferation, and differentiation; (6) highly porous, interconnected pore network for cell ingrowth, and transport of nutrients and metabolic waste; (7) ability to maintain volume and osteoconductivity over time [25,30]. These mentioned features are associated with some governing factors, including scaffold materials, designing and manufacturing as well as the surface modification technique.

4.1 Introduction of bone tissue

Bone tissue originates from mesenchymal tissue and is a specialized connective tissue that plays a supporting role. It involves many processes that are vital to the human body. The uniqueness of bone is that it can provide the mechanical stability required by bones to bear weight, exercise, and protect internal organs; it has the characteristics of strength, hardness, pressure resistance, tension, and torsion. In addition, the homeostasis of calcium levels in the blood is maintained because the mineral calcium is stored in the blood.

Bone is composed of cells and an intercellular matrix rich in organic compounds, mainly type I collagen fibers embedded in a matrix composed of proteoglycans, glycoproteins, and inorganic minerals. Collagen fibers form bundles or fibrils to resist tension, while minerals provide hardness and resist bending and compression. Bone minerals mainly exist in the form of calcium phosphate and calcium hydroxyapatite (HA) crystals. When combined with collagen fibers, bones have a specific hardness. The organic ingredients of bone include type I, III, IV collagen, glycoproteins, proteoglycans, etc.; the inorganic ingredients of bone mainly include HA nanoparticles (natural biological HA: calcium-deficient carbonate apatite) and some adsorbed on Inorganic ions (sodium, potassium, manganese, chlorine, fluorine, etc.).

Bone is a complex composite material that exists on at least five different hierarchical levels, namely whole bone level (cortical and spongy/cancellous bone), architectural level, tissue level, lamellar level, and ultrastructure [31]. Cancellous bone, that is, the inner part of bone, has a spongy structure with varying porosities between 50% and 90% and consists of a large number of trabeculae. Cortical bone, that is, the dense outer layer of bone with a porosity of less than 10%, on the other hand, is highly compact and orthotropic due to the circular nature of the osteons that make up its structure. Trabecula grows naturally along the stress direction, allowing the bone to withstand the maximum load with a minimum bone mass.

Bone naturally possesses the characteristic of mechano-transduction and trabecula grows in the direction of the principal stress. It is now widely acknowledged that loading magnitude and frequency have significant effects on bone remodeling. Young's modulus is considered to be one of the most significant characteristics in the biomechanical research on BTE scaffolds, on top of sufficient compressive strength to bear osteogenic loads during healing. The compressive strength of the cortical bone is in a range of 100–230 MPa, and of the cancellous bone is 2–12 MPa [32]. The young's modulus of the cortical bone is in the range of 3–30 GPa, and of the cancellous bone is 0.02–3 GPa [33].

Although there are a variety of different cells in bones, four main cell types ensure the integrity of its function: osteoclasts (OCLs), cells that destroy bones; osteoblasts, osteoblasts; osteocytes (OCTs), bone-maintaining cells; and endothelial cells (ECs), angiogenic cells associated with bones. They all have clear tasks and are therefore essential for maintaining healthy bone tissue. OCL is a large multinucleated cell formed by self-fusion. They are located in shallow pits on the bone surface, called resorption pits or Howship's lacunae. The main function of OCLs is the absorption of bone tissue, which can absorb strong matrix by secreting acid and collagenase. Bone resorption plays a vital role in the maintenance, repair and remodeling of bones. OCL is formed by the fusion of mononuclear precursors derived from pluripotent hematopoietic stem cells and shares more hematopoietic progenitor cells with T cells. Osteoblasts are monocytes derived from mesenchymal cells and are responsible for bone formation; they are mainly located on the surface of bones and are mononuclear, flat, flat cells. Their function is to produce the organic components of the bone matrix. When active, they show high alkaline phosphatase activity, and OBLs are eventually trapped in the matrix they produce and become OCTs. The lining cells are static flat cells covering the inner surface of the bone. Does not participate in the formation and reconstruction of bone matrix. The lining cells are derived from the osteoblast lineage and have potential osteogenic potential. A thin layer of connective tissue under the lining cells cannot be classified as osteoid. ECs are very flat; they form sidewalk-like patterns in blood vessels and play a role in various important physiological processes. Essentially, ECs secrete a variety of mediators (factors), which may cause biological responses through a variety of signal transduction mechanisms. These mediators are involved in regulating the permeability of endothelial cells and can promote chemotactic reactions such as inflammation and blood coagulation. Bone formation is an angiogenesis-dependent process, and ECs play an important role in the formation of blood vessels, providing oxygen and nutrients to the developing bone tissue. ECs interact with osteoprogenitor cells to produce specific osteoinductive factors under certain conditions, which may play a more direct role in bone development and formation.

4.2 Designing a 3D-printed scaffold for bone tissue reconstruction

Key features in the design of porous implants include careful selection of porosity, pore size and pore interconnects for satisfactory clinical results. These porous structural parameters can be controlled by AM technology and they have a profound effect on the mechanical and biological properties of scaffolds (Fig. 8.3).

4.2.1 Pore size

The pre-designed pores are arranged in a regular pattern, and their primary function is to induce osteoinduction in the porous metal scaffolds. Bone regeneration in porous implants in vivo involves the recruitment and penetration of cells from surrounding bone tissue and vascularization [34]. If new bone ingrowth is to be achieved, the pore size should not be too large or too small. At present, the effect of pore size on bone ingrowth is still controversial, and in the existing literatures, the optimal scaffold pore size for supporting bone growth varies.

According to a series of in vitro studies of scaffolds with different pore sizes, the minimum pore size of the scaffold should not be less than 100 µm (for cell proliferation and migration), and the optimal pore size is 300 µm to meet the needs of new bone and capillary formation [34]. The most suitable pore size for osteoblast growth and new bone formation is between 300 and 500 µm [35].

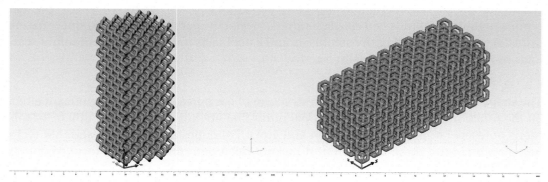

FIGURE 8.3 An example of designing the 3D model of metallic scaffold. Pore size, porosity, and pore structure together will affect the mechanical and biological properties of scaffold.

Some in vivo studies have tested the osteogenic capacity of porous scaffolds with different pore sizes. Scaffolds with smaller pores are considered to have a larger surface area and therefore have more space for ingrowth of bone tissue [30]. Itala et al. claimed that there is no apparent pore size limitation for consistent bone ingrowth [36]. More recently, Bream et al. evaluated the feasibility of early bone ingrowth into microporous Ti coating in rabbits' tibia, and it was found that new bone was formed in micropores less than 10 mm [37]. Although small holes are suitable, larger holes are considered to facilitate blood vessel formation. Kuboki et al. found that, when the pore size ranged from 300 to 400 mm, the implantation of porous hydroxyapatite scaffolds into rats showed higher alkaline phosphates activity, osteocalcin content, and bone ingrowth [38]. Naoya et al. implanted 300 mm, 600 mm, and 900 mm AM manufactured porous Ti scaffolds into rabbit tibia and they found 600 mm and 900 mm scaffolds demonstrated significantly higher bone ingrowth than 300 mm scaffolds [39].

4.2.1.1 Porosity
To increase the mass transfer, while retaining a strong supporting framework, there is a need to maintain a delicate trade-off between the porosity of the fabricated scaffold and its strength [40]. Higher porosity brings greater overall implant surface area and more space available for cellular proliferation and tissue growth [41,42]. At the same time, higher porosity increases the implant surface roughness, therefore enhances the initial stability of the implant [43]. More and deeper bone ingrowth was found in porous titanium coatings of higher porosity [44].

However, the porosity of the human trabecular bone is 70%–90%, so the porosity of the scaffold is also preferably within this range because excessive porosity tends to cause a decrease in the mechanical properties of the implant. Previous studies have shown that implants with porosity close to human bone have enhanced bone ingrowth and osteoblast activity and differentiation [45,46]. Previous reports have demonstrated that scaffolds with a porosity of 25%–42% can have compressive strength and Young's modulus similar to cortical bone, which can increase the life of the implant in vivo [18].

The elastic modulus of the implant can be controlled by adjusting the porosity [30]. The elastic modulus of human bone is between 3 and 20 GPa. In a study by Wiria et al., printed porous titanium scaffolds had elastic modulus levels comparable to natural bone, ranging from 4.8 to 13.2 GPa, and both osteoblasts and osteoblasts found in porous titanium scaffolds proliferated well and remained active [47].

4.2.1.2 Pore structure
The shape and the internal connection structure of the pores also have a significant effect on the function of the scaffold. Individual pores that are not connected to others, or tortuous pores will impede the formation and growth of bones and blood vessels. AM technology can control these factors, but it has not been determined which form of pore is most helpful for osteogenesis. According to previous studies, the pyramidal pores appear to be more suitable for cell growth than cubic and diagonal pores, and the cubic structure showed greater bone ingrowth depth than the wave structure [45].

In addition, scaffolds with irregular pore structure mimic the human trabecular structure, they enhanced cell viability, promoted cell proliferation and maturation, and promoted bone formation and ingrowth [48]. Therefore, the specific pore shape and porosity used in our research needs further exploration.

In summary, porosity, pore size, and pore structure, are key factors that will significantly influence the mechanical properties and biological performance of scaffolds such as bone ingrowth and transportation of cells and nutrients. However, the effects of these factors on scaffold performance are complicated, even conflicting to each other in certain circumstances. For example, increasing the porosity may enhance the biological processes, but it can decrease the stiffness and strength drastically [49].

4.2.1.3 Surface modification

Surface modification is a key part in the manufacture of metallic scaffolds. Ideal surface properties (microstructure and chemical compositions) are critical to the fixation of metal scaffolds with surrounding bone tissue and the extracellular matrix, and can determine the long-term success of the scaffolds [50]. The surface features of the metal scaffolds can be modified by surface modification to increase the bioactivity and biocompatibility, and enhance the biological performance [51].

At present, there are two main methods of surface modification. One is to optimize micro-roughness (blasting, acid etching, or sand blasting/etching), and the other is to apply bioactive coatings [52,53]. The former aims to increase cell attachment and proliferation by altering the microstructure and roughness of the scaffold surface, while the latter focuses on improving biocompatibility. Currently, surface coating technology is the most commonly used technique in porous metal implants [30], and different coating materials have been applied to improve the surface characteristics, including titanium nitride (TiN), titanium carbide (TiC), diamond-like carbon (DLC), hydroxyapatite (HA), zirconia as well as calcium phosphate (CaP), etc. [54–59].

The CaP coating is a bio-ceramic coating that can be used to improve the bone conduction properties of the scaffold surface [60]. The CaP coating is chemically similar to natural bone, has good biocompatibility and the ability to improve osteoblast proliferation and differentiation. CaP-coated titanium alloy implants can induce bone formation in soft tissues, and if antibiotics are incorporated into the coating, inflammation can be prevented [61].

CaP coatings can be fabricated in a variety of ways, including plasma spray, sol gel coating, and biomimetic coating technology [62–64]. Biomimetic coating involves immersing a metal implant in a simulated body fluid at physiological pH (7.4) and temperature (37°C), it has the inherent advantage of not being a line of sight technology, so that a porous metal scaffold can be successfully and homogeneously coated [65]. In addition, biomimetic CaP materials can also carry bioactive agents without compromising their biological activity.

One of the most popular bioactive agents in bone tissue engineering is morphogenetic protein 2 (BMP-2). It is an osteoinductive protein that can be administered topically to improve bone formation around the scaffold [66]. BMP-2 is one of the most potent growth

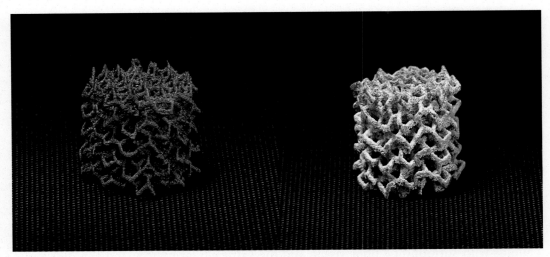

FIGURE 8.4 Comparison of Ti6Al4V scaffold *(Left)* and Ti6Al4V scaffold with biomimetic calcium phosphate coating *(Right)*.

factors for the differentiation of mesenchymal stem cells (MSC) and osteoprogenitor cells into osteoblasts [67]. Studies have shown that BMP-2 promotes the formation of new bone on titanium scaffolds [68]. In addition, BMP-2 can be bounded with CaP or CaP-based composites, which act as osteoinductive agents and induce bone formation efficiently (Fig. 8.4).

5 Summary

Emerging 3D printing technologies are enabling the fabrication of complex scaffold structures for diverse medical applications. 3D printing allows controlled material placement for configuring porous tissue scaffolds with tailored properties for desired mechanical stiffness, nutrient transport, and biological growth. Since 3D printing technology is fairly recent and there is no well-established knowledge about it in the medical field, it is necessary to research more about the subject and to explore the repercussion of the use of different printing techniques, because there are many factors that influence the final properties of the printed structure, such as the chosen material, the resolution of each technique, the time it takes to print and speed of the printing, and the computer model. Besides that, it is also necessary to evaluate the applicability of the nanomaterials in the 3D printed scaffolds, with the intent of obtaining synergetic results in the mechanical and biological properties.

References

[1] H.-W. Kang, S.J. Lee, I.K. Ko, C. Kengla, J.J. Yoo, A. Atala, A 3D bioprinting system to produce human-scale tissue constructs with structural integrity, Nat. Biotechnol. 34 (3) (2016) 312–319.

[2] K. Nune, A. Kumar, R. Misra, S. Li, Y. Hao, R. Yang, Functional response of osteoblasts in functionally gradient titanium alloy mesh arrays processed by 3D additive manufacturing, Colloids Surfaces B Biointerf. 150 (2017) 78–88.

[3] T. Rayna, L. Striukova, From rapid prototyping to home fabrication: How 3D printing is changing business model innovation, Technol. Forecast. Soc. Change 102 (2016) 214–224.

[4] S.V. Murphy, A. Atala, 3D bioprinting of tissues and organs, Nat. Biotechnol. 32 (8) (2014) 773–785.

[5] C.L. Ventola, Medical applications for 3D printing: current and projected uses, Pharm. Therapeut. 39 (10) (2014) 704.

[6] S. Kondor, C. Grant, P. Liacouras, M. Schmid, L. Michael Parsons, B. Macy, et al. Personalized surgical instruments, J. Med. Devices 7 (3) (2013).

[7] J. Jang, H.-G. Yi, D.-W. Cho, 3D printed tissue models: present and future, ACS Biomater. Sci. Eng. 2 (10) (2016) 1722–1731.

[8] G.B. Kim, S. Lee, H. Kim, D.H. Yang, Y.-H. Kim, Y.S. Kyung, et al. Three-dimensional printing: basic principles and applications in medicine and radiology, Korean J. Radiol. 17 (2) (2016) 182–197.

[9] T. Billiet, M. Vandenhaute, J. Schelfhout, S Van Vlierberghe, P. Dubruel, A review of trends and limitations in hydrogel-rapid prototyping for tissue engineering, Biomaterials 33 (26) (2012) 6020-L6041.

[10] J.R. Tumbleston, D. Shirvanyants, N. Ermoshkin, R. Janusziewicz, A.R. Johnson, D. Kelly, et al. Continuous liquid interface production of 3D objects, Science 347 (6228) (2015) 1349–1352.

[11] S.F.S. Shirazi, S. Gharehkhani, M. Mehrali, H. Yarmand, H.S.C. Metselaar, N.A. Kadri, et al. A review on powder-based additive manufacturing for tissue engineering: selective laser sintering and inkjet 3D printing, Sci. Technol. Adv. Mater. 16 (3) (2015) 033502.

[12] J. Kruth, P. Mercelis, J. Van Vaerenbergh, L. Froyen, M. Rombouts, Binding mechanisms in selective laser sintering and selective laser melting, Rapid Prototyping. J. 11 (1) (2005) 26–36.

[13] K.V. Wong, A. Hernandez, A review of additive manufacturing, Int. Sch. Res. Notices 2012 (2012) Article ID 208760.

[14] J. Bohandy, B. Kim, F. Adrian, Metal deposition from a supported metal film using an excimer laser, J. Appl. Phys. 60 (4) (1986) 1538–1539.

[15] E.M. Sachs, J.S. Haggerty, M.J. Cima, P.A. Williams, Three-dimensional printing techniques, US Pat. 5,340,656 (1994).

[16] S. Mobini, A. Ayoub. Bone tissue engineering in the maxillofacial region: the state-of-the-art practice and future prospects, Regen. Reconstr. Restor. 1 (1) (2016) 8.

[17] S.F. Badylak, D. Taylor, K. Uygun, Whole-organ tissue engineering: decellularization and recellularization of three-dimensional matrix scaffolds, Ann. Rev. Biomed. Eng. 13 (2011) 27–53.

[18] S. Bose, M. Roy, A. Bandyopadhyay, Recent advances in bone tissue engineering scaffolds, Trends Biotechnol. 30 (10) (2012) 546–554.

[19] I. Armentano, M. Dottori, E. Fortunati, S. Mattioli, J. Kenny, Biodegradable polymer matrix nanocomposites for tissue engineering: a review, Polym. Degrad. Stab. 95 (11) (2010) 2126–2146.

[20] S. Van Vlierberghe, P. Dubruel, E. Schacht, Biopolymer-based hydrogels as scaffolds for tissue engineering applications: a review, Biomacromolecules 12 (5) (2011) 1387–1408.

[21] S. Yang, K.-F. Leong, Z. Du, C.-K. Chua, The design of scaffolds for use in tissue engineering. Part I. Traditional factors, Tissue Eng. 7 (6) (2001) 679–689.

[22] M. Geetha, A.K. Singh, R. Asokamani, A.K. Gogia, Ti based biomaterials, the ultimate choice for orthopaedic implants–a review, Progr. Mater. Sci. 54 (3) (2009) 397–425.

[23] M. Tamaddon, S. Samizadeh, L. Wang, G. Blunn, C. Liu, Intrinsic osteoinductivity of porous titanium scaffold for bone tissue engineering, Int. J. Biomater. 2017 (2017) Article ID 5093063.

[24] A. Yousefi, M.E. Hoque, R.G. Prasad, N. Uth, Current strategies in multiphasic scaffold design for osteochondral tissue engineering: a review, J. Biomed. Mater. Res. A. 103 (7) (2015) 2460–2481.

[25] K. Alvarez, H. Nakajima, Metallic scaffolds for bone regeneration, Materials 2 (3) (2009) 790–832.

[26] C. Elias, J. Lima, R. Valiev, M. Meyers, Biomedical applications of titanium and its alloys, Jom. 60 (3) (2008) 46–49.

[27] A. Sicilia, S. Cuesta, G. Coma, I. Arregui, C. Guisasola, E. Ruiz, et al. Titanium allergy in dental implant patients: a clinical study on 1500 consecutive patients, Clin. Oral Implant. Res. 19 (8) (2008) 823–835.

[28] J. Parthasarathy, B. Starly, S. Raman, A. Christensen, Mechanical evaluation of porous titanium (Ti6Al4V) structures with electron beam melting (EBM), J. Mech. Behav. Biomed. Mater. 3 (3) (2010) 249–259.

[29] P.H. Warnke, T. Douglas, P. Wollny, E. Sherry, M. Steiner, S. Galonska, et al. Rapid prototyping: porous titanium alloy scaffolds produced by selective laser melting for bone tissue engineering, Tissue Eng. Part C Methods 15 (2) (2008) 115–124.

[30] X. Wang, S. Xu, S. Zhou, W. Xu, M. Leary, P. Choong, et al. Topological design and additive manufacturing of porous metals for bone scaffolds and orthopaedic implants: A review, Biomaterials 83 (2016) 127–141.

[31] M. Liebschner, M. Wettergreen, Optimization of bone scaffold engineering for load bearing applications, Topics Tissue Eng. (2003) 1–39.

[32] M.A. Surmeneva, R.A. Surmenev, E.A. Chudinova, A. Koptioug, M.S. Tkachev, S.N. Gorodzha, et al. Fabrication of multiple-layered gradient cellular metal scaffold via electron beam melting for segmental bone reconstruction, Mater. Des. 133 (2017) 195–204.

[33] X.-Y. Zhang, G. Fang, J. Zhou, Additively manufactured scaffolds for bone tissue engineering and the prediction of their mechanical behavior: A review, Materials 10 (1) (2017) 50.

[34] V. Karageorgiou, D. Kaplan, Porosity of 3D biomaterial scaffolds and osteogenesis, Biomaterials 26 (27) (2005) 5474–5491.

[35] A. Cheng, A. Humayun, D.J. Cohen, B.D. Boyan, Z. Schwartz, Additively manufactured 3D porous Ti-6Al-4V constructs mimic trabecular bone structure and regulate osteoblast proliferation, differentiation and local factor production in a porosity and surface roughness dependent manner, Biofabrication 6 (4) (2014) 045007.

[36] A.I. Itälä, H.O. Ylänen, C. Ekholm, K.H. Karlsson, H.T. Aro, Pore diameter of more than 100 μm is not requisite for bone ingrowth in rabbits, J. Biomed. Mater. Res. 58 (6) (2001) 679–683.

[37] A. Braem, A. Chaudhari, M.V. Cardoso, J. Schrooten, J. Duyck, J. Vleugels, Peri-and intra-implant bone response to microporous Ti coatings with surface modification, Acta biomaterialia 10 (2) (2014) 986–995.

[38] Y. Kuboki, Q. Jin, H. Takita, Geometry of carriers controlling phenotypic expression in BMP-induced osteogenesis and chondrogenesis, JBJS 83 (1_suppl_2) (2001) S105–S115.

[39] N. Taniguchi, S. Fujibayashi, M. Takemoto, K. Sasaki, B. Otsuki, T. Nakamura, et al. Effect of pore size on bone ingrowth into porous titanium implants fabricated by additive manufacturing: an in vivo experiment, Mater. Sci. Eng. C 59 (2016) 690–701.

[40] G. Ryan, A. Pandit, D.P. Apatsidis, Fabrication methods of porous metals for use in orthopaedic applications, Biomaterials 27 (13) (2006) 2651–2670.

[41] V.K. Balla, S. Bodhak, S. Bose, A. Bandyopadhyay, Porous tantalum structures for bone implants: fabrication, mechanical and in vitro biological properties, Acta biomaterialia 6 (8) (2010) 3349–3359.

[42] H. Jeon, H. Lee, G. Kim, A surface-modified poly (ε-caprolactone) scaffold comprising variable nanosized surface-roughness using a plasma treatment, Tissue Eng. Part C Method. 20 (12) (2014) 951–963.

[43] W. Xue, B.V. Krishna, A. Bandyopadhyay, S. Bose, Processing and biocompatibility evaluation of laser processed porous titanium, Acta biomaterialia 3 (6) (2007) 1007–1018.

[44] B.J. Story, W.R. Wagner, D.M. Gaisser, S.D. Cook, A.M. Rust-Dawicki, In vivo performance of a modified CSTi dental implant coating, Int. J. Oral Maxillofac. Implant. 13 (6) (1998).

[45] J.E. Biemond, T.S. Eufrásio, G. Hannink, N. Verdonschot, P. Buma, Assessment of bone ingrowth potential of biomimetic hydroxyapatite and brushite coated porous E-beam structures, J. Mater. Sci Med. 22 (4) (2011) 917–925.

[46] J. Markhoff, J. Wieding, V. Weissmann, J. Pasold, A. Jonitz-Heincke, R. Bader, Influence of different three-dimensional open porous titanium scaffold designs on human osteoblasts behavior in static and dynamic cell investigations, Materials 8 (8) (2015) 5490–5507.

[47] F.E. Wiria, J.Y.M. Shyan, P.N. Lim, F.G.C. Wen, J.F. Yeo, T. Cao, Printing of titanium implant prototype, Mater. Des. 31 (2010) S101–S105.

[48] J. Lv, Z. Jia, J. Li, Y. Wang, J. Yang, P. Xiu, et al. Electron beam melting fabrication of porous Ti6Al4V scaffolds: cytocompatibility and osteogenesis, Adv. Eng. Mater. 17 (9) (2015) 1391–1398.

[49] L.J. Gibson, M.F. Ashby, Cellular Solids: Structure and Properties, Cambridge University Press, (1999).

[50] R.A. Gittens, T. McLachlan, R. Olivares-Navarrete, Y. Cai, S. Berner, R. Tannenbaum, et al. The effects of combined micron-/submicron-scale surface roughness and nanoscale features on cell proliferation and differentiation, Biomaterials 32 (13) (2011) 3395–3403.

[51] S.A. Yavari, J. van der Stok, Y.C. Chai, R. Wauthle, Z.T. Birgani, P. Habibovic, et al. Bone regeneration performance of surface-treated porous titanium, Biomaterials 35 (24) (2014) 6172–6181.

[52] Q. Chen, G.A. Thouas, Metallic implant biomaterials, Mater. Sci. Eng. Rep. 87 (2015) 1–57.

[53] R. Singh, N.B. Dahotre, Corrosion degradation and prevention by surface modification of biometallic materials, J. Mater. Sci. Med. 18 (5) (2007) 725–751.

[54] P. Cheang, K. Khor, Addressing processing problems associated with plasma spraying of hydroxyapatite coatings, Biomaterials 17 (5) (1996) 537–544.

[55] H.A. Ching, D. Choudhury, M.J. Nine, N.A.A. Osman, Effects of surface coating on reducing friction and wear of orthopaedic implants, Sci. Technol. Adv. Mater. 15 (1) (2014) 014402.

[56] F. Koch, D. Weng, S. Krämer, S. Biesterfeld, A. Jahn-Eimermacher, W. Wagner, Osseointegration of one-piece zirconia implants compared with a titanium implant of identical design: a histomorphometric study in the dog, Clin. Oral Implant. Res. 21 (3) (2010) 350–356.

[57] J. Langhoff, K. Voelter, D. Scharnweber, M. Schnabelrauch, F. Schlottig, T. Hefti, et al. Comparison of chemically and pharmaceutically modified titanium and zirconia implant surfaces in dentistry: a study in sheep, Int. J. Oral Maxillofac. Surg. 37 (12) (2008) 1125–1132.

[58] P. Liu, J. Smits, D.C. Ayers, J. Song, Surface mineralization of Ti6Al4V substrates with calcium apatites for the retention and local delivery of recombinant human bone morphogenetic protein-2, Acta biomaterialia 7 (9) (2011) 3488–3495.

[59] R.K. Roy, K. Lee, Biomedical applications of diamond-like carbon coatings: A review, J. Biomed. Mater. Res. B Appl. Biomater. 83 (1) (2007) 72–84.

[60] R.Z. LeGeros, Properties of osteoconductive biomaterials: calcium phosphates, Clin. Orthop. Relat. Res. 395 (2002) 81–98.

[61] P. Habibovic, J. Li, C.M. Van Der Valk, G. Meijer, P. Layrolle, C.A. Van Blitterswijk, et al. Biological performance of uncoated and octacalcium phosphate-coated Ti6Al4V, Biomaterials 26 (1) (2005) 23–36.

[62] I. Denry, L.T. Kuhn, Design and characterization of calcium phosphate ceramic scaffolds for bone tissue engineering, Dental Mater. 32 (1) (2016) 43–53.

[63] D.H. Nguyen, C.W. Wu, J.J. Huang, C.S. Chang, M.H. Cheng, Simultaneous left maxillary and right mandibular reconstructions with a split osteomyocutaneous peroneal artery-based combined flap, Head Neck. 35 (2) (2013) E39–E43.

[64] Z. Zyman, J. Weng, X. Liu, X. Zhang, Z. Ma, Amorphous phase and morphological structure of hydroxyapatite plasma coatings, Biomaterials 14 (3) (1993) 225–228.

[65] F. Barrere, C.M. van der Valk, R.A. Dalmeijer, G. Meijer, C.A. van Blitterswijk, K. de Groot, et al. Osteogenecity of octacalcium phosphate coatings applied on porous metal implants, J. Biomed. Mater. Res. 66 (4) (2003) 779–788.

[66] P. Boyne, S.D. Jones, Demonstration of the osseoinductive effect of bone morphogenetic protein within endosseous dental implants, Implant Dentist. 13 (2) (2004) 180–184.

[67] H. Cheng, W. Jiang, F.M. Phillips, R.C. Haydon, Y. Peng, L. Zhou, et al. Osteogenic activity of the fourteen types of human bone morphogenetic proteins (BMPs), JBJS 85 (8) (2003) 1544–1552.

[68] J. van der Stok, M. Koolen, M. de Maat, S. Amin Yavari, J. Alblas, P. Patka, et al. Full regeneration of segmental bone defects using porous titanium implants loaded with BMP-2 containing fibrin gels, Eur. Cells Mater. 2015 (29) (2015) 141–154.

9

Clinical practice (Graz, Austria and Gießen, Germany)

Jürgen Wallner[a,b], Michael Schwaiger[a], Philipp Streckbein[c], Wolfgang Zemann[a]

[a]DEPARTMENT OF ORAL AND MAXILLOFACIAL SURGERY, MEDICAL UNIVERSITY OF GRAZ, GRAZ, AUSTRIA; [b]DEPARTMENT OF CRANIO-MAXILLOFACIAL SURGERY, AZ MONICA AND THE UNIVERSITY HOSPITAL ANTWERP, ANTWERP, BELGIUM; [c]DEPARTMENT OF ORAL- AND CRANIO-MAXILLO-FACIAL SURGERY, UNIVERSITY HOSPITAL GIEßEN, GIEßEN, GERMANY

1 Clinical centers in Austria

Austria is a country with about 8.8 million people. The country has a total of eight specialized departments for oral and maxillofacial surgery including four university clinics located in Vienna, Graz, Innsbruck, and Salzburg.

The specialized subject of oral and maxillofacial surgery is strongly dominated through its practical surgical activity. In Austria oral and maxillofacial surgery involves the surgical treatment of hard and soft tissues in the oral cavity, the face and the head and neck area such as the surgical treatment of facial trauma and malformations, the correction of dentofacial discrepancies, and the microvascular reconstruction of expanded facial defects.

Although the number of inhabitants in Austria is quite small compared to other European countries the treated number of maxillofacial cases in the country's university clinics can be compared worldwide to other specialized departments of much bigger countries. This is especially true for the clinical centers in Innsbruck, which is, due to frequent ski and mountain tourism in winter and/or summer, one of Europe's leading trauma centers [1–3] or the university clinic in Salzburg which is internationally known for their high specialization in microvascular surgery when treating reconstructive cases [4–6].

The Medical University of Graz is a tertiary clinical center in Styria in the very south of Austria. The university has a high scientific focus and involves a university clinic and several newly built up research centers that have strongly expanded in the last years. The department of oral and maxillofacial surgery is the only specialized department in the greater surrounding area of Styria. The department comprises general primary and specialized care in the various surgical subfields of maxillofacial surgery such as oral surgery, trauma surgery, microvascular facial soft and hard tissue reconstruction, the surgical correction of congenital skeletal dentofacial malformations/malocclusions and head and neck tumor resections. The latter three are under a specialized focus at the department.

Computer-Aided Oral and Maxillofacial Surgery. http://dx.doi.org/10.1016/B978-0-12-823299-6.00009-2

Being localized in a catchment area of over 1.5 million people, more than 20,000 patients are treated by the division's facilities every year.

Among others, the department of oral and maxillofacial surgical in Graz is working together with the technical university to investigate computer aided surgical technologies for the diagnosis and treatment support and to implement further developed computer-aided technologies in the surgical practical clinical routine [7–10]. The gathered knowledge about digital workflow procedures, image based computing or navigated surgery is used in the clinical practice to increase treatment quality and efficiency as also in research projects together with both other medical university departments and the industry.

Due to the continuous development of medical technologies and computer-supported methods, an ongoing increasing number of cases is today clinically treated by the support of such computer-assisted planning and/or visualization modules especially in facial reconstructive cases [11–14]. These cases involve complex bone fractures in anatomical areas of limited intraoperative view, the resection of tumors, cysts, or other pathologies and the microvascular tissue transfer. Further, clinically relevant areas of use are skeletal dentofacial malformations that are corrected by orthognathic surgical procedures [15,16].

Apart from that, individually generated patient-specific facial implants that are planned and manufactured by computer-aided support are increasingly used in the clinical routine as a high-end treatment option in complex bone trauma or reconstructive cases and have become the gold standard in that field in the last years [17–19].

2 Clinical imaging modalities used for computer-aided oral and maxillofacial surgery

In the past 2 decades, the discipline of maxillofacial surgery has undergone a remarkable rate of computer-based technological innovation. This is mainly related to (1) the continuously ongoing technical developments for clinical medicine and (2) the complex three-dimensional (3D) anatomy of the face in combination with (3) the need of surgical precision, and (4) an increasing number of requests for morphological 3D visualized surgery [20,21]. Therefore, the needed advanced technological and computer-based assistance is mostly based on 3D surface reconstructions or volume renderings of anatomical structures generated by segmentation algorithms [22] that build the basis for a huge range of computer-aided technologies and procedures that can be used in oral and maxillofacial surgery.

These segmentation approaches and segmentation algorithms are software tools and functions that are used on digital radiological image data mainly from computed tomography (CT) or positron emission tomography (PET/CT) scans and magnet resonance imaging (MRI) [23–26]. Due to the enlargement of medical image data in the most clinical centers—at least in the western world—the accuracy of new image scanner generations and the low time consumption of 3D image reconstruction [27], there is a rapidly growing interest in image data generation during the clinical routine and also in virtual segmentation automata and computer-based 3D medical image analysis [28,29]. These increasing interests seem to continuously push the development of computer-aided technologies to higher levels and try to increasingly implement these technologies in the clinical routine.

Since the clinical used radiological imaging modalities like CT or PET/CT are widely used in diagnostics, clinical studies, treatment planning procedures and their scientific evaluations, automatic algorithms for image analysis play a vital role in various computer-aided medical applications and create the functional basis of computer-aided medical technologies. Therefore, these algorithms have become an invaluable tool in medicine, especially in terms of surgical diagnosis and treatment planning support in three dimensions [30]. Typically, segmentation is the first step in a medical image analysis pipeline, and therefore incorrect segmentation affects any subsequent steps heavily. However, automatic medical image segmentation is still known to be one of the most complex problems in image analysis [31]. Therefore, to this day, image-based delineation of the anatomical region of interest is often adapted manually or semi-manually, especially in regions with limited contrast and for organs or tissues with large variations in geometry.

This is a challenging task, since it is time consuming and requires a lot of empirical knowledge. Furthermore, the process of semi-automatic segmentation is prone to errors, highly operator-dependent and not really reproducible. All these limitations emphasize the need for accurate, automatic algorithms. In the past years, deep learning approaches have made a large impact in the field of image processing and analysis, outperforming the state of the art in many visual recognition tasks [32]. In this context, artificial neural networks have also been applied successfully to medical image processing tasks such as segmentation.

Clinical image modalities that are mainly used in oral and maxillofacial surgery are simple X-ray scans, head and neck ultrasound, CT and cone-beam computed tomography (CBCT), MRI, or PET scans. These image modalities all work digitally and are clinically widely used during diagnosis and treatment planning and post-operative follow ups in all oral and maxillofacial subfields [33,34]. In this context CT and CBCT scans, which consume by far the lowest amount of time for a full image scan and the according image data generation, are mainly used for hard tissue assessments such as in dental or bony trauma, reconstruction, or skeletal dentofacial malformation/malocclusion cases or in emergency cases to create a fast image series overview of the regions of interest. Head and neck ultrasound and MRI scans are predominantly used for soft tissue assessments to visualize the expansion and size of tumors, cysts or pathologic lesions, but also to determine the exact localization of blood vessels, muscles, or lymph nodes and their relation to other anatomical structures of interest. Positron emission tomography (PET) with the glucose analog fluorine [18-F] 2-fluorodeoxyglucose (FDG) is a very effective image modality mainly used in the pre- and postoperative diagnostic in oral and maxillofacial oncology [33]. FDG PET reveals the biochemical differences between normal and malignant tissues and supports the localization of primary and metastatic tumor types [35]. To visualize both functional biomechanical processes and anatomical localization, FDG PET and CT data can be combined into [18-F] 2-fluorodeoxyglucose positron emission tomography and computed tomography image fusion scans (F^{18}-FDG PET/CT or PET/CT) which is probably today the most advanced computer-aided technology performed routinely in every days clinical practice on patients. From the image modality point of view, combined PET/CT is today the clinical gold standard in preoperative tumor staging and surgical treatment planning [36,37] especially in oro-pharyngeal oncology, although the procedure is highly expensive compared to normal head and neck CT scans. Image modality combinations between PET and MRI scans (PET/MRI) do also exist; however are usually not routinely performed for clinical follow-up procedures, since there is, because of technical-physical reasons, only a weak bony contrast displayed in such image series that constitutes a disadvantage in the surgical diagnostic procedures. In PET/CT image series various studies have shown high sensitivity and specificity in the detection of nodal metastases, up to 100% in some reports, in contrast to the 75% sensitivity and 80% specificity of the CT/MRI scan [38,39].

In that context, combined PET/CT scanning offers many advantages for the clinical routine in both the preoperative tumor staging and in the postoperative oncologic follow-up [40]. These advantages are mainly related to the CT based combined visualization of the anatomical tumor localization and the PET based visualization of the tumor metabolism. Therefore, one single PET/CT full body scan can replace additional radiological investigations [36].

However, independent from the image modality, the clinical image scans are routinely visualized two-dimensionally on screens included in big computer workstation and have to be manually assessed by a radiological or/and a surgical expert. Since automatic image segmentation has been increasingly investigated in oral and maxillofacial surgery during the last years [21,41], an automatic diagnostic image based detection in image data scans such as the PET/CT could potentially localize a tumor in the PET/CT images independently from manual assessments. Although such deep learning networks have already been tested to automatically detect tumor in PET/CT scans [42], such computer-aided procedures are currently at the stage of early research and by far not ready for clinical use.

Due to the high contrast values, nearly all computer-aided methods that are currently clinically used, build up on CT or CBCT-data scans. The scans are usually of high resolution with good contrast values with slices not exceeding 1.5 mm to ensure clear and highly accurate anatomical images [7,9,17,41]. High-resolution MRI scans are also performed in the clinical routine, but usually only on special surgical requests to exactly assess and focus on soft tissue structures, if for example tumor boarders have to be detected very accurately in cases when neoplastic lesions are localized close to important anatomical structures, which can potentially be infiltrated.

Image-based segmentation modules that are usually included in industrial and licensed software packages are clinically used on CT data basis for further image processing such as operation planning, 3D printing of patient-specific anatomical structure templates or patient-specific implants for facial reconstructions. Although, clinical computer-aided surgical planning methods based on MRI image data have also been described and tested [43,44], they still remain on a scientific level of research.

3 Use and practice of clinical computer-aided methods and technologies

In the oral and maxillofacial field, computer-aided technologies constitute currently an important step in the diagnosis and treatment support of complex surgical cases in the clinical routine. The used computer-aided technologies are today mostly based on segmentation processes that are used on clinical CT-data consisting out of digital imaging and communications in medicine (DICOM) files [28,45,46]. In that context, the biological structures of interest in the face and skull—including both soft and hard tissues but practically used much more in hard than soft tissues—can virtually be localized, quantified, and visualized to simulate (1) an interactive treatment planning, (2) complex surgical procedures and/or (3) therapeutic surgical outcomes in three dimensions [47,48]. Further, image-based segmentation can be used to generate (4) 3D printed models by using an appropriate printer to support diagnosis and treatment pathways, such as the creation of anatomical templates for the preoperative orientation of osteosynthesis material adaption [45], for example, for patients with oral-maxillofacial deformities/malocclusion or for reconstructions after tumor resections. If functionally stable, these computer-based procedures increase a precise preoperative representation of treatment goals, a shortened treatment or operation time, and a more accurate therapeutic outcome and improve the treatment quality [24,49,50].

In today's clinical practice computer-aided technologies in maxillofacial surgery are mainly used for a patient-specific approach, which means that these technologies are used to try to create a personal medicine individually for each patient. In that context, the main computer-aided patient-specific approaches are (1) image-based virtual surgical planning and 3D visualization (based on CT-DICOM files and algorithmic segmentations), (2) 3D printed models (polymer made based on CT-DICOM files by the support of 3D printers in-house or by an industry partner), (3) virtual planning and manufacturing of surgical cutting guides and splints (CT-DICOM based titanium or polymer made), and (4) virtual planning and manufacturing of patient-specific implants (titanium made).

In the clinical practice, the most frequent and most important clinical use of computer-aided technologies is most probably referred to the following three points: (1) the planning and manufacturing of patient-specific implants (PSIs) for bone reconstruction (complex orbital and midfacial trauma surgery, defect surgery), (2) the production of anatomical surgical templates/models for the specific orientation/adaption of osteosynthesis materials in reconstructive cases (head and neck tumor surgery, expanded trauma surgery), and (3) the 3D operation planning with or without computer-guided intraoperative support (dental splints, surgical cutting guides) in skeletal dentofacial malformation/malocclusion cases (orthognathic surgery).

Independently of these procedures, a digital workflow has to be performed when computer-aided procedures are used. This workflow can be described as "clinical computer-aided design and computer-aided manufacturing – CAD/CAM workflow" and is defined as follows:

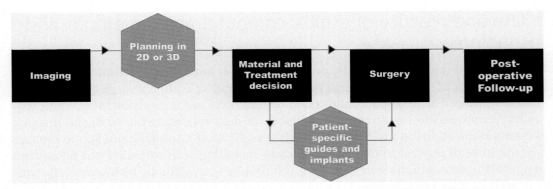

FIGURE 9.1 Overview about the clinical computer-aided design and computer-aided manufacturing—CAD/CAM workflow.

- Digital imaging modality (mainly CT or CBCT scans, DICOM based)—virtual planning (image data based) in 2D or 3D—material (titanium or polymer) and treatment decision
- Patient-specific guides/splints and/or implants (dependent on the treatment plan and surgical procedure manufactured by the industry partner and transferred to the clinical center)
- Surgery, postoperative follow up (digital follow up with image modality by CT or CBCT scans or others and additional clinical follow up)

Fig. 9.1 gives a graphical overview about this workflow.

There are some specific computer-aided procedures that are especially important in today's clinical practice. These procedures and methods are described in the next paragraphs including the surrounding information.

3.1 Planning and manufacturing of patient-specific implants (PSI) for bone reconstruction in complex defect surgery

CAD/CAM-based PSIs are a newly developed technology introduced to and routinely used in the clinical practice within the last years. PSIs can be used in the defect reconstruction of nearly every bone in the facial skeleton. This means that a complete digital workflow is used in the clinic to create a CAD/CAM-based personalized implant for reconstruction exactly fitting to the patients defect in the facial skeleton. PSIs are frequently used in the lateral and middle face, as these areas are central parts of bone defects after traffic and sports accidents, but also in the lower face for mandibular reconstruction after pathological defects such as after osteonecrosis or removals of expanded cysts, when a bone transplant from another anatomical location of the own body is not indicated or cannot be used.

However, clinically, PSIs are especially used in complex orbital and mid-facial fractures due to the limited operative access, the limited space in the operation field and in parallel the need of highly precise reconstruction and surgical treatment in these anatomical areas to avoid functional and aesthetic impairments.

In that context, the orbital is a common site for facial fractures [51] that cause both serious functional and aesthetic impairments [52]. Overall, these fractures represent more than 40% of all facial fractures in contemporary cranio-maxillofacial trauma. Surgically, the treatment is difficult due to the high complexity of the orbital anatomy and the limited intraoperative view [53]. Therefore, meticulous 3D CT image scans and clinical examinations are indispensable for an appropriate treatment planning, in order to restore orbital volume and shape. Consequently, inaccurate surgical techniques may lead to visual disturbances such as double vision, miss-positioning of the eye, unstable fracture healings, enophthalmos (permanent recession of the globe into the orbit) or infraorbital and optical nerve injuries [54], which are disastrous for the patient.

In complex reconstructions such as complex mid-facial and orbital fractures PSIs represent a key step towards safer clinical practice, increased intraoperative control and simplify operative procedures through the possibility of pre-operative virtual operation planning and life like implant design simulation [55,56]. By means of a complete digital planning and design workflow, PSIs are today routinely available for the clinical practice [17] and are used to achieve stable reconstructions mainly in complex orbital fractures that typically involve at least two orbital walls and/or widely expand over the orbital floor.

In any case, a PSI is personalized manufactured according to the defect. Therefore, a digital planning workflow is carried out by both the operating surgeon and the technician from the manufacturing company (industrial partner). Industrial partner for clinical PSI planning and manufacturing are for example the professional medical device companies KLS Martin—https://www.klsmartin.com/de/, Johnson & Johnson Synthes—https://www.jnjmedicaldevices.com/de-DE/synthes-tuttlingen-gmbh or Stryker—https://www.stryker.com/at/en/index.html. In Austria, the first of the companies named above is most probably used in most of the cases when industry support regarding PSI planning and manufacturing is needed.

To reconstruct the defect, the patient's CT data set has to be uploaded to the server of the industrial partner. After a technical image data quality check the PSI is virtually planned on the computer. This starts with a first planning outline by the technician and proceeds then further by the design adaption made by the operating surgeon. The communication between surgeon and technician is usually made via web meetings and assessments of 3D proposals. The technical software used to design the implants is mainly done by Geomagic Freeform (3D Systems— https://de.3dsystems.com/software/geomagic-freeform). In the design process, the technician proposes an outline using a 3D file format such as 3D.pdf files that are send to the surgeon for check-up. The operating surgeon adapts and validates the outlines in web meetings, online messages or via phone calls. In some cases, final design adaptions are made directly in an online web meeting when using the design software by both the surgeon and the technician.

In unilateral facial defects (defect affecting only one side of the face), the defect is virtually reconstructed on the computer by mirroring the healthy side which is not affected

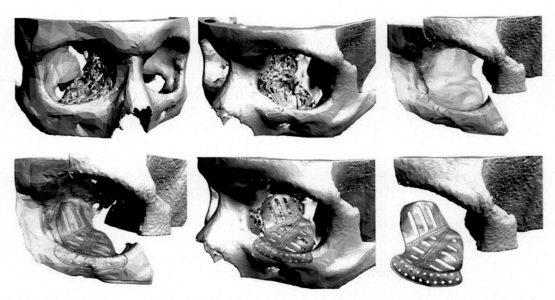

FIGURE 9.2 PSI used to reconstruct the left orbit after a heavy orbital trauma. The completed image segmentation and virtual planning is shown. The PSI was designed according to the right orbital geometry that was mirrored to the left side.

to the defected side. In bilateral facial defects (defect affecting both sides of the face) or in defects that cross the midline the virtual defect reconstruction is based on earlier existing image data of the patient without defects or has to be orientated on the surrounding anatomical tissues. Fig. 9.2 shows the completed virtual planning of a PSI used to reconstruct the left orbit after a heavy orbital trauma. After the virtual PSI design is completed, the planning has to be approved by the operating surgeon. After virtual PSI design approval, a titanium made PSI is manufactured by the industry partner and after technical industrial approval sent to the clinical center where the operation is performed (Figs. 9.3 and 9.4). The whole planning and transfer procedure takes time and can be estimated to approximately 5–7 working days in some cases even more. The financial costs of one PSI per patient depending on the size and geometry is between 4000 and 7000 Euros. Such additional financial costs influence the budget of the hospital. In Austria, such additional costs have to be paid by the clinical center and are not refunded. Apart from the frequent use of PSIs in the orbit and the midface, PSIs can also, as already mentioned earlier, be used for the reconstruction of defects caused by expanded trauma or osteonecrosis, for example, in the upper or lower jaw as an alternative for harvested bone transplants taken from the own body which constitute the first choice in defect reconstruction (Fig. 9.5).

However, although PSIs are known to clinically provide safe functional and aesthetic results and make clinical operating procedures in complex cases more efficient, the needed digital planning and design workflow still consumes high financial and personnel resources. The digital workflow procedure can be time consuming and erroneous especially in cases of expanded defects or in cases where inexperienced surgeons are involved [18].

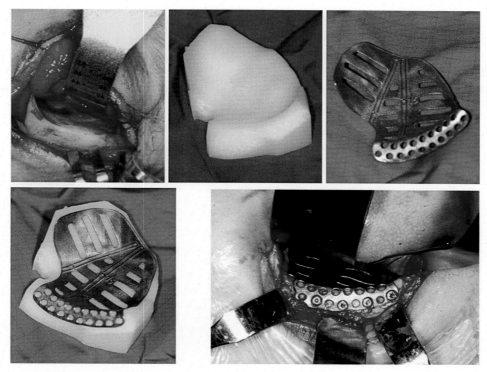

FIGURE 9.3 Intraoperative situation of the PSI insertion in the left orbit via a minimal invasive access. The PSI is made out of titanium. The pictures are taken from the same patient displayed in Fig. 9.2.

Therefore, the creation of efficient virtual workflows and three dimensional (3D) design templates is highly relevant for maxillofacial defect reconstruction [19]. However, an efficient and time saving digital PSI design workflow requires clinical training cases, training templates and planning experience, which is currently difficult to become, because there is a lack of accessible data in that field [57].

Up until now, absolutely no available clinical data or data libraries exist that offer valid training cases for PSI design planning or provide a variety of successful designed orbital PSIs as control group samples that can be used by clinicians for training purposes and/or by researchers for the investigation and further development of software tools or PSI in-house productions with 3D printers.

3.2 Production of anatomical surgical templates/models for the specific orientation/adaption of osteosynthesis materials in head and neck tumor surgery and expanded trauma surgery

The production of surgical anatomical templates/models was already clinically performed in the past for many years to achieve milled models showing naturally the patient's bone structure anatomy. However, the accuracy, form and geometry of these models where

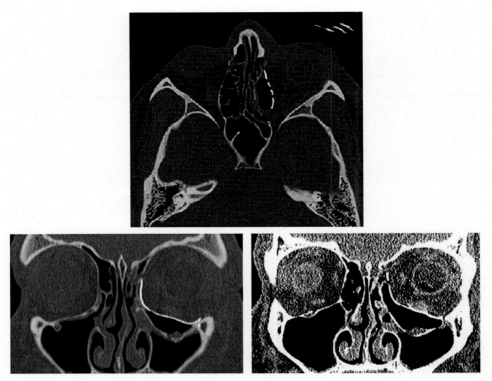

FIGURE 9.4 Postoperative radiological follow-up after operation from the patient case shown in Fig. 9.2. The reconstructed orbit on the left side shows the same geometry than on the right side. For the reconstruction the left side was mirrored from the right side. The PSI fits anatomically perfectly to the surrounding bone anatomical structures and reconstructs an expanded defect that includes two walls of the left orbit.

FIGURE 9.5 Virtual PSI planning for the reconstruction of an expanded defect of the lower jaw. A PSI was planned and manufactured to reconstruct the mandible on the left side. A microvascular bone transplant harvested from the hip or the leg, which is normally the first treatment choice in such cases was not used due to the patient's negotiation regarding transplant harvesting.

limited because of technical reasons. Today, recently introduced and commercially available computer-aided 3D printers replaced the big and heavy stereolithographic milling machines that were used in the past for surgical model production. In general, the different available types of 3D printer techniques are (1) stereolithography, (2) laser sintering, (3) poly jet, and (4) metal 3D printing. In-house clinical 3D model and template production is mostly done on the polymer-based 3D printing poly jet technology. Similar to the other clinically used computer-aided methods, the 3D printed medical models are made from threshold image based segmentations carried out on clinical CT data. Computer software that can be used for such image-based segmentation are commercially available in more or less user-friendly software packages such as provided by Materialise (https://www.materialise.com/de). Alternatives to license based software packages are multifunctional open-source based software platforms such as 3D Slicer (https://www.slicer.org/), Meshlab (https://www.meshlab.net/), MeVisLab (https://www.mevislab.de/), Meshmixer (http://www.meshmixer.com/), Blender (https://www.blender.org/), and others. These open-source based software platforms include a huge range of different image modification options that offer functions far beyond simple threshold segmentation, however without being ISO certificated for a medical usage.

Clinically 3D anatomical models are printed to provide visual and tactile information for the diagnosis and/or surgical treatment process such as the planning of the surgical access, the establishment of bone cutting lines (osteotomy), the assessment and prediction of bone movements after osteotomy and others. Further 3D printed models are used for a better clinical communication between radiologists and surgeons or between doctors and patients to increase the anatomical visualization and imagination in the region of interest. Moreover, anatomical 3D models are used for didactic purposes in student teaching lessons or in the training of young surgeons. However, the most important use regarding printed 3D models is the preparation of complex surgical treatments and the anatomical orientation of osteosynthesis materials. Especially when bony structures have to be replaced, anatomical 3D models can provide a "preview" of the achieved final result (surgery model simulation). In cases where bone structures are planned to be cut over a wide distance, the bone is replaced by a transplant harvested from the own body. To fix the harvested bone to the defect surgical osteosynthesis materials such as plates and screws are used. To fit best to the surrounding anatomy, the osteosynthesis materials can be adapted or orientated on the anatomical model that is used as a surgical template prior to the operation. Today and different to the past, any anatomical form and geometry can be created with high accuracy by 3D printers. This includes hollow forms, complex shapes, very thin walls, or undercuts which are, for example, present in the anatomy of the orbital or midfacial structures.

Clinically, printed 3D models can lead to a decrease of the overall operation time and reduce therefore financial hospital costs. It has been found that on average about 43 minutes can approximately be reduced when surgical models are included in the operation plan or the surgical treatment [58]. Time-based cost savings have been estimated with about 1000US$ per patient when 3D anatomical models where included in the operation plan [59].

Today patient-specific 3D anatomical templates/models have become standard in clinical practice and are increasingly used to plan surgical procedures, to better understand individual anatomy and implant prefabrication especially in complex or rare surgical cases. This is not limited to oral and maxillofacial surgery. This is also the cases for the surgical orthopedic and trauma field, where time saving values of one-third to one-half of the overall operation time where detected in surgical hand trauma cases when printed surgical 3D models are involved.

3.3 3D operation planning with or without computer based intraoperative support (dental splints, cutting guides) in orthognathic surgery

Computer-aided 3D operation planning, that is, from a technical point of view, mainly based on threshold image segmentation, has become routine in clinical practice, especially in orthognathic surgery within the last years. The reason therefore may be the 3D software programs available for operation planning that have continuously been further developed to achieve high usability and functionality and push the level of user-friendliness to the highest grade. In the last years, these developments were pushed by big medical industrial companies to integrate certain license-based 3D software programs as quickly as possible in the clinical practice on a commercial basis. Today, these programs exist in nearly every clinical center for oral and maxillofacial surgery to plan preoperatively the movements of the facial skeleton (upper and/or lower jaw and/or chin) for surgical procedures where skeletal dentofacial malformations/malocclusions are corrected. In such operations, the facial bones in the upper and/or lower jaw and/ or chin are cut (osteotomy) to move them in certain directions that have been planned before. This surgical procedures influences facial hard and soft tissues and lead to correct a positioned upper and/or lower jaw and facial profile. Due to the changes in the skin and bone profile, many patients have postoperatively a different facial appearance than preoperatively.

Today, commonly used virtual 3D surgical planning programs in orthognathic surgery are the ones provided by KLS Martin (IPS Case Designer—https://www.klsmartin.com/en/products/individual-patient-solutions/ips-casedesigner/) or in similar form and function by Materialse (https://www.materialise.com/de). Within these software packages, the skeletal movements including the soft tissue prediction of the face can be simulated according to the surgical treatment plan. On CT or CBCT scan basis the pre- and postoperative situation of patients with skeletal dentofacial malformations/malocclusion can be compared and the treatment plan individually assessed (Figs. 9.6 and 9.7). The program offers the surgeon the possibility to virtually move the skeletal bones of the jaws and/or the chin in real time directly on the screen. Additionally to these virtual planning procedure surgical cutting guides, splints and/or patient-specific individualized plates that are based on the planned situation and the virtually moved facial bones can be ordered from the company.

To date, the clinically used virtual planning software packages are highly developed, functional stable and can be run easily on computer hardware that is commonly present

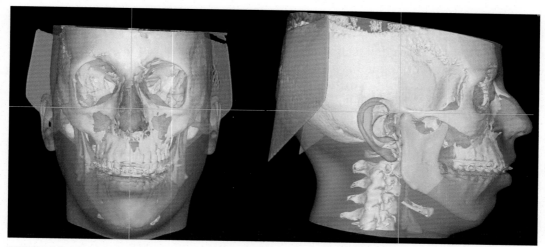

FIGURE 9.6 Preoperative CBCT image based 3D visualization taken out of the clinical planning program (IPS Case designer, KLS Martin) of a case where a skeletal dentofacial malformation/malocclusion is planned to be surgically corrected by movements of the upper and lower jaw and the chin. The 3D visualization of the program shows hard and soft tissues of the patient that can be superimposed.

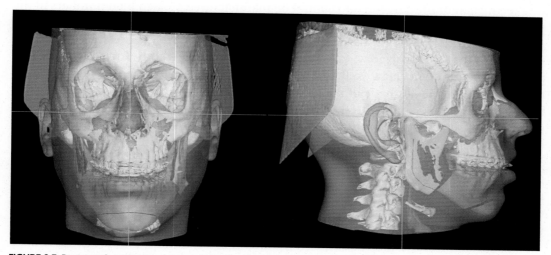

FIGURE 9.7 Postperative CBCT image based 3D visualization taken out of the clinical planning program (IPS Case designer, KLS Martin) of a case where a skeletal dentofacial malformation/malocclusion is planned to be surgically corrected. The 3D visualization shows the predicted hard and soft tissues after the operation. The surgical movements of the upper and lower jaw and the chin are simulated by superimposition to give the surgeon preoperatively an idea of the final postoperative result.

in clinical centers. However, although all jaw and/or chin movements that can clinically be performed during surgery can be simulated and visualized with these software packages, a clinical investigation of the patient is still necessary before the computer-aided planning is started.

3D virtual software packages are today most probably those computer-aided methods in every day's clinical practice in oral and maxillofacial surgery that are used more frequently than computer-aided technologies in other maxillofacial subfields. In big clinical centers, nearly every orthognathic patient case is planned by the support of such virtual 3D planning tools. The amount of orthognathic cases in big reference centers of Europe can achieve up to nearly 1000 patients per year, as this is, for example, the case at the department of cranio-maxillofacial surgery in Antwerp, Belgium. Through the computer software support a much higher amount of cases can be treated than without virtual 3D planning. This is the reason, because the needed surgical operation splints that are based on the individual planning of every patient can directly be 3D printed or ordered in high numbers from the industry partner. The surgical splints are used during the operation (and sometimes also for a few days postoperatively), to secure the position between upper and lower jaw in the corrected new position - that was pre-operatively planned - after the bone cuts (osteotomy) are performed and before the bones are fixed again with plates and screws. The osteotomies can be performed with the support of individually pre-planned cutting guides provided by the industry or by free hand. During the operation, the surgical splints are fixed in the mouth and positioned between the teeth of the upper and lower jaw. Without the use of such computer software technologies the needed surgical splints would have to be made by a technician or the surgeon and cannot be manufactured in such high numbers in the same time than with the computer-aided support of 3D virtual planning programs.

Further, virtual planning programs give immediately a 3D overview of all skeletal movements that are involved when a surgical treatment plan is completed. Since the surgical movements of the facial skeleton are clinically limited in their amount and influence the function and the aesthetic of the facial bones (hard tissues) and the surrounding soft tissues like the muscles and the skin, highly accurate 3D computer-aided planning is especially important in asymmetric and complex skeletal dentofacial malformation/malocclusion cases.

Apart from the virtual planning in orthognathic surgery computer-aided software programs are clinically also used in dento-alveolar implant surgery. A therefore easily available and clinically routinely used very common software package is for example provided the Simplant software (https://www.dentsplysirona.com/en/explore/implantology/simplant.html).

All 3D virtual planning software packages that are now available for a clinical use are certified medical products provided by the industry and can be used for clinical and patient treatment purposes without restrictions.

3.3.1 Steps of 3D orthognathic surgery planning

The use of digital planning software changed the clinical routine in orthognathic surgery procedures tremendously. Having all needed patient information in a single software package to adequately virtually plan and simulate osteotomies and skeletal jaw movements speeds up the planning process and leads to a potential surgical reduced failure rate [60]. The pre-operative acquisition of CT- or CBCT-scans of the patient is mandatory.

Additionally, clinical photographic set up in standardized positions is needed to evaluate the patient's natural head position, which leads to reliable and standardized soft tissue analysis [61,62]. Further, the usage of 2D or 3D cephalometric measurements optimizes the skeletal analysis to a maximum [63–65]. Scanning plaster models or using intraoral scans to generate virtual upper and lower jaw teeth models enables the surgeon to create a full virtual augmented model of the patient's skeletal and dental situation. There is no doubt that the therapeutic occlusion (position of upper and lower jaw when teeth are in contact) is still a challenge. Haptic feedback to define the most feasible post-operative occlusion is still not replaceable. Therefore, the workflow includes 3D-printed or plaster models to adjust the occlusion manually. After the definition of the post-OP occlusion the alignment of the models is turned back into the virtual world via 3D scans (3D-scanner, 3D-X-ray) to generate a STL data set, from which an operation splint (for fixating the correct upper and lower position during the operation) can be manufactured using a 3D printer.

Having created the augmented model, the virtual positioning of the scull according to the natural head position is the next step. Virtual surgery starts with defining the osteotomy lines in the upper and lower jaw. Upper and/or lower jaw movements are made after choosing the modus of the virtual surgery. This could be the movement of the upper and/or the lower jaw. Taking all soft- and hard tissue information into account, the movements are performed, and the software documents all translational and rotational movements. Finally, when the facial skeleton has been brought in the correct position, the surgical splints are generated which leads to respective STL datafiles. 3D printed or milled, the splints are ready to transport all information into to operation room, except the vertical positioning of the jaws. This fact leads to the need of a skeletal fixed reference (e.g., LeFort1 plane or Glabella-pin) to transfer the vertically planned positioning into the surgery.

The digital alignment of the tooth bearing jaws into the therapeutic occlusion and the vertical positioning should be addressed in future development. One idea is to manufacture individual plates (individually manufactured and adapted plates that define the skeletal movements) to position the upper jaw.

The virtual simulation of facial soft tissue movements is still not reliable but gives a principle impression of the postoperative result. Providing a patient-individual algorithm that simulates the soft tissue movements according to the skeletal jaw movements could be a solution of this planning issue for the upcoming future.

3.3.2 Medical planning of orthognathic cases in the clinical routine

After anamnestic finding of the subjective wishes of the patient, the first step in clinical routine is collecting the information about the patient's actual soft and hard tissues position. Therefore, a CBCT or CT scan of the patient's skull is performed in central occlusion. Impressions of the patient's dentition (plaster models or intraoral scans) are taken. Additionally, 2D photographs following a standard picture set (extraoral and intraoral) are taken and analyzed according to Rob Mulié s facial harmony [66–69]. The respective vertical analysis categorizes the patient into short, normal, and long face type. The sagittal analysis defines corridors for the facial harmony and the respective need to harmonize the profile of the patient. To gain information about the skeletal deformity, the analysis of the cephalometric image (2D or 3D) provides respective measurements [63]. The synopsis of these findings is subjectively and objectively a solid base for the virtual planning procedure.

The next step is the definition of the planned therapeutic occlusion using the patient's plaster models or 3D printed models. In some cases, this step is challenging due to preoperative limitations in aligning the dentition into a stable postoperative occlusion and should be in consent with the orthodontist who is responsible for the postoperative final alignment.

Transferring CBCT/CT data, scanned plaster models/intraoral scans and the defined final occlusion into the virtual planning software is mandatory to generate an augmented model of the patient. The software packages that are commonly available for orthognathic virtual planning procedures are user friendly and guide through all steps, since they are fully lincensed products from a medical company. From there on the virtual surgery procedure starts. Defining the virtual osteotomy planes in the upper and lower jaw on the computer screen is the next step. Subsequently, the surgeon chooses the jaw which will be firstly moved: maxilla (upper jaw) first or mandible (lower jaw) first (independently of the modus operandi in the operation theatre). Taking all information about the patient's skeletal position, the soft tissues and the subjective wishes of the patient into account, all skeletal movements are made within a full virtual setting until the final hard and soft tissue position. The final position is usually the skeletal position (upper, lower jaw), where both a correct dental occlusion and a facial soft tissues harmony can be achieved.

Finally, the decision of how the surgeon will operate (maxilla fist or mandible first) influences the splint-production (generating STL-Files and splint manufacturing). These finally generated STL-datasets are the end result of the complete virtual planning process and enable the user to 3D-print or mill (computer aided design/computer aided manufacturing—CAD/CAM) the respective final splint that is used in the patient at the time of surgery.

4 Limitations of computer-aided technologies and procedures

Although treatment outcome and life quality have been found to increase when using computer-aided surgery in the clinical maxillofacial field [24,49,50], there are some limitations to think of before implementing such technologies to the clinical practice. This is especially true when they are newly developed. Independently from the computer-aided method or technology that is introduced or used at a clinical center an exact cost-efficiency calculation should be made in advance to avoid unplanned occurring limitations resulting in high financial costs, existing licenses agreements on newly introduced services, complete dependencies from industrial partners or missing usability.

The main limitations of computer-aided surgery in oral and maxillofacial surgery are (1) high financial costs for hard- and software, (2) missing hardware or computer power to run software functions quickly, efficiently, and in high resolution, (3) continuously further developed license and permission agreements necessary for the use of the technologies, (4) human and time resources that have to be clinically available for the use of computer-aided technologies (virtual planning procedures, program installations, virtual meetings, time of software use, computer loading times, additional image data acquirements, time consuming complex program functions, missing knowledge to use specific computer software packages, etc.), (5) transfer times from ordered surgical equipment that is based on computer-aided surgery planning such as personalized implants or intraoperative splints. These transfer or shipping times could delay surgical patient scheduling or if a treatment cannot be delayed for medical reasons lead to a second surgery, and (6) today, most of the clinically used computer-aided technologies, especially the ones based on computer software have a CE mark or ISO certification licensed by the industry or are certified medical products that create a certain dependency from the industry, if there are limited existing alternatives for the provided computer-aided service. If computer-aided technologies that are used in the clinical practice do not have CE marks or ISO certifications, it would not be allowed to use products based on such technologies on the patient or intraoperatively. For example, it would not be allowed to print a segmentation based osteosynthesis material for an intraoperative use with these technologies. This is one of the main reasons why open-source-based computer-aided technologies such as open-source segmentation platforms for 3D visualizations, 3D printing processes and surgery planning procedures that can potentially be used in the clinical practice, are more or less still subject of research, except in some limited cases [7,9]. Additional limitation reasons are the complex software functions or user-unfriendly software design and usability that are more found in open-source-based technologies than in industrial licensed software packages. The functional instability of computer software packages, which is also often found in open-source software, further limits the implementation of especially newly developed computer-aided technologies in clinical practice. The functional instability is usually related to technical reasons that occur when software packages are functionally overloaded or when they are not developed to the very end and are released too early as beta versions.

5 Future perspectives

Future perspectives of computer-aided oral and maxillofacial surgery may be the increase of functional stability of open-source-based computer programs to be used clinically in a more efficient way. However, this will need further technical development in that field. Further perspectives, especially for smaller clinical centers, are the reduction of financial costs of computer-aided methods provided by the industry and the reduction of human and time resources needed to be provided in the clinical practical for the use of computer software processes, since clinical doctors should usually mainly work on the patient and not on the computer. A further perspective may be the use of patient-specific MRI image data instead of CT scans for computer software packages. Since MRI images visualize soft tissues more accurately than CT scans, automatic segmentations could be performed on vessels, muscles, lymph nodes, or tumors in anatomical 3D visualizations or in operation planning procedures such as tumor resections or pathological head and neck lesions.

Additionally, a clinical implementation of functional stable mixed reality 3D visualization technologies based on radiological image data such as augmented reality see-trough displays, that work clinically without separate screens or workstations directly on the patient could improve medical diagnosis and treatment pathways. Additional further future perspectives are the implementation of in-house manufactured polymers made PSIs instead of titanium to achieve a digital PSI design and manufacturing process located completely in the clinical center where the patient is treated. If an appropriate design software is available, such PSIs could be completely designed and manufactured in-house without industry support, time-consuming transfer procedures, or expensive implant costs per patient.

Finally, an additional future perspective of computer-aided technologies in oral and maxillofacial surgery is related to a recently released medical image-processing platform named Studierfenster (www.studierfenster.at). This platform offers multiple functions for medical image-based processing on an open-source and license free basis, however without being a certified medical product. Studierfenster may currently be used for educational, research, and/or informational purposes. However, the use of this platform is completely free and available for everybody.

Although many computer-aided methods and technologies presently exist that are increasingly tried to be implemented in the clinical practice, it has to be pointed out that at the present stage, further scientific development is needed in all the named fields earlier, until such computer-aided technologies that are big topics of current research can be clinically routinely used, provide a real additional beneficial value for the clinical practice or can even replace commonly used medical diagnostic or therapeutic methods.

Acknowledgment

This work was supported by the Austrian Science Fund (FWF) KLI 678-B31: "enFaced: Virtual and Augmented Reality Training and Navigation Module for 3D-Printed Facial Defect Reconstructions." At the time of writing, J.W. was with the Department of Cranio-Maxillofacial Surgery, AZ Monica and the University Hospital Antwerp, Antwerp, Belgium as orthognathic clinical research fellow.

References

[1] R. Gassner, T. Tuli, O. Hächl, A. Rudisch, H. Ulmer, Cranio-maxillofacial trauma: a 10 year review of 9,543 cases with 21,067 injuries, J. Craniomaxillofac. Surg. 31 (1) (2003) 51–61.

[2] F. Kloss, K. Laimer, M. Hohlrieder, H. Ulmer, W. Hackl, A. Benzer, et al. Traumatic intracranial haemorrhage in conscious patients with facial fractures-a review of 1959 cases, J. Craniomaxillofac. Surg. 36 (7) (2008) 372–377.

[3] A. Kraft, E. Abermann, R. Stigler, C. Zsifkovits, F. Pedross, F. Kloss, et al. Craniomaxillofacial trauma: synopsis of 14,654 cases with 35,129 injuries in 15¦years, Craniomaxillofac. Trauma Reconstr. 5 (1) (2012) 41–50.

[4] A.J. Gaggl, H. Bürger, M Chiari, Reconstruction of the nose with a new double flap technique: microvascular osteocutaneous femur and microvascular chondrocutaneous ear flap—first clinical results, Int. J. Oral Maxillofac. Surg. 41 (5) (2012) 581–586.

[5] F. Borumandi, H. Bürger, C. Brandtner, A. Gaggl, Osteocutaneous femur perforator flap for salvage reconstruction of the nasal septum and columella, Plast. Reconstr. Surg. 131 (5) (2013) 854e–855e.

[6] K. Zeman-Kuhnert, A.J. Gaggl, C. Brandtner, A.-I. Wittig-Draenert, G.B. Bottini, J. Wittig, Donor site morbidity after microvascular medial femoral condylar flap procurement for facial reconstruction, Int. J. Oral Maxillofac. Surg. 49 (5) (2020) 569–575.

[7] J. Wallner, M. Schwaiger, K. Hochegger, C. Gsaxner, W. Zemann, J. Egger, A review on multiplatform evaluations of semi-automatic open-source based image segmentation for cranio-maxillofacial surgery, Comput. Methods Programs Biomed. 182 (2019) 105102.

[8] A. Pepe, G.F. Trotta, P. Mohr-Ziak, C. Gsaxner, J. Wallner, V. Bevilacqua, et al. Marker-less registration approach for mixed reality-aided maxillofacial surgery: a pilot evaluation, J. Digit. Imaging 32 (6) (2019) 1008–1018.

[9] J. Wallner, K. Hochegger, X. Chen, I. Mischak, K. Reinbacher, M. Pau, et al. Clinical evaluation of semi-automatic open-source algorithmic software segmentation of the mandibular bone: Practical feasibility and assessment of a new course of action, PLoS One 13 (5) (2018) e0196378.

[10] J. Egger, J. Wallner, M. Gall, X. Chen, K. Schwenzer-Zimmerer, K. Reinbacher, et al. Computer-aided position planning of miniplates to treat facial bone defects, PLoS One 12 (8) (2017) e0182839.

[11] H. Kim, T.G. Son, J. Lee, H.A. Kim, H. Cho, W.S. Jeong, et al. Three-dimensional orbital wall modeling using paranasal sinus segmentation, J. Craniomaxillofac. Surg. 47 (6) (2019) 959–967.

[12] D. Koper, M. Ter Laak-Poort, B. Lethaus, K. Yamauchi, L. Moroni, P. Habibovic, et al. Cranioplasty with patient-specific implants in repeatedly reconstructed cases, J. Craniomaxillofac. Surg. 47 (5) (2019) 709–714.

[13] A.M. Goodson, M.A. Kittur, P.L. Evans, E.M. Williams, Patient-specific, printed titanium implants for reconstruction of mandibular continuity defects: A systematic review of the evidence, J. Craniomaxillofac. Surg. 47 (6) (2019) 968–976.

[14] T. Numajiri, D. Morita, H. Nakamura, S. Tsujiko, R. Yamochi, Y. Sowa, et al. Using an in-house approach to computer-assisted design and computer-aided manufacturing reconstruction of the maxilla, J. Oral Maxillofac. Surg. 76 (6) (2018) 1361–1369.

[15] Y. Yamaguchi, K. Yamauchi, H. Suzuki, S. Saito, S. Nogami, T. Takahashi, The accuracy of maxillary position using a computer-aided design/computer-aided manufacturing intermediate splint derived via surgical simulation in bimaxillary orthognathic surgery, J. Craniofac. Surg. 31 (4) (2020) 976–979.

[16] K. Li, J. Li, W. Du, C. Xu, B. Ye, E. Luo, Computer-aided design and manufacturing cutting and drilling guides with prebent titanium plates improve surgical accuracy of skeletal class III malocclusion, Plast. Reconstr. Surg. 145 (5) (2020) 963e–974e.

[17] T. Gander, H. Essig, P. Metzler, D. Lindhorst, L. Dubois, M. Rücker, et al. Patient specific implants (PSI) in reconstruction of orbital floor and wall fractures, J. Craniomaxillofac. Surg. 43 (1) (2015) 126–130.

[18] J. Nilsson, N. Hindocha, A. Thor, Time matters—Differences between computer-assisted surgery and conventional planning in cranio-maxillofacial surgery: A systematic review and meta-analysis, J. Craniomaxillofac. Surg. 48 (2) (2020) 132–140.

[19] T.H. Farook, N.B. Jamayet, J.Y. Abdullah, J.A. Asif, Z.A. Rajion, M.K. Alam, Designing 3D prosthetic templates for maxillofacial defect rehabilitation: A comparative analysis of different virtual workflows, Comput. Biol. Med. 118 (2020) 103646.

[20] M.J. Zinser, H.F. Sailer, L. Ritter, B. Braumann, M. Maegele, J.E. Zoller, A paradigm shift in orthognathic surgery? A comparison of navigation, computer-aided designed/computer-aided

manufactured splints, and "classic" intermaxillary splints to surgical transfer of virtual orthognathic planning, J. Oral Maxillofac. Surg. 71 (12) (2013) 2151e1–2151e21.

[21] S. Mazzoni, G. Badiali, L. Lancellotti, L. Babbi, A. Bianchi, C. Marchetti, Simulation-guided navigation: a new approach to improve intraoperative three-dimensional reproducibility during orthognathic surgery, J. Craniofac. Surg. 21 (6) (2010) 1698–1705.

[22] D. Zukic, A. Vlasak, T. Dukatz, J. Egger, D. Horinek, C. Nimsky. Segmentation of vertebral bodies in MR images. 17th International Workshop on Vision, Modeling and Visualization (VMV), The Eurographics Association (2012) 135–142.

[23] S.D. Olabarriaga, A.W. Smeulders, Interaction in the segmentation of medical images: a survey, Med. Image Anal. 5 (2) (2001) 127–142.

[24] G. Orentlicher, D. Goldsmith, A. Horowitz, Applications of 3-dimensional virtual computerized tomography technology in oral and maxillofacial surgery: current therapy, J. Oral Maxillofac. Surg. 68 (8) (2010) 1933–1959.

[25] J. Egger, T. Luueddemann, R. Schwarzenberg, B. Freisleben, C. Nimsky, Interactive-cut: real-time feedback segmentation for translational research, Comput. Med. Imaging Graph. 38 (4) (2014) 285–295.

[26] J. Egger, R.R. Colen, B. Freisleben, C. Nimsky, Manual refinement system for graph-based segmentation results in the medical domain, J. Med. Syst. 36 (5) (2012) 2829–2839.

[27] M.T. McCann, M. Nilchian, M. Stampanoni, M. Unser, Fast 3D reconstruction method for differential phase contrast X-ray CT, Opt. Express 24 (13) (2016) 14564–14581.

[28] S.C. Schvartzman, R. Silva, K. Salisbury, D. Gaudilliere, S. Girod, Computer-aided trauma simulation system with haptic feedback is easy and fast for oral-maxillofacial surgeons to learn and use, J. Oral Maxillofac. Surg. 72 (10) (2014) 1984–1993.

[29] J Egger, PCG-cut: graph driven segmentation of the prostate central gland, PLoS One 8 (10) (2013) e76645.

[30] D.L. Pham, C. Xu, J.L. Prince, Current methods in medical image segmentation 1, Annu. Rev. Biomed. Eng. 2 (1) (2000) 315–337.

[31] I. Bankman, Handbook of Medical Image Processing and Analysis, Academic Press, (2008).

[32] A. Krizhevsky, Imagenet classification with deep convolutional neural networks, Advances in Neural Information Processing SystemsCurran Associates, Inc., 2012, pp. 1097–1105.

[33] D. Delbeke, Oncological applications of FDG PET imaging, J. Nucl. Med. 40 (1999) 1706–1715.

[34] E.M. Rohren, T.G. Turkington, R.E. Coleman, Clinical applications of PET in oncology, Radiology 231 (2) (2004) 305–332.

[35] M. Tatsumi, C. Cohade, Y. Nakamoto, E.K. Fishman, R.L. Wahl, Direct comparison of FDG PET and CT findings in patients with lymphoma: initial experience, Radiology 237 (2005) 1038–1045.

[36] T. Beyer, D.W. Townsend, T. Brun, P.E. Kinahan, M. Charron, R. Roddy, et al. A combined PET/CT scanner for clinical oncology, J. Nucl. Med. 41 (2000) 1369–1379.

[37] C. Cohade, R.L. Wahl, Applications of positron emission tomography/computed tomography image fusion in clinical positron emission tomographydclinical use, interpretation methods, diagnostic improvements, Semin. Nucl. Med. 33 (2003) 228–237.

[38] C.H. Terhaard, V. Bongers, P.P. van Rijk, G.J. Hordijk, F-18-fluoro-deoxyglucose positron-emission tomography scanning in detection of local recurrence after radiotherapy for laryngeal/pharyngeal cancer, Head Neck 23 (11) (2001) 933–941.

[39] R.J. Wong, D.T. Lin, H. Schöder, S.G. Patel, M. Gonen, S. Wolden, et al. Diagnostic and prognostic value of [(18)F] fluorodeoxyglucose positron emission tomography for recurrent head and neck squamous cell carcinoma, J. Clin. Oncol. 20 (20) (2002) 4199–4208.

[40] J.F. Daisne, T. Duprez, B. Weynand, M. Lonneux, M. Hamoir, H. Reychler, et al. Tumour volume in pharyngolaryngeal squamous cell carcinoma: comparison at CT, MR imaging, and FDG PET and validation with surgical specimen, Radiology 233 (1) (2004) 93–100.

[41] R. Olszewski, Three-dimensional rapid prototyping models in cranio-maxillofacial surgery: systematic review and new clinical applications, Proc. Belgian R. Acad. Med. 2 (43) (2013) e77.

[42] C. Gsaxner, P.M. Roth, J. Wallner, J. Egger, Exploit fully automatic low-level segmented PET data for training high-level deep learning algorithms for the corresponding CT data, PLoS One 14 (3) (2019) e0212550l.

[43] A. Juerchott, C. Freudlsperger, S. Zingler, M.M.E. Abdullah Saleem, J. Jende, CJ. Lux, et al. In vivo reliability of 3D cephalometric landmark determination on magnetic resonance imaging: a feasibility study, Clin. Oral Investig. 24 (3) (2020) 1339–1349.

[44] A. Juerchott, C. Freudlsperger, D. Weber, J.M.E. Jende, M.A. Saleem, Zingler, et al. In vivo comparison of MRI- and CBCT-based 3D cephalometric analysis: beginning of a non-ionizing diagnostic era in craniomaxillofacial imaging?, Eur. Radiol. 30 (3) (2020) 1488–1497.

[45] S. Raith, S. Wolff, T. Steiner, A. Modabber, M. Weber, F. Holzle, et al. Planning of mandibular reconstructions based on statistical shape models, Int. J. Comput. Assist Radiol. Surg. 21 (1) (2017) 99–112.

[46] W. Shui, M. Zhou, S. Chen, Z. Pan, Q. Deng, Y. Yao, et al. The production of digital and printed resources from multiple modalities using visualization and three-dimensional printing techniques, Int. J. Comput. Assist Radiol. Surg. 12 (1) (2017) 12–23.

[47] M. Poon, G. Hamarneh, R. Abugharbieh, Efficient interactive 3D Livewire segmentation of complex objects with arbitrary topology, Comput. Med. Imaging Graph. 32 (8) (2008) 639–650.

[48] G. Badiali, V. Ferrari, F. Cutolo, C. Freschi, D. Caramella, A. Bianchi, et al. Augmented reality as an aid in maxillofacial surgery: validation of a wearable system allowing maxillary repositioning, J. Craniomaxillofac. Surg. 42 (8) (2014) 1970–1976.

[49] S. Tucker, L.H. Cevidanes, M. Styner, H. Kim, M. Reyes, W. Proffit, et al. Comparison of actual surgical outcomes and 3-dimensional surgical simulations, J. Oral Maxillofac. Surg. 68 (10) (2010) 2412–2421.

[50] I. Barandiaran, An automatic segmentation and reconstruction of mandibular structures from CT-data. 10th International Conference on Intelligent Data Engineering and Automated Learning, Springer Press (2009) 649–655.

[51] J.W. Shin, J.S. Lim, G. Yoo, J.H. Byeon, An analysis of pure blowout fractures and associated ocular symptoms, J. Craniofac. Surg. 24 (2013) 703–707.

[52] P. Rosado, J.C. de Vicente, Retrospective analysis of 314 orbital fractures, Oral Surg. Oral Med. Oral Pathol. Oral Radiol. 113 (2012) 168–171.

[53] T.Y. Hsieh, S. Vong, E.B. Strong, Orbital reconstruction, Curr. Opin. Otolaryngol. Head Neck Surg. 23 (5) (2015) 388–392.

[54] M. Brucoli, F. Arcuri, R. Cavenaghi, A. Benech, Analysis of complications after surgical repair of orbital fractures, J. Craniofac. Surg. 22 (4) (2011) 1387–1390.

[55] H. Essig, L. Dressel, M. Rana, H. Kokemueller, M. Ruecker, N.C. Gellrich, Precision of posttraumatic primary orbital reconstruction using individually bent titanium mesh with and without navigation: a retrospective study, Head Face Med. 9 (2013) 18.

[56] P. Udhay, K. Bhattacharjee, P. Ananthnarayanan, G. Sundar, Computer-assisted navigation in orbitofacial surgery, Indian J. Ophthalmol. 67 (7) (2019) 995–1003.

[57] T.V. Dave, S. Tiple, S. Vempati, M. Palo, M.J. Ali, S. Kaliki, et al. Low-cost three-dimensional printed orbital template-assisted patient-specific implants for the correction of spherical orbital implant migration, Indian J. Ophthalmol. 66 (11) (2018) 1600–1607.

[58] L. Yuan-Ta, H. Chun-Chi, C. Yu-Ching, C. Jia-En, W. Chia-Chun, S. Hsain-Chung, et al. Surgical treatment for posterior dislocation of hip combined with acetabular fractures using preoperative virtual simulation and three-dimensional printing model-assisted precontoured plate fixation techniques, Biomed. Res. Int. 2019 (2019) 3971571.

[59] C.R. Rogers-Vizena, S. Flath Sporn, K. Daniels, B. Padwa, P. Weinstock, Cost-benefit analysis of three-dimensional craniofacial models for midfacial distraction: A pilot study, Cleft Palate Craniofac. J. 54 (5) (2017) 612–617.

[60] G.R. Swennen, Timing of three-dimensional virtual treatment planning of orthognathic surgery: a prospective single-surgeon evaluation on 350 consecutive cases, Oral Maxillofac. Surg. Clin. North Am. 26 (4) (2014) 475–485.

[61] J.W. Casselman, K. Gieraerts, D. Volders, J. Delanote, K. Mermuys, B. De Foer, et al. Cone beam CT: non-dental applications, JBR-BTR 96 (6) (2013) 333–353.

[62] H. Schaaf, C.Y. Malik, H.P. Howaldt, P. Streckbein, Evolution of photography in maxillofacial surgery: from analog to 3D photography—an overview, Clin. Cosmet. Investig. Dent. 1 (2009) 39–45.

[63] O.J. van Vlijmen, S.J. Berge, G.R. Swennen, E.M. Bronkhorst, C. Katsaros, A.M. Kuijpers-Jagtman, Comparison of cephalometric radiographs obtained from cone-beam computed tomography scans and conventional radiographs, J. Oral Maxillofac. Surg. 67 (1) (2009) 92–97.

[64] G. Ettorre, M. Weber, H. Schaaf, J.C. Lowry, M.Y. Mommaerts, H.P. Howaldt, Standards for digital photography in cranio-maxillo-facial surgery—Part I: Basic views and guidelines, J. Craniomaxillofac. Surg. 34 (2) (2006) 65–73.

[65] H. Schaaf, P. Streckbein, G. Ettorre, J.C. Lowry, M.Y. Mommaerts, H.P. Howaldt, Standards for digital photography in cranio-maxillo-facial surgery—Part II: Additional picture sets and avoiding common mistakes, J. Craniomaxillofac. Surg. 34 (7) (2006) 444–455.

[66] R. Brons, Harmony of the facial profile Part IV. Sagittal rules, Ned. Tijdschr. Tandheelkd. 104 (1) (1997) 12–15.

[67] R. Brons, Harmony of the facial profile Part I. Introduction and concept definition, Ned. Tijdschr. Tandheelkd. 103 (8) (1996) 306–308.

[68] R. Brons, Harmony of the facial profile Part II. The analysis, Ned. Tijdschr. Tandheelkd. 103 (10) (1996) 396–397.

[69] R. Brons, Harmony of the facial profile Part III. Vertical rules, Ned. Tijdschr. Tandheelkd. 103 (12) (1996) 508–510.

10

Real-time navigation system in implant dentistry

Yiqun Wu[a], Feng Wang[b], Baoxin Tao[a], KengLiang Lan[a]

aDEPARTMENT OF SECOND DENTAL CENTER, SHANGHAI NINTH PEOPLE'S HOSPITAL, COLLEGE OF STOMATOLOGY, SHANGHAI JIAO TONG UNIVERSITY SCHOOL OF MEDICINE; NATIONAL CLINICAL RESEARCH CENTER FOR ORAL DISEASES; SHANGHAI KEY LABORATORY OF STOMATOLOGY & SHANGHAI RESEARCH INSTITUTE OF STOMATOLOGY, SHANGHAI, CHINA; bDEPARTMENT OF ORAL IMPLANTOLOGY, SHANGHAI NINTH PEOPLE'S HOSPITAL, COLLEGE OF STOMATOLOGY, SHANGHAI JIAO TONG UNIVERSITY SCHOOL OF MEDICINE; NATIONAL CLINICAL RESEARCH CENTER FOR ORAL DISEASES; SHANGHAI KEY LABORATORY OF STOMATOLOGY & SHANGHAI RESEARCH INSTITUTE OF STOMATOLOGY, SHANGHAI, CHINA

1 The history of clinical application of dynamic navigation system

In the 1970s, with the development of 3D imaging technology, a dynamic navigation system was developed and combined with the stereotaxic navigation frames and computerized tomography scanning. At the end of 1980, multiple teams made efforts to optimize the navigation system software, so the tip of instruments could be mapped dynamically on the computer screen with the rapid development and maturity of the navigation system. In 1992, the Canadian medical team performed the first clinical computer-assisted navigation neurosurgery. This frameless system was called "Viewing Wand" and successfully combined the imaging diagnosis, preoperative treatment plan, and intraoperative real-time navigation. In the next 5 years, this field witnessed a gradual expansion into head and neck, spine, sinus, and arthroscopic surgery. Computer navigation system-assisted surgery was accepted as one of the standard surgical procedures for neurosurgery in the early 21st century [1]. In 2000, the first dynamic navigation system appeared in dental implant surgery. This system can also correctly combine the preoperative planning software to design the ideal implant trajectory and visualize the dental drill and patient's anatomical structure [2,3]. The popularity of cone-beam computed tomography (CBCT) in the oral clinic helps to simplify navigation steps and reduce registration time, and many manufacturers have developed navigation devices to meet the wide application of CBCT. Currently, commercial dental navigation devices include IGI (Image Navigation, Israel), Visit (University of Vienna, Austria), Robodent (Robodent, Germany), VoNavix (IVS Solutions, Germany), Treon (Medtronic Navigation, USA), Mona-Dent (IMT, Germany) and so on [4].

2 Comparison of static surgical guides and dynamic navigation systems

In general, there are two digital guided systems in the field of oral implantology: dynamic navigation systems and static surgical guides. Dynamic navigation systems can monitor bone drilling and implant placement in real-time during the entire operation. On the contrary, static surgical guides are often used for guiding implant hole preparation and implant placement. The stability, rehabilitation, aesthetics, and oral health maintenance of the soft and hard tissues around the implant are closely related to the three-dimensional positioning of the implant [5,6].

The static surgical guide uses static surgical templates to transmit the information from the pre-surgical prosthetic and surgical planning to the patient. Its advantages include the following:

1. The use of static surgical templates can better achieve the ideal implant position of rehabilitation compared with freehand surgery;
2. The static surgical process can be used to complete multiple implants in one operation, thus improving the efficiency of the entire implant surgery;
3. The immediate implantation operation can be completed to obtain a more ideal site and initial stability;
4. If the alveolar width or the occlusal gap distance of the restoration is insufficient, osteotomy can be performed according to the bone reduction guide template, and the implantation and restoration conditions can be gradually reasonable;
5. Under appropriate circumstances, the operation can still be completed with a flapless approach.

The disadvantages include the following:

1. Preoperative preparation is time-consuming, and the operation cannot be directly performed;
2. Once the guide template is created, the surgical plan cannot be changed;
3. The frequency of visits is increased, and the treatment procedure is prolonged;
4. The complete location and stability of the guide template are affected by the surrounding tissue structure;
5. It is challenging to ensure the accuracy of multiple missing teeth and edentulous jaws;
6. The use of the guide template is affected by the mouth opening of the patient. The operation is difficult to perform when the mouth is insufficiently opened;
7. It is easy to produce heat, which affects the cooling of the local implant site and the discharge of bone fragments;
8. A spacing that is too narrow affects the use of the guide template;
9. The guide template may obstruct the doctor's vision [7–14].

On the other hand, the dynamic navigation system is a technology that integrates the medical image as well as computer and stereo positioning to guide doctors to achieve precise planning and a successful operation. During the procedure, specialized instruments and software are used to fully track the bone drilling and implant placement through the navigation system and display the patient's anatomical structure and operation process in real time. Its advantages include the following:

1. The dynamic navigation system can achieve a better implant position for rehabilitation compared with freehand selection;
2. The clinical cases were extensive and included single tooth loss, multiple tooth loss, an edentulous jaw and jaw defect;
3. Patients can be scanned, scheduled and undergo the operation on the same day;
4. When the operation plan needs to be changed, surgeons can design new trajectories at any time;
5. The entire operation can be visualized in real-time, and the accuracy can be verified at any time.

The disadvantages include the following:

1. Preoperative preparation is time-consuming, and errors in the system may affect the spatial relationship between the reference points and the patient;
2. The learning curve is steep, and a training period should be provided beforehand;
3. In vitro studies comprise the majority of dynamic navigation studies, whereas in vivo studies are rare;
4. The dynamic navigation equipment is currently expensive.

Although the application of navigation in surgery has achieved excellent results, it still not popular in clinical practice due to some limitations [7,15–17].

3 Dynamic navigation system in conventional implant surgery

Compared with the static surgical guide, the dynamic navigation system can completely transfer the preoperative plan to the surgery. Through the registration and calibration procedure, the patient's image data and real position, the surgical instruments and navigation system can be unified into the same spatial coordinates to visualize the three-dimensional space. The system breaks through the limitations of traditional surgery in the field of vision, so surgeons can track the operation process and even the apical position of the implant in real time and make the operation more accurate [18,19].

Block et al. [20] divided 714 implants into three groups and calculated deviations between the preoperative design position and actual position of each implant after operation using full guide navigation (FG), partial guide navigation (PG), and freehand implant (FH) surgery. The deviations of the entry, apex, and angle of the FG group were

1.16 mm, 1.29 mm, and 2.97°, respectively, and those of the PG group were 1.31 mm, 1.52 mm, and 3.43°, respectively. The referred deviations of FH were 1.78 mm, 2.27 mm, and 6.5°, respectively. The results demonstrated the increased accuracy of navigation-guided implant surgery. The evidence obtained by other scholars is consistent; under the guidance of dynamic navigation system, the accuracy of implant surgery is improved [21–23]. When comparing two conventional computer-assisted implant surgery methods, Kaewsiri et al. conducted a randomized controlled trial by randomly grouping 60 patients who needed a single tooth implant and performed dynamic navigation and static surgical guided implant surgery. The result showed that dynamic navigation and static surgical guide could acquire same accuracy in single tooth implant surgery. In this experiment, the researchers strictly controlled the errors that may be caused by the guided surgery itself. With the exception of human factors in the static guided group, including whether the patient's mouth was sufficiently opened or the guide template is in place, these problems can be avoided completely in the group using the dynamic navigation system in contrast to the guide plate group [24].

4 Real-time navigation system in zygomatic implant surgery

Prosthetic rehabilitation of the severely resorbed maxilla continues to pose a challenge for dental implant surgeon. The main problem is insufficient bone volume at the implant site [25]. Several techniques have been introduced to treat severely resorbed maxilla, such as bone grafting [26], tilted implants [27], implants in pterygoid apophysis [28], short implants [29], and zygomatic implants [25]. Zygomatic implants were first described by Brånemark (Nobel Biocare, Sweden) in 1988 and widely used in the treatment of extremely atrophic edentulous maxilla [30]. Brian L. Schmidt et al. used zygomatic implants combined with standard implants to reconstruct maxilla after near-total or total maxillectomy, and five patients have been functioning with the prosthesis for at least 5 years [31]. A 10-year clinical and radiographic evaluation of zygomatic implants shows that the 10-year cumulative survival rate is 97.71% [32], and another report finds that survival rate of zygomatic implants in 25 studies is 97.86% after 36 months [33]. All these studies indicate that zygomatic implants can be used to rehabilitate atrophic maxilla. Compared with bone augmentation, several advantages of the use of zygomatic implants are noted: (1) There is no donor site mobility given that the bone grafting procedure is unnecessary. (2) The total treatment time is reduced without bone grafting. The classical or quad approaches of zygomatic implants can achieve immediate loading without extra time for bone grafting healing. Thus, the indications for zygomatic implants are noted as follows: (1) Treatment of severely atrophic maxilla without the use of bone augmentation regardless of whether bone remains in the anterior maxilla. (2) Treatment of partially edentulous maxilla with severe atrophy without adopting sinus lifting or grafting. (3) Maxilla reconstruction after near-total or total maxillectomy [34].

Although numerous benefits have been presented, many limitations of zygomatic implants are gradually noted. (1) Because the anatomy of the zygoma limits the placement of zygomatic implants, the implant surgery will be difficult. (2) The difficulty of placing zygomatic implants requires a well-trained surgeon, and more time is required for the doctor to learn this skill. (3) The palatal emergence profile may make patients feel excess bulk and result in prosthetic problems. Furthermore, it has been approximately 20 years since Brnemark described the classical surgical placement of zygomatic implants, and many researchers have reported some improvements and modifications.

However, the placement of zygomatic implants cannot be free of risks because the zygomatic implant placement surgery requires long drilling paths that are close to essential vascular and nerve bundles combined with an operation field that is not directly visible, potentially resulting in severe complications, including penetrating the orbital cavity and inaccurate placement [35].

The accuracy of implant placement is one of the most important factors that is related to the outcome of implantation and its rehabilitation. The following principles of implant insertion are noted: the distance from the implant to the anatomical landmarks, such as the mandibular nerve and the maxillary sinus floor, should be at least 2 mm; the distance from the implant to the adjacent roots and implant should be at least 2–3 mm. These parameter requirements for spacing implants are vitally necessary.

To improve the accuracy of zygomatic implant surgery and prevent surgical complications, some modifications have been suggested, such as a computer-aided implant surgery system that could be divided into static and dynamic guided surgery systems that are similar to digital approaches in conventional dental implant placement [36]. Vrielinck used a static guided system for zygomatic implant surgery, and high accuracy was achieved [37]. Since then, the static guided implant surgery system, that is, the surgical template, has been further developed and improved (Fig. 10.1). However, for zygomatic implant surgery, the surgical template has several limitations. First, patient with severally atrophic maxilla or edentulism meet the indication for zygomatic implant surgery, but the surgical area may not provide stable and repeatable support for surgical template. In addition, only the start of trajectory instead of the middle part could be guided by the template because the surgical template is placed on the residual bone or mucosa, which may block the visibility of the exit preparation. Moreover, slight movement of drills in the guided hole can cause obvious exit deviation. Therefore, the dynamic guided system was considered a promising substitute for guided zygomatic implant surgery mainly due to its real-time guidance and feedback. Thus, this chapter focuses on the real-time navigation system for zygomatic implant placement surgery.

The real-time navigation system was first applied in zygomatic implant surgery in 2000. Schramm et al. applied the STN navigation system [Stryker-Leibinger /Zeiss] to insert zygomatic implants according to preoperative planning. Thereafter, several attempts have been made to use dynamic guided zygomatic implant surgery both in vivo and in vitro. Model- and cadaver-based studies were performed to test its safety and efficiency.

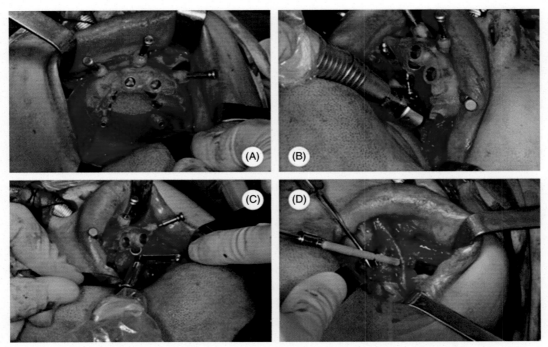

FIGURE 10.1 Static guided zygomatic implant surgery. (A) The surgical guide is fixed on its position using pin screws. (B and C) Preparation of drilling paths. (D) Placement of zygomatic implant.

Watzinger and colleagues precisely placed 10 endosteal implants in zygomas of 5 cadavers using the VISIT system [38]. Fifteen skull models underwent zygomatic implant placement using the IGOIS system developed by Chen et al., and the result showed high insertion accuracy, laying a solid foundation for in vivo research [39]. Hung et al. reported the placement of 40 zygomatic implants with the guidance of the Brainlab real-time navigation system, and high accuracy was gained with entry, apical and angle deviation values of 1.35 ± 0.75 mm, 2.15 ± 0.95 mm, and $2.05 \pm 1.02°$, respectively [40] (Fig. 10.2). The same navigation system has been used in other studies, and high insertion accuracy was also achieved [41,42]. Other navigation systems, such as VoXim [43], AccuNavi [44], ImplaNav [45], and others without specific names [46,47], were employed in zygomatic implant surgery, achieving gratifying outcomes with acceptable accuracy. The new generation navigation system X-guide developed by Nobel Biocare AB can be applied in conventional implant surgery [48] but also plays a pivotal role in zygomatic implant surgery in which a zygomatic implant was placed using a contra-angle loading handpiece tracker, which is not the same as a zygomatic implant handpiece [49]. Recent years have witnessed a sharp increase in the use of the dynamic guided system in zygomatic implant surgery. Henceforth, a new digital era with high accuracy for zygomatic implant surgery has already arrived.

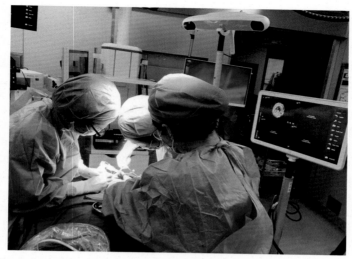

FIGURE 10.2 A panoramic view of a real-time navigation system used in zygomatic implant surgery.

5 Workflow for real-time navigation system

There are five main steps involved in the use of the real-time navigation system in zygomatic implant surgery: imaging, preoperative planning, registration, calibration, tracking, and postoperative evaluation.

5.1 Imaging

The preoperative diagnosis and surgical planning of implant surgery are inseparable from imaging technology. For zygomatic implant surgery, the acquisition of imaging information and accurate planning of surgical path are very important because the surgical area cannot be directly viewed. Therefore, computer tomography (CT) technology and preoperative planning software have become vital components to ensure the success of zygomatic implant surgery.

CT technology uses an X-ray transmitter to launch fan-shaped X-ray harness and scan the human body at a certain thickness from multiple directions. The detector at the other end of the examination component receives the X-ray passing through the plane and converts it into an electrical signal using a photoelectric converter. This electric signal is input into a computer for later processing. In image processing, the obtained layers are divided into several cubes with the same volume, which are called voxels. Due to the different densities of the components of the human body, the attenuation after X-ray exposure varies. According to the attenuation value of different angles of the selected plane, the attenuation coefficient or linear attenuation coefficient of each voxel (μ) is calculated. Then, the digital signal is input into the computer and converted into a matrix. According to the size of the value, different gray values, which are called pixels, are given and arranged in the order of the original matrix to form the CT image [50]. CT technology has made great progress in the past 50 years from the first generation of a single emitter and single receiver to the fourth generation of 256-row or even 512-row spiral CT, greatly improving the efficiency and accuracy of CT scanning.

The basic imaging principle of cone beam CT (CBCT) is the same as that of CT, but some differences are noted. First, CBCT is the integration of an X-ray transmitter and receiver that rotate around the axis located in the center of region of interest (ROI). Second, unlike CT, the irradiated object only needs to be fixed without moving. Most importantly, the X-ray beam of CBCT is a cone beam rather than fan beam, and its field of view (FOV) reaches 180° or greater. In the early stage, most of its receivers were integrated image amplifiers and charge-coupled device (II/CCD), and now flat panel detector (FDP) is widely used. The shooting results are similar to that of a curved section; thus, the fusion of multiple and multi-angle panoramic slices has only a small angle difference between them [51]. Compared with CT, CBCT has many advantages. First, unlike spiral CT, CBCT only needs to rotate one circle to obtain the image of the object, improving the efficiency, reducing the artifacts caused by the patient's micro motion, and minimizing the amount of radiation. Second, the voxels of CT are anisotropic due to the limitation of layer thickness, whereas CBCT voxels are isotropic in three orthogonal directions. Therefore, the resolution of CBCT is high. Its resolution can reach 5 line pairs per millimeter (LP/mm), whereas CT can only achieve 2–3 line pairs per millimeter (LP/mm). In addition, CBCT can perform fast, multi plane three-dimensional reconstruction to meet the different needs of oral and maxillofacial surgery.

However, CBCT cone X-ray beam easily causes noise, artifacts and scattering. For example, the dynamic range of II/CCD and FPD is lower than that of the CT detector, which results in the lower resolution accuracy of CBCT for soft tissue, such as poor resolution for liquid and solid tumors. CBCT is prone to cone beam effects, which are attributed to the reduction of resolution around the image and the production of artifacts and image distortion [50].

In general, CBCT has been selected and used by an increasing number of clinicians given its low radiation, accurate imaging and relatively low cost [52]. CBCT can provide information of bone height, width and density and has been widely used in preoperative bone quantity assessment [53]. In addition, CBCT can also be used in image-guided surgery, which will have a profound impact on the diagnosis and treatment of oral diseases [51] (Fig. 10.3).

5.2 Preoperative planning

The long-term stability of the implant is closely related to the location of the implant and requires perfect preoperative planning to achieve [36]. The basic objectives of implant planning are to evaluate the available bone mass and bone density, to mark the surrounding important anatomical structures, to select the real implants from the software catalog,

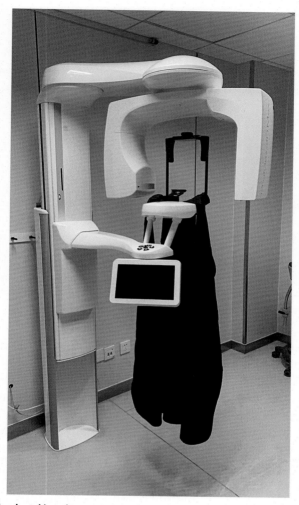

FIGURE 10.3   CBCT device for dental imaging.

and to simulate the implant surgery process [54] (Fig. 10.4). The corresponding preoperative planning software represents the bridge between image acquisition and preoperative planning [55].

In 1988, American Columbia Scientific Company developed software that can reconstruct the CT image and measure and evaluate the alveolar ridge. Then, imagemaster-101, a more advanced planning software, was released. In 1993, Columbia Scientific Company developed Simplant, dental implant planning software, to simulate the implant process in cross-section, axial and panoramic interfaces. The Material Company (Leuven, Belgium) completed the acquisition of Simplant software and further improved and promoted it. Since then, various types of dental implant planning software have emerged

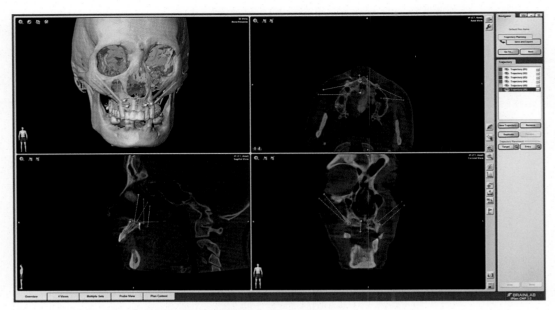

FIGURE 10.4 Implant planning interface of a real time navigation system.

[36], such as Nobel Clinician (Nobelbiocare, Sweden), InVivo5 (Anatomage, USA), and Straumann®coDiagnostiX (Straumann, Switzerland). The function of preoperative planning software is comprehensive (1) importing the image data obtained by CT as DICOM (digital imaging communications in medicine) format and then generating a 3D reconstructed model on the screen; (2) marking vital anatomical structures, such as the mandibular canal, nasal cavity, orbital base, maxillary sinus and other structures, near the zygomatic implant operation area; (3) confirming the location and length of the zygomatic implant and planning various implant trajectories; (4) selecting different surgical approaches according to position between implant and anterolateral wall of maxillary sinus; (5) adjusting the position angle of the implant and selecting the appropriate angle and height of the abutment; (6) immediately simulating the outcome of prosthesis after implant rehabilitation.

At present, the available preoperative commercial planning software in zygomatic implant surgery includes SimPlant software (Materialise NV, Leuven, Belgium) [56], Nobelclinician (Nobel Biocare Services AG, Gothenburg, Sweden) [57,58], Dental Slice software (BioParts Prototipagem Biomédica, Brasilia, Brazil) [59], SurgiCase software (Materialise NV, Leuven, Belgium) [60], and Sun UltraSPARC 10 (Sun Microsystems, Palo Alto, Calif) [38]. In addition, other software was independently developed and designed by large scientific research institutions, including the software Medplan [44,45] and Dental Helper developed by Chen et al. based on Microsoft Visual C++ 6.0 and Visualization Toolkit (Fig. 10.5). In addition, 3D modeling software, such as SolidWorks 2014 software (Dassault systems, SolidWorks corps, USA), can also be used to further refine and render the

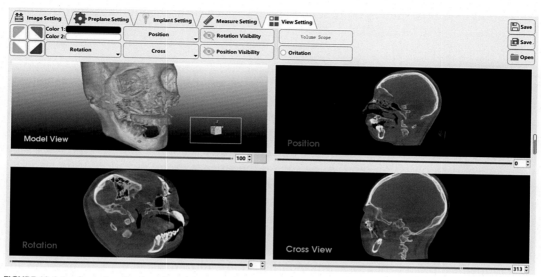

FIGURE 10.5 Implant planning interface of Dental Helper software.

zygomatic implant and maxilla models in cooperation with preoperative planning software. Yang et al. also developed the pre-operative planning software for the zygomatic implant surgery robot, and the robot system interface was added to realize the interaction among the robot, the computer and the surrounding equipment [48].

To achieve the desired function and aesthetic effect, the implant should be inserted precisely based on the position, direction, and angle. Based on the consensus of the 4th European Congress of Osseointegration, scanning prosthesis or virtual tooth arrangement can be used as a guide for implant location [61], and the principle of a "prosthesis-guided implant treatment" protocol has been widely accepted and applied in the preoperative planning of implant location. First, facial skeleton data are commonly acquired by MSCT or CBCT. After reconstruction, a 3D virtual model is displayed. Then, the ideal position of prosthesis is acquired by a double scan technique: patients are scanned twice with and without a radiographic template in the mouth. After merging with the facial skeleton, the planned denture is displayed in the same image [62]. Occasionally, a dentition model or soft tissue are also necessary; these features are acquired using a laser scan or intra-oral scanner and then merged with former models using surfaced, fiducials, or voxel-based approaches [63]. Then, an integrated virtual patient is obtained with almost all the required information. Finally, the zygomatic implant entrance and apical point are easily planned depending on the fused model to attain the ideal prosthesis position and sufficient bone-to-implant contact at the zygoma bone [64].

5.3 Registration

Registration is regarded as a key element for accurate navigation due to its direct influence on the all later procedures [65]. Studies have focused on the comparison of different registration methods, such as bone screws, laser surface scanning, fiducials on the prothesis, and anatomical landmarks.

5.3.1 Types and applications of registration markers

The registration mark is a stable and straightforward identification that can be recognized in virtual and real patients and used for intraoperative registration, including (1) percutaneous bone-implant screws; (2) dental splints mounted on the teeth; (3) identification of corresponding structures that are obvious in the imaging data scanning depending on the craniofacial anatomy of the patient; and (4) laser surface scanning matches the soft tissue in the image data based on random points on the surface of the face skin. If no artificial marker is available, the patient's anatomical characteristics can also be used as a marker to complete the registration. Markers are typically classified as non-invasive and invasive. Anatomic location, occlusal splint, and surface laser scanning are non-invasive markers. In contrast, bone anchor titanium screws are invasive markers. Before CT scanning, invasive markers are firmly fixed on the patient's skull and remained in place until the surgery was complete. Similarly, before acquiring image data, non-invasive markers must be applied to patients and set in their position effectively, or natural anatomical markers should be used as a tag. The number and distribution of titanium screws have an important impact on the accuracy of surgery. Most scholars have accepted the basic registration principle proposed by West. The theory is as follows:

1. The positioning screws should be evenly and widely distributed.
2. The center of the registration combination should be close to the main operation area.
3. The positioning screws should not be arranged in a linear or nearly linear combination.
4. As many positioning screws as possible should be placed in the surgical site.
5. However, there is no clear clinical guidance on the distribution and number of applications for each registration method [66–69].

Numerous labeled and unlabeled registration markers are available, and each technology has its own accuracy and clinical practicability.

5.3.1.1 Bone implant markers

Bone implant markers typically refer to self-tapping screws for percutaneous implantation of bone around the surgical area to obtain stable retention and clear image data. Clinically, the number and distribution of registration screws have a significant impact on surgical accuracy. Stable accuracy can be obtained following West's registration principle, which has been widely recognized and demonstrated to be a feasible registration method. The registration screws can be inserted under local anesthesia into various locations, such as the frontozygomatic process, jaw, zygoma, and the lower part of the anterior nasal spine. The main advantage of using screws as markers is that they do not need to be shifted between image acquisition and surgery and are suitable for edentulous cases where dental splints are not sufficient to meet the requirement. However, screw insertion is an invasive procedure with risks of infection, scarring and prolonged irritation, which are poorly tolerated by patients [70–73].

5.3.1.2 Dental splint

The dental splint provides a noninvasive and simple registration method. However, in the clinical environment, the following practical problems must be considered:

1. Splint loosening or incorrect placement will lead to unforeseen errors in the imaging processor or the subsequent registration process;
2. In a periodontitis patients, the stability of the teeth is low, and even the use of an appropriate splint will lead to inaccurate results; and
3. Dental splints cannot be used in the edentulous jaw.

In addition to these considerations, some previous studies have demonstrated that the clinical application of dental splints in the oral cavity has acceptable accuracy. However, as long as the dental splint goes beyond the anterior nasal spine and approaches or reaches the middle and upper part of the face, such as zygoma, orbital floor, temporal bone, frontal bone, the error is greater than 3 mm, which is not acceptable in clinic. Therefore, when the navigation is limited to the area below the midface, we believe that splints represent a feasible and accurate method [70,73,74] (Figs. 10.6 and 10.7).

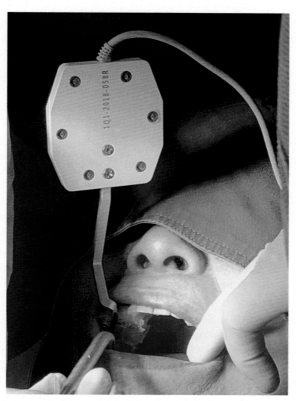

FIGURE 10.6 Dental splint is locked in the patient's maxilla dentition.

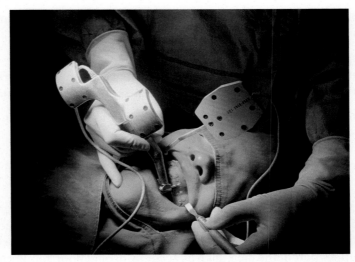

FIGURE 10.7 Registration procedure of the Dcarer system using a drill tip to contact several concaved points on the splint.

5.3.1.3 Bony landmarks

Numerous similarities exist between bony marks and surface matching. All patients have a reference point. There is no need to repeat the imaging scan before the operation. Uncertain parts can be selected. However, given that the position of the reference point is small and separated from the facial bones, the precise area that can be obtained is relatively small and limited to the center surface. In addition, the accuracy is significantly lower than invasive marking or skin surface matching. In the current situation, the accuracy obtained by bone markers alone is unrealistic in clinical practice [74,75].

5.3.1.4 Laser surface scanning

In previous studies, laser surface scanning is sufficiently accurate for clinical applications. Given its non-invasive features, its use is considered more practical. In addition, artificial marks do not need to be applied before image acquisition. However, in several in vitro studies, only the hard bone surface of the skull model is scanned. Due to the lack of soft tissue and although the results showed that laser surface scanning seems to be the most accurate registration technology, it is crucial to recognize that soft tissue has a significant influence on the accuracy of laser surface scanning, especially via clinical tissue swelling and shape change with movement. In clinical application, due to the vigorous muscle activity of the face and the uneven surface of the facial features, the error of this method is greater than 3 mm, demonstrating that it is unsuitable for the facial region [75,76].

Bone screws are widely applied in dynamic navigation zygomatic implant surgery. Before surgery, fiducial screws are first inserted under general anesthesia prior to MSCT or CBCT scanning. In general, four to six screws are placed in anterior nasal spine, two to four are placed in the midpalatal suture, and one to two are placed in the bilateral maxillary

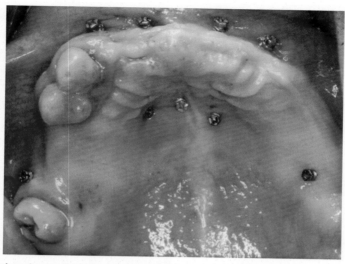

FIGURE 10.8 Bone-anchored screw fiducial markers are distributed in a polygon shape.

tuberosity (Fig. 10.8). When encountering maxillary ablation defects, surgeon may find it difficult to select optimal positions. The mastoid process and supraorbital ridge on the surgical side could be chosen as an adequate quantity of bone for registration and screw fixation unless the number of fiducials on the residual bone needs to be increased. After general anesthesia, a skull reference frame is secured on the patient's head (Fig. 10.9). Then, surgeons select a registration point, such as the center of screws, in a specific order using the planning software. During the operation, the registration procedure was performed by contacting the registration points separately in the former order using a probe;

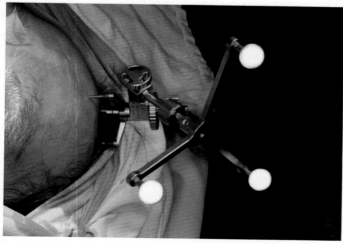

FIGURE 10.9 A skull reference frame is steadily fixed on the skull.

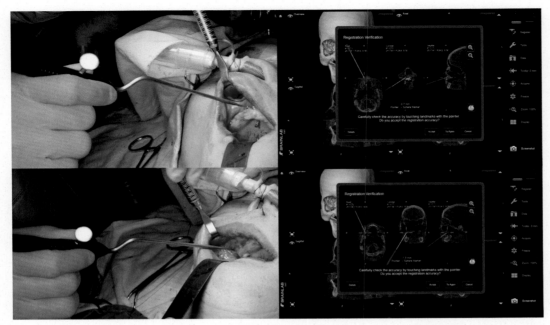

FIGURE 10.10 Registration procedure of the Brainlab CMF system. (A and C) The centers of fiducial screw are separately touched by the probe in the registration procedure. (B and D) The corresponding computer interface of the real-time navigation system.

thus, a connection between the virtual image and the patient was established (Fig. 10.10). Once the procedure was accomplished, the accuracy of registration, which is calculated as fiducial registration error (FRE), was exhibited on the screen. If the FRE is not acceptable, the entire procedure should be performed again. Given that the registration procedure is performed manually, the process of registration point selection and intra-operative contact could cause deviation. Once the reference frame fixed on the patient or handpiece moves and the reflective ball is contaminated, the registration procedure should also be conducted once again. Moreover, the anchorage of bone screws occasionally is displaced during open flap surgeries, suggesting that all screws need to be regularly assessed to ensure high accuracy for registration.

5.4 Calibration

For drill-path preparation, calibration should be executed before initial drilling. This procedure aims to track the position of the handpiece. Pivot calibration should be performed to identify the offset value for the tip of instrument, which is also loaded to a reference frame (Fig. 10.11). During calibration of the axis of surgical drills, the drill is inserted into calibration holes that are the same diameter on the calibration instrument, and the direction of the vector of drill could be obtained (Fig. 10.12). All these processes are executed

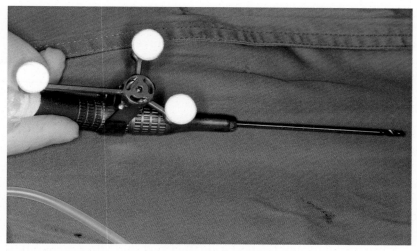

FIGURE 10.11 A handpiece loaded the reference frame for real-time tracking.

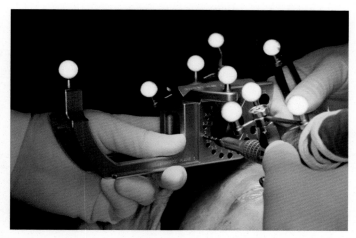

FIGURE 10.12 The calibration procedure is completed by the selection of holes of an appropriate diameter and inserting the handpiece to the bottom.

in the vision field of the infrared camera. Because the drill path needs to be prepared by drills and the length and diameter are incrementally increased, the calibration procedure should be re-performed to reduce the calibration error.

However, the calibration block of Brainlab system is occasionally cumbersome, and other navigation systems tried to replace the calibration instrument to optimize this procedure. The implant drill bit is placed perpendicular to the center target on the Go Plate, which is a calibration plastic plate, to determine its tip and axis [48]. The Navident navigation system combines a calibration plate with a jaw tag, which is initially set to track patient, and the surgeon simply uses the drill to place a dimple on it [77]. To some extent, the required perpendicular position makes it difficult to repeat and ensure steadiness after long-term surgery. Therefore, compared with the calibration block, poor results may be achieved with axis calibration (Fig. 10.14).

5.5 Tracking

After registration and calibration, the surgical drill is displayed on the screen by combining the image and planned trajectories. During surgery, because the zygomatic implant bed is prepared individually, other planned trajectories could be concealed, avoiding unnecessary interference. In addition, it is better to use the probe or calibrated surgical instruments to detect the trajectory entrance and marker on the patient. For all of the drilling procedures, surgeons are supposed to adjust the direction and angle of drilling to make the path as accurate as possible. When approaching the end of path, the length of path should be measured to avoid penetrating the facial skin. After preparation, the zygomatic implant of the planned length is inserted manually or with the help of the handpiece (Fig. 10.13).

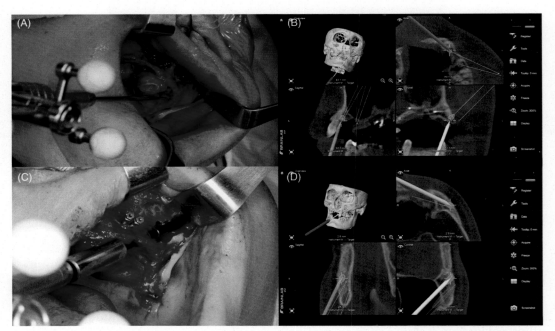

FIGURE 10.13 (A) Preparation of the entrance of the zygomatic implant drilling path. (B) Corresponding computer interface of the entrance preparation. (C) Preparation of the exit of zygomatic implant drilling path. (D) Corresponding computer interface of the exit preparation.

5.6 Postoperative evaluation

Postoperative evaluation is indispensable for clinical outcome. Generally speaking, the goal of the primary evaluation using the real-time navigation system is accuracy, including entry, apical and angular deviation, between the planned and placed zygomatic implants. After surgery, a MSCT or CBCT with the same parameters as preoperative planning is performed and merged with the preoperative image containing the planning trajectory based on the maxillary sinus or the skull, which will not change in the short term. The deviations could be detected at this point. The distance between the center point of the implant entry and apex is measured in millimeters. The line connecting the center point of entry and apex points of each implant is defined as the axis line and is measured in degrees (Fig. 10.14). In addition to accuracy, the success rate and whether surgical and prosthetic complications occurred should also be appraised. According to a systematic review [78], zygomatic implant-related biological complications include sinusitis, fungal infection in the maxilla sinus, intraoral soft tissue infection, loss of osseointegration, formation of fistula, extraoral infection with the apex of implant, and fenestration of alveolar mucosa. Surgical complications include orbital involvement and intracranial placement, infraorbital nerve and zygomaticofacial nerve paresthesia, difficulty with speech, facial or periorbital hematoma and lip laceration and bruising. Prosthetic complications include implant and prosthesis fractures. All these associated complications call for meticulous assessment and treatment.

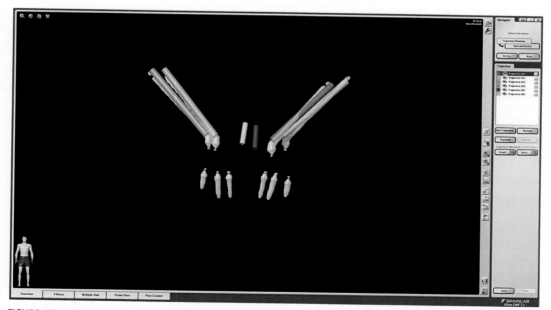

FIGURE 10.14 The CT images obtained preoperatively and postoperatively are merged to evaluate the implant accuracy.

6 Clinical outcome of real-time navigation system

The evaluation indications are mentioned above. Although several studies reported that zygomatic implants were placed under guidance of the navigation system [38,45,46,79], few presented data are related to accuracy. Hung et al. measured the accuracy of zygomatic implants inserted with the help of image-guided navigation systems, and the entry deviation, apical deviation and angle deviation were 1.35 ± 0.75 mm, 2.15 ± 0.95 mm, and 2.05 ± 1.02 degrees, respectively [40]. Another study reported 1.07 ± 0.15 mm, 1.20 ± 0.46 mm and 1.37 ± 0.21° as average entry, apical and angle deviation values, respectively [41]. For conventional implants, the real-time navigation system has gained impressive results with increased accuracy compared with free-hand surgery [80,81]. However, to our best knowledge, no study has compared these methods for zygomatic implant surgery, and more studies should focus on this comparison further.

Numerous factors affect accuracy. Widmann et al. reported navigation system errors, including technical errors, imaging errors, registration errors, application errors, and human errors [82]. The placement of fiducial screws, selection of registration points and the tool calibration procedure may obviously influence the accuracy [83]. To avoid these error as much as possible, more clinical practice and a deeper understanding of the mechanism of the real-time navigation system are extremely important. A 2-mm error is defined as "acceptable" range for brain and sinus surgery. For zygomatic implant surgery, due to the limitation of zygoma width and thickness, the safe distance between the implant and the key anatomical structure (lateral orbital wall) is set at 2 mm or greater in the preoperative planning, and the error of registration accuracy of 2 mm remains a large risk threshold. Theoretically, the accuracy currently achieved meets the requirements of zygomatic implant surgery; before the accuracy is further improved, the safe distance from the orbit should be 3 mm [83].

According to published systematic reviews, the success rate of zygomatic implants ranges from 94% to 100% for both the classical and quad approaches [78,84]. However, no study has focused on the accumulated success rate of real-time navigated zygomatic implant surgery, and more attention should be given to this topic in the future.

7 Advantages and disadvantages of a real-time navigation system in zygomatic implant surgery

The most obvious advantage of the real-time navigation system is the precise implant insertion. Under the guidance of the navigation system, improved accuracy has been attained in contrast with free-hand manipulation [76,85,86]. Furthermore, planned trajectories could be adjusted further to suit the specific intraoral condition detected during surgery, and the entry point can be changed by probing the ideal position. Unfortunately, the exit position cannot be changed intraoperatively in navigation software, and this change must be made using planning software. The navigation system allows the surgeon to simply look at the screen, and the requirement of back and neck bending for a prolonged time is reduced [48]. The integration of virtual guidance and the real surgical field require the use of augmented reality technology in the navigated surgery [87] given that the perception of volatile intraoral and surgical instrument conditions have the same importance. Finally, in some areas with limited direct visualization or areas in which it is difficult to place a static guide template, the navigation system allows surgeon to perform implant holes preparation and insert implants [48].

The disadvantages of real-time navigation system are as follows. First, errors from registration, calibration, and tracking lead to mistakes in the transformation of spatial relationship. The process is time consuming, and extra effort is required during the planning stage and surgical procedure [88]. Moreover, necessary training is required given the learning curve described. Although no learning curve has been established for the use of the navigation system in zygomatic implant surgery, for conventional implant surgery, the surgeon becomes practiced after 10–20 implant surgeries [85]. In addition, a capital cost is associated with the navigation system following the integrated digital workflow and maintenance charge. Bone screws remain the gold standard in the registration procedure, resulting in additional injury and pain for patients. Alternative registration methods, such as anatomical landmarks, are suggested to replace screws [48], but the accuracy remains inferior to the former to date. Finally, human studies in accordance with its clinical application are still rare. Further studies are needed to access the safety and efficiency before generalized use of the system.

8 Major error factors of dynamic navigation system

The main errors in dynamic navigation surgery can be classified as technical errors, imaging errors, registration errors, application errors, and human errors. The primary sources of error are listed further: the distance between the optical system and tracking equipment; the position, angle, and stability of the dynamic reference frame; the position, angle, and looseness of the registration point measured by the probe; the thickness of the acquired image data and the deformation in the process of image import and reconstruction; the positioning registration mark error (FLE), the registration mark registration error (FRE) and the target registration error (TRE) caused by the registration method and the registration process; and the accuracy of the navigation equipment. For "novices" who are new to the navigation system, it may be challenging to get started given the more complicated operating procedures. In particular, the surgical field of view needs to be transferred from the patient's mouth to the real-time 3D image display during the operation, which increases operational discomfort. Computer dynamic navigation system-assisted mandibular edentulous implant surgery has also encountered challenges because the temporomandibular joint has a specific range of mobility. At present, the reference frame can only be fixed on the mandible with a titanium nail to obtain real-time oral tracking under dynamic navigation. However, when titanium screws are used as invasive markers, sufficient bone and space are needed to place reference frame and markers, which will reduce the visual field and area of surgery. Different registration methods also cause differences in surgical accuracy. It is necessary to understand the characteristics of these methods and select appropriate indications for operation. The anatomical landmark needs to be registered on a significant anatomical structure. When a registration mark is adhered to the skin, care should be taken to ensure that it does not easily fall off and move during the operation. The registration screw for bone implantation requires an area with good bone mass to provide sufficient retention force [89–91].

9 Application of the dynamic navigation system in teaching and its learning curve

Accurate implant placement should be the goal of all implants and not just a criterion. If a promising method is available to improve the accuracy of implant placement, all patients should benefit from it. In surgery fields, such as laparoscopic surgery, endovascular surgery, or surgical endoscopy, computer-guided simulation has been used to train and evaluate the surgical capability and capability development. In these entirely different surgical fields, the operation level and learning curve have been improved through training using computer-guided simulation systems [92–96]. In recent years, computer-assisted implant surgery has reached the stage of simplification and improvement. Because implant surgery has a high technical sensitivity, the dynamic navigation training system can provide novices with teaching tools for the early development of clinical implant skills, and the interactive model can use biofeedback to develop neural pathways and improve doctors' proficiency in implant surgery. It may be beneficial to obtain better clinical results and provide predictable accuracy results in the early clinical stage. Therefore, the accuracy and efficiency of the clinical workflow can be improved based on the skills and precision of the patients' clinical work process. According to Janina et al., beginners significantly improved speed and angle deviation during the first three attempts to place implants using the dynamic navigation system. Another study showed that three surgeons achieved better implant accuracy as the number of surgeries increased, and the accuracy stabilized after 20 practices. The dynamic navigation system can be used to improve the accuracy training level of beginners [97–99].

A recent study on the learning curve of navigation system-assisted implantation demonstrated that after 20 clinical trials of real-time navigation system-assisted implant placement, the accuracy of implants could be significantly improved, and the stop point error of conventional implants can be reduced to 0.96 mm. The angle error is reduced to 3.63. The navigation preoperative planning software, surgical registration, and intraoperative equipment operation all exhibit high technical sensitivity, and the guidance of experienced technicians is required to perform the system's functions to minimize the implant error.

10 Current limitations of dynamic navigation systems

The mobility of the mandible leads to some problems in the navigation of the mandible region. The synchronization of the intraoperative and preoperative imaging data is complicated. Therefore, it is challenging to use dynamic navigation in mandible surgery.

At present, most of the dynamic navigation systems used in implant surgery use a dental splint or bone-implant titanium screw as marker. However, the markers used have specific limitations. The dental splint is mainly clamped on the teeth to stabilize the markers, but it cannot be used in patients with severe periodontitis or dentition loss. Titanium screw markers need to be implanted in specific areas according to the West principle [100–102].

Moreover, invasive markers require sufficient bone mass, which may cause discomfort to patients after implantation. In addition, the craniomaxillofacial soft tissue is prone to deformation during the operation, resulting in deformation of the image data. Due to the different resolutions of image detection technology, the simulation effect of soft tissue surgery (skin, muscle, tumor) is not as accurate as bone tissue. Thus, preoperative image data cannot reflect the shape of the soft tissue during the process in real-time. In addition, changes in the form of the diseased soft tissue cannot be obtained clearly in real time during the operation. Large navigation errors are prone to occur, which limits the application of surgical navigation technology in soft tissue surgery [103–105].

11 Modifications and further developments of real-time navigation systems

Based on problems noted in clinical applications, some modifications of the entire system have been assessed in various studies. The mouse and keyboard could represent a latent infection medium during operation, and an assistant is recommended to exclusively control the computer to reduce this risk. When a surgeon who performs the operation fails to transfer his idea to the computer in a short period of time, a more gratuitous interaction and long operation time are noted. A Long Short-Term Memory (LSTM) recurrent neural network-based camera was developed to recognize certain gestures by the surgeon. For example, moving the right hand and waving the left hand opens preoperative files, and the tracking system will be active upon downward movement of the left hand. To some extent, this method helps to alleviate complex manipulation of the navigation system [106]. Moreover, automatic recognition of fiducial markers in the DICOM image may promote registration accuracy. A mean-shift algorithm was adapted. Compared with free-hand selection by an experienced surgeon, the automatic selection method earned an accuracy that ranged from 0.373 to 0.847 mm, meeting the requirement of clinical use [107]. During the operation period, some researchers combined the navigation system with an ultrasonic instrument for implant bed preparation. This method reduced soft tissue damage and eliminated the difficulties of using a zygomatic drill when drilling on an oblique surface [108].

It has been 20 years since Schramm first applied computer-aided technology to zygomatic implant surgery [79]. As digital technology continues to improve, the function of preoperative planning software is becoming increasingly comprehensive. The 3D reconstruction accuracy is further improved, and the calculation speed has improved. Moreover, humanization of the operation interface has been further improved. All these enhancements highlight the availability and value of the navigation system in the area of implant surgery.

In recent years, as the most automatic technology product, the robot has been widely applied in dental implant surgery. In 2002, Brief et al. designed a robot [109] to assist the operator in implant path planning and implantation. Kim et al. designed a 3-DOF (degrees of freedom) mechanical arm [110] and a 6-DOF robot and coordinate machine to prepare the robot implant hole after two-stage registration [111]. A novel breakthrough was reported in 2017 and 2018 when the Yomi implant surgery robot was listed and certified, respectively, by the FDA [112]. A surgical robot integrates a series of technologies, including a visual navigation and mechanical sensor, with an error of only 0.2–0.3mm, providing a new foundation for the development of a dental implant surgical robot [113]. A navigation system and a commercial mechanical arm was built by Chen et al. and achieved accurate zygomatic implant placement with entry, apical, and angle deviation values of 2.34 mm ± 0.79 mm, 2.57 mm ± 1.73 mm, and 2.76 ± 1.39°, respectively [114] (Fig. 10.15).

Remarkable progress using the real-time navigation system as a novel approach guarantee predictable outcomes with high accuracy for zygomatic implant surgery, highlighting its further clinical value and commodity after randomized clinical trials with larger sample sizes and advanced enhancements are achieved in the future.

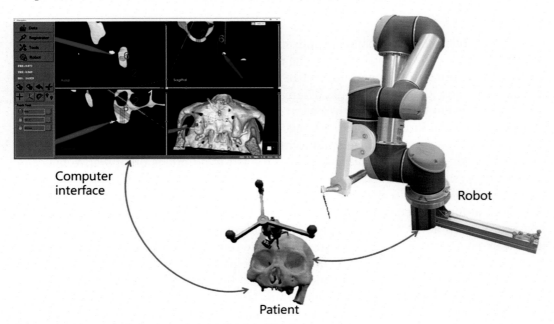

Computer interface

Robot

Patient

FIGURE 10.15 The surgical robot control system for dental implant surgery.

References

[1] J. D'Haese, J. Ackhurst, D. Wismeijer, et al. Current state of the art of computer-guided implant surgery, Periodontol. 2000 73 (1) (2017) 121–133.

[2] C. Xiaojun, Y. Ming, L. Yanping, et al. Image guided oral implantology and its application in the placement of zygoma implants, Comput. Methods Progr. Biomed. 93 (2) (2009) 162–173.

[3] M. Vercruyssen, T. Fortin, G. Widmann, et al. Different techniques of static/dynamic guided implant surgery: modalities and indications, Periodontol. 2000 66 (1) (2014) 214–227.

[4] R.E. Jung, D. Schneider, J. Ganeles, et al. Computer technology applications in surgical implant dentistry: a systematic review, Int. J. Oral Maxillofac. Implants 24 (Suppl.) (2009) 92–109.

[5] D. Buser, W. Martin, U.C. Belser, Optimizing esthetics for implant restorations in the anterior maxilla: anatomic and surgical considerations, Int. J. Oral Maxillofac. Implants 19 (Suppl.) (2004) 43–61.

[6] D.P. Tarnow, S.C. Cho, S.S. Wallace, The effect of inter-implant distance on the height of inter-implant bone crest, J. Periodontol. 71 (4) (2000) 546–549.

[7] J. Gargallo-Albiol, S. Barootchi, O. Salomó-Coll, H.L. Wang, Advantages and disadvantages of implant navigation surgery. A systematic review, Ann. Anat. 225 (2019) 1–10.

[8] F. Bover-Ramos, J. Vina-Almunia, J. Cervera-Ballester, M. Penarrocha-Diago, B. Garcia-Mira, Accuracy of implant placement with computer-guided surgery: a systematic review and meta-analysis comparing cadaver, clinical, and in vitro studies, Int. J. Oral Maxillofac. Implants 33 (1) (2018) 101–115.

[9] M. Colombo, C. Mangano, E. Mijiritsky, M. Krebs, U. Hauschild, T. Fortin, Clinical applications and effectiveness of guided implant surgery: a critical review based on randomized controlled trials, BMC Oral Health 17 (1) (2017) 150.

[10] N.E. Farley, K. Kennedy, E.A. McGlumphy, N.L. Clelland, Split-mouth comparison of the accuracy of computer-generated and conventional surgical guides, Int. J. Oral Maxillofac. Implants 28 (2) (2013) 563–572.

[11] V. Moraschini, G. Velloso, D. Luz, E.P. Barboza, Implant survival rates, marginal bone level changes, and complications in full-mouth rehabilitation with flapless computer-guided surgery: a systematic review and meta-analysis, Int. J. Oral Maxillofac. Surg. 44 (7) (2015) 892–901.

[12] Y.N. Raico Gallardo, I.R.T. da Silva-Olivio, E. Mukai, S. Morimoto, N. Sesma, L. Cordaro, Accuracy comparison of guided surgery for dental implants according to the tissue of support: a systematic review and meta-analysis, Clin. Oral Implants Res. 28 (5) (2017) 602–612.

[13] V. Arisan, C.Z. Karabuda, T. Ozdemir, Implant surgery using bone- and mucosa-supported stereolithographic guides in totally edentulous jaws: surgical and post-operative outcomes of computer-aided vs. standard techniques, Clin. Oral Implants Res. 21 (9) (2010) 980–988.

[14] T.T. Zhang, J. Hu, Research progress of digital guide and dynamic navigation in dental implantation [J], Int. J. Stomatol. 46 (01) (2019) 99–104.

[15] G. Pellegrino, V. Taraschi, T. Vercellotti, et al. Three-dimensional implant positioning with a piezosurgery implant site preparation technique and an intraoral surgical navigation system: case report, Int. J. Oral Maxillofac. Implants 32 (3) (2017) e163–e165.

[16] J. Brief, D. Edinger, S. Hassfeld, G. Eggers, Accuracy of image-guided implantology, Clin. Oral Implants Res. 16 (2005) 495–501.

[17] J. Hoffmann, C. Westendorff, G. Gomez-Roman, et al. Accuracy of navigation-guided socket drilling before implant installation compared to the conventional freehand method in a synthetic edentulous lower jaw model[J], Clin. Oral Implants Res. 16 (5) (2005) 609–614.

[18] P. Pietruski, M. Majak, E. Swiatek-Najwer, et al. Accuracy of experimental mandibular osteotomy using the image guided sagittal saw, Int. J. Oral Maxillofac. Surg. 45 (6) (2016) 793–800.

[19] I. Azarmehr, K. Stokbro, R.B. Bell, et al. Surgical navigation: A systematic review of indications, treatments, and outcomes in oral and maxillofacial surgery, Int. J. Oral Maxillofac. Surg. 75 (9) (2017) 1987–2005.

[20] M.S. Block, R.W. Emery, D.R. Cullum, et al. Implant placement is more accurate using dynamic navigation, J. Oral Maxillofac. Surg. 75 (7) (2017) 1377–1386.

[21] C.K. Chen, D.Y. Yuh, R.Y. Huang, et al. Accuracy of implant placement with a navigation system, a laboratory guide, and freehand drilling, Int. J. Oral Maxillofac. Implants 33 (6) (2018) 1213–1218.

[22] A. Jorba-Garcia, R. Figueiredo, A. Gonzalez-Barnadas, et al. Accuracy and the role of experience in dynamic computer guided dental implant surgery: an in-vitro study, Med. Oral Patol. Oral Cir. Bucal 24 (1) (2019) e76–e83.

[23] G. Pellegrino, V. Taraschi, Z. Andrea, et al. Dynamic navigation: a prospective clinical trial to evaluate the accuracy of implant placement, Int. J. Comput. Dentist. 22 (2) (2019) 139–147.

[24] D. Kaewsiri, S. Panmekiate, K. Subbalekha, et al. The accuracy of static vs. dynamic computer—assisted implant surgery in single tooth space: a randomized controlled trial, Clin. Oral Implants Res. 30 (6) (2019) 505–514.

[25] B.R. Chrcanovic, A.R. Pedrosa, A.L.N. Custódio, Zygomatic implants: a critical review of the surgical techniques, Oral Maxillofac. Surg. 17 (1) (2013) 1–9.

[26] C. Aparicio, W. Ouazzani, A. Aparicio, V. Fortes, R. Muela, A. Pascual, et al. Extrasinus zygomatic implants: Three year experience from a new surgical approach for patients with pronounced buccal concavities in the edentulous maxilla, Clin. Implant Dent. Relat. Res. 12 (1) (2010) 55–61.

[27] M.S. Block, C.J. Haggerty, G.R. Fisher, Nongrafting implant options for restoration of the edentulous maxilla, J. Oral Maxillofac. Surg. 67 (4) (2009) 872–881.

[28] T.J. Balshi, G.J. Wolfinger, S.F. Balshi Ii, Analysis of 356 pterygomaxillary implants in edentulous arches for fixed prosthesis anchorage, Int. J. Oral Maxillofac. Implant. 14 (3) (1999) 398–406.

[29] P. Malo, M. de Araujo Nobre, B. Rangert, Short implants placed one-stage in maxillae and mandibles: a retrospective clinical study with 1 to 9 years of follow-up, Clin. Implant Dent. Relat. Res. 9 (1) (2007) 15–21.

[30] J.P. Becktor, S. Isaksson, P. Abrahamsson, L. Sennerby, A. Sahlgrenska, Institute of Surgical Sciences DoB, et al. Evaluation of 31 zygomatic implants and 74 regular dental implants used in 16 patients for prosthetic reconstruction of the atrophic maxilla with cross-arch fixed bridges, Clin. Implant Dent. Relat. Res. 7 (3) (2005) 159–165.

[31] B.L. Schmidt, M.A. Pogrel, C.W. Young, A. Sharma, Reconstruction of extensive maxillary defects using zygomaticus implants, J. Oral Maxillofac. Surg. 62 (2) (2004) 82–89.

[32] C. Aparicio, C. Manresa, K. Francisco, W. Ouazzani, P. Claros, J.M. Potau, et al. The Long-Term Use of Zygomatic Implants: A 10-Year Clinical and Radiographic Report, Clin. Implant Dent. Relat. Res. 16 (3) (2014) 447–459.

[33] M.C. Goiato, E.P. Pellizzer, A. Moreno, H. Gennari-Filho, D.M. dos Santos, J.F. Santiago, et al. Implants in the zygomatic bone for maxillary prosthetic rehabilitation: a systematic review, Int. J. Oral Maxillofac. Surg. 43 (6) (2014) 748–757.

[34] A. D'Agostino, L. Trevisiol, V. Favero, M. Pessina, P. Procacci, P.F. Nocini, Are zygomatic implants associated with maxillary sinusitis?, J. Oral Maxillofac. Surg. 74 (8) (2016) 1562–1573.

[35] Y. Dedong, H Wei., Z. Zhiyong, W. Yiqun, Application of digital technology in implant surgery, Chin. J. Pract. Stomatol. (1) (2016) 10–14.

[36] G. Orentlicher, A. Horowitz, L. Kobren, Computer-guided dental implant treatment of complete arch restoration of edentulous and terminal dentition patients, Oral Maxillofac. Surg. Clin. N. Am. 31 (3) (2019) 399–426.

[37] L. Vrielinck, C. Politis, S. Schepers, M. Pauwels, I. Naert, Image-based planning and clinical validation of zygoma and pterygoid implant placement in patients with severe bone atrophy using

customized drill guides. Preliminary results from a prospective clinical follow-up study, Int. J. Oral Maxillofac. Surg. 32 (1) (2003) 7–14.

[38] F. Watzinger, W. Birkfellner, F. Wanschitz, F. Ziya, A. Wagner, J. Kremser, et al. Placement of endosteal implants in the zygoma after maxillectomy: a Cadaver study using surgical navigation, Plast. Reconstruct. Surg. 107 (3) (2001) 659–667.

[39] X. Chen, Y. Wu, C. Wang, Application of a surgical navigation system in the rehabilitation of maxillary defects using zygoma implants: report of one case, Int. J. Oral Maxillofac. Implant. 26 (5) (2011) e29–e34.

[40] K.F. Hung, F. Wang, H.W. Wang, W.J. Zhou, W. Huang, Y.Q. Wu, Accuracy of a real-time surgical navigation system for the placement of quad zygomatic implants in the severe atrophic maxilla: A pilot clinical study, Clin. Implant Dent. Relat. Res.. 19 (3) (2017) 458–465.

[41] K. Hung, W. Huang, F. Wang, Y. Wu, Real-time surgical navigation system for the placement of zygomatic implants with severe bone deficiency, Int. J. Oral Maxillofac. Implant. 31 (6) (2016) 1444.

[42] F. Wang, M.M. Bornstein, K. Hung, S. Fan, X. Chen, W. Huang, et al. Application of real-time surgical navigation for zygomatic implant insertion in patients with severely atrophic maxilla, J. Oral Maxillofac. Surg. 76 (1) (2018) 80–87.

[43] M.E. Kreissl, G. Heydecke, M.C. Metzger, R. Schoen, Zygoma implant-supported prosthetic rehabilitation after partial maxillectomy using surgical navigation: a clinical report, J. Prosthet. Dentist. 97 (3) (2007) 121–128.

[44] X. Chen, Y. Lin, C. Wang, G. Shen, S. Zhang, X. Wang, A surgical navigation system for oral and maxillofacial surgery and its application in the treatment of old zygomatic fractures, Int. J. Med. Robot. Comput. Assist. Surg. 7 (1) (2011) 42–50.

[45] G. Pellegrino, A. Tarsitano, F. Basile, A. Pizzigallo, C. Marchetti, Computer-aided rehabilitation of maxillary oncological defects using zygomatic implants: a defect-based classification, J. Oral Maxillofac. Surg. 73 (12) (2015) 2446e1–244e11.

[46] G. Gasparini, R. Boniello, A. Lafori, P. De Angelis, V. Del Deo, A. Moro, et al. Navigation system approach in zygomatic implant technique, J. Craniofac. Surg. 28 (1) (2017) 250–251.

[47] P. Franco, Full mouth rehabilitation of the maxilla using precise implant guided surgery (from extracting teeth to zygoma implants and immediate loading), Int. J. Oral Maxillofac. Surg. 46 (2017) 18.

[48] N. Panchal, L. Mahmood, A. Retana, R. Emery 3rd., Dynamic navigation for dental implant surgery, Atlas Oral Maxillofac. Surg. Clin. North Am. 31 (4) (2019) 539–547.

[49] A. Lopes, M. de Araujo Nobre, D. Santos, The workflow of a new dynamic navigation system for the insertion of dental implants in the rehabilitation of edentulous jaws: report of two cases, J. Clin. Med. 9 (2) (2020).

[50] C. Angelopoulos, W.C. Scarfe, A.G. Farman, A comparison of maxillofacial CBCT and medical CT, Atlas Oral Maxillofac. Surg. Clin. North Am. 20 (1) (2012) 1–17.

[51] W.C. Scarfe, A.G. Farman, What is cone-beam ct and how does it work?, Dent. Clin. North Am. 52 (4) (2008) 707–730.

[52] T. Fortin, G. Champleboux, S. Bianchi, H. Buatois, J.L. Coudert, Precision of transfer of preoperative planning for oral implants based on cone-beam CT-scan images through a robotic drilling machine, Clin. Oral Implant. Res. 13 (6) (2002) 651–656.

[53] T. Fortin, J.L. Bosson, J.L. Coudert, M. Isidori, Reliability of preoperative planning of an image-guided system for oral implant placement based on 3-dimensional images: an in vivo study, Int. J. Oral Maxillofac. Implant. 18 (6) (2003) 886–893.

[54] A.J. Voitik, CT data and its CAD and CAM utility in implant planning: part I, J. Oral Implantol. 28 (6) (2002) 302–303.

[55] M. Rubio Serrano, S. Albalat Estela, M. Penarrocha Diago, M. Penarrocha Diago, Software applied to oral implantology: update, Med. Oral Patol. Oral Cir. Bucal. 13 (10) (2008) E661–E665.

[56] J. Chow, E. Hui, P.K. Lee, W. Li, Zygomatic implants—protocol for immediate occlusal loading: a preliminary report, J. Oral Maxillofac. Surg. 64 (5) (2006) 804–811.

[57] F. Pia, P. Aluffi, M.C. Crespi, F. Arcuri, M. Brucoli, A. Benech, Intraoral transposition of pedicled temporalis muscle flap followed by zygomatic implant placement, J. Craniofac. Surg. 23 (5) (2012) e463–e465.

[58] D. De Santis, L. Trevisiol, A. Cucchi, L.C. Canton, P.F. Nocini, Zygomatic and maxillary implants inserted by means of computer-assisted surgery in a patient with a cleft palate, J. Craniofac. Surg. 21 (3) (2010) 858–862.

[59] B.R. Chrcanovic, D.R. Oliveira, A.L. Custodio, Accuracy evaluation of computed tomography-derived stereolithographic surgical guides in zygomatic implant placement in human cadavers, J. Oral Implantol. 36 (5) (2010) 345–355.

[60] L. Vrielinck, C. Politis, S. Schepers, M. Pauwels, I. Naert, Image-based planning and clinical validation of zygoma and pterygoid implant placement in patients with severe bone atrophy using customized drill guides. Preliminary results from a prospective clinical follow-up study, Int. J. Oral Maxillofac. Surg. 32 (1) (2003) 7–14.

[61] C.H. Hammerle, L. Cordaro, N. van Assche, G.I. Benic, M. Bornstein, F. Gamper, et al. Digital technologies to support planning, treatment, and fabrication processes and outcome assessments in implant dentistry. Summary and consensus statements. The 4th EAO consensus conference 2015, Clin. Oral Implant. Res. 26 (Suppl. 11) (2015) 97–101.

[62] W. Wojciechowski, P. Kownacki, S. Kownacki, A. Urbanik, Virtual planning of dental implant placement using CT double-scan technique—Own experience, Pol. J. Radiol. 72 (2007) 44–49.

[63] J.M. Plooij, T.J. Maal, P. Haers, W.A. Borstlap, A.M. Kuijpers-Jagtman, S.J. Berge, Digital three-dimensional image fusion processes for planning and evaluating orthodontics and orthognathic surgery. A systematic review, Int. J. Oral Maxillofac. Surg. 40 (4) (2011) 341–352.

[64] T.J. Balshi, G.J. Wolfinger, N.J. Shuscavage, S.F. Balshi, Zygomatic bone-to-implant contact in 77 patients with partially or completely edentulous maxillas, J. Oral Maxillofac. Surg. 70 (9) (2012) 2065–2069.

[65] H.T. Luebbers, P. Messmer, J.A. Obwegeser, R.A. Zwahlen, R. Kikinis, K.W. Graetz, et al. Comparison of different registration methods for surgical navigation in cranio-maxillofacial surgery, J. Cranio-maxillo-fac. Surg. 36 (2) (2008) 109–116.

[66] J.M. Fitzpatrick, J.B. West, The distribution of target registration error in rigid-body point-based registration, IEEE Trans. Med. Imaging 20 (9) (2001) 917–927.

[67] J.B. West, J.M. Fitzpatrick, S A Toms, et al. Fiducial point placement and the accuracy of point-based, rigid body registration, Neurosurgery 48 (2001) 810–816.

[68] Z. Wenbin, W. Chenhao, Y. Hongbo, et al. Effect of fiducial configuration on target registration error in image-guided cranio-maxillofacial surgery, Journal of oral and maxillofacial surgery. 39 (2011) 407–411.

[69] W. Gerlig, Z. Antoniette, S. Peter, et al. Do image modality and registration method influence the accuracy of craniofacial navigation?, J. Oral Maxillofac. Surg. 70 (2012) 2165–2173.

[70] H.T. Luebbers, P. Messmer, J.A. Obwegeser, et al. Comparison of different registration methods for surgical navigation in craniomaxillofacial surgery, J. Cranio-maxillo-fac. Surg. 36 (2) (2008) 109–116.

[71] H.T. Luebbers, Die Navigation als Hilfe bei der Versorgung von Orbitawandfrakturen. Tierexperimentelle Untersuchung am Schwarzkopfschaf. Medical Thesis, Department of Oral and Maxillofacial Surgery, Hannover Medical School, Hannover, 2004.

[72] B. Hohlweg-Majert, R. Schön, R. Schmelzeisen, N.C. Gellrich, A. Schramm, Navigational maxillofacial surgery using virtual models, World J. Surg. 29 (2005) 1530–1538.

[73] G. Wittwer, W.L. Adeyemo, K. Schicho, N. Gigovic, D. Turhani, G. Enislidis, Computer-guided flapless transmucosal implant placement in the mandible: a new combination of two innovative techniques, Oral Surg. Oral Med. Oral Pathol. Oral Radiol. Endodont. 101 (2006) 718–723.

[74] M.C. Metzger, A. Rafii, B. Holhweg-Majert, A.M. Pham, B. Strong, Comparison of 4 registration strategies for computer-aided maxillofacial surgery, Otolaryngol. Head Neck Surg. 137 (2007) 93–99.

[75] P.A. Woerdeman, P.W. Willems, H.J. Noordmans, C.A. Tulleken, J.W. van der Sprenkel, Application accuracy in frameless image-guided neurosurgery: a comparison study of three patient-to-image registration methods, J. Neurosurg. 106 (2007) 1012–1016.

[76] J. Hoffmann, C. Westendorff, G. Gomez-Roman, S. Reinert, Accuracy of navigation-guided socket drilling before implant installation compared to the conventional free-hand method in a synthetic edentulous lower jaw model, Clin. Oral Implant. Res. 16 (5) (2005) 609–614.

[77] G.A. Mandelaris, L.V. Stefanelli, B.S. DeGroot, Dynamic navigation for surgical implant placement: overview of technology, key concepts, and a case report, Compend. Continuin. Edu. Dent. 39 (9) (2018) 614–621 quiz 22.

[78] B.R. Chrcanovic, T. Albrektsson, A. Wennerberg, Survival and complications of zygomatic implants: an updated systematic review, J. Oral Maxillofac. Surg. 74 (10) (2016) 1949–1964.

[79] A. Schramm, N.C. Gellrich, R. Schimming, R. Schmelzeisen, Computer-assisted insertion of zygomatic implants (Branemark system) after extensive tumor surgery, MKG 4 (5) (2000) 292–295.

[80] S.D. Ganz, Three-dimensional imaging and guided surgery for dental implants, Dent. Clin. North Am. 59 (2) (2015) 265–290.

[81] C.A. Aydemir, V. Arisan, Accuracy of dental implant placement via dynamic navigation or the freehand method: A split-mouth randomized controlled clinical trial, Clin. Oral Implant. Res. 31 (3) (2020) 255–263.

[82] G.M.D. Widmann, R.D. Stoffner, R.M.D. Bale, Errors and error management in image-guided craniomaxillofacial surgery, Oral Surg. Oral Med. Oral Pathol. Oral Radiol. Endodontol. 107 (5) (2009) 701–715.

[83] Y. Wu, F. Wang, W. Huang, S. Fan, Real-time navigation in zygomatic implant placement: workflow, Atlas Oral Maxillofac. Surg. Clin. North Am. 31 (3) (2019) 357–367.

[84] P. Maló, A. Nobre Mde, A. Lopes, A. Ferro, S. Moss, Five-year outcome of a retrospective cohort study on the rehabilitation of completely edentulous atrophic maxillae with immediately loaded zygomatic implants placed extra-maxillary, Eur. J. Oral Implantol. 7 (3) (2014) 267–281.

[85] N. Panchal, L. Mahmood, A. Retana, R Emery 3rd., Dynamic navigation for dental implant surgery, Oral Maxillofac. Surg. Clin. North Am. 31 (4) (2019) 539–547.

[86] F.J. Kramer, C. Baethge, G. Swennen, S. Rosahl, Navigated vs. conventional implant insertion for maxillary single tooth replacement, Clin. Oral Implant. Res. 16 (1) (2005) 60–68.

[87] T.K. Huang, C.H. Yang, Y.H. Hsieh, J.C. Wang, C.C. Hung, Augmented reality (AR) and virtual reality (VR) applied in dentistry, Kaohsiung J. Med. Sci. 34 (4) (2018) 243–248.

[88] J. Dai, J. Wu, X. Wang, X. Yang, Y. Wu, B. Xu, et al. An excellent navigation system and experience in craniomaxillofacial navigation surgery: a double-center study, Sci. Rep. 6 (2016) 28242.

[89] M. Rana, H. Essig, A.M. Eckardt, et al. Advances and innovations in computer-assisted head and neck oncologic surgery, J. Craniofac. Surg. 23 (1) (2012) 272–278.

[90] M.S. Block, R.W. Emery, K. Lank, et al. Implant placement accuracy using dynamic navigation, Int. J. Oral Maxillofac. Implant. 32 (1) (2016) 92–99.

[91] Y.P. Wang, S.Q. Fan, Y.Q. Wu, Development and application of dynamic navigation system in oral implant field, Oral Dis. Prevent. Treat. 25 (10) (2017) 613–619.

[92] S.F. Kelsey, S.M. Mullin, K.M. Detre, H. Mitchell, M.J. Cowley, A.R. Gruentzig, et al. Effect of investigator experience on percutaneous transluminal coronary angioplasty, Am. J. Cardiol. 53 (1984) 56C–64C.

[93] G.P. Pisano, R.M.J. Bohmer, A.C. Edmondson, Organizational differences in rates of learning: evidence from the adoption of minimally invasive cardiac surgery, Manage. Sci. 47 (2001) 752e68.

[94] R. Aggarwal, S.A. Black, J.R. Hance, A. Darzi, N.Z. Cheshire, Virtual reality simulation training can improve inexperienced surgeons' endo-vascular skills, Eur. J. Vasc. Endovasc. Surg. 31 (2006) 588–593.

[95] R. Aggarwal, T.P. Grantcharov, J.R. Eriksen, et al. An evidence-based virtual reality training program for novice laparoscopic surgeons, Ann. Surg. 244 (2006) 310–314.

[96] E.G. Verdaasdonk, L.P. Stassen, M.P. Schijven, J. Dankelman, Construct validity and assessment of the learning curve for the SIMENDO endoscopic simulator, Surg. Endosc. 21 (2007) 1406–1412.

[97] M. Cassetta, F. Altieri, M. Giansanti, et al. Is there a learning curve in static computer-assisted implant surgery? A prospective clinical study, Int. J. Oral Maxillofac. Surg. 49 (10) (2020) 1335–1342, doi: 10.1016/j.ijom.2020.03.007.

[98] J. Golob Deeb, S. Bencharit, K. Carrico, et al. Exploring training dental implant placement using computer-guided implant navigation system for predoctoral students: A pilot study, Eur. J. Dent. Educ. 23 (2019) 415–423.

[99] M.S. Block, R.W. Emery, K. Lank, et al. Accuracy using dynamic navigation, Int. J. Oral Maxillofac. Implant. 32 (2017) 92.

[100] M. Liu, G.W. Sun, E.Y. Tang, New development of computer navigation technology in oral and maxillofacial surgery, Chin. J. Stomatol. Res. 11 (03) (2017) 174–177.

[101] M. Ershad, A. Ahmadian, N. Dadashi Serej, H. Saberi, K. Amini Khoiy, Minimization of target registration error for vertebra in image-guided spine surgery, Int. J. Comput. Assist. Radiol. Surg. 9 (1) (2014) 29–38.

[102] C.S. Yang, D.S. Jiang, H.H. Zhou, J.Y. Wu, Z.J. Song, S.L. Zhang, Ultrasound and CT image fusion based on optical localization: key technology research and preliminary application of craniomaxillofacial soft tissue navigation, J. Tissue Eng. Reconstruct. Surg. 12 (02) (2016) 98–101.

[103] S. Sukegawa, T. Kanno, A. Shibata, et al. Use of an intraoperative navigation system for retrieving a broken dental instrument in tshe mandible: a case report, J. Med. Case Rep. 11 (1) (2017) 14.

[104] M.N. Van Oosterom, P. Meershoek, G.H. KleinJan, et al. Navigation of fluorescence cameras during soft tissue surgeryis it possible to use a single navigation setup for various open and laparoscopic urological surgery applications?, J. Urol. 199 (4) (2018) 1061–1068.

[105] X.W. Lu, L.J. Li, Application progress of computer aided navigation technology in oral and maxillofacial surgery [J], J. Oral Maxillofac. Prosthodont. 20 (05) (2019) 309–312.

[106] C. Qin, X. Ran, Y. Wu, X. Chen, The development of non-contact user interface of a surgical navigation system based on multi-LSTM and a phantom experiment for zygomatic implant placement, Int. J. Comput. Assist. Radiol. Surg. 14 (12) (2019) 2147–2154.

[107] C. Qin, Z. Cao, S. Fan, Y. Wu, Y. Sun, C. Politis, et al. An oral and maxillofacial navigation system for implant placement with automatic identification of fiducial points, Int. J. Comput. Assist. Radiol. Surg. 14 (2) (2019) 281–289.

[108] G. Pellegrino, A. Tarsitano, V. Taraschi, T. Vercellotti, C. Marchetti, Simplifying zygomatic implant site preparation using ultrasonic navigation: a technical note, Int. J. Oral Maxillofac. Implant. 33 (3) (2018) e67–e71.

[109] J. Brief, S. Haßfeld, et al. Robot assisted dental implantology, Int. Poster J. Dentist. Oral Med. 4 (1) (2002) 109.

[110] G. Kim, H. Seo, S. Im, D. Kang, S. Jeong, (Eds.), A study on simulator of human-robot cooperative manipulator for dental implant surgery. IEEE, 2009.

[111] X. Sun, F.D. McKenzie, S. Bawab, J. Li, Y. Yoon, J.K. Huang, Automated dental implantation using image-guided robotics: registration results, Int. J. Comput. Assist. Radiol. Surg. 6 (5) (2011) 627–634.

[112] Z.S. Haidar, Autonomous robotics: a fresh era of implant dentistry... is a reality, J. Oral Res. 6 (9) (2017) 230–231.

[113] R. Xie, The study on accurary of the dental implantology robotic system [Master]: Fourth Military Medical University, Xi'an, China, 2016.

[114] F. Shengchi, C. Zhenggang, Q. Chunxia, W. Feng, H. Wei, C. Xiaojun, et al. The accuracy of surgical automatic robotic assisted implants placement in edentulous maxilla—an in vitro study, Clin. Oral Implant. Res. 29 (S17) (2018) 283.

Index

Note: Page numbers followed by "f" indicate figures, "t" indicate tables.

Printed in the United States
by Baker & Taylor Publisher Services